GOSPEL STUDIES SERIES
Volume 2

The New Testament

Made Easier

Part I

Matthew, Mark, Luke & John

GOSPEL STUDIES SERIES
Volume 2

The New Testament

Made Easier

Part I
Matthew, Mark, Luke & John

by

David J. Ridges

BONNEVILLE BOOKS™

Springville, Utah

ISBN: 1-55517-638-0
v.1

Published by Cedar Fort Inc.
www.cedarfort.com

Distributed by:

Typeset by Kristin Nelson
Cover design by Nicole Cunningham
Cover design © 2002 by Lyle Mortimer

Printed in the United States of America
10 9 8 7 6 5 4 3 2 1

Printed on acid-free paper

Library of Congress Control Number: 2002115030

Introduction

Welcome to the *Gospel Studies Series* on the New Testament. In this volume, we will study the life of Christ as taught in the Four Gospels—Matthew, Mark, Luke and John. It is interesting to note that only 31 days of the Savior's life and ministry are covered in the Four Gospels. Volume three of this Personal Gospel Study Series will deal with Acts through Revelation.

We will use the King James version of the Bible as published and used by the Church of Jesus Christ of Latter-day Saints as our basic text. As is the case with other volumes in this *Gospel Studies Series*, it is anticipated that you will use your own copy of the scriptures as the main text for your studies. This is intended to be a quick-reference, "user-friendly," basic study of this portion of the New Testament. The notes given in parentheses within the verses are provided as helps toward understanding, and also for you to use as desired to make notes in your own scriptures.

—David J. Ridges

TABLE OF CONTENTS

FOREWORD

Over many years of teaching in the Church and for the Church Educational System, I have found that members of the Church encounter some common problems when it comes to understanding the scriptures. One problem is understanding the language of the scriptures themselves. Another is understanding symbolism. Another common concern is how best to mark their own scriptures and perhaps make brief notes in them. Yet another concern is how to understand what the scriptures are actually teaching. In other words, what are the major messages etc. being taught by the Lord through His prophets?

This book is designed to address each of the concerns mentioned above for the Gospels of Matthew, Mark, Luke, and John in the New Testament. The Bible text of the Gospels is included in its entirety and serves as the basic text for this work. The format is intentionally simple and is intended to help readers to:

- Gain instant basic understanding of these scriptures as they read, through the use of brief explanatory notes in parentheses within the verses. This paves the way for even deeper testimony and understanding later.
- Better understand the beautiful language of the King James Version of the Bible. This is accomplished in this book with in-the-verse notes which define difficult Old English terms.
- Mark their scriptures and put brief notes in the margins which will help them understand now and remember later what particular passages of scripture teach.
- Better understand the symbolism of the parables of Jesus as well as many other passages where symbolism is used.
- Get a feel for the background and setting in which events and teachings take place as recorded by Matthew, Mark, Luke and John. A basic understanding of Jewish culture in the days of the Savior is vital. Notes between verses help with these issues.

Over the years, one of the most common expressions of gratitude from my students has been "Thanks for the notes you had us put in our scriptures". This book is dedicated to that purpose.

Sources for the notes given in this work are as follows:

- The Standard Works of the Church of Jesus Christ of Latter-day Saints.
- Footnotes in the Latter-day Saint version of the King James Bible.
- The Joseph Smith Translation of the Bible, designated as JST in this book.
- The Bible Dictionary in the back of our Bible.
- Strong's Exhaustive Concordance of the Bible.
- Various Bible dictionaries.
- The New Testament Student Manual provided for our Institutes of Religion.
- Various translations of the Bible, including the Martin Luther edition of the German Bible, which Joseph Smith said was the most correct of any then available.
- Jesus the Christ, by Apostle James E. Talmage.
- Doctrinal New Testament Commentary, Vol. 1, by Apostle Bruce R. McConkie.
- Other sources as noted in the text.

It is hoped by the author that this book will serve effectively as a teacher to members of the Church as they seek to increase their understanding of the life of the Savior during his mortal ministry and to strengthen their testimony of him. Above all, if this work serves to bring increased understanding and testimony of the Atonement of Christ, all the efforts to put it together will have been far more than worth it. A special thanks goes to my wife, Janette, and my children who have encouraged me every step of the way.

—David J. Ridges

THE GOSPEL OF MATTHEW

The Gospel of Matthew was written by the Apostle Matthew. He was sometimes called Levi (Mark 2:14; Luke 5:27). He lived in Capernaum, in Galilee, and worked as a tax collector, or "publican" until he was called by the Savior to follow Him. Matthew wrote primarily to a Jewish audience. In order to appeal to the Jews, who placed great emphasis on the Old Testament, he places particular emphasis on how the Savior's life fulfilled Old Testament prophecy. For more information about Matthew, see Bible Dictionary (in the back section of your Bible), page 729.

Note: You will often see words in *italics* in the King James version of the Bible. King James, of England, assembled a group of scholars to make a new translation of the Bible. It was completed in 1611 AD. Whenever the translators for this version of the Bible did not know what a word or phrase should be, based on the ancient manuscripts they were studying, they requested that it be printed in italics.

MATTHEW 1

1 The book of the generation (genealogy) of Jesus Christ, the son of (descendent of) David, the son of Abraham.

Note: The genealogy of Christ, given here by Matthew, is that of the legal successors to the throne of David, not a strict father-to-son genealogy. It includes living successors such as grandson, nephew etc. Luke's genealogy of the Savior, as given in Luke 3:23-38, is a strict father-to-son genealogy.

2 Abraham begat Isaac (was the father of Isaac); and Isaac begat Jacob; and Jacob begat Judas and his brethren;

3 And Judas begat Phares and Zara of Thamar; and Phares begat Esrom; and Esrom begat Aram;

4 And Aram begat Aminadab; and Aminadab begat Naasson; and Naasson begat Salmon;

5 And Salmon begat Booz of Rachab; and Booz begat Obed of Ruth; and Obed begat Jesse;

6 And Jesse begat David the king; and David the king begat Solomon of her (Bathsheba) *that had been the wife* of Urias;

7 And Solomon begat Roboam; and Roboam begat Abia; and Abia begat Asa;

8 And Asa begat Josaphat; and Josaphat begat Joram; and Joram begat Ozias;

9 And Ozias begat Joatham; and Joatham begat Achaz; and Achaz begat Ezekias;

10 And Ezekias begat Manasses; and Manasses begat Amon; and Amon begat Josias;

11 And Josias begat Jechonias and his brethren, about the time they were carried away to Babylon:

12 And after they were brought to Babylon, Jechonias begat Salathiel; and Salathiel begat Zorobabel;

13 And Zorobabel begat Abiud; and Abiud begat Eliakim; and Eliakim

begat Azor;

14 And Azor begat Sadoc; and Sadoc begat Achim; and Achim begat Eliud;

15 And Eliud begat Eleazar; and Eleazar begat Matthan; and Matthan begat Jacob;

16 And Jacob begat Joseph the husband of Mary, of whom was born Jesus, who is called Christ (Greek: the "Anointed One").

Note: Joseph would have been the political king of the Jewish nation at this time if the Romans had not been in power. See *Jesus the Christ*, p. 87.

17 So all the generations from Abraham to David are fourteen generations; and from David until the carrying away into Babylon are fourteen generations; and from the carrying away into Babylon unto Christ are fourteen generations.

18 ¶ Now the birth of Jesus Christ was on this wise (happened this way): When as his mother Mary was espoused (among the Jews, being espoused was a much more serious obligation than our "engagement"; during the espousal period, the bride-to-be lived with her family or friends; communication between her and her husband-to-be was carried on by a friend) to Joseph, before they came together (before they were married), she was found with child of the Holy Ghost.

Note: In Jewish culture at this time, an unmarried woman found to be expecting a child was subject to being stoned to death.

19 Then Joseph her husband, being a just (righteous; fair) man, and not willing to make her a publick example (which would protect his own reputation, but could subject Mary to execution by stoning), was minded to put her away privily (privately, so as to avoid embarrassing her, and to avoid putting her life in danger).

20 But while he thought on these things, behold, the angel of the Lord appeared unto him in a dream, saying, Joseph, thou son of David (descendant of David), fear not to take unto thee Mary thy wife (don't be afraid to marry Mary): for that (the child) which is conceived in her is of the Holy Ghost.

21 And she shall bring forth a son, and thou shalt call his name JESUS: for he shall save his people from their sins (i.e., Mary is expecting the promised Messiah).

Note: Joseph was a kind man and the angel came and put his mind at ease *after* he made the decision to be merciful to Mary.

22 Now all this was done, that it might be fulfilled (that prophecy would be fulfilled) which was spoken of the Lord by the prophet, saying,

23 Behold, a virgin shall be with child, and shall bring forth a son, and they shall call his name Emmanuel, which being interpreted is, God with us.

24 Then Joseph being raised from sleep did as the angel of the Lord had bidden him, and took unto him his wife (Joseph obeyed the angel immediately, probably with great relief and joy):

25 And knew her not (had no sexual relationship) till she had brought forth her firstborn son: and he called his name JESUS.

Note: Joseph and Mary went on to have at least six children of their own. See Mark 6:3. In fact, the Greek text of this verse indicates that there were at least three sisters plus the four brothers mentioned.

MATTHEW 2

1 Now when Jesus was born in Bethlehem of Judaea in the days of Herod the king (see Bible Dictionary, page 700-701, for background information on Herod the Great), behold, there came wise men (no doubt inspired men of God; perhaps prophets) from the east to Jerusalem,

2 Saying, Where is he that is born King of the Jews? for we have seen his star in the east, and are come to worship him..

3 When Herod the king had heard *these things*, he was troubled, and all Jerusalem with him.

4 And when he had gathered all the chief priests and scribes of the people together, he demanded of them where Christ should be born.

5 And they said unto him, In Bethlehem of Judaea: for thus it is written by the prophet,

6 And thou Bethlehem, in the land of Juda, art not the least among the princes of Juda: for out of thee shall come a Governor (Christ), that shall rule my people Israel.

7 Then Herod, when he had privily (privately) called the wise men, enquired of them diligently what time the star appeared.

8 And he sent them to Bethlehem, and said, Go and search diligently for the young child; and when ye have found him, bring me word again, that I may come and worship him also.

9 When they had heard the king, they departed; and, lo, the star, which they saw in the east, went before them, till it came and stood over where the young child was.

10 When they saw the star, they rejoiced with exceeding great joy.

Note: By the time the wise men arrived in Jerusalem, Jesus was already a young child.

11 And when they were come into the house, they saw the young child with Mary his mother, and fell down, and worshipped him: and when they had opened their treasures, they presented unto him gifts; gold, and frankincense, and myrrh (frankincense and myrrh were also costly gifts and were used as incense).

12 And being warned of God in a dream that they should not return to Herod, they departed into their own country another way.

13 And when they were departed, behold, the angel of the Lord appeareth to Joseph in a dream, saying, Arise, and take the young child and his mother, and flee into Egypt, and be thou there until I bring thee word: for Herod will seek the young child to destroy him.

14 When he arose, he took the young child and his mother by night, and departed into Egypt (this would be a long and difficult journey, but Joseph and Mary were obedient):

15 And was there until the death of Herod: that it might be fulfilled which was spoken of the Lord by the prophet (Hosea 11:1), saying, Out of Egypt have I called my son.

16 ¶ Then Herod, when he saw that he was mocked of the wise men, was exceeding wroth (very angry), and sent forth, and slew all the children (Greek: male babies) that were in Bethlehem, and in all the coasts thereof, from two years old and under, according to the time which he had diligently enquired of the wise men.

Note: John the Baptist was also a small child at this time, just six months older than Jesus. He lived in the vicinity of Bethlehem when Herod gave his murderous order to kill all the babies two years old and younger in the Bethlehem area. John's father, Zacharias, was killed-see Matthew 23:35- because he would not tell where John was hiding. The Prophet Joseph Smith gives us more information about this. "When Herod's edict went forth to destroy the young children, John was about six months older than Jesus, and came under this hellish edict, and Zacharias caused his mother to take him into the mountains, where he was raised on locusts and wild honey. When his father refused to disclose his hiding place, and being the officiating high priest at the Temple that year, was slain by Herod's order, between the porch and the altar, as Jesus said." (Teachings of the Prophet Joseph Smith, p. 261.)

17 Then was fulfilled that which was spoken by Jeremy (Jeremiah) the prophet, saying,

18 In Rama was there a voice heard, lamentation, and weeping, and great mourning, Rachel weeping *for* her children, and would not be comforted, because they are not.

19 But when Herod was dead, behold, an angel of the Lord appeareth in a dream to Joseph in Egypt,

20 Saying, Arise, and take the young child and his mother, and go into the land of Israel: for they are dead which sought the young child's life.

21 And he arose, and took the young child and his mother, and came into the land of Israel.

22 But when he heard that Archelaus did reign in Judaea in the room of (in place of) his father Herod, he was afraid to go thither (there): notwith-standing, being warned of God in a dream, he turned aside into the parts of Galilee:

23 And he came and dwelt in a city called Nazareth: that it might be fulfilled which was spoken by the prophets, He shall be called a Nazarene.

MATTHEW 3

1 In those days came John the Baptist, preaching in the wilderness of Judaea,

2 And saying, Repent ye: for the kingdom of heaven is at hand (is near; is now available to you).

3 For this (Christ) is he that was spoken of by the prophet Esaias (Isaiah), saying, The voice of one crying in the wilderness, Prepare ye the way of the Lord, make his paths straight.

4 And the same John had his raiment (clothing) of camel's hair, and a leathern girdle about his loins; and his meat (food) was locusts and wild honey.

Note: The Bible generally uses the word "meat" to mean any kind of food. The word "flesh" is used when referring to meat, such as beef, chicken, lamb, etc.

5 Then went out to him Jerusalem, and all Judaea, and all the region round about Jordan (i.e., people from all over came to the Jordan River to see John the Baptist),

6 And were baptized of him in Jordan (the Jordan River), confessing their sins.

7 But when he saw many of the Pharisees and Sadducees (religious leaders among the Jews) come to his baptism, he said unto them, O generation of vipers, who hath warned you to flee from the wrath to come?

Note: Pharisees believed in the resurrection. Sadducees did not. Consequently, there was much arguing and disagreement between the two groups.

8 Bring forth therefore fruits meet (necessary) for repentance:

9 And think not to say within yourselves, We have Abraham to *our* father (as our ancestor): for I say unto you, that God is able of these stones to raise up children (descendants) unto Abraham.

Note: The Jews had a belief that, since they were direct descendants of Abraham, they were automatically entitled to the highest position in heaven in the afterlife, and, that all other people, no matter how good they were, could attain only second class status in heaven.

10 And now also the axe is laid unto the root of the trees (trees often represent people in the scriptures): therefore every tree which bringeth not forth good fruit (every person who does not live righteously) is hewn (cut) down, and cast into the fire.

11 I indeed baptize you with water unto repentance: but he (Christ) that cometh after me is mightier than I, whose shoes I am not worthy to bear: he shall baptize you with the Holy Ghost, and *with* fire:

Note: In the scriptures, the Holy Ghost is often compared to fire. The symbolism comes from the use of fire to purify gold. The gold ore is put in a container and fire is used to heat the container. The ore melts, the impurities float to the top, and the pure gold settles to the bottom. The impurities are then discarded and pure gold remains. Thus, the gold is purified by fire. Similarly, the Holy Ghost purifies us, if we allow it. Example: We commit sin. The Holy Ghost points it out and causes our conscience to burn within us. We respond by repenting. Thus we are purified, bit by bit.

12 Whose fan (used to blow the chaff away from the kernels of wheat on the

threshing floor) is in his hand, and he will throughly purge (cleanse) his floor (the earth), and gather his wheat (the righteous) into the garner (the barn); but he will burn up the chaff (the wicked) with unquenchable fire.

13 ¶ Then cometh Jesus from Galilee to Jordan unto John, to be baptized of (by) him.

14 But John forbad him, saying, I have need to be baptized of thee, and comest thou to me?

15 And Jesus answering said unto him, Suffer (allow) *it to be so* now: for thus it becometh us to fulfil all righteousness (do the will of the Father). Then he suffered him.

16 And Jesus, when he was baptized, went up straightway out of the water: and, lo, the heavens were opened unto him, and he (John the Baptist) saw the Spirit of God descending like a dove, and lighting upon him (the Savior): (The Joseph Smith Translation [JST] gives verses 15-17 as follows: "And Jesus, answering, said unto him, Suffer me to be baptized of thee, for thus it becometh us to fulfill all righteousness. Then he suffered him. And John went down into the water and baptized him. And Jesus when he was baptized, went up straightway out of the water; and John saw, and lo, the heavens were opened unto him, and he saw the Spirit of God descending like a dove and lighting upon Jesus. And lo, he heard a voice from heaven, saying, This is my beloved Son, in whom I am well pleased. Hear ye him.")

Note: The Prophet Joseph Smith taught that the Holy Ghost does not transform himself into a dove.

Teachings of the Prophet Joseph Smith, pages 275-276.

17 And lo a voice from heaven, saying, This is my beloved Son, in whom I am well pleased.

MATTHEW 4

1 Then was Jesus led up of the Spirit into the wilderness to be tempted of the devil (JST: "to be with God").

2 And when he had fasted forty days and forty nights, he was afterward an hungred.

3 And when the tempter (Satan) came to him, he said, If thou be the Son of God, command that these stones be made bread (temptation to yield to physical appetite).

4 But he answered and said, It is written, Man shall not live by bread alone, but by every word that proceedeth out of the mouth of God.

5 Then the devil taketh him up into the holy city (Jerusalem), and setteth him on a pinnacle of the temple (JST "Then Jesus was taken up into the holy city and the Spirit setteth him on the pinnacle of the temple"),

6 And saith unto him (JST "Then the devil came unto him and said"), If thou be the Son of God, cast thyself down: for it is written, He shall give his angels charge concerning thee: and in their hands they shall bear thee up, lest at any time thou dash thy foot against a stone (temptation to yield to vanity, pride).

7 Jesus said unto him, It is written again, Thou shalt not tempt the Lord thy God.

8 Again, the devil taketh him (JST "And again, Jesus was in the Spirit,

6

and it taketh him") up into an exceeding high mountain, and sheweth him all the kingdoms of the world, and the glory of them;

9 And saith unto him (JST "And the devil came unto him again, and said"), All these things will I give thee, if thou wilt fall down and worship me (temptation to yield to materialism and power).

10 Then saith Jesus unto him, Get thee hence, Satan: for it is written, Thou shalt worship the Lord thy God, and him only shalt thou serve.

11 Then the devil leaveth him, and, behold, angels came and ministered unto him.

12 Now when Jesus had heard that John (the Baptist) was cast into prison, he departed into Galilee;

13 And leaving Nazareth, he came and dwelt in Capernaum, which is upon the sea (Sea of Galilee) coast, in the borders of Zabulon and Nephthalim (the area where Zebulon and Naphtali, two of the Twelve Tribes, settled when Joshua brought the Children of Israel into the promised land):

14 That it might be fulfilled which was spoken by Esaias (Isaiah) the prophet, saying,

15 The land of Zabulon, and the land of Nephthalim, by the way of the sea, beyond Jordan, Galilee of the Gentiles;

16 The people which sat in darkness saw great light (the Savior and His gospel); and to them which sat in the region and shadow of death (spiritual darkness) light is sprung up.

17 From that time Jesus began to preach, and to say, Repent: for the kingdom of heaven is at hand.

18 And Jesus, walking by the sea of Galilee, saw two brethren, Simon called Peter, and Andrew his brother, casting a net into the sea: for they were fishers (fishermen; they earned their living by fishing).

19 And he saith unto them, Follow me, and I will make you fishers of men.

20 And they straightway (immediately) left *their* nets, and followed him.

21 And going on from thence, he saw other two brethren, James *the son* of Zebedee, and John his brother, in a ship with Zebedee their father, mending their nets; and he called them.

22 And they immediately left the ship and their father, and followed him.

23 And Jesus went about all Galilee, teaching in their synagogues (church buildings), and preaching the gospel of the kingdom, and healing all manner of (all kinds of) sickness and all manner of disease among the people.

24 And his fame went throughout all Syria: and they brought unto him all sick people that were taken with (who had) divers (various) diseases and torments, and those which were possessed with devils, and those which were lunatick, and those that had the palsy; and he healed them.

25 And there followed him great multitudes of people from Galilee, and *from* Decapolis, and *from* Jerusalem, and *from* Judaea, and *from* beyond Jordan.

MATTHEW 5

Note: Matthew, chapters 5, 6 and 7, are known as "The Sermon on the Mount". Many people consider these chapters to contain a series of desirable ethical behaviors, and indeed they do. But there is much more. The righteous behaviors stressed here by the Master are those which lead to celestial glory and exaltation.

1 And seeing the multitudes, he went up into a mountain: and when he was set, his disciples came unto him:

Note: You may wish to make a cross reference here to 3 Nephi 12:1-3, wherein we are told that the Sermon on the Mount which follows is addressed to members of the Church, and is a series of instructions for entering celestial glory.

2 And he opened his mouth, and taught them, saying,

3 Blessed *are* the poor in spirit (who come unto me. 3 Nephi 12:3): for theirs is the kingdom of heaven (celestial glory).

4 Blessed *are* they that mourn (for their sins; in other words, those who repent): for they shall be comforted (by the Holy Ghost).

5 Blessed *are* the meek: for they shall inherit the earth (this earth will become the celestial kingdom; see D&C 130:8-9).

6 Blessed *are* they which do hunger and thirst after righteousness: for they shall be filled (with the Holy Ghost; 3 Nephi 12:6).

7 Blessed *are* the merciful: for they shall obtain mercy.

8 Blessed *are* the pure in heart: for they shall see God.

9 Blessed *are* the peacemakers: for they shall be called the children of God (another term for those who inherit the celestial kingdom).

10 Blessed *are* they which are persecuted for righteousness' sake: for theirs is the kingdom of heaven (celestial glory).

11 Blessed are ye, when *men* shall revile you (mock you, ridicule you for your righteous beliefs and lifestyle), and persecute you, and shall say all manner of evil against you falsely, for my sake (because you follow the Savior).

12 Rejoice, and be exceeding glad: for great is your reward in heaven: for so persecuted they the prophets which were before you (who lived before you came to earth).

13 Ye are the salt of the earth: but if the salt have lost his savour (its ability to improve flavor, to thus improve life), wherewith shall it be salted? it is thenceforth good for nothing, but to be cast out, and to be trodden under foot of men.

14 Ye are the light of the world. A city that is set on an hill cannot be hid.

Note: In the Holy Land, cities were built upon the hills, saving valuable land in the valleys for agricultural and pasture use.

15 Neither do men light a candle, and put it under a bushel, but on a candlestick; and it giveth light unto all that are in the house.

16 Let your light so shine before men, that they may see your good works, and glorify your Father which is in heaven.

17 Think not that I am come to destroy the law (of Moses), or the prophets (the Old Testament): I am not

come to destroy, but to fulfil.

Note: The Savior was accused by the Jews of trying to destroy all the laws and teachings of the Law of Moses. In fact, the rituals, teachings and animal sacrifices taught by the Law of Moses all were designed by God to point peoples' minds toward the Savior and His Atonement, to His atoning sacrifice for us. A good example of this is found in Leviticus 14:1-9. We will take the time here to examine these verses and make notes about the Atonement symbolism in them.

Leviticus 14
The message and symbolism here is the power of the Atonement of Christ to cleanse and heal people from very serious sins. Leprosy is described in Webster's New World Dictionary, Second College Edition, as follows: "...a chronic infectious disease...that attacks the skin, flesh, nerves, etc.; it is characterized by nodules, ulcers, white scaly scabs, deformities, and wasting of body parts,..."

1 And the LORD spake unto Moses, saying,
2 This shall be the law of the leper (a person with leprosy; symbolic of a person with very serious sins) in the day of his cleansing: He shall be brought unto the priest (the Lord's authorized servant):
3 And the priest shall go forth out of the camp; and the priest shall look, and, behold (see), *if* the plague of leprosy be healed in the leper (in other words, see if the person has truly repented [the symbolism]);
4 Then shall the priest command to take for him (the sinner) that is to be cleansed two birds alive *and* clean, and cedar wood, and scarlet, and hyssop (the two live birds represent the Savior and the sinner; cedar wood represents the cross upon which they crucified the Savior; scarlet and hyssop were involved in the events leading up to and including the crucifixion; see Matthew 27:28 and John 19:29):
5 And the priest shall command that one of the birds (represents the Savior) be killed in an earthen vessel (represents this earth) over running water (can represent the "Living Water", John 4:10 and 14, in other words, cleansing and giving new life):
6 As for the living bird (represents the leper; symbolic of sinners), he (the priest, representing the Father) shall take it, and the cedar wood, and the scarlet, and the hyssop, and shall dip them and the living bird in the blood of the bird *that was* killed over the running water (symbolic of the blood of the Lamb; the Savior's Atonement):
7 And he shall sprinkle upon him (symbolic of a sinner who has repented) that is to be cleansed from the leprosy seven times (seven is a number which symbolically represents perfection), and shall pronounce him clean, and shall let the living bird loose (freed from the bondage of sin) into the open field (representing wide field of new opportunities because of being cleansed from sin).
8 And he that is to be cleansed shall wash his clothes, and shave off all his hair (symbolic of becoming like a newborn baby, i.e., being "born again"), and wash himself in water (symbolic of baptism), that he may be clean: and after that he shall come into the camp (symbolic of rejoining the

covenant people of the Lord), and shall tarry abroad out of his tent seven days.

9 But it shall be on the seventh day, that he shall shave all his hair off his head and his beard and his eyebrows, even all his hair he shall shave off (symbolic of new birth): and he shall wash his clothes, also he shall wash his flesh in water (baptism), and he shall be clean (through proper repentance, the Savior's Atonement makes us clean).

Such Atonement symbolism and teaching is found much in the Old Testament. We will now return to Matthew, chapter 5.

18 For verily I say unto you, Till heaven and earth pass, one jot or one tittle (tiny bit) shall in no wise pass from the law (Law of Moses), till all be fulfilled.

19 Whosoever therefore shall break one of these least commandments, and shall teach men so, he shall be called the least in the kingdom of heaven (will be punished): but whosoever shall do and teach *them*, the same shall be called great in the kingdom of heaven (will gain a great reward in the next life).

20 For I say unto you, That except your righteousness shall exceed *the righteousness* of the scribes (Jewish religious leaders who explain and interpret the scriptures) and Pharisees, ye shall in no case enter into the kingdom of heaven. (The scribes and Pharisees claim to be righteous but are wicked.)

21 Ye have heard that it was said by them of old time, Thou shalt not kill; and whosoever shall kill shall be in danger of the judgment (punishments of God):

22 But I say unto you, That whosoever is angry with his brother without a cause shall be in danger of the judgment: and whosoever shall say to his brother, Raca (a term of derision, such as "You stupid idiot!"), shall be in danger of the council: but whosoever shall say, Thou fool, shall be in danger of hell fire. (In other words, don't put others down, as if you didn't have any imperfections yourself.)

23 Therefore if thou bring thy gift to the altar (JST Matthew 5:25. "Therefore, if ye shall come unto me, or shall desire to come unto me,"), and there rememberest that thy brother hath ought against thee (you have contention with someone close to you);

24 Leave there thy gift before the altar, and go thy way; first be reconciled to (make peace with) thy brother, and then come and offer thy gift.

25 Agree with (make peace with) thine adversary (the person you have contention with) quickly, whiles thou art in the way with him (while you have the opportunity); lest at any time the adversary deliver thee to the judge, and the judge deliver thee to the officer, and thou be cast into prison. (If you don't try to make peace, it does a lot of damage to you, yourself.)

26 Verily I say unto thee, Thou shalt by no means come out thence, till thou hast paid the uttermost farthing. (You pay dearly for holding grudges etc. in terms of lack of peace for yourself.)

27 Ye have heard that it was said by them of old time, Thou shalt not

commit adultery:

28 But I say unto you, That whosoever looketh on a woman to lust after her hath committed adultery with her already in his heart.

29 And if thy right eye (symbolic of specific temptation, bad environment, friends, bad habit, specific sin, etc.) offend thee (puts you in spiritual danger), pluck it out, and cast it from thee: for it is profitable for thee that one of thy members should perish, and not *that* thy whole body should be cast into hell.

Note: Body parts in verses 29 and 30 are symbolic of choices, behaviors etc. which could cause you to lose salvation.

30 And if thy right hand offend thee, cut *it* off, and cast it from thee: for it is profitable for thee that one of thy members should perish, and not *that* thy whole body should be cast into hell. (JST Matthew 5:34. "And now this I speak, a parable concerning your sins; wherefore, cast them from you, that ye may not be hewn down and cast into the fire.")

31 It hath been said, Whosoever shall put away (divorce) his wife, let him give her a writing of divorcement (a legal divorce):

Note: Verses 31 and 32 deal with divorce. Clearly, marriage and family involve sacred promises which are very serious. In an ideal society, there would seldom if ever be a divorce. In cases where divorce has taken place, verse 32 can sometimes be misunderstood to teach that anyone who gets a

divorce and then remarries is now living in adultery, except where fornication was involved in leading up to the divorce.

A very important principle about following the Brethren, our General Authorities, can be taught here. Even if you don't completely understand verse 32, you can understand the Brethren. The principle is: What do the Brethren do? Do they ever allow a worthy divorced person to be sealed to another spouse, in the temple? Answer: "Yes." Would they allow such a thing if such sealing led automatically to adultery? Answer: "No. It would be a mockery of most sacred ordinances." Conclusion: There must be some things we don't understand about verse 32.

With this conclusion in mind, we might wonder at the meaning of specific words in verse 32. For instance, the word "fornication" is usually used with respect to sexual sin between unmarried individuals. Why, then, is it used in this verse where married people are involved? One possibility is that the word "fornication" is often used in the scriptures to mean total disloyalty, breaking covenants, etc. See, for example, Revelation 14:8, 17:2, 19:2. The word "adultery" is likewise often used in the sense of total disloyalty to God, apostasy etc. This is mentioned on page 604 of the Bible Dictionary, in the back of your LDS Bible, under the topic, "Adultery," where it says: "While adultery is usually spoken of in the individual sense, it is sometimes used to illustrate the apostasy of a nation or a whole people from the ways of the Lord, such as Israel forsaking her God and going after strange gods and strange practices. (Ex. 20:14; Jer. 3:7-10; Matt. 5:27-32; Luke 18:11;)."

32 But I say unto you, That whosoever shall put away (divorce) his wife, saving for (except for) the cause of fornication, causeth her to commit adultery: and whosoever shall marry her that is divorced committeth adultery. (See notes above)

33 Again, ye have heard that it hath been said by them of old time, Thou shalt not forswear thyself (commit perjury; make false promises), but shalt perform unto the Lord thine oaths (keep your word):

34 But I say unto you, Swear (make contracts, promises, etc.) not at all; neither by heaven; for it is God's throne:

35 Nor by the earth; for it is his footstool: neither by Jerusalem; for it is the city of the great King.

36 Neither shalt thou swear by thy head, because thou canst not make one hair white or black.

Note: It was common among the Jews to make agreements, contracts, etc. so complex that they were easy to get out of, legally. For instance, if one promised "by the full moon" that a chariot for sale was in top shape, and it wasn't, one could later say to the irate customer that the moon wasn't actually a full moon on the day of the contract, rather, was a day or two away from its full phase. Thus, the one giving his word was legally exempt from keeping it.

37 But let your communication be, Yea, yea; Nay, nay: for whatsoever is more than these cometh of evil. (In other words, if you make a promise, keep it.)

38 Ye have heard that it hath been said, An eye for an eye, and a tooth for a tooth:

Note: This could be considered a rather high law, as given in Exodus 21:24-25, Leviticus 24:20, etc. In effect, it meant "...only *one* eye for an eye, only *one* tooth for a tooth, only *one* cow for a cow, only *one* sheep for a sheep." Many people tended to get revenge, kill off a whole village in retaliation for the death of a sheep or other wrong against themselves. Now, the Savior will give a much higher law, a law requiring even more self control and forgiving. Keeping such higher laws develops Christlike qualities in us. These higher laws are designed by the Lord to lead us along the path towards exaltation, as stated in verse 45, "That ye may be the children of (successful followers of) your Father which is in heaven:" In other words, this is a vital part of our education toward becoming gods.

39 But I say unto you, That ye resist not evil: but whosoever shall smite thee on thy right cheek, turn to him the other also.

40 And if any man will sue thee at the law, and take away thy coat, let him have *thy* cloke also.

41 And whosoever shall compel thee to go a mile, go with him twain.

Note: Often, we tend to look at these

verses and think in terms of extremes. For instance, if attacked by a mob, intent on severely harming or killing us, we might be hesitant to give them a head start by "turning the other cheek". In fact, D&C 98:31 seems to give different instructions for situations where life is in immediate danger. If we look at the Savior's words in terms of daily living, we see and experience that exercising self-control on our part, returning good for evil, does much good in our relationships with others.

42 Give to him that asketh thee, and from him that would borrow of thee turn not thou away.

43 Ye have heard that it hath been said, Thou shalt love thy neighbour, and hate thine enemy.

44 But I say unto you, Love your enemies, bless them that curse you, do good to them that hate you, and pray for them which despitefully use you, and persecute you;

45 That ye may be the children of your Father which is in heaven (that you may become gods): for he maketh his sun to rise on the evil and on the good, and sendeth rain on the just (the righteous) and on the unjust (the wicked). (He shows love and kindness for all.)

46 For if ye love them which love you, what reward have ye? do not even the publicans the same? (Publicans were Jews who worked for the Roman government as tax collectors. They were hated by the Jews and were excommunicated when they accepted such employment. See Bible Dictionary, page 755)

47 And if ye salute your brethren only, what do ye more *than others*? do not even the publicans so?

Note: As we become more successful in developing the Christlike qualities given in the above commandments, we draw closer to fulfilling the startling yet wonderful commandment given next in verse 48.)

48 Be ye therefore perfect, even as your Father which is in heaven is perfect. (JST Matt. 5:50 "Ye are therefore commanded to be perfect, even as your Father who is in heaven is perfect." The word "perfect", as used here, means complete, finished, fully developed, as stated in Matt. 5:48, footnote b. This denotes our actively pursuing the path leading to exaltation, eventually becoming "fully developed", and thus makes this commandment attainable for us.)

MATTHEW 6

1 Take heed that ye do not your alms (righteous deeds; contributions to the poor, etc.) before men, to be seen of them (your main motive for doing them): otherwise ye have no reward of your Father which is in heaven.

2 Therefore when thou doest *thine* alms, do not sound a trumpet before thee, as the hypocrites (people who want to look righteous but do not want to be righteous) do in the synagogues and in the streets, that they may have glory of men. Verily I say unto you, They have their reward (the reward of having people think they are righteous).

3 But when thou doest alms (give offerings for the poor etc.), let not thy

left hand know what thy right hand doeth:

4 That thine alms may be in secret: and thy Father which seeth in secret himself shall reward thee openly.

5 And when thou prayest, thou shalt not be as the hypocrites *are*: for they love to pray standing in the synagogues (church buildings where the Jews worshiped) and in the corners of the streets, that they may be seen of men. Verily I say unto you, They have their reward.

6 But thou, when thou prayest, enter into thy closet, and when thou hast shut thy door, pray to thy Father which is in secret; and thy Father which seeth in secret shall reward thee openly.

7 But when ye pray, use not vain (useless, meaningless, ineffective) repetitions, as the heathen (non-Jews, non-Christians) *do*: for they think that they shall be heard for their much speaking.

8 Be not ye therefore like unto them: for your Father knoweth what things ye have need of, before ye ask him.

Note: The Savior now gives us what is commonly known as "The Lord's Prayer". It is a beautiful example of prayer and may be considered to be one example of appropriate prayer, rather than a rigid form to be followed without deviation.

9 After this manner therefore pray ye: Our Father which art in heaven, Hallowed (sacred, holy) be thy name.

10 Thy kingdom come. Thy will be done in earth, as *it is* in heaven.

11 Give us this day our daily bread.

12 And forgive us our debts (sins, faults, offenses–see Matt. 6:12, footnote a), as we forgive our debtors. (This is an important formula for our obtaining forgiveness for our own sins.)

13 And lead us not into temptation (we should avoid purposely putting ourselves into temptation) , but deliver us from evil: For thine is the kingdom, and the power, and the glory, for ever. Amen.

14 For if ye forgive men their trespasses (their sins against you), your heavenly Father will also forgive you:

15 But if ye forgive not men their trespasses, neither will your Father forgive your trespasses. (This is a very simple guide to obtaining forgiveness ourselves.)

Note: The Savior now reminds us again that our internal motives are what really count in pursuing the path to exaltation.

16 Moreover when ye fast, be not, as the hypocrites (people who want to look righteous but don't want to be righteous), of a sad countenance: for they disfigure their faces, that they may appear unto men to fast. Verily I say unto you, They have their reward (people look at them and think that they are righteous).

17 But thou, when thou fastest, anoint thine head, and wash thy face;

18 That thou appear not unto men to fast, but unto thy Father which is in secret: and thy Father, which seeth in secret, shall reward thee openly.

Note: Another reminder about priorities is presented now.

19 Lay not up for yourselves treasures upon earth, where moth and rust doth corrupt, and where thieves break through and steal:

20 But lay up for yourselves treasures in heaven, where neither moth nor rust doth corrupt, and where thieves do not break through nor steal:

Note: In the Book of Mormon, Jacob 2:17-19, we find the following counsel about obtaining personal wealth which can go along with these teachings of the Savior in the Sermon on the Mount:

17 Think of your brethren like unto yourselves, and be familiar with all and free with your substance, that they may be rich like unto you.

18 But before ye seek for riches, seek ye for the kingdom of God.

19 And after ye have obtained a hope in Christ ye shall obtain riches, if ye seek them; and ye will seek them for the intent to do good—to clothe the naked, and to feed the hungry, and to liberate the captive, and administer relief to the sick and the afflicted.

21 For where your treasure is, there will your heart be also.

22 The light of the body is the eye: if therefore thine eye be single (Matt. 6:22, footnote b, healthy, sincere, without improper motives. JST ...single to the glory of God...), thy whole body shall be full of light. (What you watch, read, intentionally look at etc., strongly affects your spiritual well-being.)

23 But if thine eye be evil (intentionally takes in evil things), thy whole body shall be full of darkness. If therefore the light that is in thee be darkness, how great is that darkness (spiritual darkness)!

24 ¶ No man can serve two masters: for either he will hate the one, and love the other; or else he will hold to the one, and despise the other. Ye cannot serve God and mammon (worldly sins, pleasures, desires).

Note: We learn from the wording in JST Matt. 6:25-27, that the Savior now turns from the multitude, and addresses verses 25-34 specifically to His Apostles and some disciples, telling them how they will be taken care of by the Father while on their missions. If you do not understand this, you might mistakenly consider some of the counsel in verses 25 to 34 to apply to all people. For instance, you might quit working and trust the Lord to take care of you, thinking that if you have sufficient faith etc., all your needs will be taken care of. Some people and groups have misapplied these verses with sad results. JST Matt. 6:25-27 reads as follows:

25 And, again, I say unto you, Go ye into the world, and care not for the world; for the world will hate you, and will persecute you, and will turn you out of their synagogues.

26 Nevertheless, ye shall go forth from house to house, teaching the people; and I will go before you.

27 And your heavenly Father will provide for you, whatsoever things ye need for food, what ye shall eat; and for raiment, what ye shall wear or put on.

25 Therefore I say unto you (the Savior's Apostles and disciples, who

are now being given instructions to take the gospel to all the world), Take no thought for your life, what ye shall eat, or what ye shall drink; nor yet for your body, what ye shall put on. Is not the life more than meat (food [in our Bible's language, "meat" means food in general, "flesh" means meat as we use the word]), and the body than raiment (clothing)?

26 Behold the fowls of the air: for they sow not (don't plant crops), neither do they reap (harvest crops), nor gather into barns; yet your heavenly Father feedeth them. Are ye (the Savior's Apostles and disciples) not much better than they?

27 Which of you by taking thought can add one cubit (about 18 inches) unto his stature (physical height)?

28 And why take ye thought for raiment (clothing)? Consider the lilies of the field, how they grow; they toil not, neither do they spin (weave cloth):

29 And yet I say unto you, That even Solomon in all his glory was not arrayed (dressed) like one of these.

30 Wherefore, if God so clothe the grass of the field, which to day is, and to morrow is cast into the oven, *shall he* not much more *clothe* you, O ye of little faith?

Note: Just a reminder about why our Bible sometimes has words in *italics*: When the translators of the King James Version [1611 AD] of the Bible–the one we use–didn't know the meaning of a word or phrase in the ancient manuscripts from which they were translating, they requested that their "best guess" be printed in *italics* to alert the reader that they didn't know for sure.

31 Therefore take no thought, saying, What shall we eat? or, What shall we drink? or, Wherewithal shall we be clothed?

32 (For after all these things do the Gentiles seek:) for your heavenly Father knoweth that ye have need of all these things.

33 But seek ye first the kingdom of God, and his righteousness; and all these things shall be added unto you. (Cross-reference this with Jacob 2:17-19 as given between verses 20 and 21 above.)

34 Take therefore no thought for the morrow: for the morrow shall take thought for the things of itself (in other words, the Lord will take care of the Apostles' physical needs while they are on missions). Sufficient unto the day is the evil thereof (The New International Version of the Bible translates this sentence to read, "Each day has enough trouble of its own." The Apostles and disciples are being told that they will have enough daily troubles in preaching the gospel, without the distraction of worrying about their physical needs.)

MATTHEW 7

1 Judge not, that ye be not judged (judged harshly on Judgment Day, etc.).

Note: Obviously, there are situations in which we must judge, or we would constantly be victims of foolishness and deceit. JST Matt. 7:1-2 adds important clarity to this verse, as follows:

1 Now these are the words which Jesus taught his disciples that they should say unto the people.

2 Judge not unrighteously, that ye be not judged; but judge righteous judgment.

2 For with what judgment ye judge, ye shall be judged: and with what measure ye mete (give out to others), it shall be measured to you again.

3 And why beholdest thou the mote (tiny speck; imperfection) that is in thy brother's eye, but considerest not the beam (large wooden beam; symbolic of shortcomings, faults) that is in thine own eye?

4 Or how wilt thou say to thy brother, Let me pull out the mote out of thine eye; and, behold, a beam is in thine own eye?

5 Thou hypocrite, first cast out the beam out of thine own eye; and then shalt thou see clearly to cast out the mote out of thy brother's eye.

Note: JST Matt. 7:4-8 clarifies the three verses above as follows:

4 And again, ye shall say unto them, Why is it that thou beholdest the mote that is in thy brother's eye, but considerest not the beam that is in thine own eye?

5 Or how wilt thou say to thy brother, Let me pull out the mote out of thine eye; and canst not behold a beam in thine own eye?

6 And Jesus said unto his disciples, Beholdest thou the scribes, and the Pharisees, and the priests, and the Levites? They teach in their synagogues, but do not observe the law, nor the commandments; and all have gone out of the way, and are under sin.

7 Go thou and say unto them, Why teach ye men the law and the commandments, when ye yourselves are the children of corruption?

8 Say unto them, Ye hypocrites, first cast out the beam out of thine own eye; and then shalt thou see clearly to cast out the mote out of thy brother's eye.

6 Give not that which is holy unto the dogs, neither cast ye your pearls before swine (be careful with whom you share sacred things), lest they trample them under their feet, and turn again and rend you (they may turn on you and try to destroy your testimony)

Note: The Lord next invites us to feel free to ask for help from Him.

7 Ask, and it shall be given you; seek, and ye shall find; knock, and it shall be opened unto you:

Note: The words "ask", "seek", and "knock" remind us that work is required on our part.

8 For every one that asketh receiveth; and he that seeketh findeth; and to him that knocketh it shall be opened.

9 Or what man is there of you, whom if his son ask bread, will he give him a stone?

10 Or if he ask a fish, will he give him a serpent?

11 If ye then, being evil, know how to give good gifts unto your children, how much more shall your Father which is in heaven give good things to them that ask him?

Note: The Savior gives what is known as "The Golden Rule" in the next verse.

12 Therefore all things whatsoever ye would that men should do to you, do ye even so to them: for this is the law and the prophets (the "law " means the first five books of the Old Testament, and the "prophets" means the inspired writings of Old Testament prophets. The meaning of the phrase "for this is the law and the prophets" is that a major focus of the law and the prophets was to teach us to be good to each other.)

13 Enter ye in at the strait (spelled this way, the word "strait" means narrow, reminding us that this gate has limited access, and requires faith, repentance, baptism and personal righteousness for entrance) gate: for wide is the gate, and broad is the way (there are many ways to be wicked), that leadeth to destruction, and many there be which go in thereat:

Note: In the next verse we find the words "strait" and "narrow" used together. This is often referred to as "the strait and narrow path", meaning the "narrow and narrowing path". The message here is that the more righteous you become, the more you restrict your behaviors away from evil and toward personal righteousness. The imagery is that the less you wander back and forth toward the outer edges of the path, seeing how close you can get to temptation and evil, the "narrower" your chosen path becomes. There is a bit of a caution here: As you become more righteous, you discover inappropriate personal behaviors which you didn't even notice before. Sometimes, faithful saints become discouraged and think

"It's no use. I'll never be perfect!" as these so-called "smaller" imperfections come to light. Actually, you might want to rejoice in the fact that your path has become sufficiently "narrow" that you notice these imperfections. Then, go ahead and work on overcoming them.

14 Because strait is the gate, and narrow is the way, which leadeth unto life (eternal life, exaltation), and few there be that find it.

15 Beware of false prophets (anyone who teaches false philosophies, behaviors etc., by word, example, deed, etc.), which come to you in sheep's clothing (they seem harmless), but inwardly they are ravening (very dangerous) wolves.

16 Ye shall know them by their fruits (what they ultimately produce). Do men gather grapes of thorns, or figs of thistles (can you harvest good food from weeds)?

17 Even so every good tree bringeth forth good fruit; but a corrupt tree bringeth forth evil fruit.

Note: "Tree" is used here to symbolize people.

18 A good tree cannot bring forth evil fruit, neither *can* a corrupt tree bring forth good fruit.

19 Every tree that bringeth not forth good fruit is hewn down, and cast into the fire (symbolic of the burning of the wicked at the Second Coming; also symbolic of the final judgment).

20 Wherefore (therefore) by their fruits ye shall know them.

Note: The Lord now emphasizes again that the gate is "strait" (narrow), in other words, we must keep the commandments in order to enter celestial glory.

21 Not every one that saith unto me, Lord, Lord, shall enter into the kingdom of heaven (celestial glory); but he that doeth the will of my Father which is in heaven.

22 Many will say to me in that day (judgment day), Lord, Lord, have we not prophesied in thy name? and in thy name have cast out devils? and in thy name done many wonderful works?

23 And then will I profess unto them, I never knew you (JST "And then will I say, Ye never knew me"): depart from me, ye that work iniquity (commit sin; disobey the laws of God).

24 Therefore whosoever heareth these sayings of mine, and doeth them, I will liken him unto a wise man, which built his house (symbolic of his life) upon a rock (symbolic of Christ, who is the "rock" of our salvation, see Hymn # 258):

25 And the rain descended, and the floods came, and the winds blew (trials and difficulties of life), and beat upon that house (his life); and it fell not: for it was founded upon a rock (Christ).

26 And every one that heareth these sayings of mine (in other words, who is accountable), and doeth them not, shall be likened unto a foolish man, which built his house upon the sand (worldly ways, priorities etc.):

27 And the rain descended, and the floods came, and the winds blew, and beat upon that house (his life); and it fell: and great was the fall of it.

28 And it came to pass, when Jesus had ended these sayings, the people were astonished at his doctrine:

29 For he taught them as one having authority, and not as the scribes (the main teachers and interpreters of the law among the Jews who rose in great opposition to the Savior. See Bible Dictionary, page 770).

MATTHEW 8

1 When he was come down from the mountain (after giving the Sermon on the Mount), great multitudes followed him.

2 And, behold, there came a leper and worshipped him, saying, Lord, if thou wilt, thou canst make me clean (heal me).

Note: Leprosy is described in Webster's New World Dictionary, Second College Edition, as follows: "...a chronic infectious disease...that attacks the skin, flesh, nerves, etc.; it is characterized by nodules, ulcers, white scaly scabs, deformities, and wasting of body parts,..."

3 And Jesus put forth *his* hand, and touched him, saying, I will; be thou clean. And immediately his leprosy was cleansed.

Note: Every time you read of a physical healing of the sick, performed by the Savior, you can consider it symbolic of His ability to heal us spiritually, through His Atonement. Thus, every healing will remind you of the Master's power to heal you spiritually, through your repentance and His forgiving you. In this case of the healing of a leper, leprosy could be symbolic of very serious sin which can gradually destroy us spiritually.

4 And Jesus saith unto him (the leper who had been healed), See thou tell no man (keep this spiritual experience very private); but go thy way, shew thyself to the priest, and offer the gift that Moses commanded, for a testimony unto them (keep the requirements of the Law of Moses with respect to the cleansing of lepers).

5 And when Jesus was entered into Capernaum, there came unto him a centurion (a Roman soldier in charge of 100 soldiers), beseeching him,

Note: The Romans were gentiles, and thus were considered by the Jews to be inferior in the eyes of God, compared to the Jews, who considered themselves to be God's only chosen people. All others, despite their best efforts, were considered to be second class citizens in the Kingdom of God.

6 And saying, Lord, my servant lieth at home sick of the palsy, grievously tormented.

7 And Jesus saith unto him, I will come and heal him.

8 The centurion answered and said, Lord, I am not worthy that thou shouldest come under my roof: but speak the word only, and my servant shall be healed.

9 For I am a man under authority, having soldiers under me: and I say to this *man*, Go, and he goeth; and to another, Come, and he cometh; and to my servant, Do this, and he doeth *it*.

10 When Jesus heard it, he marvelled, and said to them that followed, Verily I say unto you, I have not found so great faith, no, not in Israel.

11 And I say unto you, That many shall come from the east and west (many foreigners, including Gentiles), and shall sit down with (be saved along with) Abraham, and Isaac, and Jacob, in the kingdom of heaven (celestial glory).

12 But the children of the kingdom (those Jews who considered themselves to be elite, above all other peoples) shall be cast out into outer darkness: there shall be weeping and gnashing of teeth.

13 And Jesus said unto the centurion, Go thy way; and as thou hast believed, *so* be it done unto thee. And his servant was healed in the selfsame hour.

14 And when Jesus was come into Peter's house, he saw his wife's mother laid, and sick of a fever (Peter's mother-in-law was very ill).

15 And he touched her hand, and the fever left her: and she arose, and ministered unto them (attended to their needs).

16 When the even (evening) was come, they brought unto him many that were possessed with devils: and he cast out the spirits with *his* word, and healed all that were sick (symbolic of the Atonement's power to cleanse and heal):

17 That it might be fulfilled which was spoken by Esaias (Isaiah) the prophet, saying, Himself (he, himself; Christ) took our infirmities, and bare *our* sicknesses (see Isaiah 53:5, Alma 7:12).

Note: From the above verse and cross-references, we learn that the Savior's

Atonement works not only for our sins, but also for our infirmities, meaning our shortcomings, imperfections, etc., as we strive to live righteously.

18 Now when Jesus saw great multitudes about him, he gave commandment to depart unto the other side (of the Sea of Galilee).

19 And a certain scribe (a leader among the Jews) came, and said unto him, Master, I will follow thee whithersoever thou goest.

20 And Jesus saith unto him, The foxes have holes, and the birds of the air *have* nests; but the Son of man hath not where to lay *his* head (in other words, following the Savior can require difficult personal sacrifices).

21 And another of his disciples said unto him, Lord, suffer me (allow me) first to go and bury my father.

22 But Jesus said unto him, Follow me; and let the dead bury their dead (there is probably more to the story here, but the message is clear, that following the Savior requires real commitment to Him and His instructions).

23 And when he was entered into a ship, his disciples followed him.

Note: We now read of the experience during the storm which was the inspiration for Hymn # 105, Master the Tempest is Raging. In these next verses we will again be clearly taught that Christ has power over the elements.

24 And, behold, there arose a great tempest (storm) in the sea, insomuch that the ship was covered with the waves: but he (the Savior) was asleep.

Note: One can imagine the stress on the disciples in the ship, being in such danger while the Master slept. Also, we are reminded that the Savior could get very, very tired and weary. In Mosiah 3:7, we read: " And lo, he shall suffer temptations, and pain of body, hunger, thirst, and fatigue, even more than man can suffer, except it be unto death;" We might also imagine the dilemma faced by the frightened disciples, knowing how tired the Savior was, in deciding which one of them should attempt to awaken the sleeping Master.

25 And his disciples came to *him*, and awoke him, saying, Lord, save us: we perish.

26 And he saith unto them, Why are ye fearful, O ye of little faith? Then he arose, and rebuked the winds and the sea; and there was a great calm.

27 But the men marvelled, saying, What manner of man is this, that even the winds and the sea obey him (the disciples are still learning about the Savior and who He really is)!

28 And when he was come to the other side into the country of the Gergesenes (an area on the eastern side of the Sea of Galilee; see Talmage, *Jesus the Christ*, pages 323-324) , there met him two possessed with devils, coming out of the tombs, exceeding fierce, so that no man might pass by that way.

29 And, behold, they (the evil spirits) cried out, saying, What have we to do with thee, Jesus, thou Son of God? art thou come hither to torment us before

the time?

Note: There are many things that can be learned about evil spirits, based on this incident. Apostle Bruce R. McConkie summarized these things as follows:

(1) That evil spirits, actual beings from Lucifer's realm, gain literal entrance into mortal bodies;

(2) That they then have such power over those bodies as to control the physical acts performed, even to the framing of the very words spoken by the mouth of those so possessed;

(3) That persons possessed by evil spirits are subjected to the severest mental and physical sufferings and to the basest sort of degradation—all symbolical of the eternal torment to be imposed upon those who fall under Satan's control in the world to come;

(4) That devils remember Jesus from pre-existence, recognize him as the One who was then foreordained to be the Redeemer, and know that he came into mortality as the Son of God;

(5) That the desire to gain bodies is so great among Lucifer's minions as to cause them, not only to steal the mortal tabernacles of men, but to enter the bodies of animals;

(6) That the devils know their eventual destiny is to be cast out into an eternal hell from whence there is no return;

(7) That rebellious and worldly people are not converted to the truth by observing miracles; and

(8) That those cleansed from evil spirits can then be used on the Lord's errand to testify of his grace and goodness so that receptive persons may be led to believe in him.

(Bruce R. McConkie, *Doctrinal New Testament Commentary*, 3 vols. [Salt Lake City: Bookcraft, 1965-1973], Vol. 1, p. 311)

30 And there was a good way off from them an herd of many swine (pigs) feeding.

31 So the devils besought (asked) him, saying, If thou cast us out, suffer (allow) us to go away into the herd of swine.

32 And he said unto them, Go. And when they were come out, they went into the herd of swine: and, behold, the whole herd of swine ran violently down a steep place into the sea, and perished in the waters.

33 And they (the herdsmen) that kept them (the pigs) fled, and went their ways into the city, and told every thing, and what was befallen to the possessed of the devils.

34 And, behold, the whole city came out to meet Jesus: and when they saw him, they besought (asked) *him* that he would depart out of their coasts (they asked Jesus to leave).

Note: It is sad that the people of the city asked the Savior to leave, rather than inviting Him to stay and teach them His gospel. Perhaps they didn't want another economic disaster–Mark 5:13 tells us there were 2000 swine.

MATTHEW 9

1 And he entered into a ship, and passed over (went back over to the west side of the Sea of Galilee), and came into his own city (Nazareth).

2 And, behold, they brought to him a man sick of the palsy, lying on a bed:

and Jesus seeing their faith said unto the sick of the palsy; Son, be of good cheer; thy sins be forgiven thee.

3 And, behold, certain of the scribes (religious leaders among the Jews who claimed the right to interpret the scriptures and had great power in the Jewish culture) said within themselves, This *man* blasphemeth (is acting with total disrespect for God and sacred things; a crime punishable by death in the Jewish society).

4 And Jesus knowing their thoughts (the scribes' thoughts) said, Wherefore (why) think ye evil in your hearts?

5 For whether (which) is easier, to say, *Thy* sins be forgiven thee; or to say, Arise, and walk? (Any person could say "Your sins are forgiven.", because there is no immediate proof as to whether or not he speaks with authority. But, if a person says "Arise and walk.", there will be immediate evidence as to whether or not he is a fake.)

6 But that ye may know that the Son of man (the Son of "Man of Holiness" [Heavenly Father's name in Adam's language], in other words, the Son of God; see Moses 6:57) hath power on earth to forgive sins, (then saith he to the sick of the palsy,) Arise, take up thy bed, and go unto thine house.

7 And he (the man healed of palsy) arose, and departed to his house.

8 But when the multitudes saw *it*, they marvelled, and glorified God, which had given such power unto men.

9 And as Jesus passed forth from thence, he saw a man, named Matthew, sitting at the receipt of custom (Matthew was a tax collector): and he saith unto him, Follow me. And he arose, and followed him.

10 And it came to pass, as Jesus sat at meat (eating a meal) in the house, behold, many publicans (Jews who worked for the Romans as tax collectors; see Bible Dictionary, p. 755) and sinners came and sat down with him and his disciples.

11 And when the Pharisees (religious leaders among the Jews; see Bible Dictionary, p. 751) saw *it*, they said unto his disciples, Why eateth your Master with publicans and sinners?

12 But when Jesus heard *that*, he said unto them (the Pharisees), They that be whole need not a physician, but they that are sick.

13 But go ye and learn what *that* meaneth, I will have mercy, and not sacrifice (quoting Hosea 6:6; the Pharisees were very strict in living the letter of the Law of Moses, including proper animal sacrifice, but did not often show mercy): for I am not come to call the righteous, but sinners to repentance.

14 Then came to him the disciples of John (followers of John the Baptist, who was in prison by this time and soon to be beheaded by Herod), saying, Why do we and the Pharisees fast oft, but thy disciples fast not?

15 And Jesus said unto them, Can the children of the bridechamber mourn, as long as the bridegroom is with them? but the days will come, when the bridegroom shall be taken from them, and then shall they fast.

Note: Understanding a bit of Jewish culture will help with the last verse. Wedding imagery is involved. Jesus is the bridegroom, or groom, as we would say it. Faithful followers are the bride. "Bridechamber" would be the place where the wedding feast is held and, symbolically, would be the land of Israel where the Savior was performing His mortal mission. While the groom and the bride are together, much celebrating and feasting–hearing and understanding the Savior's teachings–would take place. It would not make sense to mourn and fast at this time. But, when the Savior is crucified and taken from them, the "children of the bridechamber", the faithful saints, will mourn and fast.

Note: Next, Jesus will teach that people who are set in their ways do not usually accept new ideas, in this case, the true gospel.

16 No man putteth (sews) a piece of new cloth (the true gospel) unto an old garment (piece of clothing; symbolic of people set in their ways with false religions and philosophies), for that which is put in to fill it up taketh from the garment, and the rent (rip, tear) is made worse.

17 Neither do men put new wine (symbolic of the true gospel) into old bottles (symbolic of people): else the bottles break, and the wine runneth out, and the bottles perish: but they put new wine into new bottles, and both are preserved.

18 While he spake these things unto them, behold, there came a certain ruler (Luke 8:41 tells us his name was Jairus and that he was a ruler in a synagogue), and worshipped him, saying, My daughter is even now dead: but come and lay thy hand upon her, and she shall live.

19 And Jesus arose, and followed him, and *so did* his disciples.

20 And, behold, a woman, which was diseased with an issue of blood twelve years (who had been hemorrhaging for twelve years, see Matt. 9:20, footnote a), came behind *him*, and touched the hem of his garment:

21 For she said within herself, If I may but touch his garment, I shall be whole (healed).

22 But Jesus turned him about, and when he saw her, he said, Daughter, be of good comfort; thy faith hath made thee whole. And the woman was made whole from that hour.

23 And when Jesus came into the ruler's house, and saw the minstrels (musicians) and the people (mourners–often paid) making a noise,

24 He said unto them, Give place: for the maid (the ruler's daughter) is not dead, but sleepeth. And they laughed him to scorn (ridiculed Jesus).

25 But when the people were put forth (had been sent out of the house), he went in, and took her by the hand, and the maid arose.

26 And the fame hereof went abroad into all that land.

27 And when Jesus departed thence, two blind men followed him, crying, and saying, *Thou* Son of David (it was widely taught among the Jews that the Messiah would be a descendant of King David; thus, these blind men were acknowledging Jesus as the promised Messiah), have mercy on us.

28 And when he was come into the house, the blind men came to him: and Jesus saith unto them, Believe ye that I am able to do this? They said unto him, Yea, Lord.

29 Then touched he their eyes, saying, According to your faith be it unto you.

30 And their eyes were opened (they were healed); and Jesus straitly charged them (strictly instructed them), saying, See *that* no man know *it*.

31 But they, when they were departed, spread abroad his fame in all that country.

32 As they went out, behold, they brought to him a dumb man (one who could not speak) possessed with a devil (an evil spirit).

33 And when the devil was cast out, the dumb spake: and the multitudes marvelled, saying, It was never so seen in Israel.

34 But the Pharisees (religious leaders among the Jews) said, He casteth out devils through the prince of the devils (the Pharisees, who seem good at missing the point, miss it again, and accuse Jesus of working for Satan and using the devil's power to cast out other devils).

35 And Jesus went about all the cities and villages, teaching in their synagogues, and preaching the gospel of the kingdom, and healing every sickness and every disease among the people (symbolic of the power of the Atonement to cleanse and heal all our spiritual ills).

36 But when he saw the multitudes, he was moved with compassion on them, because they fainted, and were scattered abroad, as sheep having no shepherd (they didn't really know where they were going).

37 Then saith he unto his disciples, The harvest truly is plenteous (there are so many people who need the true gospel), but the labourers (missionaries, etc.) *are* few;

38 Pray ye therefore the Lord of the harvest, that he will send forth labourers into his harvest.

MATTHEW 10

Note: This chapter contains much specific instruction and training for the newly-called Twelve Apostles.

1 And when he had called unto *him* his twelve disciples (the Twelve Apostles), he gave them power *against* unclean spirits, to cast them out, and to heal all manner of sickness and all manner of disease.

2 Now the names of the twelve apostles are these; The first, Simon, who is called Peter, and Andrew his brother; James *the son* of Zebedee, and John his brother;

3 Philip, and Bartholomew; Thomas, and Matthew the publican (tax collector); James *the son* of Alphaeus, and Lebbaeus, whose surname (last name; family name) was Thaddaeus;

4 Simon the Canaanite, and Judas Iscariot, who also betrayed him.

5 These twelve Jesus sent forth, and commanded them, saying, Go not into the way of the Gentiles, and into *any* city of the Samaritans enter ye not: (In other words, don't go to the Gentiles yet.)

6 But go rather to the lost sheep of the house of Israel.

7 And as ye go, preach, saying, The kingdom of heaven is at hand (is available to you now).

8 Heal the sick, cleanse the lepers, raise the dead, cast out devils: freely ye have received, freely give.

9 Provide neither gold, nor silver, nor brass in your purses,

10 Nor scrip (a bag containing food and provisions) for *your* journey, neither two coats, neither shoes, nor yet staves: for the workman is worthy of his meat (the Lord will take care of you).

11 And into whatsoever city or town ye shall enter, enquire who in it is worthy; and there abide till ye go thence (stay with a worthy person while there).

12 And when ye come into an house, salute it (Luke 10:5 helps with this; it says "...into whatsoever house ye enter, first say, Peace be to this house").

13 And if the house be worthy, let your peace come upon it: but if it be not worthy, let your peace return to you.

14 And whosoever shall not receive you, nor hear your words, when ye depart out of that house or city, shake off the dust of your feet (as a witness that they have had an opportunity to accept the gospel).

15 Verily I say unto you, It shall be more tolerable for the land of Sodom and Gomorrha (Old Testament cities which were destroyed completely because of wickedness) in the day of judgment, than for that city. (It is a very serious thing to reject the Lord's servants.)

16 Behold, I send you forth as sheep in the midst of wolves: be ye therefore wise as serpents (use honest cunning and common sense), and harmless as doves (be without guile).

17 But beware of men: for they will deliver you up to the councils (arrest you and turn you over to local courts), and they will scourge (flog, whip) you in their synagogues;

18 And ye shall be brought before governors and kings for my sake (because of me and my work), for a testimony against them and the Gentiles.

19 But when they deliver you up (arrest you), take no thought how or what ye shall speak: for it shall be given you (by the Spirt) in that same hour what ye shall speak.

20 For it is not ye that speak, but the Spirit of your Father which speaketh in you.

21 And the brother shall deliver up the brother to death, and the father the child: and the children shall rise up against *their* parents, and cause them to be put to death (you will see much wickedness during your missions).

22 And ye shall be hated of all *men* for my name's sake (because of the work you do for me): but he that endureth (remains faithful) to the end (can mean "goal" or "purpose", as well as "to the end of mortal life") shall be saved.

23 But when they persecute you in this city, flee ye into another: for verily I say unto you, Ye shall not have gone over the cities of Israel, till the Son of man (Christ, Son of Man of Holiness–see Moses 6:57) be come (there is so much missionary work to be done that it will not all be finished before the second coming–see McConkie, *Doctrinal New Testament Commentary*, Vol. 1, p. 332).

24 The disciple is not above *his* master, nor the servant above his lord (just as the Savior will go through

much of persecution, so also His servants will go through much).

25 It is enough for the disciple that he be (become, see Matt. 10:25, footnote a) as his master, and the servant as his lord (the reward of faithful servants of the Savior is to be joint heirs with Christ, exalted like He is). If they have called the master of the house (Christ) Beelzebub, how much more *shall they call* them of his household (if they call Me the devil, don't you think you can expect similar treatment)?

26 Fear them not therefore (they can't take away your exaltation): for there is nothing covered (evil that is hidden, done in secret), that shall not be revealed; and hid, that shall not be known (see 2 Nephi 9:14).

27 What I tell you in darkness (private), *that* speak ye in light (in public): and what ye hear in the ear (what I whisper to you), *that* preach ye upon the housetops (preach to everybody).

28 And fear not them which kill the body, but are not able to kill the soul (don't fear those who may kill you but can't take your salvation from you): but rather fear (respect) him (God, see McConkie, *Doctrinal New Testament Commentary*, Vol. 1, p. 334) which is able to destroy both soul and body in hell.

Note: The Savior now reminds the Twelve (and us) that the Father is aware of all things and is always aware of our concerns, needs, and desires.

29 Are not two sparrows sold for a farthing? and one of them shall not fall on the ground without your Father (being aware of it).

30 But the very hairs of your head are all numbered (the Father literally knows everything about you and can bless you as needed).

31 Fear ye not therefore, ye are of more value than many sparrows.

32 Whosoever therefore shall confess (make covenants with me, see Matt. 10:32, footnote a) me before men, him will I confess (acknowledge, accept) also before my Father which is in heaven.

33 But whosoever shall deny me before men, him will I also deny before my Father which is in heaven.

Note: In the next verses, the Savior tells the Twelve that, on some occasions, the gospel will divide and separate people from others, even loved ones sometimes.

34 Think not that I am come to send peace on earth: I came not to send peace, but a sword.

35 For I am come to set a man at variance against (in opposition to) his father, and the daughter against her mother, and the daughter in law against her mother in law.

36 And a man's foes *shall* be they of his own household (will be family members).

37 He that loveth father or mother more than me is not worthy of me: and he that loveth son or daughter more than me is not worthy of me (we must follow Christ no matter what the cost).

38 And he that taketh not his cross (whatever sacrifices are necessary), and followeth after me, is not worthy of me.

39 He that findeth his life (follows priorities less important than the gospel) shall lose it (shall not gain exaltation): and he that loseth his life for my sake (prioritizes on the gospel above all else) shall find it (will gain exaltation).

40 He that receiveth you receiveth me, and he that receiveth me receiveth him that sent me (Heavenly Father).

41 He that receiveth a prophet (accepts and sustains Church leaders) in the name of a prophet shall receive a prophet's reward (exaltation); and he that receiveth a righteous man in the name of a righteous man shall receive a righteous man's reward.

Note: Finally, the Savior reminds His apostles and us, as His disciples (followers), that charity and service must accompany the above-mentioned attributes, if we want to attain exaltation.

42 And whosoever shall give to drink unto one of these little ones a cup of cold water only in the name of a disciple, verily I say unto you, he shall in no wise lose his reward.

MATTHEW 11

1 And it came to pass, when Jesus had made an end of commanding his twelve disciples, he departed thence to teach and to preach in their cities.

2 Now when John (John the Baptist, who is in prison at this time) had heard in the prison the works of Christ, he sent two of his disciples (John's faithful followers),

3 And said unto him (John the Baptist's disciples asked Jesus), Art thou he that should come (are you the promised Messiah?), or do we look for another?

4 Jesus answered and said unto them, Go and shew John again those things which ye do hear and see:

5 The blind receive their sight, and the lame walk, the lepers are cleansed, and the deaf hear, the dead are raised up, and the poor have the gospel preached to them. (John the Baptist will realize that this is the Savior, when he hears what He has been doing.)

6 And blessed is *he*, whosoever shall not be offended in me.

7 And as they (John's disciples) departed, Jesus began to say unto the multitudes concerning John (the Baptist), What went ye out into the wilderness to see? A reed shaken with the wind (a man who was timid and afraid of opposition)?

8 But what went ye out for to see? A man clothed in soft raiment (clothing; in other words, a man pampered by easy living)? behold, they that wear soft *clothing* are in kings' houses.

9 But what went ye out for to see? A prophet? yea, I say unto you, and more than a prophet. (Jesus has tender feelings for John the Baptist, and bears witness of John's divine calling and mission.)

10 For this is *he*, of whom it is written (prophesied), Behold, I send my messenger (John the Baptist) before thy (the Savior) face, which shall prepare thy way before thee (John is the messenger sent by God to prepare the way before me).

11 Verily I say unto you, Among them that are born of women there

hath not risen a greater than John the Baptist: notwithstanding he that is least in the kingdom of heaven is greater than he.

Note: Verse 11, above, can be a bit confusing, but the Prophet Joseph Smith explains it to us. He tells us that John the Baptist is the greatest prophet, born of woman, but that He, Christ, who is considered by the Jews to be the least in the kingdom, is above John the Baptist. See *Teachings of the Prophet Joseph Smith*, pages 275-276.

12 And from the days of John the Baptist until now the kingdom of heaven suffereth violence, and the violent take it by force (violent people have done much to harm the work of the Lord, see Matt. 11:12, footnote a).

13 For all the prophets (the Old Testament prophets) and the law (the first five books of the Old Testament) prophesied until John (prophesied of things leading up to this time).

14 And if ye will receive *it* (accept my word about who John is), this is Elias, which was for to come (John is the "Elias", the preparer-of-the-way, who was prophesied to prepare the way for me).

15 He that hath ears to hear, let him hear (he who is in tune with the Spirit will understand what has just been taught).

16 But whereunto shall I liken this generation (unto what shall I compare the present generation of people)? It is like unto children sitting in the markets, and calling unto their fellows,

17 And saying, We have piped unto you, and ye have not danced; we have mourned unto you, and ye have not lamented (the current generation is ignoring the messengers of God).

Note: Jesus now tells them that the righteous can never win, in the eyes of the wicked. No matter what the righteous do, the wicked still criticize them.

18 For John (the Baptist) came neither eating nor drinking, and they say, He hath a devil.

19 The Son of man (the Son of God, Christ; see Moses 6:57) came eating and drinking, and they say, Behold a man gluttonous, and a winebibber, a friend of publicans and sinners. But wisdom is justified of her children (actions, deeds; in other words, wise people will see through this constant criticism).

Note: Some people ask whether or not the Savior ever did come right out and say that He is the Son of God. As you study Matthew, Mark, Luke, and John, you will find many instances, including in verse 19 above, wherein He openly told people that He was the Son of God, the promised Messiah.

20 Then began he to upbraid (scold) the cities wherein most of his mighty works were done, because they repented not:

21 Woe unto thee, Chorazin! woe unto thee, Bethsaida! for if the mighty works, which were done in you, had been done in Tyre and Sidon, they would have repented long ago in sackcloth and ashes ("sackcloth and ashes" means in deep humility and mourning for their sins).

22 But I say unto you, It shall be more tolerable for Tyre and Sidon at the day of judgment, than for you (because you have the true gospel available and they don't, yet).

23 And thou, Capernaum, which art exalted unto heaven (full of pride), shalt be brought down to hell: for if the mighty works, which have been done in thee, had been done in Sodom, it would have remained until this day (would not have been destroyed).

24 But I say unto you, That it shall be more tolerable for the land of Sodom in the day of judgment, than for thee.

Note: That Jesus kept in close touch with the Father is evidenced again in these next verses.

25 At that time Jesus answered and said, I thank thee, O Father, Lord of heaven and earth, because thou hast hid these things from the wise and prudent ("old bottles" who won't accept "new wine"), and hast revealed them unto babes (humble people who are willing to accept truth).

26 Even so (let it be so), Father: for so it seemed good in thy sight.

27 All things are delivered unto me of my Father: and no man knoweth the Son, but the Father; neither knoweth any man the Father, save the Son, and *he* to whomsoever the Son will reveal *him* (JST "...and they to whom the Son will reveal himself;").

Note: The Joseph Smith Translation (JST), Matt. 11:27-28, helps us understand the above three verses, as follows: 27. And at that time, there came a voice out of heaven, and Jesus answered and said, I thank thee, O Father, Lord of heaven and earth, because thou hast hid these things from the wise and prudent, and hast revealed them unto babes. Even so, Father, for so it seemed good in thy sight! 28. All things are delivered unto me of my Father; and no man knoweth the Son, but the Father; neither knoweth any man the Father, save the Son, and they to whom the Son will reveal himself; they shall see the Father also.

28 Come unto me, all ye that labour and are heavy laden, and I will give you rest.

29 Take my yoke (my burden, my gospel; make covenants with me) upon you, and learn of me; for I am meek and lowly in heart (I am humble and love to help you): and ye shall find rest unto your souls.

30 For my yoke *is* easy, and my burden is light.

Note: Above, the Savior teaches us that the the path to exaltation is actually the easiest way as well as the happiest. The "burdens" one carries as a devout follower of the Master are nothing compared to the burdens of guilt and shame carried by those who choose wickedness as a lifestyle.

MATTHEW 12

1 At that time Jesus went on the sabbath day through the corn (grain; perhaps wheat); and his disciples were an hungred, and began to pluck the ears of corn (the heads of the grain), and to eat.

2 But when the Pharisees (religious leaders among the Jews) saw *it*, they said unto him, Behold, thy disciples do

that which is not lawful to do upon the sabbath day.

3 But he said unto them, Have ye not read what David (David, the one who killed Goliath and later became king) did, when he was an hungred, and they that were with him;

4 How he entered into the house of God, and did eat the shewbread (holy bread used for worship services, see 1 Samuel 21:6), which was not lawful for him to eat, neither for them which were with him, but only for the priests?

5 Or have ye not read in the law, how that on the sabbath days the priests in the temple profane the sabbath (break some of the sabbath rules), and are blameless (JST ..."and ye say they are blameless.")? (In other words, you allow it in some cases, but won't allow my disciples to do it; you are hypocrites.)

6 But I say unto you, That in this place is *one* greater than the temple (I am here among you and I am greater than the temple).

Note: Here, again (verse 6), Jesus tells them who He is.)

7 But if ye had known what *this* meaneth, I will have mercy, and not sacrifice (quoting Hosea 6:6), ye would not have condemned the guiltless. (In other words, all the animal sacrifices you can possibly do are of no value and are just empty ritual, if you are not merciful to others. You claim to know the scriptures, but you sure don't understand Hosea 6:6!)

Note: The Pharisees and scribes are becoming quite alarmed and puzzled that Jesus knows the Old Testament so well. Of course, as the God of the Old Testament, Christ was the one who gave the revelations to the Old Testament prophets.

8 For the Son of man (Son of Man, Son of God; Jesus; see Moses 6:57) is Lord even of the sabbath day (I am the one who gave the commandments concerning the Sabbath Day).

9 And when he was departed thence, he went into their synagogue:

10 And, behold, there was a man which had his hand withered. And they (the Jewish religious leaders) asked him (Jesus), saying, Is it lawful to heal on the sabbath days? that they might accuse him (that they might trap him and have grounds to have him arrested).

Note: The Savior is a master at answering questions with questions.

11 And he said unto them, What man shall there be among you, that shall have one sheep, and if it fall into a pit on the sabbath day, will he not lay hold on it, and lift it out? (In other words, you yourselves rescue your animals that fall into trouble on the Sabbath.)

12 How much then is a man better than a sheep (how much more important are people than sheep)? Wherefore it is lawful to do well on the sabbath days. (This direct statement, that it is ok to do good on the Sabbath, must have been quite frustrating to these hypocritical religious leaders. To them, it appeared that Jesus was speaking as if He had authority to make the laws, which, of course, he did.)

13 Then saith he to the man, Stretch forth thine hand. And he stretched *it* forth; and it was restored whole, like as the other. (The man's hand was healed, and it was done on the Sabbath, in front of many witnesses, in defiance of these Pharisees, these Jewish religious leaders.)

14 Then the Pharisees went out, and held a council against him, how they might destroy him.

15 But when Jesus knew *it* (that they were plotting against Him), he withdrew himself from thence: and great multitudes followed him, and he healed them all (symbolic of His power to heal all of us spiritually);

16 And charged them that they should not make him known (He asked them to keep these personal experiences with Him private):

Note: The next four verses remind us that one of Matthew's main purposes in writing his gospel was to prove that Jesus fulfilled Old Testament prophecies foretelling the coming of the Savior. In other words, Matthew wanted his audience to realize that Jesus was the promised Messiah.

17 That it might be fulfilled which was spoken by Esaias (Isaiah) the prophet, saying (in Isaiah 42:1-3),

18 Behold my servant (Christ), whom I have chosen; my beloved, in whom my soul is well pleased: I will put my spirit upon him, and he shall shew judgment (justice, fairness, mercy) to the Gentiles.

19 He shall not strive (fight, quarrel), nor cry (shout); neither shall any man hear his voice (shouting) in the streets (Jesus will be peaceable and low key as He goes forth in His mortal ministry).

20 A bruised (bent, crushed) reed shall he not break (He is not here to hurt the weak, the already bruised and broken, rather to help them and save them if they will), and smoking flax (literally a tiny spark smoldering in a bit of fire starter material) shall he not quench (symbolic of the fact that Christ will come to gently fan the tiny spark of spirituality into a flame, rather than snuffing it out), till he send forth judgment unto victory.

21 And in his name shall the Gentiles trust (a prophecy that many Gentiles will take Christ's name upon them).

22 Then was brought unto him one possessed with a devil, blind, and dumb (could not talk): and he healed him, insomuch that the blind and dumb both spake and saw.

23 And all the people were amazed, and said, Is not this the son of David (isn't this the Messiah who was prophesied to come)?

24 But when the Pharisees (corrupt Jewish religious leaders) heard *it*, they said, This *fellow* doth not cast out devils, but by Beelzebub the prince of the devils (Satan, see Bible Dictionary, p. 620; in other words, the Pharisees claim that Jesus is in partnership with the devil and uses that power to cast out devils).

25 And Jesus knew their thoughts, and said unto them, Every kingdom divided against itself is brought to desolation (destruction); and every city or house divided against itself shall not stand (will not survive):

26 And if Satan cast out Satan, he is

divided against himself; how shall then his kingdom stand?

27 And if I by Beelzebub (Satan) cast out devils, by whom do your children cast *them* out? therefore they shall be your judges.

Note: From JST Matt. 12:22-23, we learn the correct interpretation of verse 27 above:

22 And if I by Beelzebub cast out devils, by whom do *your children* cast our devils? Therefore *they* shall be your judges.

23 But if I cast out devils by the Spirit of God, then the kingdom of God is come unto you. For *they also cast out devils by the Spirit of God, for unto them is given power over devils, that they may cast them out."*

(Bold italics added for emphasis) From the words in bold italics, we find that there were righteous Jews, obviously baptized and faithful, who were enabled by the Spirit of God to cast out evil spirits. See McConkie, *Doctrinal New Testament Commentary*, Vol. 1, p. 269.

28 But if I cast out devils by the Spirit of God, then the kingdom of God is come unto you (then you know that I am the promised Messiah and am making the kingdom of God available to you).

29 Or else how can one enter into a strong man's house, and spoil (plunder, rob) his goods, except he first bind the strong man? and then he will spoil his house (one must truly have the power of God over devils in order to cast them out).

30 He that is not with me is against me; and he that gathereth not with me (does not join with me) scattereth abroad (works against me).

31 Wherefore I say unto you, All manner of sin and blasphemy (evil speaking of and evil behavior toward sacred things) shall be forgiven unto men (JST "who receive me and repent"): but the blasphemy *against* the *Holy* Ghost (denying the Holy Ghost) shall not be forgiven unto men.

Note: Simply put, denying the Holy Ghost means knowing full well, by the power of the Holy Ghost, that God exists, that the Church is true etc., then going completely against that sure knowledge, trying to destroy the Church and knowledge of God. In other words, it means becoming like Satan, thinking like he does and acting like he does. See D&C 76:31-35. See also *Teachings of the Prophet Joseph Smith*, page 358.

32 And whosoever speaketh a word against the Son of man (Jesus; Son of Man of Holiness [Heavenly Father] see Moses 6:57), it shall be forgiven him: but whosoever speaketh against the Holy Ghost (denies the Holy Ghost–see note between verses 31 and 32), it shall not be forgiven him, neither in this world, neither in the *world* to come.

33 Either make the tree good, and his fruit good; or else make the tree corrupt, and his fruit corrupt: for the tree is known by *his* fruit. (Jesus is rebuking the Pharisees for accusing Him of being evil, yet doing good in the healing of the man in verse 22. He is saying to them to make up their

minds. Anybody knows that a bad tree doesn't give good fruit. If I'm doing good, I must be a "good tree".)

34 O generation of vipers (you poisonous serpents! This is exactly what John the Baptist called them in Matt. 3:7.), how can ye, being evil, speak good things? for out of the abundance of the heart the mouth speaketh (you can tell what is in your hearts by the evil which comes out of your mouths).

35 A good man out of the good treasure of the heart bringeth forth good things: and an evil man out of the evil treasure bringeth forth evil things.

36 But I say unto you, That every idle word (gossip; unjust criticism, profanity, etc., see Matt. 12:36 footnotes b and c) that men shall speak, they shall give account thereof in the day of judgment.

37 For by thy words (righteous words) thou shalt be justified (saved; approved by God on judgment day), and by thy words ("idle words", wicked words) thou shalt be condemned (stopped; cast out on judgment day).

38 Then certain of the scribes (lawyers, interpreters of the religious laws among the Jews [usually Pharisees]) and of the Pharisees (religious leaders among the Jews) answered, saying, Master, we would see a sign from thee (show us a sign which proves that you are the Messiah, the Christ).

39 But he answered and said unto them, An evil and adulterous generation seeketh after a sign; and there shall no sign be given to it, but the sign of the prophet Jonas (if I do give you a

sign, it will not be what you want, as in the case when Jonah was swallowed by the whale):

40 For as Jonas (Jonah) was three days and three nights in the whale's belly; so shall the Son of man (I, Christ; Son of man means Son of Man of Holiness, meaning Son of Heavenly Father–see Moses 6:57) be three days and three nights in the heart of the earth (I will be in the tomb for three days and three nights).

41 The men of Nineveh (the city to which Jonah finally went and preached) shall rise in judgment with this generation, and shall condemn it: because they repented at the preaching of Jonas (Jonah); and, behold, a greater than Jonas is here (the Son of God is here among you right now; you have no excuse for not repenting!).

Note: These scribes and Pharisees do indeed understand that Jesus is telling them that He is the Son of God. *The Joseph Smith Translation* of the Bible confirms this fact in JST Mark 3:21 as follows: "An then came certain men unto him, accusing him, saying, Why do ye receive sinners, **seeing thou makest thyself the Son of God**." (bold added for emphasis.)

42 The queen of the south (the Queen of Sheba, a famous queen who visited Solomon to learn from him, see 1 Kings 10:1-13) shall rise up in the judgment with this generation, and shall condemn it: for she came from the uttermost parts of the earth to hear the wisdom of Solomon; and, behold (JST "ye behold", i.e., before your very eyes you are seeing), a greater

than Solomon *is* here (the Son of God is greater than Solomon and you are seeing me here right now, and if you had the good sense the Queen of Sheba had, you would be seeking my help rather than trying to destroy me).

Note: Verses 43-45, which come next, may seem at first to be a bit out of context with the foregoing verses. However, in verses 31 and 32 above, the Savior taught that the sin against the Holy Ghost cannot be forgiven in this life or in the life to come. In verses 33 to 42, Jesus is warning these wicked Jewish leaders that they are seeing things which make them very accountable! They are actually seeing the Savior in person, among them, witnessing His teachings and miracles, perhaps feeling His Spirit, and yet denying it and seeking to destroy Him and his work among them. Next, in verses 43-45, He continues His warning to them by giving an illustration which explains why a person who denies the Holy Ghost can't be forgiven. In effect, a person who denies the Holy Ghost (see the note between verses 31 and 32 above) deliberately invites Satan and his evil spirits into his soul (his "house"), and associates with them until he thinks, acts, and becomes like Satan, and thus qualifies to live with him and his evil spirits forever as a son of perdition. **We will use the JST for clarification, after we have read verses 43-45.**

43 When the unclean spirit is gone out of a man, he walketh through dry places, seeking rest, and findeth none.

44 Then he saith, I will return into

my house from whence I came out; and when he is come, he findeth *it* empty, swept, and garnished.

45 Then goeth he, and taketh with himself seven other spirits more wicked than himself, and they enter in and dwell there: and the last *state* of that man is worse than the first. Even so shall it be also unto this wicked generation.

Note: As stated above, we will now use JST Matthew 12:37-39 to help us understand verses 43-45.

37 (Note: This verse is entirely missing from the Bible.) Then came some of the scribes (Jewish religious leaders who specialized in interpreting the gospel doctrines and laws) and said unto him, Master, it is written that, Every sin shall be forgiven; but ye say, Whosoever speaketh against the Holy Ghost shall not be forgiven. And they asked him, saying, How can these things be? (In other words, what you, Jesus, are teaching contradicts our traditional written doctrines.)

38 And he said unto them, When the unclean spirit is gone out of a man (because he has repented etc.), he (the evil spirit) walketh through dry places, seeking rest and findeth none; but when a man speaketh against the Holy Ghost (the man reverts back to his evil ways to the extent of denying the Holy Ghost), then he (the evil spirit) saith, I will return into my house (the man in whom the evil spirit used to reside) from whence I came out; and when he (the evil spirit) is come, he findeth him (the man in whom the evil spirit formerly resided) empty, swept and garnished (was cleansed from sin, with

a sure testimony given him by the Holy Ghost, but who is now speaking against that testimony from the Holy Ghost); for the good spirit (the Holy Ghost) leaveth him unto himself.

39 Then goeth the evil spirit, and taketh with himself seven other spirits more wicked than himself; and they enter in and dwell there (with the man who has denied the Holy Ghost); and the last end of that man is worse than the first (the man is worse off now than he was before he gained a sure testimony from the Holy Ghost). Even so shall it be also unto this wicked generation.

Note: Elder Bruce R. McConkie helps us understand the above three verses as follows: "JST. Matt. 12:37-39. Having already taught that every sin shall be forgiven except the sin against the Holy Ghost, Jesus now illustrates why. In effect he says: 'If you gain a perfect knowledge of me and my mission, it must come by revelation from the Holy Ghost; that Holy Spirit must speak to the spirit within you; and then you shall know, nothing doubting. But to receive this knowledge and revelation, you must cleanse and perfect your own soul; that is, your house must be clean, swept, and garnished. Then if you deny me by speaking against the Holy Ghost who gave you your revelation of the truth, that is if you come out in open rebellion against the perfect light you have received, the Holy Ghost will depart, leaving you to yourself. Your house will now be available for other tenancy, and so the evil spirits and influences you had once conquered will return to plague

you. Having completely lost the preserving power of the Spirit, you will then be worse off than if you had never received the truth; and many in this generation shall be so condemned.'"

Doctrinal New Testament Commentary, Volume 1, page 276.

46 While he yet talked to the people, behold, *his* mother and his brethren (Mary and some family members, see Matt. 12, footnote 46a) stood without (outside), desiring to speak with him.

47 Then one said unto him, Behold (look), thy mother and thy brethren stand without (outside), desiring to speak with thee.

48 But he answered and said unto him that told him, Who is my mother? and who are my brethren? (In other words, who is my family? This is a teaching moment.)

49 And he stretched forth his hand toward his disciples (followers), and said, Behold (you are seeing) my mother and my brethren! (My followers are my family. This answers the question Christ posed in verse 48. See also the answer in verse 50.)

50 (The JST adds an important sentence to the first of this verse. JST "And he gave them charge concerning her [asked them to take good care of his mother while he continued on his mission], saying, I go my way, for my Father hath sent me.") For whosoever shall do the will of my Father which is in heaven, the same is my brother, and sister, and mother.

MATTHEW 13

Note: The Savior will now use a

number of parables to illustrate his teachings. A parable is a story which is used to teach us about real life situations. The Prophet Joseph Smith said: "I have a key by which I understand the scriptures. I enquire, what was the question which drew out the answer, or caused Jesus to utter the parable?" *Teachings of the Prophet Joseph Smith*, pages 276-277.

1 THE same day went Jesus out of the house, and sat by the sea side.

2 And great multitudes were gathered together unto him, so that he went into a ship, and sat; and the whole multitude stood on the shore.

3 And he spake many things unto them in parables, saying, Behold, a sower (a farmer) went forth to sow (plant seeds);

4 And when he sowed, some *seeds* fell by the way side, and the fowls (birds) came and devoured them up:

5 Some fell upon stony places (where there was only a thin layer of dirt, see Matt. 13:5a), where they had not much earth: and forthwith (immediately) they sprung up, because they had no deepness of earth:

6 And when the sun was up, they were scorched; and because they had no root, they withered away (dried up and died).

7 And some fell among thorns; and the thorns sprung up, and choked them:

8 But other fell into good ground, and brought forth fruit, some an hundredfold, (a hundred times what was planted) some sixtyfold,· some thirtyfold. (Christ will explain this parable starting with verse 18.)

9 Who hath ears to hear, let him hear

(those who are spiritually mature and in tune will understand what I am saying).

10 And the disciples came, and said unto him, Why speakest thou unto them (the multitude in verse 2) in parables?

11 He answered and said unto them, Because it is given unto you to know the mysteries of the kingdom of heaven (because you want to learn spiritual things), but to them it is not given (because they do not want to learn of spiritual things).

Note: JST Matt.13:10-11 helps us understand the above two verses as well as verses which follow:

"10 For whosoever receiveth, to him shall be given, and he shall have more abundance;

11. But whosoever continueth not to receive, from him shall be taken away even that he hath."

The point is that these people don't want to understand the Savior's teachings.

12 For whosoever hath, to him shall be given, and he shall have more abundance: but whosoever hath not, from him shall be taken away even that he hath.

13 Therefore (for this reason) speak I to them in parables: because they seeing see not; and hearing they hear not, neither do they understand (they don't understand spiritual things because they don't want to).

14 And in them is fulfilled the prophecy of Esaias (Isaiah), which saith, By hearing ye shall hear, and shall not understand; and seeing ye

shall see, and shall not perceive (you are so far gone spiritually that you can't understand spiritual things):

15 For this people's heart is waxed gross (they have become hard-hearted), and *their* ears are dull of hearing (they are deaf to spiritual things), and their eyes they have closed (they don't want to see spiritual things); lest at any time they should see with *their* eyes, and hear with *their* ears, and should understand with *their* heart, and should be converted, and I should heal them (these people are intentionally avoiding conversion to Christ).

16 But blessed *are* your eyes, for they see: and your ears, for they hear.

17 For verily I say unto you, That many prophets and righteous *men* have desired to see *those things* which ye see, and have not seen *them*; and to hear *those things* which ye hear, and have not heard *them*.

18 Hear ye therefore the parable of the sower (I will explain the parable of the sower to you).

19 When any one heareth the word of the kingdom, and understandeth it not, then cometh the wicked *one*, and catcheth away that which was sown in his heart. This is he which received seed by the way side.

20 But he that received the seed into stony places, the same is he that heareth the word, and anon (immediately) with joy receiveth it;

21 Yet hath he not root in himself, but dureth (lasts) for a while: for when tribulation or persecution ariseth because of the word (the gospel), by and by he is offended.

22 He also that received seed among the thorns is he that heareth the word (the gospel); and the care of this world, and the deceitfulness of riches, choke the word, and he becometh unfruitful (does not remain faithful).

23 But he that received seed into the good ground is he that heareth the word, and understandeth *it*; (this takes work and commitment) which also beareth fruit (lives the gospel, remains faithful), and bringeth forth, some an hundredfold, some sixty, some thirty.

Note: Joseph Smith gives additional insights about the parable of the sower as follows: "But listen to the explanation of the parable of the Sower: 'When any one heareth the word of the Kingdom, and understandeth it not, then cometh the wicked one, and catcheth away that which was sown in his heart.' Now mark the expression— that which was sown in his heart. This is he which receiveth seed by the way side. Men who have no principle of righteousness in themselves, and whose hearts are full of iniquity, and have no desire for the principles of truth, do not understand the word of truth when they hear it. The devil taketh away the word of truth out of their hearts, because there is no desire for righteousness in them. 'But he that receiveth seed in stony places, the same is he that heareth the word, and anon, with joy receiveth it; yet hath he not root in himself, but dureth for a while; for when tribulation or persecution ariseth because of the word, by and by, he is offended. He also that receiveth seed among the thorns, is he that heareth the word; and the care of this world, and the deceitfulness of riches choke the word, and he becometh unfruitful. But he that received seed into the good ground, is he that heareth the word, and understandeth it, which also beareth fruit, and bringeth forth, some an hundred fold, some sixty, some thirty.' Thus the Savior Himself explains unto His disciples the parable which He put forth, and left no mystery or darkness upon the minds of those who firmly believe on His words.

We draw the conclusion, then, that the very reason why the multitude, or the world, as they were designated by the Savior, did not receive an explanation upon His parables, was because of unbelief. To you, He says (speaking to His disciples) it is given to know the mysteries of the Kingdom of God. And why? Because of the faith and confidence they had in Him." *Teachings of the Prophet Joseph Smith*, p. 97.

24 Another parable put he forth unto them, saying, The kingdom of heaven is likened unto a man (Christ, see verse 37) which sowed (planted) good seed (faithful followers of Christ, verse 38) in his field (the world, verse 38)):

25 But while men slept, his enemy (the devil, verse 39) came and sowed tares (wicked people, verse 38) among the wheat (faithful members of the Church), and went his way.

Note: A tare is a weed that looks very much like wheat while it is growing. Often, the roots of tares intertwine with the roots of the wheat while both are growing.

26 But when the blade was sprung up, and brought forth fruit, then appeared the tares also.

27 So the servants of the householder (Christ) came and said unto him, Sir,

didst not thou sow (plant) good seed (wheat) in thy field? from whence then hath it tares (where did the tares come from)?

28 He said unto them, An enemy hath done this. The servants said unto him, Wilt thou then that we go and gather them up (would you like us to weed out the tares now)?

29 But he said, Nay (No); lest (for fear that) while ye gather up the tares, ye root up also the wheat with them.

Note: There are several messages here in verse 29. One message might be that there are usually insincere and unrighteous members living among the righteous members of wards and branches of the Church. Another message could be that each of us has some "tares" in our own lives and personalities and we would be wise to weed them out as our righteous attributes mature. Jacob 5:65-66 in the Book of Mormon reminds us that as the good in people grows, the bad can gradually be cleared away. See also D&C 86:6.

30 Let both grow together until the harvest: and in the time of harvest I will say to the reapers (harvesters, angels in verse 39), Gather ye together first the tares (the wicked), and bind them in bundles to burn them: but gather the wheat (the righteous) into my barn (my kingdom).

Note: D&C 86:7 changes the order of the harvesting, as does JST Matt. 13:29. The correct order is that the wheat is gathered first, then the tares are gathered, bundled (bound), and burned. This is significant doctrinally, because it indicates that, at the Second

Coming, the righteous will be taken up first (D&C 88:96), and then the wicked will be burned.

31 Another parable put he forth unto them, saying, The kingdom of heaven is like to a grain of mustard seed, which a man took, and sowed in his field:

32 Which indeed is the least (smallest) of all seeds: but when it is grown, it is the greatest among herbs, and becometh a tree, so that the birds of the air (symbolic of angels, see *Teachings of the Prophet Joseph Smith*, p. 159) come and lodge in the branches thereof.

Note: Joseph Smith explained this parable. " And again, another parable put He forth unto them, having an allusion to the Kingdom that should be set up, just previous to or at the time of the harvest, which reads as follows—'The Kingdom of Heaven is like a grain of mustard seed, which a man took and sowed in his field: which indeed is the least of all seeds: but, when it is grown, it is the greatest among herbs, and becometh a tree, so that the birds of the air come and lodge in the branches thereof.' Now we can discover plainly that this figure is given to represent the Church as it shall come forth in the last days." For more of the Prophet's explanation, see *Teachings of the Prophet Joseph Smith*, pages 98-99 and page 159.

33 Another parable spake he unto them; The kingdom of heaven is like unto leaven (an ingredient such as yeast, which, when mixed into bread dough, causes the whole loaf to rise), which a woman took, and hid in three measures of meal, till the whole was leavened.

Note: Joseph Smith explained that the "leaven" in verse 33 could be compared to the true Church as it expands into the whole world. See *Teachings of the Prophet Joseph Smith*, pages 100 and 102.

34 All these things spake Jesus unto the multitude in parables; and without a parable spake he not unto them:

35 That it might be fulfilled which was spoken by the prophet, saying, I will open my mouth in parables; I will utter things which have been kept secret from the foundation of the world.

36 Then Jesus sent the multitude away, and went into the house: and his disciples came unto him, saying, Declare (explain) unto us the parable of the tares of the field (verses 24-30).

37 He answered and said unto them, He that soweth (plants) the good seed (wheat; righteousness) is the Son of man (Christ; Son of Man of Holiness-see Moses 6:57);

38 The field is the world; the good seed are the children of the kingdom (faithful members of the Church; the righteous); but the tares are the children of the wicked *one* (followers of Satan; the wicked);

39 The enemy that sowed them is the devil; the harvest is the end of the world; and the reapers (harvesters) are the angels.

40 As therefore the tares (the wicked) are gathered and burned in the

fire; so shall it be in the end of this world (the wicked will be burned at the Second Coming).

Note: People often ask how the wicked will be burned. D&C 5:19 along with 2 Nephi 12:10, 19 and 21, explain that the wicked will be burned by the brightness of the glory of Christ, who comes in full glory at the time of the Second Coming.

41 The Son of man (Christ) shall send forth his angels, and they shall gather out of his kingdom all things that offend, and them which do iniquity (the wicked);

42 And shall cast them into a furnace of fire (the burning at the Second Coming-see note above): there shall be wailing (bitter crying) and gnashing (grinding) of teeth.

43 Then shall the righteous shine forth as the sun (symbolic of celestial glory for the righteous saints) in the kingdom of their Father. Who hath ears to hear, let him hear (those who are spiritually in tune will understand what I am saying).

44 Again, the kingdom of heaven is like unto treasure hid in a field; the which when a man hath found, he hideth, and for joy thereof goeth and selleth all that he hath, and buyeth that field. (It is worth the sacrificing of whatever it takes to join the Church and to remain faithful.)

45 Again, the kingdom of heaven is like unto a merchant man, seeking goodly pearls:

46 Who, when he had found one pearl of great price, went and sold all that he had, and bought it.

47 Again, the kingdom of heaven is like unto a net, that was cast into the sea, and gathered of every kind (the missionary work of the Church gathers all kinds of converts, some sincere who remain faithful, others who are not sincere etc.): (This verse also exemplifies that all people will get a chance to join with the Savior's church, whether in this life or in the spirit world.)

48 Which, when it was full, they drew to shore, and sat down, and gathered the good into vessels, but cast the bad away.

49 So shall it be at the end of the world: the angels shall come forth, and sever the wicked from among the just (the righteous),

50 And shall cast them (the wicked) into the furnace of fire (the burning of the wicked): there shall be wailing (bitter anguish) and gnashing (grinding) of teeth (symbolic of the extreme suffering of the wicked as they face the consequences of their evil choices).

51 Jesus saith unto them, Have ye understood all these things? They say unto him, Yea, Lord.

52 Then said he unto them, Therefore every scribe (Jewish leaders, generally enemies of Christ, who determined correct interpretation of the scriptures among their people) *which is* instructed unto the kingdom of heaven (who has been converted and become a true follower of Christ, see Matt. 13:52, footnote b) is like unto a man *that is* an householder, which bringeth forth (throws out) out of his treasure *things* new and old (has to throw out many previously held

beliefs; see Sperry Symposium, 1983, p. 101).

53 And it came to pass, *that* when Jesus had finished these parables, he departed thence.

54 And when he was come into his own country (Nazareth), he taught them in their synagogue, insomuch that they were astonished, and said, Whence hath this *man* this wisdom, and *these* mighty works?

55 Is not this the carpenter's son? is not his mother called Mary? and his brethren, James, and Joses, and Simon, and Judas?

56 And his sisters, are they not all with us? Whence then hath this *man* all these things? (Isn't this Joseph and Mary's son? We know the family. How could he possibly be saying and doing such incredible things?)

57 And they were offended in him (embarrassed and offended by what he was doing). But Jesus said unto them, A prophet is not without honour, save (except) in his own country, and in his own house.

58 And he did not many mighty works there because of their unbelief.

MATTHEW 14

Note: In verse one, we meet "Herod the tetrarch", also known as Herod Antipas. His father, Herod the Great, was the ruler who commanded that all the infant boys at Bethlehem be killed, in an unsuccessful attempt to kill the Christ child. See Matt. 2:16. Upon the death of Herod the Great, his kingdom was divided among three of his sons, Antipas, Archelaus, and Philip. Herod the tetrarch was the wicked ruler who ordered the death of John the Baptist about two years ago as we begin this

chapter. Herod has heard of Jesus' fame and is afraid that John the Baptist has come back from the dead.

1 AT that time Herod the tetrarch heard of the fame of Jesus,

2 And said unto his servants, This is John the Baptist; he is risen from the dead (he has come back from the dead); and therefore mighty works do shew forth themselves in him.

3 For Herod had laid hold on (arrested) John, and bound him, and put *him* in prison for Herodias' sake, his brother Philip's wife. (Herod was an immoral man who married Herodias, his own brother, Philip's, wife).

4 For John (the Baptist) said unto him (Herod the tetrarch), It is not lawful for thee to have her (it was wrong for you to marry her).

5 And when he (Herod) would have put him (John the Baptist) to death, he feared the multitude, because they counted him as a prophet (considered John the Baptist to be a prophet).

6 But when Herod's birthday was kept, the daughter of Herodias (the daughter's name was Salome; see Bible Dictionary, p. 768) danced before them, and pleased Herod.

7 Whereupon he promised with an oath to give her whatsoever she would ask.

8 And she, being before instructed of her mother (Herodias, who hated John the Baptist because he boldly told her she was living in adultery with Herod), said, Give me here John Baptist's head in a charger (on a platter).

9 And the king was sorry: nevertheless for the oath's sake, and them which sat with him at meat (because he

had promised to her in front of all those at his birthday party), he commanded *it* (John's head) to be given *her*.

10 And he sent, and beheaded John in the prison.

11 And his head was brought in a charger, and given to the damsel: and she brought *it* to her mother.

12 And his disciples (John's followers) came, and took up the body, and buried it, and went and told Jesus.

13 When Jesus heard *of it*, he departed thence by ship into a desert place apart: and when the people had heard *thereof*, they followed him on foot out of the cities.

14 And Jesus went forth, and saw a great multitude, and was moved with compassion toward them, and he healed their sick.

15 And when it was evening, his disciples came to him, saying, This is a desert place, and the time is now past; send the multitude away, that they may go into the villages, and buy themselves victuals (food).

16 But Jesus said unto them, They need not depart; give ye them to eat.

17 And they say unto him, We have here but five loaves (of bread), and two fishes.

18 He said, Bring them hither to me.

19 And he commanded the multitude to sit down on the grass, and took the five loaves, and the two fishes, and looking up to heaven, he blessed, and brake, and gave the loaves to *his* disciples, and the disciples to the multitude.

20 And they did all eat, and were filled: and they took up of the fragments that remained twelve baskets full.

21 And they that had eaten were about five thousand men, beside (in addition to) women and children.

22 And straightway Jesus constrained (instructed) his disciples to get into a ship, and to go before him (go on ahead of him) unto the other side (of the Sea of Galilee), while he sent the multitudes away.

23 And when he had sent the multitudes away, he went up into a mountain apart (to be alone) to pray: and when the evening was come, he was there alone.

24 But the ship was now in the midst of the sea, tossed with waves: for the wind was contrary.

25 And in the fourth watch of the night (between 3 AM and 6 AM) Jesus went unto them, walking on the sea.

26 And when the disciples saw him walking on the sea, they were troubled, saying, It is a spirit; and they cried out for fear (they thought they were seeing a ghost).

27 But straightway (immediately) Jesus spake unto them, saying, Be of good cheer; it is I; be not afraid.

28 And Peter answered him and said, Lord, if it be thou, bid (ask) me come unto thee on the water.

29 And he said, Come. And when Peter was come down out of the ship, he walked on the water, to go to Jesus.

30 But when he saw the wind boisterous, he was afraid; and beginning to sink, he cried, saying, Lord, save me.

31 And immediately Jesus stretched forth *his* hand, and caught him, and said unto him, O thou of little faith, wherefore (why) didst thou doubt?

32 And when they were come into the ship, the wind ceased. (Once again, the Lord's power over the elements is

displayed.)

33 Then they that were in the ship came and worshipped him, saying, Of a truth (for sure) thou art the Son of God.

34 And when they were gone over (had crossed the Sea of Galilee from east to west), they came into the land of Gennesaret (on the northwestern side of the Sea of Galilee).

35 And when the men of that place had knowledge of him, they sent out (spread the word) into all that country round about, and brought unto him all that were diseased;

36 And besought him that they might only touch the hem of his garment: and as many as touched were made perfectly whole.

Note: Every physical healing performed by the Savior is symbolic of his power and desire to heal us spiritually, in order that we might come to the Father through him and his Atonement.

MATTHEW 15

Note: The Savior began his three year formal ministry at age 30. With the feeding of the 5000 in chapter 14, we begin our study of the last year of his earthly ministry. By this time, the hatred and jealousy of the Jewish religious leaders had grown to the point that they sent a delegation all the way from Jerusalem to Galilee to challenge Jesus and to try to discredit him. The scribes were the most powerful and influential of these leaders. Perhaps it would be helpful for you at this point to read a description of the scribes, given by one of the foremost biblical scholars. Here it is.

"A foremost actor in a New Testament list of characters is the scribe. He is found in Jerusalem, Judea, and Galilee and is not new to Jewish life and culture. Present in Babylon and also throughout the dispersion, he is spokesman of the people; he is the sage; he is the man of wisdom, the rabbi who received his ordination by the laying on of hands. His ability to cross-examine and to question is renowned. Dignified and important, he is an aristocrat among the common people who have no knowledge of the law. Regarding faith and religious practice, he is the authority and the last word; and as a teacher of the law, as a judge in ecclesiastical courts, is the learned one who must be respected, whose judgment is infallible. He travels in the company of the Pharisees, yet he is not necessarily a member of this religious party. He holds office and has status. His worth is beyond that of all the common folk and they must honor him, for he is to be praised by God and by angels in heaven. In fact, so revered are his words regarding law and practice that he must be believed though his statements contradict all common sense, or though he pronounce that the sun does not shine at noon day when in fact it is visible to the naked eye." (See Edersheim, The Life and Times of Jesus the Messiah, 1:93–94.)

1 THEN came to Jesus scribes and Pharisees (wicked religious leaders of the Jews), which were of Jerusalem, saying,

2 Why do thy disciples transgress

(sin against) the tradition of the elders (laws and customs established over the centuries by Jewish religious leaders, not necessarily the laws of God)? for they wash not their hands when they eat bread.

Note: The Savior will now teach a major lesson, namely, that inner cleanliness of mind and spirit are far more important than outward physical cleanliness.

3 But he answered and said unto them, Why do ye also transgress the commandment of God by your tradition?

4 For God commanded, saying, Honour thy father and mother: and, He that curseth father or mother, let him die the death (the penalty, given by Moses for failing to honor one's father and mother, was death).

5 But ye say, Whosoever shall say to *his* father or *his* mother, *It is* a gift, by whatsoever thou (the parents) mightest be profited (helped) by me;

6 And honour not his father or his mother, *he shall be free* (of obligation to help his parents). Thus have ye made the commandment of God ("Honor thy father and thy mother", Exodus 20:12) of none effect by your tradition.

Note: The Savior here challenges the wicked practice, approved by the Jewish leaders, of gaining freedom from taking care of their aging parents by saying "It is a gift.", (verse 5). By formally saying this, they could make their material means, time etc. off limits to their elderly parents who needed their help. This practice is called "Corban" in Mark 7:11.

7 *Ye* hypocrites (people who want to appear righteous but like to do evil), well did Esaias (Isaiah) prophesy of you, saying,

8 This people draweth nigh unto me with their mouth, and honoureth me with *their* lips; but their heart is far from me.

9 But in vain (it does no good) they do worship me, teaching *for* doctrines the commandments of men.

10 And he called the multitude, and said unto them, Hear, and understand:

11 Not that which goeth into the mouth defileth a man; but that which cometh out of the mouth, this defileth a man.

Note: This is a stinging rebuke to these wicked Jewish leaders. Jesus said to the multitude who have gathered around, within the hearing of the scribes and Pharisees, that the teachings which come out of the scribes' mouths and influence daily behavior of their people defile, or, in other words, make filthy. His disciples are worried about his bold scolding of the scribes as evidenced by the next verse.

12 Then came his disciples, and said unto him, Knowest thou that the Pharisees were offended, after they heard this saying?

13 But he answered and said, Every plant, which my heavenly Father hath not planted, shall be rooted up (everything which is false will ultimately be exposed and destroyed).

14 Let them alone: they be blind leaders of the blind. And if the blind lead the blind, both shall fall into the ditch (ultimately, they and their followers will get caught up with).

15 Then answered Peter and said unto him, Declare unto us this parable (please explain what you just said).

16 And Jesus said, Are ye also yet without understanding?

17 Do not ye yet understand, that whatsoever entereth in at the mouth goeth into the belly, and is cast out into the draught (eventually leaves the body)?

18 But those things which proceed out of the mouth come forth from the heart; and they defile (make filthy) the man (because they show what he is really like).

19 For out of the heart proceed evil thoughts, murders, adulteries, fornications, thefts, false witness, blasphemies:

20 These are *the things* which defile a man: but to eat with unwashen hands (verse 2) defileth not a man.

21 Then Jesus went thence, and departed into the coasts (borders) of Tyre and Sidon (a bit north and then west of the Sea of Galilee).

22 And, behold, a woman of Canaan (a Gentile, non-Israelite, probably a descendent of Ham; see Bible Dictionary, p. 629) came out of the same coasts (from the same area), and cried unto him, saying, Have mercy on me, O Lord, *thou* Son of David (thou Messiah, who was prophesied to be a descendent of King David); my daughter is grievously vexed (is very sick) with a devil.

23 But he answered her not a word. And his disciples came and besought him, saying, Send her away; for she crieth after us.

24 But he answered and said, I am not sent but unto the lost sheep of the house of Israel.

Note: As he states here, Jesus' mortal mission was limited to the house of Israel, specifically, the Jews. This limitation will be done away with later, as exemplified by Mark 16:15 and Peter's dream in Acts 10:9-48.

25 Then came she and worshipped him, saying, Lord, help me.

26 But he answered and said, It is not meet (appropriate, necessary) to take the children's bread (the gospel nourishment designated at this time for the Jews-see note above), and to cast *it* to dogs.

Note: The word "dogs" in this context means "little dogs" or household pets [a term of endearment]. A Bible scholar named Dummelow explains as follows:

""'The rabbis often spoke of the Gentiles as dogs. ...

... [Jesus] says not 'dogs,' but 'little dogs,' i.e. house-hold, favourite dogs, and the woman cleverly catches at the expression, arguing that if the Gentiles are household dogs, then it is only right that they should be fed with the crumbs that fall from their master's table." (Dummelow, Commentary, pp. 678–79.)

27 And she said, Truth, Lord: yet the dogs eat of the crumbs which fall from their masters' table.

28 Then Jesus answered and said unto her, O woman, great is thy faith: be it unto thee even as thou wilt. And her daughter was made whole from that very hour.

29 And Jesus departed from thence, and came nigh unto the sea of Galilee; and went up into a mountain, and sat down there.

30 And great multitudes came unto him, having with them *those that were* lame, blind, dumb (not able to speak), maimed, and many others, and cast them down at Jesus' feet; and he healed them:

31 Insomuch that the multitude wondered, when they saw the dumb to speak, the maimed to be whole, the lame to walk, and the blind to see: and they glorified the God of Israel.

32 Then Jesus called his disciples *unto him*, and said, I have compassion on the multitude, because they continue with me now three days (they have been following me for three days), and have nothing to eat: and I will not send them away fasting (hungry), lest they faint in the way (collapse on the way home).

33 And his disciples say unto him, Whence should we have so much bread in the wilderness, as to fill so great a multitude (where can we get enough bread to feed such a large group)?

34 And Jesus saith unto them, How many loaves have ye? And they said, Seven, and a few little fishes.

35 And he commanded the multitude to sit down on the ground.

36 And he took the seven loaves and the fishes, and gave thanks, and brake *them*, and gave to his disciples, and the disciples to the multitude.

37 And they did all eat, and were filled: and they took up of the broken *meat* (food) that was left seven baskets full.

38 And they that did eat were four thousand men, beside (plus) women and children.

39 And he sent away the multitude, and took ship, and came into the coasts (borders) of Magdala (near the north-western shore of the Sea of Galilee).

MATTHEW 16

1 THE Pharisees (Jewish religious leaders who believed in resurrection) also with the Sadducees (Jewish religious leaders who did not believe in resurrection) came, and tempting desired him that he would shew them a sign from heaven.

Note: The Pharisees and the Sadducees were usually enemies, but here we see them teamed up together against the Savior.

2 He answered and said unto them, When it is evening, ye say, *It will be* fair weather: for the sky is red.

3 And in the morning, *It will be* foul weather to day: for the sky is red and lowring (threatening), O ye hypocrites (people who want to appear righteous but like to be evil), ye can discern the face of the sky (you can predict the weather by looking at the sky); but can ye not *discern* (JST tell) the signs of the times (the obvious fulfillment of prophecies about Christ's mortal ministry, which, if paid attention to, would present these hypocrites with sure evidence that this Jesus against whom they were fighting is the promised Messiah)?

4 A wicked and adulterous generation seeketh after a sign; and there shall no sign be given unto it, but the

sign of the prophet Jonas (just as Jonah spent three days and three nights in the whale's belly, so also will Christ spend three days and three nights in the tomb, see JST Mark 8:12). And he left them, and departed.

5 And when his disciples were come to the other side, they had forgotten to take bread.

6 Then Jesus said unto them, Take heed and beware of the leaven of the Pharisees and of the Sadducees.

Note: Here the Master Teacher uses the setting to teach and warn his disciples against the evil doctrines (verse 12) of the Pharisees and Sadducees. He compares these doctrines to leaven [yeast] which is put in bread dough to make it rise. As the leaven works its way through the entire lump of dough, it influences everything. So also with these hypocritical Jewish leaders, who are influencing everything in Jewish society. At first, the disciples did not understand what Jesus was saying.

7 And they reasoned among themselves, saying, *It is* because we have taken no bread.

8 *Which* when Jesus perceived, he said unto them, O ye of little faith, why reason ye among yourselves, because ye have brought no bread (you are missing the point)?

9 Do ye not yet understand, neither remember the five loaves of the five thousand, and how many baskets ye took up (Matt. 14:20)?

10 Neither the seven loaves of the four thousand, and how many baskets ye took up (Matt. 15:37)?

11 How is it that ye do not under-

stand that I spake it (what I said about leaven, yeast) not to you concerning bread, (but, rather) that ye should beware of (watch out for) the leaven (influence) of the Pharisees and of the Sadducees?

12 Then understood they (the apostles) how that he bade *them* (warned them) not (to) beware of the leaven (yeast) of bread, but of the doctrine of the Pharisees and of the Sadducees (Hypocritical Jewish religious leaders).

Note: In other words, just as a little bit of yeast can spread itself throughout the whole lump of bread dough, and thus influence it all, so also can the evil influence of corrupt religious leaders, such as the Pharisees and Sadducees, spread throughout the whole nation.

11 How is it that ye do not understand that I spake it not to you concerning bread, that ye should beware of the leaven of the Pharisees and of the Sadducees?

12 Then understood they how that he bade *them* not beware of the leaven of bread, but of the doctrine of the Pharisees and of the Sadducees.

13 When Jesus came into the coasts of (area around) Caesarea Philippi (about 15 to 20 miles north of the Sea of Galilee), he asked his disciples, saying, Whom do men say that I the Son of man ("Son of God", "Son of Man of Holiness", see Moses 6:57) am?

14 And they said, Some *say that thou art* John the Baptist: some, Elias (Elijah); and others, Jeremias (Jeremiah), or one of the prophets.

15 He saith unto them, But whom

say ye that I am?

16 And Simon Peter answered and said, Thou art the Christ, the Son of the living God.

17 And Jesus answered and said unto him, Blessed art thou, Simon Bar-jona (son of a man named Jonah): for flesh and blood (man) hath not revealed *it* unto thee, but my Father which is in heaven (you have received your testimony of me through revelation).

18 And I say also unto thee, That thou art Peter, and upon this rock (the "rock" of revelation, see TPJS, p. 274; also, Christ is the "rock" upon which the Church is based, see Matt. 16:18, footnote a) I will build my church; and the gates of hell shall not prevail (win) against it. (Satan's kingdom absolutely will not win against Christ's kingdom, a very comforting fact!)

19 And I will give unto thee the keys (including the sealing power) of the kingdom of heaven (Peter is authorized to serve as the president of the Church after the Savior leaves): and whatsoever thou shalt bind (seal) on earth shall be bound in heaven: and whatsoever thou shalt loose (unseal) on earth shall be loosed in heaven.

20 Then charged he his disciples that they should tell no man that he was Jesus the Christ.

Note: Apostle Bruce R. McConkie explained verse 20, above, as follows: " For the time being, to avoid persecution and because the available hearers were not prepared to heed their witness, the apostles were restrained from bearing witness of the divine Sonship of their Master."

(Bruce R. McConkie, *Doctrinal New Testament Commentary*, Vol. 1 p. 390.)

21 From that time forth began Jesus to shew unto his disciples, how that he must go unto Jerusalem, and suffer many things of the elders and chief priests and scribes, and be killed, and be raised again the third day.

22 Then Peter took him, and began to rebuke (scold) him, saying, Be it far from thee, Lord: this shall not be unto thee (this can't happen to you!).

23 But he turned, and said unto Peter, Get thee behind me, Satan: thou art an offence unto me: for thou savourest (cherish) not the things that be of God, but those that be of men. (You must not try to stop me from following through with the Atonement.)

24 Then said Jesus unto his disciples, If any *man* will come after me, let him deny himself (put off worldly concerns), and take up his cross (sacrifice whatever is necessary), and follow me.

Note: JST Matt. 16:26 gives verse 24 above as follows: " And now for a man to take up his cross, is to deny himself of all ungodliness, and every worldly lust, and keep my commandments."

25 For whosoever will save his life (live his own life rather than following me) shall lose it: and whosoever will lose his life (sacrifice his own comforts and desires) for my sake shall find it.

26 For what is a man profited, if he shall gain the whole world, and lose his own soul? or what shall a man give in exchange for his soul?

27 For the Son of man shall come in the glory of his Father with his angels;

and then he shall reward every man according to his works. (Those who sacrifice whatever is necessary to truly follow me will find the reward more than worth it.)

28 Verily I say unto you, There be some standing here, which shall not taste of death, till they see the Son of man coming in his kingdom. (Some will be translated and will continue living on earth, doing the work of the Lord until He comes again. The Apostle John is the only one of these men whom we know by name as having been translated. See D&C 7.)

Note: For more information about translated beings, see 3 Nephi 28.

MATTHEW 17

Note: It is now near October, and the Savior will be crucified the following April, thus ending his mortal ministry. Three of his apostles, Peter, James, and John are already taking on the role of First Presidency. They will experience tremendous additional training now as the Master takes them with him up on the mountain which is referred to as the Mount of Transfiguration. There, they will see Christ transfigured before their eyes, will hear the Father's voice, and will see, among others, the great prophets Moses and Elijah, from whom they will receive additional priesthood keys. From JST Mark 9:3, we learn that John the Baptist was also there.

1 AND after six days Jesus taketh Peter, James, and John his brother, and bringeth them up into an high mountain apart,

2 And was transfigured before them: and his face did shine as the sun, and his raiment (clothing) was white as the light.

3 And, behold, there appeared unto them Moses and Elias (Elijah) talking with him.

4 Then answered Peter, and said unto Jesus, Lord, it is good for us to be here: if thou wilt, let us make here three tabernacles (small booths, typically used among the Jews for private worship during the annual Feast of Tabernacles); one for thee, and one for Moses, and one for Elias (Elijah).

5 While he yet spake, behold, a bright cloud overshadowed them: and behold a voice out of the cloud, which said, This is my beloved Son, in whom I am well pleased; hear ye him.

6 And when the disciples heard it, they fell on their face (a show of humility), and were sore (very) afraid.

7 And Jesus came and touched them, and said, Arise, and be not afraid.

8 And when they had lifted up their eyes, they saw no man, save (except) Jesus only.

Note: Apostle Bruce R. McConkie summarizes what took place on the Mount of Transfiguration in the following quote: " From the New Testament accounts and from the added light revealed through Joseph Smith it appears evident that:

(1) Jesus singled out Peter, James, and John from the rest of the Twelve; took them upon an unnamed mountain; there he was transfigured before them, and they beheld his glory. Testifying later, John said, "We beheld his glory, the glory as of the only begotten of the

Father" (John 1:14); and Peter, speaking of the same event, said they "were eyewitnesses of his majesty." (2 Pet. 1:16.)

(2) Peter, James, and John, were themselves "transfigured before him" (Teachings, p. 158), even as Moses, the Three Nephites, Joseph Smith, and many prophets of all ages have been transfigured, thus enabling them to entertain angels, see visions and comprehend the things of God. (Mormon Doctrine, pp. 725-726.)

(3) Moses and Elijah—two ancient prophets who were translated and taken to heaven without tasting death, so they could return with tangible bodies on this very occasion, an occasion preceding the day of resurrection—appeared on the mountain; and they and Jesus gave the keys of the kingdom to Peter, James, and John. (Teachings, p. 158.)

(4) John the Baptist, previously beheaded by Herod, apparently was also present. It may well be that other unnamed prophets, either coming as translated beings or as spirits from paradise, were also present.

(5) Peter, James, and John saw in vision the transfiguration of the earth, that is, they saw it renewed and returned to its paradisiacal state—an event that is to take place at the Second Coming when the millennial era is ushered in. (D. & C. 63:20-21; Mormon Doctrine, pp. 718-719.)

(6) It appears that Peter, James, and John received their own endowments while on the mountain. (Doctrines of Salvation, vol. 2, p. 165.) Peter says that while there, they "received from God the Father honour and glory,"

seemingly bearing out this conclusion. It also appears that it was while on the mount that they received the more sure word of prophecy, it then being revealed to them that they were sealed up unto eternal life. (2 Pet. 1:16-19; D. & C. 131:5.)

(7) Apparently Jesus himself was strengthened and encouraged by Moses and Elijah so as to be prepared for the infinite sufferings and agony ahead of him in connection with working out the infinite and eternal atonement. (Jesus the Christ, p. 373.) Similar comfort had been given him by angelic visitants following his forty-day fast and its attendant temptations (Matt. 4:11), and an angel from heaven was yet to strengthen him when he would sweat great drops of blood in the Garden of Gethsemane. (Luke 22:42-44.)

(8) Certainly the three chosen apostles were taught in plainness "of his death and also his resurrection" (I. V. Luke 9:31), teachings which would be of inestimable value to them in the trying days ahead.

(9) It should also have been apparent to them that the old dispensations of the past had faded away, that the law (of which Moses was the symbol) and the prophets (of whom Elijah was the typifying representative) were subject to Him whom they were now commanded to hear.

(10) Apparently God the Father, overshadowed and hidden by a cloud, was present on the mountain, although our Lord's three associates, as far as the record stipulates, heard only his voice and did not see his form."

(Bruce R. McConkie, *Doctrinal New*

Testament Commentary, Vol. 1 p. 399.)

9 And as they came down from the mountain, Jesus charged (instructed) them, saying, Tell the vision to no man, until the Son of man (Christ; Son of Man of Holiness, see Moses 6:57) be risen again from the dead.

10 And his disciples asked him, saying, Why then say the scribes that Elias must first come?

Note: Here, Peter, James, and John seem to be asking the Savior to clear up some doctrinal confusion in their own minds about Elias. They had been taught by their scriptures that Elias would come and prepare the way for the Lord. Yet, they had just seen Elias [Elijah] on the Mount and this was after the Savior had come, in fact, was near the end of the Master's mortal ministry. It is helpful for us, as we study these scriptures, to be aware that the name "Elias" has many meanings. See Bible Dictionary, p. 663. Thus, here, in this setting as explained by the Savior, Elias can mean John the Baptist who came before Jesus and prepared the way for him. It can also mean Elijah who ministered on the Mount of Transfiguration and would yet appear in the Kirtland Temple (D&C 110:13-15). It is also helpful to read JST Matt. 17:10-14 in the back of our Bible, pages 803-804, concerning Elias.

11 And Jesus answered and said unto them, Elias truly shall first come, and restore all things.

12 But I say unto you, That Elias is come already, and they knew him not,

but have done unto him whatsoever they listed. Likewise shall also the Son of man suffer of them.

13 Then the disciples understood that he spake unto them of John the Baptist.

14 And when they were come to the multitude, there came to him a *certain* man, kneeling down to him, and saying,

15 Lord, have mercy on my son: for he is lunatick, and sore vexed (very sick and troubled): for ofttimes he falleth into the fire, and oft into the water.

16 And I brought him to thy disciples, and they could not cure him.

17 Then Jesus answered and said, O faithless and perverse generation, how long shall I be with you? how long shall I suffer you (put up with you)? bring him hither to me.

18 And Jesus rebuked the devil; and he departed out of him: and the child was cured from that very hour.

Note: This is another reminder that Christ has power over Satan and his kingdom. Also, we are reminded here, as elsewhere, that the Savior has power to heal whatever ails us, symbolic of his power to save all who will follow him.

19 Then came the disciples to Jesus apart (privately), and said, Why could not we cast him out?

20 And Jesus said unto them, Because of your unbelief: for verily I say unto you, If ye have faith as a grain of mustard seed, ye shall say unto this mountain, Remove hence to yonder place; and it shall remove; and nothing

shall be impossible unto you.

21 Howbeit (however) this kind goeth not out but by prayer and fasting.

22 And while they abode in Galilee, Jesus said unto them, The Son of man (Christ; Son of Man of Holiness, see Moses 6:57) shall be betrayed into the hands of men:

23 And they shall kill him, and the third day he shall be raised again. And they were exceeding sorry.

24 And when they were come to Capernaum (Peter's home town on the northern edge of the Sea of Galilee), they (temple tax collectors) that received tribute *money* (annual temple tax of a half shekel, required from every male, twenty years old and older) came to Peter, and said, Doth not your master pay tribute (the temple tax)?

25 He saith, Yes. And when he (Peter) was come into the house, Jesus prevented him (spoke to him first, before he had a chance to mention the temple tax to Jesus), saying, What thinkest thou, Simon (Peter)? of whom (from whom) do the kings of the earth take custom (collect taxes) or tribute? of their own children, or of strangers (others)?

26 Peter saith unto him, Of strangers. Jesus saith unto him, Then are the children (of kings) free (exempt).

Note: There is a subtle play on words at work here. Jesus is the Son of the King (Heavenly Father). He is also the King, the Messiah. He is even the rightful political King of the Jews if the Romans had not been in political power at the time, because Joseph, Mary's husband, was the rightful heir to the political throne of the Jews. Thus, Jesus, as King and as the Son of the King (Elohim) should not have to pay this tax. Approaching it from another angle, since Jesus is a King in many ways, his children (his followers, the apostles etc.) including Peter, should not have to pay this tribute either.

27 Notwithstanding (nevertheless), lest we should offend them (in order to keep the peace), go thou to the sea (Sea of Galilee, which is probably just a few hundred feet or less away), and cast an hook (go fishing), and take up the fish that first cometh up (the first one you catch); and when thou hast opened his mouth, thou shalt find a piece of money (a one shekel [four-drachma] coin, the exact amount to pay the temple tax for Christ and Peter; see NIV Bible, Matt. 17:27): that take, and give unto them (the temple tax collectors) for me and thee.

MATTHEW 18

1 AT the same time came the disciples unto Jesus, saying, Who is the greatest in the kingdom of heaven?

2 And Jesus called a little child unto him, and set him in the midst of them,

3 And said, Verily I say unto you, Except ye be converted, and become as little children, ye shall not enter into the kingdom of heaven (celestial glory).

4 Whosoever therefore shall humble himself as this little child, the same is greatest in the kingdom of heaven.

5 And whoso shall receive one such little child in my name receiveth me.

6 But whoso shall offend (lead astray, cause to commit sin) one of these little ones which believe in me, it were better for him that a millstone (a large, heavy stone used to grind grain in a flour mill) were hanged about his neck, and *that* he were drowned in the depth of the sea.

7 Woe unto the world because of offences! for it must needs be that offences come; but woe to that man by whom the offence cometh!

Note: Sometimes people think that, since there needs to be opposition in all things (2 Nephi 2:11), they are helping the Lord's plan by being wicked, tempting others to sin etc. Verse 7, above, shows such thinking to be very wrong!

8 Wherefore if thy hand (friend; see JST explanation below) or thy foot (friend) offend thee, cut them off, and cast *them* from thee: it is better for thee to enter into life halt or maimed, rather than having two hands or two feet to be cast into everlasting fire.

9 And if thine eye (your own family members; see JST explanation below) offend thee, pluck it out, and cast *it* from thee: it is better for thee to enter into life with one eye, rather than having two eyes to be cast into hell fire.

Note: JST Matt. 18:9 explains the symbolism of "hand", "foot", and "eye" in verses 8 and 9 above as follows: " And a man's hand is his friend, and his foot, also; and a man's eye, are they of his own household."

10 Take heed that ye despise not one of these little ones; for I say unto you, That in heaven their angels do always behold the face of my Father which is in heaven (they will be saved in the celestial kingdom; see D&C 137:10).

11 For the Son of man is come to save that which was lost. (The JST for this verse reads: " For the Son of man is come to save that which was lost, and to call sinners to repentance; but these little ones have no need of repentance, and I will save them.")

12 How think ye (what do you think)? if a man have an hundred sheep, and one of them be gone astray, doth he not leave the ninety and nine, and goeth into the mountains, and seeketh that which is gone astray (God does everything he can to bring back the strays [sinners])?

13 And if so be that he find it, verily I say unto you, he rejoiceth more of that *sheep*, than of the ninety and nine which went not astray. (There is much joy when a stray returns to the fold.)

14 Even so it is not the will of your Father which is in heaven, that one of these little ones should perish.

15 Moreover if thy brother shall trespass against thee, go and tell him his fault between thee and him alone (keep it private; don't gossip about it; see D&C 20:80): if he shall hear thee (responds positively), thou hast gained thy brother.

16 But if he will not hear *thee* (will not accept your efforts to make peace), *then* take with thee one or two more (as witnesses that you have tried to work the matter out with him), that in the mouth of two or three witnesses every word may be established.

17 And if he shall neglect to hear them (if he won't respond favorably to

that effort on your part), tell *it* unto the church (go to the authorities of the church): but if he neglect to hear the church, let him be unto thee as an heathen man and a publican (go ahead and excommunicate him).

18 Verily I say unto you, Whatsoever ye (the apostles) shall bind on earth shall be bound in heaven: and whatsoever ye shall loose on earth shall be loosed in heaven.

19 Again I say unto you, That if two of you shall agree on earth as touching any thing that they shall ask, it shall be done for them of my Father which is in heaven.

20 For where two or three are gathered together in my name, there am I in the midst of them.

21 Then came Peter to him, and said, Lord, how oft shall my brother sin against me, and I forgive him? till seven times?

22 Jesus saith unto him, I say not unto thee, Until seven times: but, Until seventy times seven. (In other words, forgive him every time he repents. See D&C 98:40.)

Note: This doctrine of forgiving is a most important one for our own salvation. When we forgive, we free ourselves of the heavy burdens of hatred, grudges, bitterness, pity parties etc. Nephi is a great example to us in 1 Nephi 7:21 where he "frankly forgave" his brothers. The Savior goes on now to teach Peter and all of us the importance of our forgiving others if we want the Lord to forgive us.

23 Therefore is the kingdom of heaven likened unto a certain king, which would take account of his servants (see who is in debt to him etc.).

24 And when he had begun to reckon (check the accounting records), one was brought unto him, which owed him ten thousand talents.

Note: One calculation of this amount, based on an average day's wage today, yields a debt of three hundred million dollars, or sixty million day's work which, of course, is an impossible debt to repay. A person who starts full time work at age 15 and works six days a week for 55 years, would have 17,160 days of work in his or her lifetime.

25 But forasmuch as he had not to pay, his lord commanded him to be sold, and his wife, and children, and all that he had, and payment to be made. (This can be symbolic of the fact that we would lose family and all that counts [see 2 Nephi 9:8-9] without the Atonement and its power to free us and cleanse us so that we can enter exaltation and dwell in family units forever.)

26 The servant therefore fell down, and worshipped him, saying, Lord, have patience with me, and I will pay thee all.

27 Then the lord of that servant was moved with compassion, and loosed him, and forgave him the debt (symbolic of the Atonement).

28 But the same servant went out, and found one of his fellowservants, which owed him an hundred pence (an amount equivalent to about 100 days' wages; see Matt. 20:2): and he laid hands on him, and took *him* by the throat, saying, Pay me that thou owest.

29 And his fellowservant fell down

at his feet, and besought him, saying, Have patience with me, and I will pay thee all.

30 And he would not: but went and cast him into prison, till he should pay the debt.

31 So when his fellowservants saw what was done, they were very sorry, and came and told unto their lord (the king in verse 23) all that was done.

32 Then his lord, after that he had called him (the man who refused to forgive the relatively small debt of 100 days' wages), said unto him, O thou wicked servant, I forgave thee all that debt, because thou desiredst me:

33 Shouldest not thou also have had compassion on thy fellowservant, even as I had pity on thee?

34 And his lord was wroth (angry; righteous indignation), and delivered him to the tormentors , till he should pay all that was due unto him.

Note: Symbolically, "tormentors" would represent the punishment of the wicked who are eventually turned over to the buffetings of Satan [D&C 82:21] to pay for their own sins. Even after they have paid the penalty for their own sins, the highest degree of glory they can enter is the Telestial [D&C 76:84-85]. Also, this parable teaches the interplay between the Law of Justice and the Law of Mercy. The Law of Mercy allows us to be forgiven of unfathomable debt to God, through obedience to the gospel, including forgiving others. However, if we, through our actions, refuse the Law of Mercy, then the Law of Justice takes over and we bear the burden of our sins as explained in D&C 19:15-18.)

35 So likewise shall my heavenly Father do also unto you, if ye from your hearts forgive not every one his brother their trespasses. (This is fair warning to us about forgiving others and quite an answer to Peter's question in verse 21, wherein he asked how often he should forgive others.)

MATTHEW 19

1 AND it came to pass, *that* when Jesus had finished these sayings, he departed from Galilee, and came into the coasts (borders) of Judæa beyond Jordan (getting close to Jerusalem but still east of the Jordan River);

2 And great multitudes followed him; and he healed them there.

3 The Pharisees (religious leaders of the Jews) also came unto him, tempting him (trying to trap him so they could arrest him), and saying unto him, Is it lawful for a man to put away (divorce) his wife for every cause?

4 And he answered and said unto them, Have ye not read, that he (Heavenly Father) which made *them* at the beginning made them male and female,

5 And said, For this cause (marriage and family) shall a man leave father and mother, and shall cleave to (stick to, be faithful to) his wife: and they twain (two) shall be one flesh?

6 Wherefore they are no more twain (two people), but one flesh (one family unit). What therefore God hath joined together, let not man put asunder (take apart).

7 They say unto him, Why did Moses then command to give a writing of divorcement (a legal certificate of divorce), and to put her away (divorce

her)?

8 He saith unto them, Moses because of the hardness of your hearts suffered (allowed) you to put away (divorce) your wives: but from the beginning it was not so.

9 And I say unto you, Whosoever shall put away his wife, except *it be* for fornication, and shall marry another, committeth adultery: and whoso marrieth her which is put away doth commit adultery.

Note: Refer to the note between Matthew, chapter five, verses 31 and 32 for help with verse nine, above.

10 His disciples say unto him, If the case of the man be so with *his* wife, it is not good to marry (if this is such a serious matter, it would be better not to risk getting married).

11 But he said unto them, All *men* cannot receive this saying, save *they* to whom it is given.

12 For there are some eunuchs (men who are physically unable to have children), which were so born from *their* mother's womb: and there are some eunuchs, which were made eunuchs of men (men who have been surgically rendered incapable of having children; see Bible Dictionary, p. 667): and there be eunuchs, which have made themselves eunuchs for the kingdom of heaven's sake. He that is able to receive *it*, let him receive *it*.

Note: Verse 12 above seems incomplete and fragmentary. We don't know what it really means. Concerning this verse, Apostle Bruce R. McConkie said "Some added background and additional information is needed to understand fully what is meant by this teaching about eunuchs." *Doctrinal New Testament Commentary*, Vol. 1, p. 549.

13 Then were there brought unto him little children, that he should put *his* hands on them, and pray: and the disciples rebuked them (those who brought the little children to Jesus).

14 But Jesus said, Suffer (allow) little children, and forbid them not, to come unto me: for of such is the kingdom of heaven.

15 And he laid *his* hands on them, and departed thence.

16 And, behold, one (the rich young man in verse 22) came and said unto him, Good Master (Teacher; see NIV Bible), what good thing shall I do, that I may have eternal life (exaltation)?

Note: This rich young man seems to believe that doing one "good thing" will secure exaltation for him. We see this thinking on his part again in verse 18 when he asks which commandment he should keep in order to attain exaltation.

17 And he said unto him, Why callest thou me good? *there is* none good but one, *that is*, God (Jesus wants no glory for himself, rather, gives all credit and glory to the Father): but if thou wilt enter into life (exaltation), keep the commandments.

18 He saith unto him, Which? Jesus said, Thou shalt do no murder, Thou shalt not commit adultery, Thou shalt not steal, Thou shalt not bear false witness,

19 Honour thy father and *thy* mother: and, Thou shalt love thy neighbour as

thyself.

20 The young man saith unto him, All these things have I kept from my youth up: what lack I yet?

21 Jesus said unto him, If thou wilt be perfect, go and sell that thou hast, and give to the poor, and thou shalt have treasure in heaven: and come and follow me.

22 But when the young man heard that saying, he went away sorrowful: for he had great possessions (was very rich).

23 Then said Jesus unto his disciples, Verily ("Listen carefully, this is an important point.") I say unto you, That a rich man shall hardly (it is "hard" for him, not "almost impossible") enter into the kingdom of heaven (celestial kingdom).

24 And again I say unto you, It is easier for a camel to go through the eye of a needle, than for a rich man to enter into the kingdom of God.

Note: There is a rumor going around that the "eye of a needle" was a small gate in the walls of Jerusalem, used for entry into the city by night, after the main gates were closed. The rumor states that it was very difficult for a camel to get down and scrunch through the gate. Scholars indicate that this rumor has no truth to it. They indicate that the word "needle", as used in verse 24, refers to an ordinary sewing needle in the original Bible languages.

25 When his disciples heard *it*, they were exceedingly amazed, saying, Who then can be saved?

26 But Jesus beheld *them*, and said unto them, With men this (being saved) is impossible; but with God (with the help of God, through the Atonement) all things are possible.

Note: The JST gives additional insights for verse 26, above. "But Jesus beheld their thoughts, and said unto them, With men this is impossible; but if they will forsake all things for my sake, with God whatsoever things I speak are possible."

27 Then answered Peter (this is old English and means that Peter asked a question) and said unto him, Behold, we have forsaken all, and followed thee; what shall we have therefore (what will our reward be)? (The answer to Peter's question is given in verses 28 and 29.)

28 And Jesus said unto them, Verily (listen very carefully, this is an important point) I say unto you, That ye which have followed me, in the regeneration (JST resurrection) when the Son of man (Christ; Son of Man of Holiness-see Moses 6:57) shall sit in the throne of his glory (in exaltation), ye also shall sit upon twelve thrones (you, too, will be exalted), judging the twelve tribes of Israel.

Note: Apostle Bruce R. McConkie explains the judging referred to in verse 28 above in the following quote:
Apostles to Judge House of Israel
Christ is the great judge of all the earth. "The Father judgeth no man, but hath committed all judgment unto the Son." (John 5:22.) In due course, every living soul shall stand before his judgment bar, be judged according to his

own works, and awarded a place in the mansions that are prepared. (Mormon 3:20.)

Under Christ a great hierarchy of judges will operate, each functioning in his assigned sphere. John saw many judges sitting upon thrones. (Rev. 20:4.) Paul said the saints would judge both the world and angels. (1 Cor. 6:2-3.) The elders are to sit in judgment on those who reject them. (D. & C. 75:21-22; Matt. 10:14-15.) Daniel saw that judgment would be given to the saints. (Dan. 7:22.) The Nephite Twelve will be judged by the Twelve from Jerusalem and then in turn will judge the Nephite nation. (1 Ne. 12:9-10; 3 Ne. 27:27; Mormon 3:19.) And the Twelve who served with our Lord in his ministry shall judge the whole house of Israel. (D. & C. 29:12.) No doubt there will be many others of many dispensations who will sit in judgment upon the peoples of their days and generations—all judging according to the judgment which Christ shall give them, "which shall be just." (3 Ne. 27:27.) *Doctrinal New Testament Commentary*, Vol. 1, p. 558-559.

29 (This is a continuation of the answer to Peter's question in verse 27.) And every one that hath forsaken (given up) houses, or brethren, or sisters, or father, or mother, or wife, or children, or lands, for my name's sake, shall receive an hundredfold, and shall inherit everlasting life (exaltation).

30 But many *that are* first (JST Mark 10:30-31 "who make themselves first"; prideful behavior) shall be last; and the last (those who consider them-selves least, and who are humbly obedient) *shall be* first (highest up in the celestial kingdom).

MATTHEW 20

1 FOR the kingdom of heaven is like unto a man *that* is an householder, which went out early in the morning to hire labourers into his vineyard.

2 And when he had agreed with the labourers for a penny a day (a day's wages), he sent them into his vineyard.

Note: When we see the word "penny", we think of a coin of very little worth. This misunderstanding can distract us as we read this parable. The King James Bible (the one we use) transla-tors consistently used the word "penny" for "denarius". A denarius is a Roman silver coin (see Bible Dictionary, p. 734). It was worth a days wages and thus was a significant amount of money.

3 And he went out about the third hour, and saw others standing idle in the marketplace,

4 And said unto them; Go ye also into the vineyard, and whatsoever is right I will give you. And they went their way.

5 Again he went out about the sixth and ninth hour, and did likewise.

6 And about the eleventh hour he went out, and found others standing idle, and saith unto them, Why stand ye here all the day idle?

7 They say unto him, Because no man hath hired us. He saith unto them, Go ye also into the vineyard; and whatsoever is right, *that* shall ye receive.

8 So when even (the end of the day) was come, the lord of the vineyard saith unto his steward, Call the labourers, and give them *their* hire (wages), beginning from the last unto the first.

9 And when they came that *were hired* about the eleventh hour, they received every man a penny (a full day's wages).

10 But when the first (those who began working at the beginning of the day, verse 2) came, they supposed that they should have received more (than those who hadn't worked all day); and they likewise received every man a penny (a full day's wages; see note by verse 2 above).

11 And when they had received *it*, they murmured (complained) against the goodman of the house (the householder who hired them, verse 1),

12 Saying, These last have wrought (worked) *but* one hour, and thou hast made them equal unto us, which have borne (had to put up with) the burden and heat of the day.

13 But he answered one of them, and said, Friend, I do thee no wrong: didst not thou agree with me for a penny? (I kept my part of the agreement and gave you full payment as we agreed upon.)

14 Take *that* thine *is*, and go thy way: I will give unto this last (the workers who started at the eleventh hour, verses 6 &7) , even as unto thee.

15 Is it not lawful for me to do what I will with mine own? Is thine eye evil, because I am good (are you jealous because I am generous to others; NIV Bible)?

16 So the last shall be first, and the first last: for many be called, but few chosen (all are "called" or invited to come to exaltation, but few are chosen to receive it because they don't overcome sins).

Note: The Parable of the Laborers, as Matt. 20:1-16 is called, is very rich in symbolism and presents an opportunity for you to improve your skill in recognizing symbolism in the scriptures as you read and study them. We will repeat verses 1-16 here and call your attention to some of the symbolism with notes in parentheses. As is the case with symbolism, there are many ways it can be interpreted, so the following is just one possibility for your consideration.

1 FOR the kingdom of heaven (celestial glory) is like unto a man (Heavenly Father) *that is* an householder, which went out early in the morning to hire labourers (faithful saints who have been active in the Church all their lives) into his vineyard (the earth).

2 And when he had agreed with the labourers for a penny a day (full pay, exaltation), he sent them into his vineyard (the earth).

3 And he went out about the third hour, and saw others standing idle (people who had not yet joined the Church or become active) in the marketplace,

4 And said unto them; Go ye also into the vineyard ("Join the church, get active, go to work."), and whatsoever is right I will give you ("I will be fair with you."). And they went their way (they joined the Church and remained faithful to the end of their lives).

5 Again he went out about the sixth and ninth hour, and did likewise (others joined the Church or became active later in their lives and remained faithful in the work).

6 And about the eleventh hour (representing people who find the truth and join the Church or get active near the end of their lives and remain faithful and work hard to the end) he went out, and found others standing idle, and saith unto them, Why stand ye here all the day idle?

7 They say unto him, Because no man hath hired us. He saith unto them, Go ye also into the vineyard; and whatsoever is right, *that* shall ye receive.

8 So when even (judgment day) was come, the lord of the vineyard (Heavenly Father) saith unto his steward (Christ, who is the final judge-see John 5:22), Call the labourers , and give them *their* hire (give them their reward), beginning from the last unto the first.

9 And when they came that *were hired* about the eleventh hour, they received every man a penny (those who became faithful saints much later in life [not "deathbed" repentance] were given exaltation).

10 (In these next verses, lifelong saints are cautioned not to become jealous or feel unfairly treated since they have "bourne the burden and heat of the day" [verse 12], i.e., sacrificed etc. all their lives to be obedient, when they see converts or reactivated saints get the same reward they have worked longer to achieve.) But when the first (those who had been active all their lives) came, they supposed that they should have received more; and they likewise received every man a penny.

11 And when they had received it, they murmured against the goodman of the house (the Father),

12 Saying, These last have wrought (worked) *but* one hour (haven't worked nearly as long as we have to gain exaltation), and thou hast made them equal unto us, which have borne the burden and heat of the day.

13 But he answered one of them, and said, Friend, I do thee no wrong: didst not thou agree with me for a penny (exaltation)?

14 Take *that* thine *is* (take your exaltation-by the way, the Lord is being very patient with these complainers at this point; if they don't repent of this bad attitude, they will lose their exaltation as indicated in verse 16), and go thy way: I will give unto this last, even as unto thee.

15 Is it not lawful for me to do what I will with mine own? Is thine eye evil, because I am good (are you jealous and sinning in your heart because I am forgiving and generous)?

16 So the last shall be first, and the first last (it is possible to lose exaltation because of a bad attitude such as that demonstrated by the workers in verses 10-15): for many be called, but few chosen.

17 And Jesus going up to Jerusalem took the twelve disciples apart (aside where they could be alone) in the way, and said unto them,

18 Behold, we go up to Jerusalem; and the Son of man (Christ, Son of Man of Holiness [Heavenly Father]; see Moses 6:57) shall be betrayed unto the chief priests and unto the scribes,

and they (religious leaders of the Jews) shall condemn him to death,

19 And shall deliver him to the Gentiles (the Romans) to mock, and to scourge, and to crucify *him*: and the third day he shall rise again (be resurrected).

20 Then came to him the mother of Zebedee's children (James and John's mother) with her sons, worshipping *him*, and desiring a certain thing of him.

21 And he said unto her, What wilt thou? She saith unto him, Grant that these my two sons (James and John) may sit, the one on thy right hand, and the other on the left, in thy kingdom.

22 But Jesus answered and said, Ye know not what ye ask. Are ye able to drink of the cup that I shall drink of, and to be baptized with the baptism that I am baptized with (can you remain faithful at all costs)? They (James and John) say unto him, We are able.

23 And he saith unto them, Ye shall drink indeed of my cup, and be baptized with the baptism that I am baptized with: but to sit on my right hand, and on my left, is not mine to give, but *it shall be given to them* for whom it is prepared of my Father (it is not to be given as a matter of favoritism or mere request, rather it will be given to those who earn it according to the laws established by the Father).

24 And when the ten (the other ten in the Quorum of Twelve) heard it, they were moved with indignation (angry) against the two brethren (apostles James and John).

Note: This is a reminder that these apostles are still learning and maturing in their work and callings, just as each of us is. It is also a view of the Savior's tenderness and patience, as he teaches them yet another lesson.

25 But Jesus called them *unto him*, and said, Ye know that the princes (kings, leaders etc.) of the Gentiles (non-Israelites) exercise dominion (power and authority) over them, and they that are great (those leaders) exercise authority upon them (the gentiles).

26 But it shall not be so among you: but whosoever will be great among you, let him be your minister;

27 And whosoever will be chief among you, let him be your servant:

28 Even as the Son of man (Christ) came not to be ministered unto, but to minister, and to give his life a ransom for many (to redeem many).

29 And as they departed from Jericho (about 25 miles from Jerusalem), a great multitude followed him.

30 And, behold, two blind men sitting by the way side, when they heard that Jesus passed by, cried out, saying, Have mercy on us, O Lord, *thou* Son of David (you Messiah who are, as prophesied, a descendent of King David).

31 And the multitude rebuked (scolded) them, because they should hold their peace (keep quiet): but they cried the more, saying, Have mercy on us, O Lord, *thou* Son of David.

32 And Jesus stood still, and called them, and said, What will ye that I shall do unto you?

33 They say unto him, Lord, that our eyes may be opened.

34 So Jesus had compassion *on them*, and touched their eyes: and immediately their eyes received sight, and they followed him.

MATTHEW 21
Note: These next verses lead up to what is known as "the Triumphal Entry", the day when Jesus rode into Jerusalem accompanied by throngs of people shouting "Hosanna to the Son of David", in other words, celebrating and cheering Jesus as the promised Messiah who would save them and free them from their enemies. The Passover was underway and throngs of Jewish pilgrims had arrived in Jerusalem from many lands to join in Passover celebration and worship. This begins the last week of the Savior's mortal life.

1 AND when they drew nigh (near) unto Jerusalem, and were come to Bethphage (on the east side of the Mount of Olives), unto the mount of Olives, then sent Jesus two disciples,
2 Saying unto them, Go into the village over against you (ahead of you), and straightway (immediately) ye shall find an ass (donkey) tied, and a colt (a young male donkey) with her: loose (untie) *them*, and bring *them* unto me.
3 And if any *man* say ought unto you (questions you about what you are doing), ye shall say, The Lord hath need of them; and straightway (immediately) he will send them.
4 All this was done, that it might be fulfilled which was spoken by the prophet (Zachariah; see Zach. 9:9), saying,

5 Tell ye the daughter of Sion, Behold, thy King cometh unto thee, meek, and sitting upon an ass, and a colt the foal (offspring) of an ass.

Note: In Hebrew symbolism, a donkey represents humility and submission. Thus, the Savior's riding into Jerusalem on a donkey is symbolic of his humility and submission to the coming suffering and crucifixion.

6 And the disciples went, and did as Jesus commanded them,
7 And brought the ass, and the colt, and put on them their clothes (JST Matt. 21:5 "...brought the colt, and put on it their clothes; and Jesus took the colt and sat thereon; and they followed him."; see also Luke 19:30) , and they set *him* thereon.

Note: Here is a seldom-noticed miracle. Luke 19:30 informs us that the colt had never been ridden before. Yet, the Master sat on it with no trouble from the colt, reminding us that Jesus has power over the animal kingdom too.

8 And a very great multitude spread their garments in the way; others cut down branches from the trees (from palm trees-John 12:13), and strawed (spread) them in the way.

Note: In Jewish symbolism, palm branches symbolized triumph and victory. Thus, in cutting palm branches and excitedly waving them and spreading them on the ground in front of the Savior, the crowd was enthusiastically expressing their belief that Jesus would bring them military triumph and victory over their Roman enemies.

9 And the multitudes that went before, and that followed, cried, saying, Hosanna to the Son of David: Blessed is he that cometh in the name of the Lord; Hosanna in the highest.

Note: The word "Hosanna" means "Lord, save us, now!" (See Bible Dictionary, pages 704-705) and ties in with the symbolism of palm branches mentioned above.

10 And when he was come into Jerusalem, all the city was moved (everyone in the city was excited about him), saying, Who is this?

11 And the multitude said, This is Jesus the prophet of Nazareth of Galilee.

12 And Jesus went into the temple of God, and cast out all them that sold and bought in the temple, and overthrew the tables of the moneychangers, and the seats of them that sold doves,

Note: John tells us (John 2:14-17) that Jesus cleansed the temple at the beginning of his ministry. Now, three years later, Jesus cleanses the temple again. This is the second time and the temple crowd obviously hadn't learned their lesson the first time.

13 And said unto them, It is written, My house shall be called the house of prayer; but ye have made it a den of thieves.

14 And the blind and the lame came to him in the temple; and he healed them.

Note: It is interesting that Jesus didn't immediately leave the temple, after having cleansed it. No doubt there was potential danger to him from the authorities. Nevertheless, he remained for a considerable time to heal people who came to him. This must have been extremely frustrating to the Jewish religious leaders who "were sore displeased" (verse 15).

15 And when the chief priests and scribes (Jewish religious leaders) saw the wonderful things that he did, and the children (JST Matt. 21:13 "children of the kingdom", in other words, faithful adult members of the Church) crying in the temple, and saying, Hosanna ("Save now", see Bible Dictionary, pages 704-705) to the Son of David; they were sore (very) displeased,

16 And said unto him, Hearest thou what these (the "children of the kingdom" in verse 15) say? (In other words, do you realize how dangerous it is to you for them to be calling you the Messiah!) And Jesus saith unto them, Yea; have ye never read, Out of the mouth of babes and sucklings thou hast perfected praise? (In other words, among other possible interpretations, Jesus is saying "You are supposed to know the scriptures. Haven't you ever read that from child-like faithful members come true praises of God?)

17 And he left them, and went out of the city into Bethany; and he lodged there.

18 Now in the morning as he returned into the city, he hungered (was hungry).

19 And when he saw a fig tree in the

way (by the road), he came to it, and found nothing thereon, but leaves only, and said unto it, Let no fruit grow on thee henceforward for ever. And presently (immediately) the fig tree withered away.

Note: The fig tree is symbolic of the hypocritical Jewish religious leaders who pretend to look official but do not produce the fruit of the gospel. It is also symbolic of the Jewish nation, the covenant people, who are "barren" as far as the gospel is concerned. See Talmage, *Jesus the Christ*, p. 443.

20 And when the disciples saw *it*, they marvelled, saying, How soon is the fig tree withered away!

21 Jesus answered and said unto them, Verily I say unto you, If ye have faith, and doubt not, ye shall not only do this *which is done* to the fig tree, but also if ye shall say unto this mountain, Be thou removed, and be thou cast into the sea; it shall be done.

22 And all things, whatsoever ye shall ask in prayer, believing, ye shall receive. (See D&C 46:30, 50:30)

23 And when he was come into the temple, the chief priests and the elders of the people (the Jewish religious leaders who are trying to trap him) came unto him as he was teaching, and said, By what authority doest thou these things? and who gave thee this authority?

24 And Jesus answered and said unto them, I also will ask you one thing, which if ye tell me, I in like wise will tell you by what authority I do these things.

25 The baptism of John (the Baptist),

whence was it? from heaven, or of men (did John the Baptist have authority from heaven, or was he just another man)? And they reasoned with themselves, saying, If we shall say, From heaven; he (Jesus) will say unto us, Why did ye not then believe him?

26 But if we shall say, Of men; we fear the people; for all hold John as a prophet. (If we say John the Baptist was just an ordinary man, the people will mob us, because they consider him to be sent from God.)

27 And they answered Jesus, and said, We cannot tell. And he said unto them, Neither tell I you by what authority I do these things.

Note: The following parable is known as The Parable of the Two Sons. The second son in the parable represents the hypocritical Jewish religious leaders who claim to agree to do the work of the Lord, but do not do it.

28 But what think ye? A *certain* man had two sons; and he came to the first, and said, Son, go work to day in my vineyard.

29 He answered and said, I will not: but afterward he repented, and went.

30 And he came to the second, and said likewise. And he answered and said, I go, sir: and went not.

31 Whether of them twain (which of the two) did the will of *his* father? They say unto him, The first. Jesus saith unto them, Verily I say unto you, That the publicans (hated Jewish tax collectors) and the harlots (prostitutes) go into the kingdom of God before you.

32 For John (the Baptist) came unto

you in the way of righteousness, and ye believed him not: but the publicans and the harlots (sinners) believed him (repented): and ye, when ye had seen it, repented not afterward (like the first son in the above parable), that ye might believe him.

Note: In this next parable, known as the Parable of the Wicked Husbandmen, the Savior clearly compares the wicked Jewish religious leaders to the wicked husbandmen who kill the owner's son in an attempt to take the kingdom from him. The notes in parentheses in the parable represent one possible interpretation of it.

33 Hear another parable: There was a certain householder (Heavenly Father), which planted a vineyard (had the earth created and put people on it), and hedged it round about (set up protections for it), and digged a wine-press in it (planned on a good harvest), and built a tower (so people could watch for enemies), and let it out to husbandmen (stewards who were supposed to take good care of it), and went into a far country (heaven):

34 And when the time of the fruit (harvest time) drew near, he sent his servants (prophets) to the husbandmen, that they might receive the fruits of it.

35 And the husbandmen took his servants (prophets), and beat one, and killed another, and stoned another.

36 Again, he sent other servants (prophets) more than the first: and they (the wicked husbandmen) did unto them likewise.

37 But last of all he sent unto them his son (Christ), saying, They will reverence my son.

38 But when the husbandmen saw the son, they said among themselves, This is the heir; come, let us kill him, and let us seize on his inheritance.

39 And they caught him, and cast *him* out of the vineyard, and slew *him* (crucified him).

40 When the lord (Christ) therefore of the vineyard cometh, what will he do unto those husbandmen?

41 They (the chief priests and elders in verse 23) say unto him (Jesus), He will miserably destroy those wicked men, and will let out his vineyard unto other husbandmen (righteous religious leaders), which shall render him the fruits in their seasons.

42 Jesus saith unto them, Did ye never read in the scriptures, The stone (Christ) which the builders rejected, the same is become the head of the corner (the capstone or cornerstone): this is the Lord's doing, and it is marvellous in our eyes?

43 Therefore say I unto you (Jewish religious leaders), The kingdom of God shall be taken from you, and given to a nation (Gentiles) bringing forth the fruits thereof.

44 And whosoever shall fall on this stone (Christ) shall be broken: but on whomsoever it shall fall, it will grind him to powder.

45 And when the chief priests and Pharisees had heard his parables, they perceived that he spake of them.

Note: "...they perceived that he spake of them" in verse 45 above is very important to our understanding of what is going on here. Some people think that the Jewish religious leaders did not really understand who Jesus was etc. That is not true. They did indeed understand who Jesus was and set out to kill him. On the cross, when Christ said "Father, forgive them for they know not what they do" (Luke 23:34), he was obviously referring to the Roman soldiers and perhaps others, but not the Jewish religious leaders. This fact is confirmed again in JST Matt. 21:47 below, where it says the same thing, "they perceived that he spake of them."

46 But when they sought to lay hands on him, they feared the multitude, because they took him for a prophet. (They were afraid the people would mob them if they arrested Jesus.)

Note: The JST contains over two hundred added words of explanation for this parable. They are included here:

47 And when the chief priests and Pharisees had heard his parables, they perceived that he spake of them.

48 And they said among themselves, Shall this man think that he alone can spoil this great kingdom? And they were angry with him

49 But when they sought to lay hands on him, they feared the multitude, because they learned that the multitude took him for a prophet.

50 And now his disciples came to him, and Jesus said unto them, Marvel ye at the words of the parable which I spake unto them?

51 Verily, I say unto you, I am the stone, and those wicked ones reject me.

52 I am the head of the corner. These Jews shall fall upon me, and shall be broken.

53 And the kingdom of God shall be taken from them, and shall be given to a nation bringing forth the fruits thereof; (meaning the Gentiles.)

54 Wherefore, on whomsoever this stone shall fall, it shall grind him to powder.

55 And when the Lord therefore of the vineyard cometh, he will destroy those miserable, wicked men, and will let again his vineyard unto other husbandmen, even in the last days (the restoration through the Prophet Joseph Smith), who shall render him the fruits in their seasons.

56 And then understood they the parable which he spake unto them, that the Gentiles (the wicked Gentiles in the last days) should be destroyed also, when the Lord should descend out of heaven (the Second Coming) to reign in his vineyard, which is the earth and the inhabitants thereof.

MATTHEW 22

1 AND Jesus answered and spake unto them again by parables, and said,

Note: Jesus will give more parables, but this next one, the Parable of the Marriage of the King's Son, will be the last one directed specifically to the Jewish religious leaders and rulers who have been aggressively trying to trap him all day (see chapter 21 above). The parable is a direct warning to the murderous Jewish rulers who have killed past prophets and now seek to arrest and kill Jesus. Notes in parentheses provide one possible interpretation of the parable.

2 The kingdom of heaven is like unto a certain king (Heavenly Father), which made a marriage ("marriage" symbolizes an opportunity to make covenants; the "bride" for this marriage would be those who are willing to become righteous saints by making and keeping covenants) for his son (Christ),

3 And sent forth his servants (prophets, missionaries, members etc.) to call them that were bidden (invited) to the wedding: and they would not come.

4 Again, he sent forth other servants, saying, Tell them which are bidden, Behold, I have prepared my dinner: my oxen and *my* fatlings (the very best) are killed, and all things *are* ready: come unto the marriage. (In other words, I have a great gospel feast prepared for you.)

5 But they made light of it, and went their ways, one to his farm, another to his merchandise: (Some ignored the invitation.)

6 And the remnant (the wicked Jewish religious leaders and rulers in Matt. 21:23) took his servants, and entreated *them* spitefully (treated them cruelly), and slew *them*. (Some violently opposed the Lord's servants who brought the invitation to come to the feast.)

7 But when the king heard *thereof*, he was wroth (angry): and he sent forth his armies, and destroyed those murderers, and burned up their city. (This was partially fulfilled when the Roman armies devastated the Jews,

especially about 70 to 73 AD.)

8 Then saith he to his servants, The wedding (the gospel, the true Church) is ready, but they which were bidden (the covenant people who were in a state of wickedness and apostasy at the time of Christ) were not worthy.

9 Go ye therefore into the highways, and as many as ye shall find, bid to the marriage. (Go to all the world and invite everyone.)

10 So those servants went out into the highways, and gathered together all as many as they found, both bad and good: and the wedding was furnished with guests.

11 And when the king came in to see the guests, he saw there a man which had not on a wedding garment (one who had had time and opportunity to properly prepare for meeting the Savior, but had not):

12 And he saith unto him, Friend, how camest thou in hither not having a wedding garment (not having made and kept covenants; personal righteousness—see Rev. 19:8)? And he was speechless (was without excuse—see 2 Nephi 9:14).

13 Then said the king to the servants, Bind him hand and foot, and take him away, and cast *him* into outer darkness; there shall be weeping and gnashing of teeth. (The wicked cannot remain in the presence of God and must be punished for their sins.)

14 For many are called, but few *are* chosen. (In fact, all are "called" to come unto Christ, but few are "chosen" to remain with him forever, because they do not make themselves worthy.)

15 Then went the Pharisees (Jewish

religious leaders), and took counsel how they might entangle (trap) him in *his* talk.

16 And they sent out unto him (Christ) their disciples (their loyal, wicked followers) with the Herodians (a political party among the Jews [see Bible Dictionary, p. 701] who normally opposed the Pharisees, but now joined with them in opposing Chirst), saying, Master, we know that thou art true, and teachest the way of God in truth, neither carest thou for any *man*: for thou regardest not the person of men.

Note: This is dripping with sarcasm and false flattery. These men are going to try to get Jesus to say something against the Roman government so they can get him arrested and executed for treason.

17 Tell us therefore, What thinkest thou? Is it lawful to give tribute (pay taxes) unto Cæsar (the Roman emperor), or not?

18 But Jesus perceived their wicked-ness, and said, Why tempt ye me, ye hypocrites?

19 Shew me the tribute money. And they brought unto him a penny (a Roman denarius, about the equivalent of a day's pay).

20 And he saith unto them, Whose is this image (picture) and superscription (the writing on the coin)?

21 They say unto him, Cæsar's. Then saith he unto them, Render (give) therefore unto Cæsar the things which are Cæsar's; and unto God the things that are God's.

22 When they had heard these words, they marvelled (were amazed), and left him, and went their way.

23 The same day came to him the Sadducees, which say that there is no resurrection, and asked him,

Note: The Sadducees were another influential group of religious leaders among the Jews. They did not believe in the resurrection, and were normally enemies of the Pharisees who did believe in resurrection. The Sadducees have now joined forces with the Pharisees in attempting to do away with Jesus.

24 Saying, Master, Moses said, If a man die, having no children, his brother shall marry his wife, and raise up seed unto his brother (have children for his dead brother; plural marriage was in practice at this time).

25 Now there were with us seven brethren (brothers): and the first, when he had married a wife, deceased (died), and, having no issue (children), left his wife unto his brother:

26 Likewise the second also, and the third, unto the seventh. (Each of the six brothers likewise married her, but died, without her having any children.)

27 And last of all the woman died also (she probably ate her own cooking).

28 Therefore in the resurrection whose wife shall she be of the seven? for they all had her (had her as a wife).

Note: Here is a major doctrinal point. Many religions use these next two verses to prove that there is no such thing as eternal marriage and family in the next life. On the contrary, the simple fact that the Sadducees asked the Savior the question "Whose wife will she be when they are all resurrected?", is proof that the Savior had indeed preached marriage in the resurrection, in other words, eternal marriage. Otherwise, their question would not make any sense at all!

29 Jesus answered and said unto them, Ye do err, not knowing the scriptures, nor the power of God.

30 For in the resurrection they neither marry, nor are given in marriage, but are as the angels of God in heaven (see D&C 132:15-17).

Note: Here again, correct doctrine needs to be understood. After everyone from this earth is resurrected, there will be no more eternal marriages performed for them, because such marriages have to be done by mortals for themselves, or by mortals who serve as proxies for those who have died–see D&C 128:15 & 18. Brigham Young said: "And when the Millennium is over, ...all the sons and daughters of Adam and Eve, *down to the last of their posterity* (bold added for emphasis), who come within the reach of the clemency of the Gospel,[will] have been redeemed in hundreds of temples through the administration of their children as proxies for them." *Discourses of Brigham Young*, p. 395. Since there will be no mortals left on earth after the resurrection is completed, there would be no one left to serve as proxies for eternal marriages.

31 But as touching the resurrection of the dead, have ye not read that which was spoken unto you by God, saying,

32 I am the God of Abraham, and the God of Isaac, and the God of Jacob? God is not the God of the dead, but of the living. (In other words, you Sadducees should believe in resurrection.)

33 And when the multitude heard this, they were astonished at his doctrine.

34 But when the Pharisees had heard that he had put the Sadducees to silence, they were gathered together. (The Pharisees now take over again, since the Sadducees were unsuccessful.)

35 Then one of them, which was a lawyer, asked him a question, tempting him (trying to trap Jesus), and saying,

36 Master, which is the great commandment in the law? ("The law", as used here, means the first five books of the Old Testament, i.e., Genesis, Exodus, Leviticus, Numbers, Deuteronomy.)

37 Jesus said unto him, Thou shalt love the Lord thy God with all thy heart, and with all thy soul, and with all thy mind (Deuteronomy 6:5).

38 This is the first and great commandment.

39 And the second is like unto it, Thou shalt love thy neighbour as thyself (Leviticus 19:18).

40 On these two commandments hang all the law and the prophets. (All the other commandments are based on these two commandments. The "law" meant Genesis, Exodus, Leviticus, Numbers, and Deuteronomy. The "prophets" meant writings of Old

Testament prophets such as Isaiah, Jeremiah etc.)

41 While the Pharisees were gathered together, Jesus asked them,

42 Saying, What think ye of Christ? whose son is he? They say unto him, The Son of David (a descendent of King David).

43 He saith unto them, How then doth David in spirit call him Lord (why would David, speaking under inspiration, refer to Him as "Lord?"), saying,

44 The LORD (Heavenly Father) said unto my Lord (Christ), Sit thou on my right hand, till I make thine enemies thy footstool? (See Hebrews 1:3, also see Bruce R. McConkie, *Doctrinal New Testament Commentary*, Vol. 1, p. 612.)

45 If David then call him Lord, how is he his son?

46 And no man was able to answer him a word, neither durst (dared) any *man* from that day forth ask him any more *questions*. (It was getting pretty embarrassing trying to trap Jesus with questions because he out-smarted them every time!)

MATTHEW 23

Note: In this chapter, the Jewish religious leaders, the scribes and Pharisees, get a scathing rebuke from the Savior because of their wickedness and hypocrisy.

1 THEN spake Jesus to the multitude, and to his disciples,

2 Saying, The scribes and the Pharisees sit in Moses' seat (have offices of high authority among you):

3 All therefore whatsoever they bid you observe, *that* observe and do (go ahead and do everything they ask you to do; i.e., respect the office they hold); but do not ye after their works (don't behave like they do): for they say, and do not (they are hypocrites).

4 For they bind heavy burdens and grievous to be borne, and lay *them* on men's shoulders (they give you all kinds of very difficult tasks to accomplish); but they *themselves* will not move them with one of their fingers (but they won't lift a finger to help).

5 But all their works they do for to be seen of men (everything they do is for show): they make broad their phylacteries, and enlarge the borders of their garments,

Note: Phylacteries were small leather boxes, beautifully crafted, which faithful Jews tied to their forehead (symbolizing loyalty to God) and left arm (to be near the heart). Inside these small leather boxes were four tiny scrolls containing Exodus 13:2-10, Exodus 13:11-17, Deuteronomy 6:4-9, and Deuteronomy 11:13-21. The scribes and Pharisees had made their phylacteries larger than normal so people could see how "righteous" they were. Likewise, they had enlarged the blue fringes on their clothing (see Numbers 15:38-39) which symbolized keeping the commandments of God.

6 And love the uppermost rooms at feasts, and the chief seats in the synagogues (church buildings),

7 And greetings in the markets, and to be called of men, Rabbi, Rabbi.

8 But be not ye (Jesus is addressing the multitude and his disciples-see

verse 1) called Rabbi: for one is your Master, *even* Christ; and all ye are brethren.

9 And call no *man* your father upon the earth: for one is your Father, which is in heaven.

10 Neither be ye called masters: for one is your Master, *even* Christ.

11 But he that is greatest among you shall be your servant. (This is the main point Christ is teaching the multitude and his disciples.)

12 And whosoever shall exalt himself (pridefully set himself up as an example) shall be abased (put down); and he that shall humble himself shall be exalted.

13 But woe unto you, scribes and Pharisees, hypocrites! for ye shut up the kingdom of heaven against men (you make so many nit-picky rules that nobody could get into heaven): for ye neither go in yourselves (you won't get to heaven yourselves), neither suffer (allow) ye them that are entering to go in (and you won't let anyone else in either!).

14 Woe unto you, scribes and Pharisees, hypocrites! for ye devour widows' houses (foreclose on widows' mortgages and take their houses from them via technicalities of the law) and, and for a pretence (for show) make long prayer: therefore ye shall receive the greater damnation.

15 Woe unto you, scribes and Pharisees, hypocrites! for ye compass sea and land to make one proselyte (you travel far and wide to get one convert), and when he is made (when he joins your church), ye make him twofold more the child of hell than yourselves.

Note: In verses 16-24, Jesus points out several examples of the hypocritical, nit-picky, laden-with-details rules which these religious leaders have forced upon their people. They have made so many rules that nobody can figure them out and follow them all properly, which puts these leaders in a position of constant power over the people.

16 Woe unto you, ye blind guides, which say, Whosoever shall swear (make vows, promises, covenants) by the temple, it is nothing; but whosoever shall swear by the gold of the temple, he is a debtor!

17 Ye fools and blind: for whether (which) is greater (more important), the gold, or the temple that sanctifieth the gold (makes the gold holy)?

18 And, Whosoever shall swear by the altar, it is nothing; but whosoever sweareth by the gift that is upon it, he is guilty (of sin, according to your rules).

19 Ye fools and blind: for whether (which) is greater (more important), the gift, or the altar that sanctifieth the gift?

20 Whoso therefore shall swear by the altar, sweareth by it, and by all things thereon.

21 And whoso shall swear by the temple, sweareth by it, and by him that dwelleth therein.

22 And he that shall swear by heaven, sweareth by the throne of God, and by him that sitteth thereon. (More of their impossible rules.)

23 Woe unto you, scribes and Pharisees, hypocrites! for ye pay tithe of mint and anise (dill) and cummin

(you weigh out the tiniest amounts of seeds and spices with exactness to see how much tithing you should pay on them) , and have omitted (left out) the weightier (more important) *matters* of the law, judgment (fairness), mercy, and faith: these ought ye to have done, and not to leave the other undone.

24 Ye blind guides, which strain at a gnat (Greek: "strain out a gnat"), and swallow a camel.

Note: Both gnats (Leviticus 11:23) and camels (Leviticus 11:4) were "unclean" and thus forbidden as food for the Jews. The JST adds more to this verse: "Ye blind guides, who strain at a gnat, and swallow a camel; who make yourselves appear unto men that ye would not commit the least sin, and yet ye yourselves, transgress the whole law.

25 Woe unto you, scribes and Pharisees, hypocrites! for ye make clean the outside of the cup and of the platter, but within they are full of extortion (greed) and excess (self-indulgence-see Matt. 23:25a, b).

26 *Thou* blind Pharisee, cleanse first that *which is* within the cup and platter, that the outside of them may be clean also.

27 Woe unto you, scribes and Pharisees, hypocrites! for ye are like unto whited sepulchres (whitewashed graves, tombs), which indeed appear beautiful outward, but are within (inside) full of dead *men's* bones, and of all uncleanness.

28 Even so ye also outwardly appear righteous unto men, but within ye are full of hypocrisy and iniquity (wickedness).

29 Woe unto you, scribes and Pharisees, hypocrites! because ye build the tombs of the prophets, and garnish (decorate) the sepulchres (graves, tombs) of the righteous (you appear to honor ancient prophets, such as Abraham, Moses, Isaiah, Jeremiah etc.),

30 And say, If we had been (lived) in the days of our fathers (ancestors), we would not have been partakers with them in the blood of the prophets (we wouldn't have killed prophets like they did).

31 Wherefore ye be witnesses unto yourselves, that ye are the children of them which killed the prophets. (You are just like your ancestors!)

32 Fill ye up then the measure of your fathers (go ahead and fill your lives with sin just like your ancestors did).

33 Ye serpents (you are like Satan-Revelation 12:9), ye generation of vipers (poisonous snakes), how can ye escape the damnation of hell?

34 Wherefore, behold, I (Christ is clearly stating that he is the Lord, the promised Messiah) send unto you prophets, and wise men, and scribes: and *some* of them ye shall kill and crucify; and *some* of them shall ye scourge (whip, beat) in your synagogues (churches), and persecute *them* from city to city:

35 That upon you may come all the righteous blood shed upon the earth (you have murderous hearts and deserve the punishments which will come upon you), from the blood of righteous Abel unto the blood of Zacharias (John the Baptist's father) son of Barachias, whom ye slew

between the temple and the altar.

Note: Zacharias was the father of John the Baptist. Joseph Smith tells us that when King Herod ordered all the babies two years old and younger killed in Bethlehem and surrounding area (see Matt. 2:16), Zacharias sent Elizabeth and John "into the mountains" to hide. "When his father refused to disclose his hiding place...[he] was slain by Herod's order, between the porch and the altar..." of the temple. See *Teachings of the Prophet Joseph Smith*, p. 261. Apparently, from what Jesus is saying to the scribes and Pharisees in verse 35, these evil leaders must have had a hand in getting Zacharias killed.

36 Verily I say unto you, All these things shall come upon this generation.

37 O Jerusalem, Jerusalem, *thou* that killest the prophets, and stonest them which are sent unto thee, how often would I have gathered thy children together, even as a hen gathereth her chickens under *her* wings, and ye would not! (You wouldn't let me gather and protect you.)

38 Behold, your house is left unto you desolate.

39 For I say unto you, Ye shall not see me henceforth, till ye shall say, Blessed *is* he that cometh in the name of the Lord. (You won't see me until the second coming.)

Note: The JST adds the following:

39 For I say unto you, that ye shall not see me henceforth, and know that I am he of whom it is written by the prophets, until ye shall say,

40 Blessed is he who cometh in the name of the Lord, in the clouds of heaven, and all the holy angels with him.

41 Then understood his disciples that he should come again on the earth, after that he was glorified and crowned on the right hand of God.

MATTHEW 24

Note: This chapter is very well known among Christians because it contains so many prophecies which will be fulfilled before the Savior's second coming. These prophecies are known as "the signs of the times". Many of them are being fulfilled in our day and bear witness to us that the second coming is near. However, since we do not know how close it is, we should plan on living a full lifetime and keeping our lives in order, so that when we meet the Savior, whether at our death, or at his coming, we will be prepared.

1 AND Jesus went out, and departed from the temple (in Jerusalem): and his disciples came to *him* for to shew (show) him the buildings of the temple.

2 And Jesus said unto them, See ye not all these things? verily I say unto you, There shall not be left here one stone upon another, that shall not be thrown down. (The temple will be destroyed. The Romans destroyed much, culminating with the final conquering of Jerusalem about 70 AD.)

3 And as he sat upon the mount of Olives (located just outside of Jerusalem), the disciples came unto

him privately, saying, Tell us, when shall these things be (the things Jesus had just prophesied)? and what *shall be* the sign of thy coming, and of the end of the world?

Note: The disciples asked Jesus two questions: 1. "When shall these things be?", meaning the things which will happen to Jerusalem, the Jews, and the early Christians following the crucifixion. 2. What shall be the sign of thy coming, and of the end of the world?", meaning the "signs of the times" preceding his Second Coming.

4 And Jesus answered and said unto them, Take heed (be careful) that no man deceive you.

5 For many shall come in my name, saying, I am Christ; and shall deceive many.

6 And ye shall hear of wars and rumours of wars: see that ye be not troubled (don't let the signs of the times cause undue fear or panic in you): for all *these things* must come to pass, but the end is not yet.

7 For nation shall rise against nation, and kingdom against kingdom: and there shall be famines, and pestilences, and earthquakes, in divers places.

8 All these are the beginning of sorrows.

9 Then shall they deliver you up to be afflicted, and shall kill you: and ye shall be hated of all nations for my name's sake.

10 And then shall many be offended (many will leave the church), and shall betray one another, and shall hate one another.

11 And many false prophets shall rise, and shall deceive many.

Note: Many people, when they read "false prophets", think only of false ministers and preachers of false doctrines and philosophies. They would be wise not to limit their understanding to these types, rather to include any famous, influential individuals who gather followers and lead them astray. This can include politicians, movie stars, singers, gang leaders, etc.

12 And because iniquity (wickedness) shall abound (will be everywhere), the love of many shall wax (grow) cold.

13 But he that shall endure unto the end, the same shall be saved.

14 And this gospel of the kingdom shall be preached in all the world for a witness unto all nations (one of the last major signs which will happen before the Savior's Second Coming); and then shall the end (of wickedness) come. (The Millennium will then begin).

15 When ye therefore shall see the abomination of desolation, spoken of by Daniel the prophet (in Dan. 11:31; 12:11), stand in the holy place, (whoso readeth, let him understand:)

Note: "Abomination of desolation" means terrible things which will cause much destruction and misery. The abomination of desolation spoken of by Daniel was to have two fulfillments. The first occurred in 70 A.D. when Titus, with his Roman legions, surrounded Jerusalem and laid siege to conquer the Jews. This siege resulted in much destruction and terrible human misery and loss of life. In the last days, the abomination of desolation will occur again (see Joseph Smith–Matt. 1:31-32), meaning that Jerusalem will again be under siege. See Bible Dictionary, p. 601.

16 Then let them which be in Judæa flee into the mountains: (Many faithful saints heeded this warning and fled to Pella, east of Samaria, and thus escaped the Romans.)

17 Let him which is on the housetop not come down to take any thing out of his house:

18 Neither let him which is in the field return back to take his clothes.

19 And woe unto them that are with child, and to them that give suck in those days!

20 But pray ye that your flight be not in the winter, neither on the sabbath day (when city gates are closed):

21 For then shall be great tribulation, such as was not since the beginning of the world to this time, no, nor ever shall be.

22 And except those days should be shortened, there should no flesh be saved: but for the elect's sake those days shall be shortened (the Lord will stop the destructions in time so that some covenant people will remain).

23 (Now, Jesus answers their second question-see note, verse 4.) Then if any man shall say unto you, Lo, here is Christ, or there; believe it not.

24 For there shall arise false Christs, and false prophets, and shall shew (show) great signs and wonders; insomuch that, if it were possible, they shall deceive the very elect (meaning those who have made covenants with God-see JS–Matt. 1:22).

25 Behold, I have told you before.

26 Wherefore if they (false prophets, "gatherers", teachers, leaders etc.) shall say unto you, Behold, he (Christ) is in the desert; go not forth (don't go to see him): behold, he is in the secret chambers; believe it not.

27 For as the lightning ("lightning" is a mistake in the Bible; it should be "as the light of the morning cometh out of the east"; see JS–Matt. 1:26) cometh out of the east, and shineth even unto the west; so shall also the coming of the Son of man be. (In other words, when he comes for the actual Second Coming, everyone will see him. It will not be a low-key, quiet, secret coming [see verse 26].)

28 For wheresoever the carcase is, there will the eagles be gathered together.

Note: This is an unusual use of the word "carcase". Symbolically, in this context, it means "the body of the Church", in other words, the true Church with the true gospel. The "eagles" are converts, faithful members of the Church who will be gathered to the Church for nourishment in all parts of the world. See JS–Matt. 1:27. In short, this verse prophesies of the gathering of Israel in the last days prior to the Second Coming. See Bruce R. McConkie, Doctrinal New Testament Commentary, Vol. 1, pages 648-649.

29 Immediately after the tribulation of those days shall the sun be darkened, and the moon shall not give her light (can refer to spiritual darkness as well as actual things in nature etc.), and the stars shall fall from heaven,

and the powers of the heavens shall be shaken:

30 And then shall appear the sign of the Son of man in heaven (we don't know what this means): and then shall all the tribes of the earth mourn (the wicked will mourn, but the righteous will rejoice-see 2 Nephi 9:14, D&C 88:96), and they shall see the Son of man coming in the clouds of heaven with power and great glory.

Note: Even those who caused the Savior's crucifixion will see him at this time. See Revelation 1:7.

31 (These verses are not all in chronological order.) And he shall send his angels with a great sound of a trumpet, and they shall gather together his elect from the four winds, from one end of heaven to the other. (This is the final gathering of the righteous.)

32 Now learn a parable of the fig tree; When his branch is yet tender, and putteth forth leaves, ye know that summer is nigh (when a fruit tree starts putting on leaves, you know that summer is near):

33 So likewise ye, when ye shall see all these things (signs of the times being fulfilled), know that it (the Second Coming) is near, *even* at the doors.

34 Verily I say unto you, This generation ("generation" can sometimes mean "dispensation") shall not pass, till all these things be fulfilled.

35 Heaven and earth shall pass away, but my words shall not pass away (you can rely on my words completely!).

36 But of that day and hour knoweth no *man*, no, not the angels of heaven, but my Father only.

Note: On occasion we hear of people who claim to know when the Second Coming will be. Sometimes they gather others around them to await the exact day they have predicted he will come. Some say they don't know the hour and day, but they do know the month and year. Some say that the Brethren know, but are not allowed to tell us. Elder M. Russell Ballard, of the Quorum of the Twelve, said the following in a talk given March 12, 1996 at a BYU Devotional. "I do not know when He is going to come again. As far as I know, none of my brethren in the Council of the Twelve or even in the First Presidency knows. And I would humbly suggest to you, my young brothers and sisters, that if we do not know, then nobody knows,..."

37 But as the days of Noe (Noah) *were*, so shall also the coming of the Son of man (Jesus) be. (Just as the wicked in the days of Noah did not believe the Flood would come, so also the wicked in the last days will not believe the Savior will come, and thus will be caught unprepared.)

38 For as in the days that were before the flood they were eating and drinking, marrying and giving in marriage, until the day that Noe (Noah) entered into the ark,

39 And knew not until the flood came, and took them all away (destroyed them); so shall also the coming of the Son of man (Jesus) be.

40 Then shall two be in the field; the one shall be taken, and the other left. (One who is worthy will be taken up to

meet Christ [see D&C 88:96] and the other who is not worthy will be left on earth to be destroyed at his coming.)

41 Two *women shall be* grinding at the mill; the one shall be taken, and the other left.

42 Watch therefore: for ye know not what hour your Lord doth come.

43 But know this, that if the goodman (symbolic of people who will be caught off guard by the Second Coming) of the house had known in what watch (the Jews divided the night into "watches" of about four hours each; see Bible Dictionary, p. 788) the thief would come, he would have watched (would have been ready), and would not have suffered (allowed) his house to be broken up.

44 Therefore be ye also ready: for in such an hour as ye think not the Son of man cometh.

Note: In the next verses, the Savior, in effect, asks the disciples who they think the people are who will be saved at the Second Coming. He answers his own question and basically says that it will be those who are faithful to the gospel and who, as servants in the gospel, serve others with kindness and wisdom.

45 Who then is a faithful and wise servant, whom his lord hath made ruler over his household, to give them (people under his jurisdiction) meat (food, nourishment) in due season (according to their needs)?

46 Blessed *is* that servant, whom his lord when he cometh shall find so doing.

47 Verily I say unto you, That he shall make him ruler over all his goods. (They will be exalted and will become gods. See D&C 84:38, D&C 132:20.)

48 But and if that evil servant (symbolic of the wicked in the last days) shall say in his heart, My lord (Christ) delayeth his coming (similar to the wicked in 3 Nephi 1);

49 And shall begin to smite *his* fellowservants (be mean and cruel to others), and to eat and drink with the drunken;

50 The lord (Christ) of that servant shall come in a day when he looketh not for *him*, and in an hour that he is not aware of,

51 And shall cut him asunder (destroy him), and appoint *him* his portion (put him in hell) with the hypocrites (people who want to appear righteous but like to do evil): there shall be weeping and gnashing of teeth (grinding of teeth together in agony and misery).

Note: In JST Matthew 24, the Prophet Joseph Smith added about 450 words to the Bible version of Matthew 24, and rearranged the order of some verses. Thus, we are in a much better position to understand this chapter. The Prophet's revision of this chapter appears as Joseph Smith–Matthew in the Pearl of Great Price. It is included next in this book in a parallel column format so that you can compare at-a-glance the inspired contributions of the Prophet Joseph Smith with Matthew, chapter 24, as it stands in the King James version of the Bible.

Joseph Smith—Matthew & Matthew 24 Parallel Column Comparison

Prepared by David J. Ridges

Joseph Smith–Matthew (With Joseph Smith's changes in bold)	King James Bible Version Matthew 24
1 For I say unto you, that ye shall not see me henceforth **and know that I am he of whom it is written by the prophets**, until ye shall say: Blessed is he who cometh in the name of the Lord, **in the clouds of heaven, and all the holy angels with him. Then understood his disciples that he should come again on the earth, after that he was glorified and crowned on the right hand of God**.	Matthew 23:39 For I say unto you, Ye shall not see me henceforth, till ye shall say, Blessed is he that cometh in the name of the Lord.
2 And Jesus went out, and departed from the temple; and his disciples came to him, for to hear him, saying: Master, show us concerning the buildings of the temple, as thou hast said—They shall be thrown down, and left unto you desolate.	1 And Jesus went out, and departed from the temple: and his disciples came to him for to shew him the buildings of the temple.
3 And Jesus said unto them: See ye not all these things, and do ye not understand them? Verily I say unto you, there shall not be left here, upon this temple, one stone upon another that shall not be thrown down.	2 And Jesus said unto them, See ye not all these things? verily I say unto you, There shall not be left here one stone upon another, that shall not be thrown down.
4 And Jesus left them, and went upon the Mount of Olives. And as he sat upon the Mount of Olives, the disciples came unto him privately, saying: Tell us when shall these things be which thou hast said concerning the	3 And as he sat upon the mount of Olives, the disciples came unto him privately, saying, Tell us, when shall these things be? and what shall be the sign of thy coming, and of the end of the world?

Joseph Smith Matthew

Matthew 24

destruction of the temple, and the Jews; and what is the sign of thy coming, and of the end of the world, or the destruction of the wicked, which is the end of the world?

5 And Jesus answered, and said unto them: Take heed that no man deceive you;

6 For many shall come in my name, saying--I am Christ--and shall deceive many;

7 Then shall they deliver you up to be afflicted, and shall kill you, and ye shall be hated of all nations, for my name's sake;

8 And then shall many be offended, and shall betray one another, and shall hate one another;

9 And many false prophets shall arise, and shall deceive many;

10 And because iniquity shall abound, the love of many shall wax cold;

11 But he that **remaineth steadfast and is not overcome**, the same shall be saved.

12 When you, therefore, shall see the abomination of desolation, spoken of by Daniel the prophet, **concerning the destruction of Jerusalem**, then you shall stand in the holy place; whoso readeth let him understand.

4 And Jesus answered and said unto them, Take heed that no man deceive you.

5 For many shall come in my name, saying, I am Christ; and shall deceive many.

9 Then shall they deliver you up to be afflicted, and shall kill you: and ye shall be hated of all nations for my name's sake.

10 And then shall many be offended, and shall betray one another, and shall hate one another.

11 And many false prophets shall rise, and shall deceive many.

12 And because iniquity shall abound, the love of many shall wax cold.

13 But he that shall endure unto the end, the same shall be saved.

14 And this gospel of the kingdom shall be preached in all the world for a witness unto all nations; and then shall the end come.

15 When ye therefore shall see the abomination of desolation, spoken of by Daniel the prophet, stand in the holy place, (whoso readeth, let him understand:)

Joseph Smith-Matthew

13 Then let them **who are** in Judea flee into the mountains;

14 Let him who is on the housetop **flee, and not return** to take anything out of his house;

15 Neither let him who is in the field return back to take his clothes;

16 And wo unto them that are with child, and unto them that give suck in those days;

17 **Therefore**, pray ye **the Lord** that your flight be not in the winter, neither on the Sabbath day;

18 For then, **in those days**, shall be great tribulation **on the Jews, and upon the inhabitants of Jerusalem**, such as was not **before sent upon Israel, of God**, since the beginning of **their kingdom until** this time; no, nor ever shall be **sent again upon Israel**.

19 **All things which have befallen them** are only the beginning of the sorrows **which shall come upon them**.

20 And except those days should be shortened, there should none of their flesh be saved; but for the elect's sake, **according to the covenant**, those days shall be shortened.

21 **Behold, these things I have spoken unto you concerning the Jews; and again, after the tribulation of those days which shall come upon Jerusalem**, if any man shall say unto you, Lo, here is Christ, or there, believe him not;

Matthew 24

16 Then let them which be in Judaea flee into the mountains:

17 Let him which is on the housetop not come down to take any thing out of his house:

18 Neither let him which is in the field return back to take his clothes.

19 And woe unto them that are with child, and to them that give suck in those days!

20 But pray ye that your flight be not in the winter, neither on the sabbath day:

21 For then shall be great tribulation, such as was not since the beginning of the world to this time, no, nor ever shall be.

8 All these *are* the beginning of sorrows.

22 And except those days should be shortened, there should no flesh be saved: but for the elect's sake those days shall be shortened.

23 Then if any man shall say unto you, Lo, here is Christ, or there; believe it not.

Joseph Smith–Matthew

22 For **in those days** there shall also arise false Christs, and false prophets, and shall show great signs and wonders, insomuch, that, if possible, they shall deceive the very elect, **who are the elect according to the covenant**.

23 **Behold, I speak these things unto you for the elect's sake**; and you also shall hear of wars, and rumors of wars; see that ye be not troubled, for all **I have told you** must come to pass; but the end is not yet.

24 Behold, I have told you before;

25 Wherefore, if they shall say unto you: Behold, he is in the desert; go not forth: Behold, he is in the secret chambers; believe it not;

26 For as the **light of the morning** cometh out of the east, and shineth even unto the west, **and covereth the whole earth**, so shall also the coming of the Son of Man be.

27 **And now I show unto you a parable. Behold**, wheresoever the carcass is, there will the eagles be gathered together; **so likewise shall mine elect be gathered from the four quarters of the earth.**

28 **And they shall hear of wars and rumors of wars**.

29 **Behold I speak for mine elect's sake**; for nation shall rise against nation, and kingdom against kingdom; there shall be famines, and pestilences, and earthquakes, in divers places.

Matthew 24

24 For there shall arise false Christs, and false prophets, and shall shew great signs and wonders; insomuch that, if it *were* possible, they shall deceive the very elect.

6 And ye shall hear of wars and rumours of wars: see that ye be not troubled: for all *these things* must come to pass, but the end is not yet.

25 Behold, I have told you before.

26 Wherefore if they shall say unto you, Behold, *he* is in the desert; go not forth: behold, he is in the secret chambers; believe *it* not.

27 For as the lightning cometh out of the east, and shineth even unto the west; so shall also the coming of the Son of man be.

28 For wheresoever the carcase is, there will the eagles be gathered together.

7 For nation shall rise against nation, and kingdom against kingdom: and there shall be famines, and pestilences, and earthquakes, in divers places.

Joseph Smith–Matthew

30 And again, because iniquity shall abound, the love of men shall wax cold; but he that shall not be overcome, the same shall be saved.

31 And again, this Gospel of the Kingdom shall be preached in all the world, for a witness unto all nations, and then shall the end come, **or the destruction of the wicked;**

32 **(This is not the same as verse 15 in Matthew 24.) And again shall the abomination of desolation, spoken of by Daniel the prophet, be fulfilled.**

33 **And** immediately after the tribulation of those days, **the sun shall be darkened**, and the moon shall not give her light, and the stars shall fall from heaven, and the powers of heaven shall be shaken.

34 Verily, I say unto you, this generation, **in which these things shall be shown forth**, shall not pass away until all **I have told you shall** be fulfilled.

35 Although, the days will come, that heaven and earth shall pass away; yet my words shall not pass away, but all shall be fulfilled.

36 And, **as I said before, after the tribulation of those days, and the powers of the heavens shall be shaken**, then shall appear the sign of the Son of Man in heaven, and then shall all the tribes of the earth mourn; and they shall see the Son of Man coming in the clouds of heaven, with power and great glory;

Matthew 24

14 And this gospel of the kingdom shall be preached in all the world for a witness unto all nations; and then shall the end come.

29 Immediately after the tribulation of those days shall the sun be darkened, and the moon shall not give her light, and the stars shall fall from heaven, and the powers of the heavens shall be shaken:

34 Verily I say unto you, This generation shall not pass, till all these things be fulfilled.

35 Heaven and earth shall pass away, but my words shall not pass away.

30 And then shall appear the sign of the Son of man in heaven: and then shall all the tribes of the earth mourn, and they shall see the Son of man coming in the clouds of heaven with power and great glory.

Joseph Smith-Matthew	Matthew 24
37 **And whoso treasureth up my word, shall not be deceived, for the Son of Man shall come**, and he shall send his angels **before him** with **the** great sound of a trumpet, and they shall gather together **the remainder of** his elect **from the four winds**, from one end of heaven to the other.	31 And he shall send his angels with a great sound of a trumpet, and they shall gather together his elect from the four winds, from one end of heaven to the other.
38 Now learn a parable of the fig-tree—When **its** branches **are** yet tender, and **it begins to** put forth leaves, **you** know that summer is nigh **at hand**;	32 Now learn a parable of the fig tree; When his branch is yet tender, and putteth forth leaves, ye know that summer is nigh:
39 So likewise, **mine elect**, when **they** shall see all these things, **they** shall know that **he** is near, even at the doors;	33 So likewise ye, when ye shall see all these things, know that it is near, even at the doors
40 But of that day, and hour, no one knoweth; no, not the angels of **God in** heaven, but my Father only.	36 But of that day and hour knoweth no man, no, not the angels of heaven, but my Father only.
41 But as **it was in** the days of Noah, so **it** shall **be** also **at** the coming of the Son of Man;	37 But as the days of Noe were, so shall also the coming of the Son of man be.
42 For **it shall be with them**, as **it was** in the days **which** were before the flood; **for until the day that Noah entered into the ark** they were eating and drinking, marrying and giving in marriage;	38 For as in the days that were before the flood they were eating and drinking, marrying and giving in marriage, until the day that Noe entered into the ark,
43 And knew not until the flood came, and took them all away; so shall also the coming of the Son of Man be.	39 And knew not until the flood came, and took them all away; so shall also the coming of the Son of man be.
44 Then shall be fulfilled that which is written, that in the last days, two shall be in the field, the one shall be taken, and the other left;	40 Then shall two be in the field; the one shall be taken, and the other left.

Joseph Smith-Matthew

45 Two shall be grinding at the mill, the one shall be taken, and the other left;

46 **And what I say unto one, I say unto all men**; watch, therefore, for you know not at what hour your Lord doth come.

47 But know this, if the good man of the house had known in what watch the thief would come, he would have watched, and would not have suffered his house to have been broken up, **but would have been ready.**

48 Therefore be ye also ready, for in such an hour as ye think not, the Son of Man cometh.

49 Who, then, is a faithful and wise servant, whom his lord hath made ruler over his household, to give them meat in due season?

50 Blessed is that servant whom his lord, when he cometh, shall find so doing; and verily I say unto you, he shall make him ruler over all his goods.

51 But if that evil servant shall say in his heart: My lord delayeth his coming,

52 And shall begin to smite his fellow-servants, and to eat and drink with the drunken,

53 The lord of that servant shall come in a day when he looketh not for him, and in an hour that he is not aware of,

Matthew 24

41 Two *women shall* be grinding at the mill; the one shall be taken, and the other left

42 Watch therefore: for ye know not what hour your Lord doth come.

43 But know this, that if the goodman of the house had known in what watch the thief would come, he would have watched, and would not have suffered his house to be broken up.

44 Therefore be ye also ready: for in such an hour as ye think not the Son of man cometh.

45 Who then is a faithful and wise servant, whom his lord hath made ruler over his household, to give them meat in due season?

46 Blessed is that servant, whom his lord when he cometh shall find so doing.

47 Verily I say unto you, That he shall make him ruler over all his goods.

48 But and if that evil servant shall say in his heart, My lord delayeth his coming;

49 And shall begin to smite his fellowservants, and to eat and drink with the drunken;

50 The lord of that servant shall come in a day when he looketh not for him, and in an hour that he is not aware of,

Joseph Smith-Matthew	Matthew 24
54 And shall cut him asunder, and **shall** appoint him his portion with the hypocrites; there shall be weeping and gnashing of teeth.	51 And shall cut him asunder, and appoint *him* his portion with the hypocrites: there shall be weeping and gnashing of teeth.
55 **And thus cometh the end of the wicked, according to the prophecy of Moses, saying: They shall be cut off from among the people; but the end of the earth is not yet, but by and by**.	

MATTHEW 25

Note: In chapter 24, many prophecies were given which will be fulfilled as the time of the Second Coming approaches, and counsel was given to be prepared by living faithfully and serving others. Chapter 25 continues with instructions on how to prepare personally for the Second Coming.

1 THEN (the last days leading up to the time of the Second Coming) shall the kingdom of heaven be likened unto ten virgins (symbolic of members of the Church, see McConkie, *Doctrinal New Testament Commentary*, Vol. 1, pages 684-685), which took their lamps, and went forth to meet the bridegroom (groom; symbolic of Christ, see Talmage, *Jesus the Christ*, p. 578).

2 And five of them were wise, and five *were* foolish.

3 They that *were* foolish took their lamps, and took no oil with them:

4 But the wise took oil in their vessels with their lamps.

Note: All ten virgins had lamps with oil in them to begin with. But the five wise virgins carried flasks with extra oil and thus were able to "endure to the end" until the bridegroom [groom] arrived.

5 While the bridegroom tarried, they all slumbered and slept.

6 And at midnight there was a cry made, Behold, the bridegroom cometh (symbolic of the Second Coming); go ye out to meet him.

7 Then all those virgins arose, and trimmed their lamps.

8 And the foolish said unto the wise, Give us of your oil; for our lamps are gone out.

9 But the wise answered, saying, *Not so*; lest there be not enough for us and you: but go ye rather to them that sell, and buy for yourselves.

Note: To some, it may seem that the five wise virgins were not living the gospel because they would not share their supplies of oil with the five foolish virgins. The point is that their extra oil is symbolic of personal worthiness and preparedness which the righteous cannot share or give to others, such as personal righteousness, church attendance, tithe paying, moral cleanliness, Sabbath observance, keeping the commandments etc.

10 And while they (the foolish virgins) went to buy, the bridegroom came (sadly, they were unprepared, unworthy, and could not get ready in time); and they that were ready went in with him to the marriage (the marriage represents the Second Coming, see Talmage, *Jesus the Christ*, p. 578): and the door was shut.

11 Afterward came also the other virgins, saying, Lord, Lord, open to us.

12 But he answered and said, Verily I say unto you, I know you not. ("I know you not." is another way of saying "You do not know me." See Talmage, *Jesus the Christ*, p. 579.)

13 Watch therefore, for ye know neither the day nor the hour wherein the Son of man (Christ) cometh.

14 For *the kingdom of heaven is* as a man (symbolic of Christ, who will be crucified within three days) travelling

into a far country (symbolic of heaven), *who* called his own servants (disciples, apostles), and delivered unto them his goods.

15 And unto one he gave five talents, to another two, and to another one; to every man according to his several ability (in other words, each is an individual and is given a stewardship according to personal capacities, talents and abilities); and straightway took his journey.

Note: Some biblical scholars suggest that a talent was a substantial sum of money in New Testament times. See Bible Dictionary, p. 734, wherein it says a talent is a sum of money.

16 Then he that had received the five talents went and traded with the same, and made *them* other five talents. (He developed and increased his talents.)

17 And likewise he that *had received two*, he also gained other two. (He developed and increased his talents.)

18 But he that had received one went and digged in the earth, and hid his lord's money. (He did not develop and increase his talent.)

19 After a long time the lord (symbolic of Christ) of those servants cometh, and reckoneth with them (had them account for how they had used that which he gave them; symbolic of Judgment Day).

20 And so he that had received five talents came and brought other five talents, saying, Lord, thou deliveredst unto me five talents: behold, I have gained beside them five talents more.

21 His lord said unto him, Well done, *thou* good and faithful servant: thou

hast been faithful over a few things, I will make thee ruler over many things (symbolic of exaltation): enter thou into the joy of thy lord.

22 He also that had received two talents came and said, Lord, thou deliveredst unto me two talents: behold, I have gained two other talents beside them.

23 His lord said unto him, Well done, good and faithful servant; thou hast been faithful over a few things, I will make thee ruler over many things (symbolic of exaltation): enter thou into the joy of thy lord.

Note: It is significant that the reward for both the servant who had received five talents and the servant who was given two talents, was exactly the same (note the wording of the rewards in verses 21and 23). It is comforting that those with fewer talents and abilities, who do their best, will receive the same reward, exaltation, as those who currently have higher abilities.

24 Then he which had received the one talent came and said (made excuses for his lack of performance), Lord, I knew thee that thou art an hard man, reaping (harvesting) where thou hast not sown (planted), and gathering (harvesting) where thou hast not strawed (thrown or scattered seeds):

25 And I was afraid, and went and hid thy talent in the earth: lo, *there* thou hast *that is* thine.

26 His lord answered and said unto him, Thou wicked and slothful (lazy) servant, thou knewest that I reap (harvest) where I sowed (planted) not, and gather (harvest) where I have not

strawed (planted; in other words, you knew that you would someday have to account to me):

27 Thou oughtest therefore to have put my money to the exchangers, and *then* at my coming I should have received mine own with usury (interest).

28 Take therefore the talent from him, and give it unto him which hath ten talents.

29 For unto every one that hath (who have done the best they can with what they were given) shall be given, and he shall have abundance (symbolic of exaltation): but from him that hath not shall be taken away even that which he hath.

30 And cast ye the unprofitable servant (symbolic of the wicked) into outer darkness: there shall be weeping and gnashing of teeth (among other things, symbolic of the fact that the wicked will have to suffer for their own sins since they were unwilling to repent and take advantage of the Atonement, see D&C 19:15-16).

31 When the Son of man (Jesus) shall come in his glory (the Second Coming), and all the holy angels with him, then shall he sit upon the throne of his glory (he will be our King during the Millennium):

32 And before him shall be gathered all nations: and he shall separate them one from another, as a shepherd divideth *his* sheep from the goats:

33 And he shall set the sheep on his right hand, but the goats on the left.

Note: Here, in this context, sheep symbolize the righteous and goats symbolize the wicked. The right hand,

in Jewish symbolism, is the covenant hand. Thus, being on the Lord's right hand symbolizes those who have made and kept covenants.

34 Then shall the King say unto them on his right hand, Come, ye blessed of my Father, inherit the kingdom (celestial kingdom) prepared for you from the foundation of the world (as planned in the premortal council):

Note: In the next verses, the Savior will beautifully detail more ways to be righteous and prepared for the Second Coming, as were the five wise virgins.

35 For I was an hungred (hungry), and ye gave me meat (food): I was thirsty, and ye gave me drink: I was a stranger, and ye took me in:

36 Naked, and ye clothed me: I was sick, and ye visited me: I was in prison, and ye came unto me.

37 Then shall the righteous answer him, saying, Lord, when saw we thee an hungred, and fed *thee*? or thirsty, and gave *thee* drink?

38 When saw we thee a stranger, and took *thee* in? or naked, and clothed *thee*?

39 Or when saw we thee sick, or in prison, and came unto thee?

40 And the King (Christ) shall answer and say unto them, Verily (listen carefully, this is the main point) I say unto you, Inasmuch as ye have done it unto one of the least of these my brethren, ye have done it unto me. (King Benjamin talked about this kind of service to others in Mosiah 2:17.)

41 Then shall he say also unto them on the left hand (in this context, being

on the left hand of God symbolizes the wicked), Depart from me, ye cursed, into everlasting fire (hell), prepared for the devil and his angels:

42 For I was an hungred, and ye gave me no meat (food): I was thirsty, and ye gave me no drink:

43 I was a stranger, and ye took me not in: naked, and ye clothed me not: sick, and in prison, and ye visited me not.

44 Then shall they also answer him, saying, Lord, when saw we thee an hungred, or athirst, or a stranger, or naked, or sick, or in prison, and did not minister unto thee (take care of your needs)?

45 Then shall he answer them, saying, Verily (when he says "verily", it means "Listen very carefully because this is the point I am trying to teach you.") I say unto you, Inasmuch as ye did it not to one of the least of these, ye did it not to me.

46 And these shall go away into everlasting punishment: but the righteous into life eternal (celestial glory and exaltation).

MATTHEW 26

1 AND it came to pass, when Jesus had finished all these sayings, he said unto his disciples,

2 Ye know that after two days is *the feast of* the passover, and the Son of man is betrayed to be crucified.

Note: The Feast of the Passover was celebrated in the springtime at about the same time as we celebrate Easter. It commemorated the destroying angel's passing over the houses of the children of Israel in Egypt, when the firstborn of

the Egyptians were killed. The Israelites in Egypt at the time were instructed by Moses to sacrifice a lamb without blemish and to put blood from the lamb which was sacrificed on the doorposts of their houses. See Bible Dictionary, p. 672. Thus, through the blood of a lamb, the Israelites were protected from the anguish and punishment brought to the Egyptians by the destroying angel. The symbolism is clear. It is by the "blood of the Lamb" (the sacrifice of the Savior) that we are saved, after all we can do (2 Nephi 25:23). Now, at the time of Passover in Jerusalem, the "Lamb of God", Christ, will present himself to be sacrificed, that we might be saved. The Feast of the Passover brought large numbers of Jews from near and far to Jerusalem to join in the worship and celebration.

3 Then assembled together the chief priests, and the scribes, and the elders of the people (the Jewish religious leaders), unto the palace of the high priest, who was called Caiaphas,

4 And consulted that they might take Jesus by subtilty, and kill *him*. (In other words, they plotted how they might arrest Jesus as quietly as possible so that they would not stir up the people and perhaps get mobbed themselves.)

5 But they said, Not on the feast day, (not on Thursday, the day of Passover), lest there be an uproar among the people.

6 Now when Jesus was in Bethany (about two or three miles east and south of Jerusalem), in the house of Simon the leper,

Note: In verses 7-13, a woman

(Mary—see John 12:3) anoints Jesus with costly ointment. Jesus is the Messiah. "Messiah" means "the Anointed One" (Bible Dictionary, p. 731). It would seem that this woman understood what the disciples did not yet fully understand, and symbolically "anointed" the Savior in preparation for his Atoning sacrifice. This sheds light on the divine nature and spiritual sensitivity of women.

7 There came unto him a woman having an alabaster box of very precious ointment, and poured it on his head, as he sat *at meat* (at dinner).

8 But when his disciples saw *it*, they had indignation, saying, To what purpose *is* this waste (why are you wasting this expensive ointment)?

9 For this ointment might have been sold for much, and given to the poor.

10 When Jesus understood *it*, he said unto them, Why trouble ye the woman? for she hath wrought (done) a good work upon me.

11 For ye have the poor always with you; but me ye have not always. (You need to keep things in perspective.)

12 For in that she hath poured this ointment on my body, she did it for my burial. (In other words, she understands that I will be crucified and buried now.)

13 Verily I say unto you, Wheresoever this gospel shall be preached in the whole world, *there* shall also this, that this woman hath done, be told for a memorial of her.

14 Then one of the twelve, called Judas Iscariot, went unto the chief priests (the Jewish religious leaders, Christ's enemies),

15 And said *unto them*, What will ye give me, and I will deliver him unto you? And they covenanted with him for thirty pieces of silver.

Note: Thirty pieces of silver was an insult to Judas, since it was the going price for a common slave.

16 And from that time he (Judas) sought opportunity to betray him (Christ).

17 Now the first *day* (Thursday) of the *feast of* unleavened bread (part of the Passover) the disciples came to Jesus, saying unto him, Where wilt thou that we prepare for thee to eat the passover?

18 And he said, Go into the city to such a man, and say unto him, The Master saith, My time is at hand (it is time for me to be sacrificed); I will keep the passover at thy house with my disciples.

19 And the disciples did as Jesus had appointed them; and they made ready the passover.

20 Now when the even (evening) was come, he sat down with the twelve.

21 And as they did eat, he said, Verily I say unto you, that one of you shall betray me.

22 And they were exceeding sorrowful, and began every one of them to say unto him, Lord, is it I?

23 And he answered and said, He that dippeth his hand with me in the dish, the same shall betray me.

24 The Son of man goeth as it is written of him (I will perform the Atonement as prophesied in the scriptures): but woe unto that man by whom the Son of man is betrayed! it had been good for that man if he had not been born. (It would have been better for

Judas Iscariot not to have been born.)

25 Then Judas, which betrayed him, answered (asked) and said, Master, is it I? He said unto him, Thou hast said.

Note: Many versions of the Bible give "Thou hast said." as "Yes." in one form or another, which fits with JST Mark 14:30 which says "And he said unto Judas Iscariot, What thou doest, do quickly; but beware of innocent blood." It is likely that this was a whispered conversation between Jesus and Judas because Matthew, Mark, Luke and John do not indicate that the other apostles were aware of it.

Note: In the next verses, Jesus introduces the sacrament to his apostles. This is known as the "Last Supper".

26 And as they were eating, Jesus took bread, and blessed *it*, and brake *it*, and gave *it* to the disciples, and said, Take, eat; this is my body (this bread is symbolic of my body; when you partake of the sacrament bread, you are symbolically "internalizing" my gospel and making it a part of you).

27 And he took the cup (representing the blood which the Savior shed for our sins), and gave thanks, and gave *it* to them, saying, Drink ye all of it;

28 For this is my blood of the new testament ("testament" means "covenant", in other words, the new covenants, associated with the full gospel which Christ had restored), which is shed for many for the remission of sins.

29 But I say unto you, I will not drink henceforth of this fruit of the vine, until that day when I drink it new with you in my Father's kingdom. (This is the last time I will partake of the sacrament with you during my mortal life.)

30 And when they had sung an hymn, they went out into the mount of Olives (just a few minutes walk from the city wall of Jerusalem).

31 Then saith Jesus unto them, All ye shall be offended because of me this night: for it is written (in Zechariah 13:7), I will smite the shepherd (Christ), and the sheep of the flock shall be scattered abroad.

32 But after I am risen again (resurrected), I will go before you (ahead of you) into Galilee.

33 Peter answered and said unto him, Though all *men* shall be offended because of thee, yet will I never be offended.

34 Jesus said unto him, Verily I say unto thee, That this night, before the cock crow (before the rooster crows), thou shalt deny me thrice (three times).

Note: Verse 34 presents a difficult dilemma to the student of the scriptures with respect to Peter. We need clarification on this situation and until we get it from a reliable source, we are left to wonder about his denying knowing the Savior three times. Some think he denied his testimony and thus denied the Holy Ghost, which is an unpardonable sin. He did not. He denied knowing the Savior. It is out of character for Peter to be afraid of people and what they think. In fact, before this most difficult night is over, he will draw a sword and cut off an ear of one of those who arrests Christ (see verse 51). Perhaps the Savior was prophetically commanding Peter to deny knowing him on the three upcoming occasions during the night when it will be claimed that he is an associate of Jesus, in order to prevent Peter's death at this time. Perhaps it is to remind Peter that he is not as strong and committed as he thinks he is.

35 Peter said unto him, Though I should die with thee, yet will I not deny thee. Likewise also said all the disciples.

36 Then cometh Jesus with them unto a place called Gethsemane (the Garden of Gethsemane, just a few minutes walk from Jerusalem), and saith unto the disciples, Sit ye here, while I go and pray yonder.

Note: "Gethsemane" means "oil press". There is significant symbolism here. The Jews put olives into bags made of mesh fabric and placed them in a press to squeeze olive oil out of them. The first pressings yielded pure olive oil which was prized for many uses, including healing and giving light in lanterns. In fact, we consecrate it and use it to administer to the sick. The last pressing of the olives, under the tremendous pressure of additional weights added to the press, yielded a bitter, red liquid which can remind us of the "bitter cup" which the Savior partook of. Symbolically, the Savior is going into the "oil press" (Gethsemane) to submit to the "pressure" of all our sins which will "squeeze" his blood out in order that we might have the healing "oil" of the Atonement to heal us from our sins.

37 And he took with him Peter and the two sons of Zebedee (James and John), and began to be sorrowful and very heavy.

38 Then saith he unto them, My soul is exceeding sorrowful, even unto death: tarry (wait) ye here, and watch with me.

39 And he went a little further, and fell on his face (showing submission and humility in Jewish culture), and prayed, saying, O my Father, if it be possible, let this cup pass from me: nevertheless not as I will, but as thou wilt.

40 And he cometh unto the disciples, and findeth them asleep, and saith unto Peter, What, could ye not watch with me one hour?

41 Watch and pray, that ye enter not into temptation: the spirit indeed is willing, but the flesh is weak.

42 He went away again the second time, and prayed, saying, O my Father, if this cup may not pass away from me, except I drink it, thy will be done.

43 And he came and found them asleep again: for their eyes were heavy (they were very sleepy; it had been a very difficult and sleepless week for the apostles, worrying about the Savior's safety etc.).

44 And he left them, and went away again, and prayed the third time, saying the same words.

45 Then cometh he to his disciples, and saith unto them, Sleep on now, and take *your* rest: behold, the hour is at hand (the time has come), and the Son of man (Christ; in other words, "Son of Man of Holiness" [Heavenly Father], see Moses 6:57) is betrayed into the hands of sinners.

46 Rise, let us be going: behold, he is

at hand that doth betray me.

47 And while he yet spake, lo, Judas, one of the twelve, came, and with him a great multitude with swords and staves, from the chief priests and elders of the people (the religious leaders of the Jews).

48 Now he (Judas) that betrayed him gave them (the soldiers) a sign, saying, Whomsoever I shall kiss, that same is he: hold him fast. (I will kiss Jesus so you know which one he is, then arrest him and hold on to him securely.)

49 And forthwith he came to Jesus, and said, Hail, master; and kissed him.

50 And Jesus said unto him, Friend, wherefore (why) art thou come? Then came they, and laid hands on Jesus, and took him.

51 And, behold, one of them (Peter) which were with Jesus stretched out *his* hand, and drew his sword, and struck a servant of the high priest's, and smote off his ear. (Jesus healed this man's ear; see Luke 22:51.)

52 Then said Jesus unto him, Put up again thy sword into his place: for all they that take the sword shall perish with the sword.

53 Thinkest thou that I cannot now pray to my Father, and he shall presently give me more than twelve legions of angels? (Don't you realize that if I wanted to stop this, I could!)

54 But how then shall the scriptures be fulfilled, that thus it must be? (I must be crucified.)

55 In that same hour said Jesus to the multitudes, Are ye come out as against a thief with swords and staves for to take me? I sat daily with you teaching in the temple, and ye laid no hold on me.

56 But all this was done, that the scriptures of the prophets might be fulfilled. Then all the disciples forsook him, and fled (as prophesied in verse 31).

57 And they that had laid hold on Jesus led him away to Caiaphas the high priest, where the scribes and the elders were assembled.

Note: This trial during the night time was completely illegal according to the Jews' own laws.

58 But Peter followed him afar off unto the high priest's palace, and went in, and sat with the servants, to see the end.

59 Now the chief priests, and elders, and all the council, sought false witness against Jesus, to put him to death;

60 But found none: yea, though many false witnesses came, yet found they none. At the last came two false witnesses,

61 And said, This *fellow* said, I am able to destroy the temple of God, and to build it in three days.

62 And the high priest arose, and said unto him (Jesus), Answerest thou nothing (why don't you say some-thing)? what *is it which* these witness against thee?

63 But Jesus held his peace (said nothing). And the high priest answered and said unto him, I adjure thee (I place you under oath) by the living God, that thou tell us whether thou be the Christ, the Son of God.

64 Jesus saith unto him, Thou hast said (in other words, yes, I am God's Son): nevertheless I say unto you,

Hereafter shall ye see the Son of man (me) sitting on the right hand of power (God), and coming in the clouds of heaven (you will see me at my second coming)

Note: In Revelation 1:7, we are informed that those who crucified Christ will indeed see his Second Coming. Surely, that will be a sorry day for them.

65 Then the high priest rent his clothes (tore his clothes, a sign of extreme emotion), saying, He hath spoken blasphemy (great disrespect for God and our religious beliefs; blasphemy was punishable by death); what further need have we of witnesses? behold, now ye have heard his blasphemy.

66 What think ye? They answered and said, He is guilty of death.

67 Then did they spit in his face, and buffeted (hit) *him*; and others smote (hit) him with the palms of their hands,

68 Saying, Prophesy unto us, thou Christ, Who is he that smote thee? (Luke 22:54 tells us that they had put a blindfold on him before they hit him, thus they were mocking him and asking him to use his "great powers" to tell them which of them were hitting him.)

69 Now Peter sat without (outside of the trial room) in the palace: and a damsel (young lady) came unto him, saying, Thou also wast with Jesus of Galilee.

70 But he denied before *them* all, saying, I know not what thou sayest.

71 And when he was gone out into the porch, another *maid* saw him, and said unto *them* that were there, This fellow was also with Jesus of Nazareth.

72 And again he denied with an oath (strongly), I do not know the man (Christ).

73 And after a while came unto *him* they that stood by, and said to Peter, Surely thou also art *one* of them (one of Christ's followers); for thy speech bewrayeth thee (your Galilean accent gives you away).

74 Then began he to curse and to swear, *saying*, I know not the man (Jesus). And immediately the cock crew (the rooster crowed).

75 And Peter remembered the word of Jesus (in verse 34), which said unto him, Before the cock crow, thou shalt deny me thrice. And he went out, and wept bitterly.

MATTHEW 27

1 WHEN the morning was come, all the chief priests and elders of the people took counsel (plotted) against Jesus to put him to death:

2 And when they had bound him, they led *him* away, and delivered him to Pontius Pilate the governor (the Roman governor over that part of the Holy Land).

3 Then Judas, which had betrayed him, when he saw that he was condemned, repented himself (changed his mind), and brought again (returned) the thirty pieces of silver (which he had been paid to betray Jesus) to the chief priests and elders,

4 Saying, I have sinned in that I have betrayed the innocent blood. And they said, What *is that* to us? see thou *to that* (that is your problem!).

5 And he cast down (threw down) the pieces of silver in the temple, and departed, and went and hanged himself.

6 And the chief priests took the silver pieces, and said, It is not lawful (legal) for to put them into the treasury, because it is the price of blood (it is blood money, the price paid to have someone killed).

7 And they took counsel (talked it over), and bought with them (the thirty pieces of silver) the potter's field, to bury strangers (foreigners) in.

8 Wherefore that field was called, The field of blood, unto this day.

9 Then was fulfilled that which was spoken by Jeremy (Jeremiah) the prophet, saying, And they took the thirty pieces of silver, the price of him that was valued, whom they of the children of Israel did value;

10 And gave them for the potter's field, as the Lord appointed me.

11 And Jesus stood before the governor (Pontius Pilate): and the governor asked him, saying, Art thou the King of the Jews? And Jesus said unto him, Thou sayest (it is as you say, yes, I am; see John 18:37).

12 And when he was accused of the chief priests and elders, he answered nothing.

13 Then said Pilate unto him, Hearest thou not how many things they witness against thee (don't you hear what they are accusing you of)?

14 And he answered him to never a word (Jesus did not reply); insomuch that the governor marvelled greatly (was very surprised).

15 Now at *that* feast the governor was wont to release (was accustomed to releasing) unto the people a prisoner, whom they would. (It was a tradition for the governor to release a prisoner of the peoples' choice each year during the feast of the Passover.)

16 And they had then a notable (famous) prisoner, called Barabbas.

Note: The name "Barabbas" means "son of the father" (see Bible Dictionary, page 619). This may be symbolic in that the "imposter", Satan, stirred up the multitude to demand the release of an "imposter", Barabbas, while the true "Son of the Father" is punished for crimes which he did not commit.

17 Therefore when they were gathered together, Pilate said unto them (the multitude which had gathered), Whom will ye that I release unto you? Barabbas, or Jesus which is called Christ?

18 For he knew that for envy (because of hatred) they had delivered him (turned Christ over to Pilot).

19 When he (Pilate) was set down on the judgment seat, his wife sent unto him, saying, Have thou nothing to do with that just man (Jesus): for I have suffered many things this day in a dream because of him. (Pilate's wife had been warned in a dream that her husband should not allow anything bad to happen to Jesus.)

20 But the chief priests and elders persuaded the multitude that they should ask (ask for) Barabbas, and destroy Jesus.

21 The governor answered and said unto them (the multitude), Whether of the twain (which of the two) will ye

that I release unto you? They said, Barabbas.

22 Pilate saith unto them, What shall I do then with Jesus which is called Christ? *They* all say unto him, Let him be crucified.

23 And the governor said, Why, what evil hath he done? But they cried out the more (all the louder), saying, Let him be crucified.

24 When Pilate saw that he could prevail nothing (that he could not get the multitude to change their minds), but that rather a tumult was made (an uprising was in the making), he took water, and washed *his* hands before the multitude, saying, I am innocent of the blood of this just (innocent) person: see ye *to it* (it is on your heads now).

25 Then answered all the people, and said, His blood be on us, and on our children. (We and our children will take responsibility for killing Jesus.)

26 Then released he Barabbas unto them: and when he had scourged (whipped) Jesus, he delivered *him* to be crucified.

Note: "Scourging" was a very severe punishment and many prisoners did not live through it. It consisted of being whipped with a whip which was composed of leather thongs with bits of metal, bone etc. secured to the ends of the thongs.

27 Then the soldiers of the governor took Jesus into the common hall (the governor's house), and gathered unto him the whole band of *soldiers*. (The soldiers brought Jesus in front of all the soldiers to mock him.)

28 And they stripped him, and put on him a scarlet (JST: purple) robe (symbolic of royalty, mocking him for his claim to be king of the Jews).

29 And when they had platted (made, woven) a crown of thorns, they put *it* upon his head, and a reed (a stick, in mockery of a kings scepter) in his right hand: and they bowed the knee before him, and mocked him, saying, Hail, King of the Jews!

30 And they spit upon him, and took the reed, and smote (hit) him on the head.

31 And after that they had mocked him, they took the robe off from him, and put his own raiment (clothing) on him, and led him away to crucify *him*.

32 And as they came out, they found a man of Cyrene (a city in northern Africa), Simon by name: him they compelled (forced) to bear his cross (Jesus was too weak to carry his cross, because of his suffering in the Garden of Gethsemane, the whipping, etc.).

33 And when they were come unto a place called Golgotha, that is to say, a place of a skull,

34 They gave him vinegar to drink mingled with gall (designed to drug the victim of crucifixion to lessen the pain somewhat-see Talmage, *Jesus the Christ*, pages 654-655): and when he had tasted *thereof*, he would not drink.

35 And they crucified him, and parted his garments (divided his clothing up among themselves), casting lots: that it might be fulfilled which was spoken by the prophet (Psalm 22:18), They parted my garments among them, and upon my vesture (clothing) did they cast lots.

36 And sitting down they watched him there;

37 And set up over his head his accusation written (they placed a sign over his head which said), THIS IS JESUS THE KING OF THE JEWS.

38 Then were there two thieves crucified with him, one on the right hand, and another on the left.

39 And they that passed by reviled (made fun of him) him, wagging their heads (shaking their heads),

40 And saying, Thou that destroyest the temple, and buildest it in three days, save thyself. If thou be the Son of God, come down from the cross.

Note: These people obviously misunderstood what Jesus said regarding the temple. What he said is in John 2:19-21. He said that if they destroyed his body (the "temple of his body"), he would raise it up in three days (be resurrected in three days). By the time Jesus is on the cross, his statement has been misquoted and spread so that the mockers claim that he said he would destroy their massive temple in Jerusalem and rebuild it in three days.

41 Likewise also the chief priests mocking him, with the scribes and elders, said,

42 He saved others; himself he cannot save. If he be the King of Israel, let him now come down from the cross, and we will believe him.

43 He trusted in God; let him deliver him now, if he will have him: for he said, I am the Son of God.

44 The thieves also, which were crucified with him, cast the same in his teeth (said similar things to him).

Note: One of the thieves seems to have softened his attitude a bit later. The Savior said to him "Today shalt thou be with me in paradise." We will do more with this in Luke 23:43.

45 Now from the sixth hour there was darkness over all the land unto the ninth hour.

Note: In the Jewish time system, the "sixth hour" would be about noon, the "ninth hour" would be about 3 PM in our time system. We understand that Jesus was nailed onto the cross at the "third hour" which would be about 9 AM.

46 And about the ninth hour Jesus cried with a loud voice, saying, Eli, Eli, lama sabachthani? that is to say, My God, my God, why hast thou forsaken me?

Note: This had to have been a most difficult time for the Savior. Apparently, as part of the Atonement, Jesus had to experience what sinners do when they sin so much that the Spirit leaves them. At this point on the cross, we understand that all available help from the Father withdrew in order that the Savior might experience all things, including the withdrawal of the Spirit which sinners experience.

Note: There are seven recorded statements made by the Savior from the cross. The references for these statements and the statements themselves follow, and are in chronological order:

1. Luke 23:34 "Father, forgive them; for they know not what they do."

2. Luke 23:43 "Today shalt thou be with me in paradise."

3. John 19:26-27 "Woman, behold thy son!" Behold thy mother!"

4. Matthew 27:46 "My God, my God, why hast thou forsaken me?"

5. John 19:28 "I thirst."

6. John 19:30 "It is finished."

7. Luke 23:46 "Father, into thy hands I commend my spirit."

47 Some of them that stood there, when they heard *that*, said, *This* man calleth for Elias (Elijah).

48 And straightway (immediately) one of them ran, and took a spunge, and filled *it* with vinegar, and put *it* on a reed, and gave him to drink.

49 The rest said, Let be, let us see whether Elias (Elijah) will come to save him (don't help him; let's see if Elijah comes to help him).

50 Jesus, when he had cried again with a loud voice (JST: saying, Father, it is finished, thy will is done), yielded up the ghost (left his body, died).

Note: It startled some of the onlookers that Jesus had so much strength that he could speak so loudly. It was to them as if he had power to leave his body when he so chose, which indeed he did!

51 And, behold, the veil of the temple (in Jerusalem) was rent in twain (torn in two) from the top to the bottom; and the earth did quake, and the rocks rent (were torn apart);

52 And the graves were opened; and many bodies of the saints (those worthy of celestial glory) which slept (were dead) arose (were resurrected [three days later when Jesus was resurrected]),

53 And came out of the graves after his resurrection, and went into the holy city (Jerusalem), and appeared unto many.

Note: Verses 52 and 53 are out of chronological order. The resurrection of these saints did not occur until Christ's resurrection The resurrection of the saints referred to here is mentioned in D&C 133:54-55. We understand this first resurrection to have included all those worthy of celestial resurrection from Adam and Eve up to the time of Christ's resurrection. Nobody worthy of terrestrial or telestial resurrection has yet been resurrected. The next major resurrection will be at the beginning of the Millennium when those who have died since Christ's resurrection and who are worthy of celestial glory will be resurrected at the Second Coming (see D&C 88:97-98). This is often referred to as "the morning of the first resurrection."

54 Now when the centurion, and they that were with him, watching Jesus, saw the earthquake, and those things that were done, they feared greatly, saying, Truly this was the Son of God.

55 And many women were there beholding (watching) afar off, which followed Jesus from Galilee, ministering unto him:

56 Among which was Mary Magdalene, and Mary the mother of James and Joses (possibly the Savior's mother-see Mark 6:3), and the mother (named Salome, Mark 15:40) of Zebedee's children (James and John-see Mark 1:19).

57 When the even (evening) was come, there came a rich man of Arimathæa, named Joseph, who also himself was Jesus' disciple (follower):

58 He went to Pilate (the Roman governor of the area), and begged (requested) the body of Jesus. Then Pilate commanded the body to be delivered (given to Joseph of Arimathaea).

59 And when Joseph had taken the body, he wrapped it in a clean linen cloth,

Note: We understand from John 19:38-40 that Nicodemus assisted Joseph of Arimathaea and in fact brought a very costly "hundredweight" of spices for anointing the Savior's body.

60 And laid it in his own new tomb, which he had hewn out in the rock: and he rolled a great (large) stone to the door of the sepulchre (tomb), and departed.

Note: There was an urgency to quickly get Christ's body in the tomb and close the tomb, because it was evening and the Jewish Sabbath (Saturday) was about to begin.

61 And there was Mary Magdalene, and the other Mary, sitting over against (in front of) the sepulchre (tomb).

Note: Because of the approaching Sabbath, which began in the evening in the Jewish system of days, there was no time for these women to do their part in the customary preparation of a body for final burial. Luke 23:55-56 tells us that they watched as the Savior's body was laid in the tomb and then left to prepare spices for Sunday morning (Sunday was the first day of the week among the Jews. Saturday was their Sabbath) when they would return to the tomb to finish anointing the body-see Luke 24:1.

62 Now the next day (Saturday, the Jewish Sabbath), that followed the day of the preparation (part of Passover), the chief priests and Pharisees came together unto Pilate,

63 Saying, Sir, we remember that that deceiver (imposter, referring to Jesus, who they claimed was a deceiver) said, while he was yet alive, After three days I will rise again (in John 2:19-21, Jesus said that if they destroyed his body, he would raise it up again in three days).

64 Command therefore that the sepulchre (tomb) be made sure (secure) until the third day, lest his disciples (followers) come by night, and steal him away, and say unto the people, He is risen from the dead: so the last error (attempted deception) shall be worse than the first. (In other words, these wicked Jewish leaders feared that if Christ's disciples were to succeed in stealing the body and pretending that Jesus had resurrected, it would be harder for them to deal with than Christ's claim to come back to life if they killed him [John 2:19])

65 Pilate said unto them, Ye have a watch (a group of soldiers of your own): go your way, make it as sure as ye can (take your soldiers and guard the tomb).

66 So they went, and made the sepulchre (tomb) sure, sealing the stone, and

setting a watch. (They put a wax seal between the stone door and the wall of the tomb so they could tell if someone moved the stone, plus they set guards to watch the tomb for three days.)

MATTHEW 28

1 IN the end of the sabbath (after the Sabbath was over), as it began to dawn toward the first day of the week (Sunday), came Mary Magdalene and the other Mary to see the sepulchre (tomb).

Note: Up to now, Saturday was the Sabbath or holy day for the Jews. But Acts 20:7 shows us that, among the followers of Christ (the Christians), Sunday became the holy day or Sabbath, after the resurrection of the Savior.

2 And, behold, there was a great earthquake: for the angel (JST: two angels) of the Lord descended from heaven, and came and rolled back the stone from the door (from the opening into the tomb), and sat upon it.

3 His countenance (face) was like lightning, and his raiment (clothing) white as snow: (JST: And their countenance was like lightning, and their raiment white as snow.)

4 And for fear of him (JST: them) the keepers (guards) did shake, and became as dead men.

5 And the angel (JST: angels) answered and said unto the women, Fear not ye: for I (we) know that ye seek Jesus, which was crucified.

6 He is not here: for he is risen (resurrected), as he said. Come, see the place where the Lord lay.

7 And go quickly, and tell his disciples that he is risen from the dead; and, behold, he goeth before you (ahead of you) into Galilee; there shall ye see him: lo, I have told you.

Note: Jesus told his disciples he would meet them in Galilee after his crucifixion-see Matt. 26:32. A description of his meeting them there is found in John, chapter 21.

8 And they (the women in verse one) departed quickly from the sepulchre (tomb) with fear and great joy; and did run to bring his disciples word.

9 And as they went to tell his disciples, behold, Jesus met them, saying, All hail (a greeting). And they came and held him by the feet, and worshipped him.

10 Then said Jesus unto them, Be not afraid: go tell my brethren (the apostles etc.) that they (should) go into Galilee (as Jesus told them in Matt. 26:32), and there shall they see me.

11 Now when they were going, behold, some of the watch (soldiers who had been assigned to guard the tomb) came into the city, and shewed (told) unto the chief priests all the things that were done.

12 And when they (the chief priests) were assembled with the elders, and had taken counsel (had plotted together), they gave large money (bribes) unto the soldiers,

13 Saying, Say ye, His disciples came by night, and stole him away while we slept. (In other words, lie about what happened.)

14 And if this (news of Jesus' body being gone from the tomb and angels

saying that he is resurrected) come to the governor's ears, we will persuade him (we will handle him), and secure you (protect you from being executed for sleeping on guard duty).

15 So they (the soldiers) took the money (the bribes), and did as they were taught: and this saying (story) is commonly reported among the Jews until this day.

16 Then the eleven disciples (apostles) went away into Galilee, into a mountain where Jesus had appointed them.

17 And when they saw him, they worshipped him: but some doubted.

Note: The statement "but some doubted" in verse 17 undoubtably refers to people other that these apostles who met the Savior as described in John 21. Some might think that this could refer to Thomas who is some-times referred to as "doubting Thomas", but his doubt was done away with (see John 20:27-28) before they went to Galilee. Thus, "some doubted" is most likely a general comment of Matthew, contrasting the witness of the Apostles who "worshipped him" (verse 17) as opposed to some members who still doubted that he had been resurrected.

18 And Jesus came and spake unto them, saying, All power is given unto me in heaven and in earth.

19 Go ye therefore, and teach all nations, baptizing them in the name of the Father, and of the Son, and of the Holy Ghost:

20 Teaching them to observe all things whatsoever I have commanded you: and, lo, I am with you alway, *even* unto the end of the world. Amen.

THE GOSPEL OF MARK

The Gospel of Mark was written by John Mark, a missionary companion of the Apostle Paul (see Acts 12:25). Tradition has it that Mark also associated much with Peter, the apostle, and that Mark got most of his material from Peter and wrote the book of Mark from Rome. His main emphasis, as he bears witness of the Savior, seems to be the miracles performed by Jesus. Mark is the shortest of the "Four Gospels", Matthew, Mark, Luke and John, and has many of the same things as Matthew and Luke.

MARK 1

1 THE beginning of the gospel of Jesus Christ, the Son of God;

2 As it is written in the prophets (the Old Testament), Behold, I send my messenger before thy face, which shall prepare thy way before thee. (Old Testament prophets prophesied that John the Baptist would come and prepare the way for Christ's earthly ministry.)

3 The voice of one (John the Baptist) crying in the wilderness, Prepare ye the way of the Lord, make his paths straight.

4 John (the Baptist) did baptize in the wilderness, and preach the baptism of repentance for the remission of sins.

5 And there went out unto him all the land of Judea, and they of Jerusalem (many people came out to listen to John the Baptist, including people from Jerusalem), and were all baptized of him in the river of Jordan, confessing their sins.

Note: The fact that they came all the way out to the Jordan River which was several miles from major population centers, is a reminder that baptism was performed by immersion. In fact the word "baptize" means "to immerse." See Bible Dictionary, page 618.

6 And John was clothed with camel's hair, and with a girdle of a skin about his loins; and he did eat locusts and wild honey;

Note: Perhaps this rough desert clothing worn by John the Baptist might have reminded people of Elijah the Prophet in the Old Testament who wore similar clothing (see 2 Kings 1:8).

7 And preached, saying, There cometh one (Christ) mightier than I after me, the latchet of whose shoes I am not worthy to stoop down and unloose (I am not even worthy to take off his shoes for him).

8 I indeed have baptized you with water: but he (Christ) shall baptize you with the Holy Ghost. (JST: ...he shall not only baptize you with water, but with fire, and the Holy Ghost.)

9 And it came to pass in those days, that Jesus came from Nazareth of Galilee, and was baptized of (by) John in Jordan (in the Jordan River, about 25 miles from Jerusalem).

10 And straightway (immediately) coming up out of the water, he (John) saw the heavens opened, and the Spirit (the Holy Ghost) like a dove descending upon him:

Note: Joseph Smith explained that the Holy Ghost does not turn into a dove and further explained that the Holy Ghost was present to testify to John of the truthfulness of what he was doing for the Savior. (*Teachings of the Prophet Joseph Smith*, pages 275-276)

11 And there came a voice (the Father's voice) from heaven, saying, Thou art my beloved Son, in whom I am well pleased.

12 And immediately the Spirit driveth him into the wilderness.

Note: *The Joseph Smith Translation of the Bible* (JST) is very helpful in giving us correct understanding of what took place here. JST, Matthew 4:1 tells us that the Holy Ghost took Jesus into the wilderness "to be with God." JST, Mark 1:10-11 says:

10 And immediately the Spirit took him into the wilderness.

11 And he was there in the wilderness forty days, Satan seeking to tempt him; and was with the wild beasts; and the angels ministered unto him.

Satan "seeking" to tempt him is different than verse 13 (next) which would incorrectly lead us to believe that Satan did tempt Christ in the wilderness.

13 And he was there in the wilderness forty days, tempted of Satan; and was with the wild beasts; and the angels ministered unto him.

14 Now after that John was put in prison (for criticizing Herod's marriage to Herodias-see Mark 6:16-29), Jesus came into Galilee, preaching the gospel of the kingdom of God,

15 And saying, The time is fulfilled, and the kingdom of God is at hand (available to you): repent ye, and believe the gospel.

16 Now as he walked by the sea of Galilee, he saw Simon (Peter) and Andrew his brother casting a net into the sea: for they were fishers (they fished for a living).

17 And Jesus said unto them, Come ye after me, and I will make you to become fishers of men.

18 And straightway (immediately) they forsook (left) their nets, and followed him. (They immediately gave up their professional fishing business and followed Jesus.)

19 And when he had gone a little further thence, he saw James the *son* of Zebedee, and John his brother, who also were in the ship mending their nets.

20 And straightway (immediately) he called them: and they left their father Zebedee in the ship with the hired servants, and went after him (followed Jesus).

21 And they went into Capernaum; and straightway (first thing) on the sabbath day he entered into the synagogue (church building), and taught.

22 And they were astonished at his doctrine: for he taught them as one that had authority, and not as the scribes (religious leaders and teachers who interpreted the gospel for the Jews).

23 And there was in their synagogue a man with an unclean spirit (possessed by an evil spirit); and he (the evil spirit) cried out,

24 Saying, Let *us* alone; what have we to do with thee (what business is it of yours what we do?), thou Jesus of Nazareth? art thou come to destroy us (to ruin our opportunity to possess

people)? I know thee who thou art, the Holy One of God.

Note: Here we learn an important thing, namely that evil spirits (the one third who were cast out of heaven [Revelation 12:4] and are here on earth tempting us, do not have the veil over their memory of premortal life. Thus, they recognize Christ and know what he is doing.

25 And Jesus rebuked him, saying, Hold thy peace (Jesus doesn't want evil spirits bearing witness of him), and come out of him.

26 And when the unclean spirit had torn him (severely shaken him), and cried with a loud voice, he came out of him.

27 And they were all amazed, insomuch that they questioned among themselves, saying, What thing is this? what new doctrine is this? for with authority commandeth he even the unclean spirits, and they do obey him.

28 And immediately his fame spread abroad throughout all the region round about Galilee.

29 And forthwith (immediately), when they were come out of the synagogue (church), they entered into the house of Simon and Andrew, with James and John (the newly-called disciples-see verses 16-20).

30 But Simon's wife's mother (Peter's mother-in-law) lay sick of a fever, and anon (immediately) they tell him (Christ) of her.

Note: This verse (30), which mentions Peter's wife's mother, is a good reminder that the early apostles were

married and that celibacy (deliberately remaining single as a sign of loyalty to God) was not part of the gospel taught by Jesus.

31 And he came and took her by the hand, and lifted her up; and immediately the fever left her, and she ministered unto them (served them, probably including giving them something to eat).

32 And at even (evening), when the sun did set, they brought unto him all that were diseased, and them that were possessed with devils.

Note: There is beautiful symbolism in the Savior's healing of the people. While Christ's miracles of healing all kinds of sickness were literal, the symbolism is that Jesus can heal all kinds of spiritual illness, through his Atonement. Therefore, each time you read of a healing performed by the Savior, you can consider it to be a reminder that he can heal us spiritually also, through the cleansing and healing power of the Atonement.

33 And all the city was gathered together at the door.

34 And he healed many that were sick of divers (various) diseases, and cast out many devils; and suffered not (did not allow) the devils to speak, because they knew him (did not allow the evil spirits to acknowledge him in public).

Note: Perhaps the Savior's not allowing evil spirits to bear witness of him (see also verse 25) involves a principle similar to that when Satan commanded Cain to offer sacrifice to the Lord (Moses 5:18). Righteous testimony, accompanied by the witness of the Holy Ghost, cannot come from an unrighteous source.

35 And in the morning, rising up a great while before day, he (Jesus) went out, and departed into a solitary place (a place where he could be alone), and there prayed.

36 And Simon (Peter) and they that were with him followed after him.

37 And when they had found him, they said unto him, All men seek for thee (everyone is looking for you).

38 And he said unto them, Let us go into the next towns, that I may preach there also: for therefore came I forth (that is the reason I came).

39 And he preached in their synagogues (Jewish churches) throughout all Galilee, and cast out devils.

40 And there came a leper (a man with leprosy, a very painful and serious disease which caused the ends of fingers, toes, ears, nose etc. to rot away; see note by Matt. 8:2 in this book) to him, beseeching him, and kneeling down to him, and saying unto him, If thou wilt (if it is thy will), thou canst make me clean (heal me).

41 And Jesus, moved with compassion, put forth his hand, and touched him, and saith unto him, I will; be thou clean.

42 And as soon as he had spoken, immediately the leprosy departed from him, and he was cleansed.

Note: Here, again, is beautiful Atonement symbolism. The symbolism is that Christ can heal us from very serious sin and make us whole. See additional help with symbolism and leprosy in the note accompanying Matthew 5:17 in this book.

43 And he straitly charged him (very firmly told him not to tell anyone but the priest-see verse 44), and forthwith (immediately) sent him away;

44 And saith unto him, See thou say nothing to any man: but go thy way, shew thyself to the priest, and offer for thy cleansing those things which Moses commanded (see Leviticus, chapter 14), for a testimony unto them.

45 But he (the leper) went out, and began to publish it much, and to blaze abroad the matter (the leper went out and told everyone he could about his being healed), insomuch that Jesus could no more openly enter into the city (because so many people were crowding to see him), but was without (outside of the city) in desert places: and they came to him from every quarter.

MARK 2

1 AND again he entered into Capernaum after *some* days; and it was noised (made known) that he was in the house.

2 And straightway (immediately) many were gathered together, insomuch that there was no room to receive *them*, no, not so much as about the door: and he preached the word unto them.

3 And they come unto him, bringing one sick of the palsy, which was borne of four (carried by four people).

4 And when they could not come

nigh (near) unto him for the press (because of the crowd), they uncovered the roof (climbed up onto the housetop and took part of the roof off) where he (Jesus) was: and when they had broken *it* (the roof) up, they let down (lowered) the bed wherein the sick of the palsy lay.

5 When Jesus saw their faith, he said unto the sick of the palsy, Son, thy sins be forgiven thee.

6 But there were certain of the scribes (Jewish religious leaders whose position was threatened by Christ's popularity) sitting there, and reasoning in their hearts,

7 Why doth this *man* (Jesus) thus speak blasphemies (disrespectful speaking of God; mocking sacred things)? who can forgive sins but God only? (Only God can forgive sins, so why is Jesus pretending to forgive sins? This is terrible!)

8 And immediately when Jesus perceived in his spirit that they so reasoned within themselves (when Jesus read their minds), he said unto them, Why reason ye these things in your hearts (why are you thinking such thoughts)?

9 Whether is it easier to say (which is easier to say) to the sick of the palsy, *Thy* sins be forgiven thee; or to say, Arise, and take up thy bed, and walk? (In other words, which would be safer for a fake, which you think I am, to say, without being exposed as an imposter: "Your sins are forgiven." or "Be healed, pick up your bed and walk away."?)

10 But that ye may know that the Son of man (Christ; see Moses 6:57 where we see that "Son of Man of

Holiness [Heavenly Father] is another name for Jesus) hath power on earth to forgive sins, (he saith to the sick of the palsy,)

11 I say unto thee, Arise, and take up thy bed, and go thy way into thine house.

12 And immediately he arose, took up the bed, and went forth before (in front of) them all; insomuch that they were all amazed, and glorified God, saying, We never saw it on this fashion (we've never seen anything like this before!).

13 And he went forth again by the sea side (the Sea of Galilee); and all the multitude resorted (came) unto him, and he taught them.

14 And as he passed by, he saw Levi (Matthew, who will become an apostle)) the *son* of Alphæus sitting at the receipt of custom (collecting taxes-Matthew worked as a tax collector), and said unto him, Follow me. And he arose and followed him.

15 And it came to pass, that, as Jesus sat at meat (at dinner) in his house, many publicans (tax collectors-see Bible Dictionary, page 755) and sinners sat also together with Jesus and his disciples: for there were many, and they followed him (Jesus).

16 And when the scribes and Pharisees (Jewish religious leaders) saw him eat with publicans and sinners, they said unto his disciples, How is it (why is it) that he (Jesus) eateth and drinketh with publicans and sinners (something the scribes and Pharisees would never lower themselves to do)?

17 When Jesus heard it, he saith unto them, They that are whole (are well,

not sick) have no need of the physician, but they that are sick: I came not to call the righteous, but sinners to repentance. (In other words, how can I help those who need my help if I refuse to associate with them?)

18 And the disciples (followers) of John (the baptist) and of the Pharisees used to fast (go without food and drink for religious purposes): and they (the scribes and Pharisees) come (came) and say (said) unto him (Jesus), Why do the disciples of John and of the Pharisees fast, but thy disciples fast not?

19 And Jesus said unto them, Can the children of the bridechamber fast, while the bridegroom is with them? as long as they have the bridegroom with them, they cannot fast.

20 But the days will come, when the bridegroom shall be taken away from them, and then shall they fast in those days.

Note: Understanding a bit of Jewish culture will help with the last two verses. Wedding imagery is involved. Jesus is the bridegroom, or groom, as we would say it. Faithful followers are the bride. "Bridechamber" would be the place where the wedding feast is held and, symbolically, would be the land of Israel where the Savior was performing His mortal mission. While the groom and the bride are together, much celebrating and feasting–hearing and understanding the Savior's teachings–would take place. It would not make sense to mourn and fast at this time. But, when the Savior is crucified and taken from them, the "children of the bridechamber", the faithful saints, will mourn and fast.

Note: Next, Jesus will teach that people who are set in their ways do not usually accept new ideas, in this case, the true gospel.

21 No man also seweth a piece of new cloth on an old garment: else the new piece that filled it up taketh away (tears away) from the old, and the rent (tear) is made worse.

22 And no man putteth new wine into old bottles (old leather wineskins): else the new wine doth burst the bottles (the old, hardened leather containers), and the wine is spilled, and the bottles will be marred (damaged): but new wine must be put into new bottles (new leather containers which are flexible).

23 And it came to pass, that he (Jesus) went through the corn (grain) fields on the sabbath day; and his disciples began, as they went, to pluck the ears of corn (to pick some grain to eat).

24 And the Pharisees (very prominent Jewish religious leaders) said unto him, Behold, why do they (your disciples) on the sabbath day that which is not lawful (not legal according to Jewish law)?

25 And he said unto them, Have ye never read what David did, when he had need, and was an hungred (was hungry), he, and they that were with him?

26 How he went into the house of God in the days of Abiathar the high priest, and did eat the shewbread (the holy bread in the house of God), which is not lawful (legal) to eat but for the

priests, and gave also to them (his soldiers) which were with him?

27 And he (Jesus) said unto them (the Pharisees), The sabbath was made for man, and not man for the sabbath:

28 Therefore the Son of man is Lord also of the sabbath.

Note: JST Mark 2:26-27 gives clarification regarding verses 27-28 above as follows:

26 Wherefore the Sabbath was given unto man for a day of rest; and also that man should glorify God, and not that man should not eat;

27 For the Son of Man made the Sabbath day therefore the Son of Man is Lord also of the Sabbath.

In JST, verse 27, it becomes clear that Jesus was telling these Pharisees that he, himself made the Sabbath, as the Son of God, the Promised Messiah, and thus is in charge of the Sabbath and makes the rules for it.

MARK 3

1 AND he (Christ) entered again into the synagogue (Jewish church building); and there was a man there which had a withered hand.

2 And they (the Pharisees) watched him, whether he would heal him on the sabbath day; that they might accuse him. (The Pharisees were looking for reasons to have Jesus arrested.)

3 And he saith unto the man which had the withered hand, Stand forth (Stand up).

4 And he saith unto them (the Pharisees, who were trying to trap him), Is it lawful (legal) to do good on the sabbath days, or to do evil? to save life, or to kill? But they held their peace (they didn't answer his question).

5 And when he had looked round about on them (Pharisees) with anger (this is often referred to as "righteous indignation"), being grieved for the hardness of their hearts, he saith unto the man, Stretch forth thine hand. And he stretched it out: and his hand was restored whole as the other (healed, as good as his other hand).

6 And the Pharisees went forth (left), and straightway (immediately) took counsel (plotted) with the Herodians against him, how they might destroy him.

Note: The Herodians were a political party among the Jews and were normally enemies of the Pharisees. (See Bible Dictionary, page 701.) So here we have a situation where two groups, who are normally enemies, have joined together to destroy Jesus.

7 But Jesus withdrew himself with his disciples to the sea: and a great multitude from Galilee (in northern Israel) followed him, and from Judæa (in southern Israel, including Jerusalem),

8 And from Jerusalem, and *from* Idumæa, and from beyond Jordan; and they about Tyre and Sidon, a great multitude, when they had heard what great things he did, came unto him. (Multitudes of people from all over the country are now following Jesus around.)

9 And he spake to his disciples, that a small ship should wait on him (ask them to get a small boat for him) because of the multitude, lest they

should throng him (press in on him too much).

10 For he had healed many; insomuch that they pressed upon him for to touch him, as many as had plagues (diseases).

11 And unclean (evil) spirits, when they saw him, fell down before him, and cried, saying, Thou art the Son of God.

12 And he straitly charged them (gave the evil spirits strict orders) that they should not make him known (that they should not bear witness of him; see note by Mark 1:34).

13 And he goeth up into a mountain, and calleth *unto him* whom he would (those whom he wanted to come): and they came unto him.

14 And he ordained twelve (apostles), that they should be with him, and that he might send them forth to preach,

15 And to have power to heal sicknesses, and to cast out devils:

16 And Simon he surnamed Peter;

17 And James the *son* of Zebedee, and John the brother of James; and he surnamed them Boanerges, which is, The sons of thunder:

18 And Andrew, and Philip, and Bartholomew, and Matthew, and Thomas, and James the *son* of Alphæus, and Thaddæus, and Simon the Canaanite,

19 And Judas Iscariot, which also betrayed him: and they went into an house.

20 And the multitude cometh together again, so that they could not so much as eat bread (didn't even have time to eat).

21 And when his friends heard *of it*, they went out to lay hold on him (to take him away from the crowds so he could eat and get some rest; see McConkie, *Doctrinal New Testament Commentary*, Vol. 1, page 211): for they said, He is beside himself (not being reasonable, working too hard, not taking care of himself).

22 And the scribes (Jewish religious leaders, interpreters of the religious laws) which came down from Jerusalem (they came all the way from Jerusalem to Galilee to try to trap Jesus) said, He hath Beelzebub (Satan; see Bible Dictionary, page 620), and by the prince of the devils (by the power of Satan) casteth he out devils.

23 And he called them (the scribes) *unto him*, and said unto them in parables, How can Satan cast out Satan?

24 And if a kingdom be divided against itself, that kingdom cannot stand.

25 And if a house be divided against itself, that house cannot stand.

26 And if Satan rise up against himself, and be divided, he cannot stand (will not survive), but hath an end.

27 No man can enter into a strong man's house, and spoil his goods, except he will first bind the strong man; and then he will spoil his house.

28 Verily I say unto you, All sins shall be forgiven unto the sons of men (people), and blasphemies (speaking against God and holy things) wherewith soever they shall blaspheme:

29 But he that shall blaspheme against the Holy Ghost hath never forgiveness, but is in danger of eternal damnation:

Note: Simply put, denying the Holy Ghost means knowing full well, by the power of the Holy Ghost, that God exists, that the Church is true etc., then going completely against that sure knowledge, trying to destroy the Church and knowledge of God. In other words, it means becoming like Satan, thinking like he does and acting like he does. See D&C 76:31-35. See also *Teachings of the Prophet Joseph Smith*, page 358.

30 Because they said, He hath an unclean spirit. (Christ's teachings in the above verses were in response to the claims of the scribes that Jesus was doing miracles by the power of Satan, including casting out evil spirits.)

31 There came then his brethren and his mother, and, standing without (outside), sent unto him, calling him.

32 And the multitude sat about him, and they said unto him, Behold, thy mother and thy brethren without (on the outside of the crowd) seek for thee.

33 And he answered them, saying, Who is my mother, or my brethren?

34 And he looked round about on them which sat about him, and said, Behold my mother and my brethren! (In other words, all of you are my family.)

35 For whosoever shall do the will of God, the same is my brother, and my sister, and mother.

Note: JST, Matthew 12:44, adds understanding to verse 35. "And he gave them charge concerning her [asked them to take good care of his mother while he continued on his mission], saying, I go my way, for my Father hath sent me. For whosoever shall do the will of my Father which is in heaven, the same is my brother, and sister, and mother."

MARK 4

1 AND he began again to teach by the sea side: and there was gathered unto him a great multitude (a large crowd of people had gathered), so that he entered into a ship, and sat in the sea; and the whole multitude was by the sea on the land.

2 And he taught them many things by parables, and said unto them in his doctrine,

3 Hearken; Behold, there went out a sower to sow (a farmer went out to plant seeds):

4 And it came to pass, as he sowed (planted seeds), some fell by the way side (the footpath), and the fowls (birds) of the air came and devoured it up (ate the seeds).

5 And some fell on stony ground, where it had not much earth (the soil was very shallow); and immediately it sprang up (started to grow), because it had no depth of earth:

6 But when the sun was up, it was scorched; and because it had no root, it withered away (dried up and died).

7 And some fell among thorns, and the thorns grew up, and choked it, and it yielded no fruit (did not produce food).

Note: Sometimes in the scriptures, the word "thorns" is symbolic of wicked behaviors, false doctrines, wicked people, bad habits etc.

8 And other fell on good ground, and did yield fruit that sprang up and

increased; and brought forth, some thirty, and some sixty, and some an hundred.

Note: The Savior will explain this parable, starting in verse 13.

9 And he said unto them, He that hath ears to hear, let him hear (people who are spiritually in tune should pay close attention to what I am teaching).

10 And when he was alone, they that were about him with the twelve asked of him the parable.

Note: JST Mark 4:9 emphasized that the people in verse 10, who were asking Jesus for help in understanding the parable, were believers. The JST is as follows: "And when he was alone with the twelve, and they that believed in him, they that were about him with the twelve asked of him the parable."

11 And he said unto them, Unto you it is given to know the mystery (the basic teachings) of the kingdom of God (because you have a desire to learn spiritual things, you will be given understanding of the gospel): but unto them that are without (those who are outside the Church and don't want to learn about these things), all *these* things are done in parables:

12 That seeing they may see, and not perceive (not understand); and hearing they may hear, and not understand; lest at any time they should be converted, and *their* sins should be forgiven them.

Note: Verse 12 is a rather strong statement by Jesus indicating that there is truth all around us but if people don't want to pay attention to it, they won't understand it and won't get their sins forgiven.

13 And he said unto them, Know (understand) ye not this parable? and how then will ye know (understand) all parables?

14 The sower (planter, farmer; symbolic of the Savior, prophets, missionaries, members) soweth (plants) the word (teaches the gospel).

15 And these (this first group of people) are they by the way side, where the word is sown (where the gospel is taught); but when they have heard, Satan cometh immediately, and taketh away the word that was sown in their hearts (Satan gets them to quickly disregard what they have heard of the true gospel; thus, the "seeds" don't even start to grow in their hearts).

16 And these (the second group of people) are they likewise which are sown (planted) on stony ground; who, when they have heard the word (the true gospel), immediately receive it with gladness;

17 And have no root in themselves (but don't do what is necessary for the gospel to take root in their hearts), and so endure but for a time: afterward, when affliction or persecution ariseth for the word's (gospel's) sake, immediately they are offended. (Peer pressure, social, family pressure etc. causes them to reject the gospel and beginning testimony which they had.)

18 And these (the third group of people) are they which are sown among thorns; such as hear the word,

19 And the cares of this world, and the deceitfulness of riches, and the lusts of other things entering in, choke the word, and it becometh unfruitful. (Worldliness, materialism, lustfulness etc. choke the gospel out of their lives

so that it doesn't make righteous saints out of them.)

20 And these (the fourth group) are they which are sown on good ground; such as hear the word (the gospel), and receive *it* (accept it and apply it in their lives), and bring forth fruit, some thirtyfold, some sixty, and some an hundred (the gospel is very productive in their lives).

Note: The symbolism of a seed growing in one's heart and life reminds us that it takes time for the gospel to grow in our lives (as taught in Alma 32) and that we must nourish it by being faithful to the teachings of the gospel.

21 ¶ And he said unto them, Is a candle brought to be put under a bushel, or under a bed? and not to be set on a candlestick? (In other words, should the light of the gospel be hidden from people? Answer: No!)

Note: The paragraph mark, ¶, at the beginning of verse 21 in our Bible indicates that there is now a change to a new topic. You may also have noticed that some words are written in *italics* in our Bible. Example: the word "it" in verse 20 above. Italics means that the translators of the King James Version of the Bible, which we use in English, did not know what the word should be. They were meticulously honest and wanted the reader to know that they were using their best guess as to what word to use.

22 For there is nothing hid, which shall not be manifested; neither was any thing kept secret, but that it should come abroad. (All things will eventually be revealed to the righteous, who allow the "seed" to continue growing in their hearts and lives. See McConkie, *Doctrinal New Testament Commentary*, Vol 1, page 291.)

23 If any man have ears to hear, let him hear (you who are spiritually in tune, listen carefully to what I say).

24 And he said unto them, Take heed what ye hear (pay close attention to what I am teaching): with what measure ye mete (the attention and obedience you give to what I am teaching), it shall be measured to you (will determine how much more truth you get): and unto you that hear (hear and apply it in your lives) shall more be given.

25 For he that hath (JST "receiveth"), to him shall be given: and he that hath not (JST "..continueth not to receive"), from him shall be taken even that which he hath.

Note: Alma 12:9-11 summarizes what the Savior taught in verses 24-25 above:

9 And now Alma began to expound these things unto him, saying: It is given unto many to know the mysteries of God; nevertheless they are laid under a strict command that they shall not impart only according to the portion of his word which he doth grant unto the children of men, according to the heed and diligence which they give unto him.

10 And therefore, he that will harden his heart, the same receiveth the lesser portion of the word; and he that will not harden his heart, to him is given

the greater portion of the word, until it is given unto him to know the mysteries of God until he know them in full.

11 And they that will harden their hearts, to them is given the lesser portion of the word until they know nothing concerning his mysteries; and then they are taken captive by the devil, and led by his will down to destruction. Now this is what is meant by the chains of hell.

26 And he said, So is the kingdom of God (this is like the Kingdom of God), as if a man should cast seed into the ground;

27 And should sleep, and rise night and day, and the seed should spring and grow up, he knoweth not how.

28 For the earth bringeth forth fruit of herself; first the blade, then the ear, after that the full corn in the ear.

29 But when the fruit is brought forth, immediately he putteth in the sickle, because the harvest is come.

Note: This parable (verses 26-29) is only recorded in Mark. Apostle James E. Talmage interpreted it in his book *Jesus the Christ*, pages 289-290 as follows:

The sower in this story is the authorized preacher of the word of God; he implants the seed of the gospel in the hearts of men, knowing not what the issue shall be. Passing on to similar or other ministry elsewhere, attending to his appointed duties in other fields, he, with faith and hope, leaves with God the result of his planting. In the harvest of souls converted through his labor, he is enriched and made to rejoice.

This parable was probably directed more particularly to the apostles and the most devoted of the other disciples, rather than to the multitude at large; the lesson is one for teachers, for workers in the Lord's fields, for the chosen sowers and reapers. It is of perennial value, as truly applicable today as when first spoken. Let the seed be sown, even though the sower be straightway called to other fields or other duties; in the gladsome harvest he shall find his recompense.

30 And he said, Whereunto shall we liken the kingdom of God? or with what comparison shall we compare it?

31 *It is* like a grain of mustard seed, which, when it is sown in the earth, is less (smaller) than all the seeds that be in the earth:

32 But when it is sown (planted), it groweth up, and becometh greater (larger) than all herbs, and shooteth out great (big) branches; so that the fowls (birds) of the air may lodge under the shadow of it.

Note: Joseph Smith explained this parable. "And again, another parable put He forth unto them, having an allusion to the Kingdom that should be set up, just previous to or at the time of the harvest, which reads as follows—'The Kingdom of Heaven is like a grain of mustard seed, which a man took and sowed in his field: which indeed is the least of all seeds: but, when it is grown, it is the greatest among herbs, and becometh a tree, so that the birds of the air come and lodge in the branches thereof.' Now we can discover plainly that this figure is given to represent the Church as it shall come forth in the last days." For more of the Prophet's explanation, see *Teachings of the Prophet Joseph Smith*, pages 98-99 and page 159.

33 And with many such parables (stories that teach) spake (spoke) he the word (gospel) unto them, as they were able to hear it (JST able to bear it).

34 But without a parable spake he not unto them (the people): and when they were alone, he expounded (explained) all things to his disciples.

35 And the same day, when the even was come (in the evening), he saith unto them (the disciples), Let us pass over unto the other side (of the Sea of Galilee).

36 And when they had sent away the multitude, they took him even as he was in the ship. And there were also with him other little ships.

37 And there arose a great storm of wind, and the waves beat into the ship, so that it was now full (of water).

38 And he was in the hinder (back) part of the ship, asleep on a pillow: and they awake him, and say unto him, Master, carest thou not that we perish (don't you care if we drown)?

39 And he arose, and rebuked the wind (commanded the wind to stop), and said unto the sea, Peace, be still. And the wind ceased, and there was a great calm.

40 And he said unto them, Why are ye so fearful? how is it that ye have no faith?

41 And they feared exceedingly, and said one to another, What manner of man is this, that even the wind and the sea obey him?

MARK 5

1 AND they came over unto the other side of the sea (of Galilee), into the country of the Gadarenes.

2 And when he was come out of the ship, immediately there met him out of the tombs a man with an unclean spirit (who was possessed by evil spirits),

3 Who had *his* dwelling among the tombs (who lived among the tombs); and no man could bind him, no, not with chains:

4 Because that he had been often bound with fetters (leg irons) and chains, and the chains had been plucked asunder (torn apart) by him, and the fetters broken in pieces: neither could any *man* tame him.

5 And always, night and day, he was in the mountains, and in the tombs, crying, and cutting himself with stones.

6 But when he saw Jesus afar off, he ran and worshipped him (bowed down in front of him),

7 And cried with a loud voice, and said, What have I (the evil spirit) to do with thee, Jesus, *thou* Son of the most high God? I adjure (beg) thee by God, that thou torment me not.

8 For he said (Jesus had said) unto him, Come out of the man, *thou* unclean spirit.

9 And he (Jesus) asked him, What is thy name? And he (the evil spirit who was speaking for all the evil spirits who possessed the man) answered, saying, My name is Legion: for we are many.

10 And he (the evil spirit spokesman) besought him much (pleaded) that he

would not send them (the evil spirits) away out of the country.

11 Now there was there nigh (near) unto the mountains a great (large) herd of swine (pigs) feeding.

12 And all the devils besought him, saying, Send us into the swine, that we may enter into them.

13 And forthwith (immediately) Jesus gave them leave (permission). And the unclean spirits went out, and entered into the swine: and the herd ran violently down a steep place into the sea, (they were about two thousand;) and were choked (drowned) in the sea.

Note: One might wonder why Jesus allowed the evil spirits he cast out of the man to enter into the pigs. We don't know. We do wonder what the people of that area were doing raising pigs, since pork was forbidden under the Law of Moses (see Leviticus 11:7).

14 And they that fed the swine (those in charge of the herd of pigs) fled (ran away), and told it (what happened to the herd) in the city, and in the country. And they (the people who owned the swine) went out to see what it was that was done.

15 And they come to Jesus, and see him (the man) that was possessed with the devil, and had the legion (of evil spirits in him before Jesus cast them out), sitting, and clothed, and in his right mind: and they (the owners of the herd) were afraid.

16 And they that saw it (the people who had seen the whole thing as it happened) told them (the owners of the pigs) how it befell (what happened) to

him that was possessed with the devil, and also concerning the swine.

17 And they began to pray (request) him (Jesus) to depart out of their coasts (area).

Note: It would be nice if these people who owned the herd of swine had been spiritually sensitive enough to recognize the great miracle which had been performed by the Savior and had been converted. However, sadly, such was not the case. It seems that they were so set on material things that, rather than asking the Master to teach them, they simply requested that he leave their area so that they would not risk suffering another economic disaster.

18 And when he was come into the ship, he that had been possessed with the devil (evil spirits) prayed (requested) him that he might be with him. (The man healed of the evil spirits wanted to go with Jesus.)

19 Howbeit (however) Jesus suffered (allowed) him not, but saith unto him, Go home to thy friends, and tell them how great things the Lord hath done for thee, and hath had compassion on thee. (In other words, Jesus asked him to go home and be a witness of the healing so that others in that area could know of Christ.)

20 And he (the man who had been healed) departed, and began to publish (tell) in Decapolis (the country south and southeast of the Sea of Galilee) how (what) great things Jesus had done for him: and all men did marvel.

21 And when Jesus was passed over again by ship unto the other side (of the Sea of Galilee), much people gath-

ered unto him: and he was nigh (near) unto the sea.

22 And, behold, there cometh one of the rulers of the synagogue (Jewish church building), Jairus by name; and when he saw him, he fell at his feet,

23 And besought him (pleaded) greatly, saying, My little daughter lieth at the point of death: *I pray thee*, come and lay thy hands on her, that she may be healed; and she shall live.

24 And *Jesus* went with him; and much people followed him, and thronged (crowded, pushed against) him.

25 And a certain woman, which had an issue of blood (had been bleeding for) twelve years,

26 And had suffered many things of (had suffered through treatments by) many physicians, and had spent all that she had (to pay the medical bills), and was nothing bettered, but rather grew worse,

27 When she had heard of Jesus, came in the press behind (pushed her way through the crowd and came up behind Jesus), and touched his garment.

28 For she said, If I may touch but his clothes, I shall be whole (healed).

29 And straightway (immediately) the fountain (source) of her blood was dried up; and she felt in *her* body that she was healed of that plague.

30 And Jesus, immediately knowing in himself that virtue (strength) had gone out of him, turned him about in the press (crowd), and said, Who touched my clothes?

31 And his disciples said unto him, Thou seest the multitude thronging (pressing against) thee, and sayest

thou, Who touched me?

32 And he looked round about to see her that had done this thing.

33 But the woman fearing and trembling, knowing what was done in her (knowing that she had been healed), came and fell down before him, and told him all the truth (that she was the one who touched him).

34 And he said unto her, Daughter, thy faith hath made thee whole; go in peace (don't be afraid of me), and be whole (healed) of thy plague.

35 While he yet spake, there came from the ruler (Jairus, verse 22) of the synagogue's *house certain* (people) which said, Thy daughter is dead: why troublest thou the Master any further?

36 As soon as Jesus heard the word that was spoken, he saith unto the ruler of the synagogue (Jairus), Be not afraid, only believe.

37 And he suffered (allowed) no man to follow him, save (except) Peter, and James, and John the brother of James.

38 And he cometh to the house of the ruler of the synagogue, and seeth the tumult (commotion), and them that wept and wailed greatly (the mourners, who, according to Jewish custom, were to make a big scene of noise and crying when someone had died).

39 And when he was come in, he saith unto them (the mourners), Why make ye this ado (fuss), and weep? the damsel (girl) is not dead, but sleepeth.

40 And they laughed him (Jesus) to scorn (made fun of him). But when he had put them all out, he taketh the father and the mother of the damsel, and them that were with him (Peter, James and John-see verse 37), and entereth in where the damsel was

lying.

41 And he took the damsel by the hand, and said unto her, Talitha cumi; which is, being interpreted, Damsel, I say unto thee, arise.

42 And straightway (immediately) the damsel arose, and walked; for she was *of the age* of twelve years. And they were astonished with a great astonishment.

43 And he charged them straitly (instructed them firmly) that no man should know it (that he had raised her from the dead, which he did-see heading to Mark, chapter 5 in our Bible); and commanded that something should be given her to eat.

Note: We have not been told why Jesus instructed them not to tell anyone that he had actually raised her from the dead. Perhaps, as is often the case, it was a private, sacred matter for the parents and the three apostles and was to be kept extra sacred by keeping it private.

MARK 6

1 AND he went out from thence (from there), and came into his own country (his home town, Nazareth); and his disciples follow him.

2 And when the sabbath day was come, he began to teach in the synagogue (the local Jewish church building): and many hearing *him* were astonished, saying, From whence hath this *man* these things (where does this man get all these teachings)? and what wisdom is this which is given unto him, that even such mighty works are wrought (done) by his hands?

3 Is not this the carpenter, the son of Mary, the brother of James, and Joses, and of Juda, and Simon? and are not his sisters here with us? And they were offended at him (felt that Jesus was an embarrassment to them and their community).

Note: Jesus had been trained as a carpenter by Joseph, Mary's husband. The citizens of Nazareth knew the family, including Jesus, and could not accept that Jesus was anything but a common man. They were disturbed that one of their own citizens was causing such an uproar in the country.

Note: Verse three gives us information about the size of Joseph and Mary's own family, which they had after Jesus was born. They had four sons, whose names are mentioned in this verse, and at least three daughters. The Greek plural form for the word "sisters" in verse three means three or more. It is also interesting to note that it is generally believed that James, one of Christ's half-brothers mentioned in this verse, was the writer of the book of James in the New Testament. See Bible Dictionary, page 709.

4 But Jesus said unto them, A prophet is not without honour, but in his own country, and among his own kin, and in his own house.

5 And he could there (in Nazareth) do no mighty work, save (except) that he laid his hands upon a few sick folk, and healed *them*.

6 And he marvelled (was amazed) because of their unbelief. And he went round about the villages, teaching.

7 And he called *unto him* the twelve

(the twelve apostles), and began to send them forth by two and two; and gave them power over unclean (evil) spirits;

8 And commanded them that they should take nothing for *their* journey, save (except) a staff (walking stick) only; no scrip (a bag, usually made of leather and used for carrying food-see Bible Dictionary, page 770), no bread, no money in *their* purse:

9 But be shod with sandals (wear sandals); and not put on two coats.

Note: Sandals were worn by the common people in the days of the Savior and his apostles. Shoes were very expensive and were worn only by the very wealthy.

10 And he said unto them, In what place soever ye enter into an house, there abide (stay) till ye depart from that place (town or city).

11 And whosoever shall not receive you, nor hear you, when ye depart thence, shake off the dust under your feet for a testimony against them (as a witness that you tried to teach them the gospel but they rejected you). Verily I say unto you, It shall be more tolerable for Sodom and Gomorrha in the day of judgment, than for that city.

Note: We understand from the scriptures that those who have a fair set of chances to hear, understand, and accept the gospel here in mortality, but reject it, will be in a worse position in spirit prison than those who did not have a chance here. Apostle Bruce R. McConkie explains this as follows: "It shall be more tolerable in the day of judgment, for heathen nations who had no opportunity to accept the gospel in this life, than for the more enlightened races who rejected the truths of salvation when such were offered to them" *Doctrinal New Testament Commentary*, Vol. 1, page 327.

12 And they went out, and preached that men should repent.

13 And they cast out many devils, and anointed with oil many that were sick, and healed them. (See also James 5:14-15 for instructions on administering to the sick.)

14 And king Herod heard *of him*; (for his name was spread abroad [Jesus was famous]:) and he (Herod) said, That John the Baptist was risen from the dead, and therefore mighty works do shew forth themselves in him (King Herod had had John the Baptist beheaded and was now worried that Jesus was actually John the Baptist come back alive).

15 Others said, That it (Jesus) is Elias (Elijah the prophet). And others said, That it is a prophet, or as one of the prophets.

16 But when Herod heard *thereof*, he said, It is John, whom I beheaded: he is risen from the dead.

17 For Herod himself had sent forth and laid hold upon (arrested) John, and bound him in prison for Herodias' sake (as requested by his wife, Herodias), his brother Philip's wife: for he had married her (Herod had married his own brother's wife, Herodias).

18 For John had said unto Herod, It is not lawful (legal) for thee to have thy brother's wife.

19 Therefore Herodias had a quarrel

against him (was very angry at John the Baptist), and would have killed him; but she could not (could not talk her husband, King Herod, into having John killed):

20 For Herod feared John, knowing that he was a just (righteous) man and an holy, and observed (protected; see Mark 6:20, footnote b) him; and when he (Herod) heard him (John), he did many things (JST did many things for him), and heard him gladly (Herod felt that John the Baptist was a prophet and gladly listened to his teaching).

21 And when a convenient day was come, that Herod on his birthday made a supper to his lords, high captains, and chief *estates* of Galilee;

22 And when the daughter (her name was Salome; see Bible Dictionary, page 768) of the said Herodias came in, and danced, and pleased Herod and them that sat with him, the king said unto the damsel, Ask of me whatsoever thou wilt, and I will give *it* thee.

23 And he sware unto (promised) her, Whatsoever thou shalt ask of me, I will give it thee, unto the half of my kingdom.

24 And she went forth (went to her mother, Herodias), and said unto her mother, What shall I ask? And she (Herodias) said, The head of John the Baptist.

25 And she (Salome) came in straightway (immediately) with haste unto the king, and asked, saying, I will that thou give me by and by (immediately [this phrase has changed in our day to mean "eventually"]) in a charger (on a platter) the head of John the Baptist.

26 And the king was exceeding (very) sorry; yet for his oath's sake (because he had promised), and for their sakes which sat with him (because of peer pressure), he would not reject her (refuse granting her request).

27 And immediately the king sent an executioner, and commanded his (John the Baptist's) head to be brought: and he (the executioner) went and beheaded him in the prison,

28 And brought his head in a charger, and gave it to the damsel (Salome): and the damsel gave it to her mother (Herodias).

29 And when his (John's) disciples (followers) heard *of it*, they came and took up his corpse (body), and laid it in a tomb.

Note: Next, the apostles who have been out preaching and healing the sick (see verses 12 and 13), return and report what they have been doing to the Savior.

30 And the apostles gathered themselves together unto Jesus, and told him all things, both what they had done, and what they had taught.

31 And he said unto them, Come ye yourselves apart into a desert place (a quiet place where we can be alone), and rest a while: for there were many (crowds of people) coming and going, and they had no leisure (time to themselves) so much as to eat.

32 And they departed into a desert place by ship privately.

33 And the people saw them departing, and many knew him (had heard of Jesus), and ran afoot (on foot) thither (to where they figured Jesus

and his apostles were going in the ship) out of all cities, and outwent them (beat them to their destination), and came together unto him.

34 And Jesus, when he came out (of the ship), saw much people (the large crowd), and was moved with compassion toward them, because they were as sheep not having a shepherd: and he began to teach them many things.

35 And when the day was now far spent, his disciples came unto him, and said, This is a desert place, and now the time is far passed (the day is about over):

36 Send them away, that they may go into the country round about, and into the villages, and buy themselves bread: for they have nothing to eat.

37 He answered and said unto them, Give ye them to eat. And they say unto him, Shall we go and buy two hundred pennyworth of bread, and give them to eat?

Note: Christ's instruction to the apostles to feed the 5000 men, plus women and children (see Matthew 14:21) apparently startled them. In reply, they told them that enough bread to feed such a crowd would cost two hundred pennies. A penny, or Greek denarius, was an average days wage for a workman-see Mark 6:37, footnote a. In our day, assuming an average days wage to be about $150, the cost of feeding the crowd, which had gathered to hear the Savior, would be about $30,000 and would be somewhat overwhelming to the apostles.

38 He saith unto them, How many loaves (of bread) have ye? go and see. And when they knew, they say, Five, and two fishes.

39 And he commanded them to make all (the people) sit down by companies (groups) upon the green grass.

40 And they sat down in ranks, by hundreds, and by fifties.

41 And when he had taken the five loaves and the two fishes, he looked up to heaven, and blessed, and brake (broke) the loaves, and gave *them* to his disciples to set before them (the people); and the two fishes divided he among them all.

42 And they did all eat, and were filled.

43 And they took up (picked up the leftovers) twelve baskets full of the fragments (pieces of bread), and of the fishes.

44 And they that did eat of the loaves were about five thousand men (plus women and children; see Matthew 14:21).

45 And straightway (immediately) he (Jesus) constrained (asked) his disciples to get into the ship, and to go to the other side (of the Sea of Galilee) before (ahead of him) unto Bethsaida, while he sent away the people.

Note: It is helpful to remember that this is a time of training, learning faith, obedience etc. for these apostles. It was probably somewhat frustrating for them to get into the ship and leave for Bethsaida, on the northeastern side of the Sea of Galilee, leaving Jesus on the land with the multitudes who had just been fed. They may well have wondered how and when Jesus would catch up with them.

46 And when he (Jesus) had sent

them away (dismissed the crowd to go home), he departed (went) into a mountain to pray.

47 And when even (evening) was come, the ship (that his apostles were on) was in the midst of the sea, and he alone on the land.

48 And he saw them toiling in rowing; for the wind was contrary unto them (they were struggling to row against the wind and waves, still trying to get to their destination): and about the fourth watch of the night (between about 3 AM and 6 AM) he (Jesus) cometh unto them, walking upon the sea, and would have passed by them.

49 But when they saw him walking upon the sea, they supposed it had been a spirit (ghost), and cried out (in fear):

50 For (because) they all saw him, and were troubled (very worried). And immediately he talked with them, and saith unto them, Be of good cheer (be happy, rejoice, cheer up): it is I; be not afraid.

Note: There is symbolism and comfort for us in these verses. We all go through "storms" of life and it is comforting to know that God is there to help and comfort us. He invites us to trust him, cheer up and to stop being afraid.

51 And he went up unto them into the ship (got into the ship); and the wind ceased: and they were sore (very) amazed in themselves beyond measure, and wondered. (The apostles were very surprised at the power Christ had over the wind and sea.)

52 For they considered not *the miracle* of the loaves: for their heart was hardened.

Note: The miracle of feeding the 5,000 hadn't yet sunk into their hearts as far as their understanding of the Savior's power was concerned. Again, we would do well not to criticize them for taking time to learn about the Master's power, rather, we ought to realize that these great men are in intense training now and are learning rapidly. The "learning curve" is steep!

53 And when they had passed over (completed the journey), they came into the land of Gennesaret, and drew to the shore.

54 And when they (Jesus and his apostles) were (had) come out of the ship, straightway (immediately) they (the people of that area) knew (recognized) him,

55 And ran through that whole region round about, and began to carry about in beds those that were sick, where they heard he was (to where Jesus was).

56 And whithersoever (wherever) he entered, into villages, or cities, or country, they laid the sick in the streets, and besought (asked) him that they might touch if it were but the border of his garment (cloak, robe): and as many as touched him were made whole (healed).

MARK 7

1 THEN came together (working and plotting together) unto him the Pharisees, and certain of the scribes, which came from Jerusalem.

Note: The Pharisees and scribes were very influential religious leaders among the Jews. They are trying to trap Jesus and get him arrested. At this point, they have come north, all the way from Jerusalem to Galilee, to challenge Christ.

2 And when they saw some of his disciples (followers) eat bread with defiled, that is to say, with unwashen (unwashed), hands, they found fault (criticized Jesus for letting his followers eat without washing their hands first).

3 For the Pharisees, and all the Jews, except (unless) they wash *their* hands oft, eat not, holding (following) the tradition of the elders.

Note: The "tradition of the elders" consisted of thousands of rules and regulations which had developed among the Jews over the centuries. Most of these rules were not in harmony with the Law of Moses, and were, in fact, opposite to God's will. They killed the spirit of the gospel. The scribes were generally the ones who interpreted these rules and prescribed penalties for those who violated them. As an example, they had so many specific rules for Sabbath day observance that it was virtually impossible for anyone to keep them all. A few of the things the Jews were forbidden to do on the Sabbath, according to the "tradition of the elders", are summarized in the following list:

The Jews were forbidden to:
- Sweep or break a single clod (it was planting)
- Pluck one blade of grass (it was harvesting)
- Cut a mushroom (a double sin-harvesting and planting because a new mushroom would grow in its place)
- Rub the ends of wheat stalks (guilty of threshing)
- Dip a radish in salt too long (guilty of pickling)
- Rub mud off a dress (might bruise the cloth, however, if they let the mud dry and then carefully picked it off the dress so as to not bruise the fabric, it was ok.)
- Spit on the ground, then rub it with the foot (guilty of farming, watering the ground; however, it was ok to spit on a stone, because nothing would grow as a result)
- Carry a legal burden more than 2000 cubits from home
- Replace wadding if it fell out of the ear
- Wear false teeth or wear a gold plug in a tooth
- Eat an egg that was laid on the Sabbath (unless the hen had been kept for eating rather than laying eggs, in which case the egg could be eaten because it was considered to be a part of the hen that had fallen off)

See McConkie, *Mortal Messiah*, Vol. 1, pages 199-212 for many more examples.

4 And *when they* (the Jews) *come* from the market, except they wash, they eat not (if they don't ritually wash, they don't eat). And many other things (rules and laws) there be, which

they have received to hold (to do, to obey), as the washing of cups, and pots, brasen vessels, and of tables.

5 Then the Pharisees and scribes asked him, Why walk not thy disciples according to the tradition of the elders (why don't your disciples keep the rules of the tradition of the elders), but eat bread with unwashen hands?

6 He answered and said unto them, Well hath Esaias (Isaiah) prophesied of you hypocrites (people who like to do evil, but want to look righteous), as it is written, This people honoureth me with *their* lips, but their heart is far from me.

7 Howbeit (however) in vain (useless) do they worship me, teaching *for* doctrines the commandments of men.

8 For laying aside the commandment of God, ye hold the tradition of men, as the washing of pots and cups: and many other such like things ye do. (Your religious worship is useless. You don't keep God's commandments. You have replaced them with your own rules and laws.)

9 And he said unto them, Full well (absolutely) ye reject the commandment of God, that ye may keep your own tradition (tradition of the elders rules etc.).

10 For Moses said, Honour thy father and thy mother; and, Whoso curseth father or mother, let him die the death (death was the penalty given by Moses for being disrespectful or disobedient to parents; see Exodus 20:12):

11 But ye say, If a man shall say to his father or mother, *It is* Corban, that is to say, a gift, by whatsoever thou

mightest be profited by me; *he shall be free* (of obligation to care for his parents; see note in this book after Matthew 15:6).

12 And ye suffer (allow) him no more to do ought (anything) for his father or his mother;

13 Making the word of God of none effect (destroying God's commandment to honor parents) through your tradition, which ye have delivered (require people to obey): and many such like things do ye (you are guilty of doing all kinds of things like this).

14 And when he had called all the people *unto him*, he said unto them, Hearken (listen and obey) unto me every one *of you*, and understand:

15 There is nothing from without (outside) a man, that entering into him can defile him (can make him unclean, unworthy): but the things which come out of him (his thoughts, his words etc.), those are they that defile the man.

16 If any man have ears to hear, let him hear (the spiritually in tune will understand and obey).

17 And when he was entered into the house from the people (away from the crowds), his disciples asked him concerning the parable (asked him to explain the parable in verse 15).

18 And he saith unto them, Are ye so without understanding also (don't you understand either)? Do ye not perceive (recognize), that whatsoever (whatever) thing from without (outside of us) entereth into the man, it cannot defile him (make him unworthy);

19 Because it entereth not into his heart, but into the belly, and goeth out into the draught (eventually passes out of the body), purging all meats

(cleansing him from all food he has eaten)?

Note: In Bible language, "meat" means food. "Flesh" means "meat" as we now use the word.

20 And he said, That which cometh out of the man, that defileth the man (your thoughts, words, actions etc. are what can make you unclean, unworthy).
21 For from within, out of the heart of men, proceed evil thoughts, adulteries, fornications, murders,
22 Thefts, covetousness, wickedness, deceit (fraud, dishonesty), lasciviousness (pornography, lustful thinking, speaking etc.), an evil eye (envy), blasphemy (speaking crudely, rudely, disrespectfully about God and sacred things), pride, foolishness:
23 All these evil things come from within, and defile the man (make him unclean and unworthy).
24 And from thence (there) he arose, and went into the borders of Tyre and Sidon (several miles north of the Sea of Galilee, on the coast of the Mediterranean Sea), and entered into an house, and would have no man know it (wanted to have some privacy): but he could not be hid (JST But he could not deny them; for he had compassion upon all men).
25 For a certain woman, whose young daughter had an unclean (evil) spirit, heard of him, and came and fell at his feet:

Note: We would understand the "young" daughter to be over age eight, because D&C 29:46-47 tells us that

Satan does not have power over children until they begin to become accountable, which we know to be age eight-see D&C 68:25-27.

26 The woman was a Greek, a Syrophenician by nation; and she besought him that he would (asked him to) cast forth the devil out of her daughter.
27 But Jesus said unto her, Let the children (the Jews, the covenant people, Israel) first be filled: for it is not meet (appropriate) to take the children's bread (the gospel, intended for the Jews at this time in God's plan), and to cast it unto the dogs (give it to the gentiles).

Note: As he states here, Jesus' mortal mission was limited to the house of Israel, specifically, the Jews. This limitation will be done away with later, as exemplified by Mark 16:15 and Peter's dream in Acts 10:9-48.

Note: The word "dogs" in this context means "little dogs" or household pets [a term of endearment]. A Bible scholar named Dummelow explains as follows:
""The rabbis often spoke of the Gentiles as dogs. ...
... [Jesus] says not 'dogs,' but 'little dogs,' i.e. house-hold, favourite dogs, and the woman cleverly catches at the expression, arguing that if the Gentiles are household dogs, then it is only right that they should be fed with the crumbs that fall from their master's table." (Dummelow, Commentary, pp. 678–79.)

28 And she answered and said unto him, Yes, Lord: yet the dogs under the table eat of the children's crumbs.

29 And he said unto her, For this saying (you have talked me into it [he probably said this with a twinkle in his eye]) go thy way; the devil (evil spirit) is gone out of thy daughter.

30 And when she was come to her house, she found the devil gone out, and her daughter laid upon the bed.

31 And again, departing from the coasts of Tyre and Sidon, he came unto the sea of Galilee, through the midst of the coasts (borders) of Decapolis (an area south and east of the Sea of Galilee).

32 And they bring (brought) unto him one that was deaf, and had an impediment in his speech; and they beseech him (asked Jesus) to put his hand upon him (to heal the man).

33 And he took him aside from the multitude, and put his fingers into his ears (probably as a signal to the deaf man that he was going to heal his deafness), and he spit (the Jews believed that saliva had healing properties) , and touched his tongue;

34 And looking up to heaven, he sighed, and saith unto him, Ephphatha, that is, Be opened.

35 And straightway (immediately) his ears were opened (he could hear), and the string of his tongue was loosed, and he spake plain (he could speak plainly).

36 And he charged them that they should tell no man (Jesus gave them strict instructions not to tell anyone): but the more he charged them, so much the more a great deal they published *it* (told others about it);

37 And were beyond measure astonished (completely surprised), saying, He hath done all things well: he maketh both the deaf to hear, and the dumb (someone who can't talk) to speak.

MARK 8

1 IN those days the multitude being very great (large), and having nothing to eat, Jesus called his disciples *unto him*, and saith unto them,

2 I have compassion on the multitude, because they have now been with me three days, and have nothing to eat:

3 And if I send them away fasting to their own houses, they will faint by the way: for divers (some) of them came from far.

4 And his disciples answered him, From whence can a man satisfy these *men* with bread here in the wilderness (where could we get bread since there are no markets here in the wilderness)?

5 And he asked them, How many loaves have ye? And they said, Seven.

6 And he commanded the people to sit down on the ground: and he took the seven loaves, and gave thanks, and brake (broke the loaves of bread into pieces), and gave to his disciples to set before *them* (to give to the people); and they did set *them* (the pieces of bread) before the people.

7 And they had a few small fishes: and he blessed, and commanded to set them also before *them*.

8 So they did eat, and were filled: and they took up of the broken *meat* (food) that was left seven baskets.

9 And they that had eaten were about four thousand: and he sent them away (dismissed them to go home).

10 And straightway (immediately) he entered into a ship with his disciples, and came into the parts of Dalmanutha. (Bible scholars' best guess is that Dalmanutha is in Galilee, on the west shore of the Sea of Galilee.)

11 And the Pharisees (Jewish religious leaders) came forth, and began to question with him (Jesus), seeking of him a sign from heaven, tempting him (to prove that he was from God).

12 And he sighed deeply in his spirit, and saith, Why doth this generation (the wicked people living in Israel at that time) seek after a sign? verily I say unto you, There shall no sign be given unto this generation.

13 And he left them, and entering into the ship again departed to the other side (of the Sea of Galilee).

14 Now *the disciples* had forgotten to take bread, neither had they in the ship with them more than one loaf.

15 And he charged (instructed) them, saying, Take heed, beware of the leaven (the yeast or whatever which causes bread to rise) of the Pharisees, and of the leaven of Herod.

16 And they reasoned (talked) among themselves, saying, *It is* because we have no bread (he is saying this because we haven't enough bread with us).

17 And when Jesus knew it, he saith unto them, Why reason ye, because ye have no bread ? (You are missing the point.) perceive ye not yet, neither understand? have ye your heart yet hardened? (Are you still so spiritually insensitive that you can't understand the symbolism of what I say?)

18 Having eyes, see ye not (can't you see with spiritual eyes and understanding)? and having ears, hear ye not (can't you hear with spiritual ears and understanding)? and do ye not remember (can't you remember previous lessons I've taught you about how to understand spiritually)?

19 When I brake (broke) the five loaves among five thousand, how many baskets full of fragments took ye up (did you gather up)? They say unto (answered) him, Twelve.

20 And when the seven (loaves of bread) among four thousand, how many baskets full of fragments took ye up? And they said, Seven.

21 And he said unto them, How is it that ye do not understand (what I said regarding "leaven" in verse 15)?

Note: Matthew 16:11-12 finishes this account as follows:

11 How is it that ye do not understand that I spake *it* (what I said about leaven, yeast) not to you concerning bread, (but, rather) that ye should beware of (watch out for) the leaven (influence) of the Pharisees and of the Sadducees?

12 Then understood they (the apostles) how that he bade *them* not (was not warning them to) beware of the leaven (yeast) of bread, but of the doctrine (teachings) of the Pharisees and of the Sadducees (Hypocritical Jewish religious leaders).

In other words, just as a little bit of yeast can spread itself throughout the whole lump of bread dough, and thus influence it all, so also can the evil influence of corrupt religious leaders, such as the Pharisees and Sadducees, spread throughout the whole nation.

22 And he cometh to Bethsaida (just north of the Sea of Galilee); and they bring a blind man unto him, and besought (asked) him to touch him.

23 And he took the blind man by the hand, and led him out of the town; and when he had spit (the Jews had a belief that saliva had healing properties) on his eyes, and put his hands upon him, he asked him if he saw ought (anything).

24 And he looked up, and said, I see men as trees, walking (I can see, but not clearly).

25 After that he put *his* hands again upon his eyes, and made him look up: and he was restored, and saw every man clearly.

Note: Perhaps this healing of the blind man in stages is symbolic of the fact that, usually, we are healed in stages. We grow "line upon line". We are gradually healed from our spiritual sicknesses such as lack of faith, meanness, inactivity, lack of charity, lustful thinking etc. until we see "clearly" as did the blind man.

26 And he sent him away to his house, saying, Neither go into the town, nor tell it (that I healed you) to any in the town.

27 And Jesus went out, and his disciples, into the towns of Cæsarea Philippi (an area north and a bit to the east of the Sea of Galilee): and by the way (as they were traveling) he asked his disciples, saying unto them, Whom do men say that I am?

28 And they answered, John the Baptist: but some say, Elias (Elijah); and others, One of the prophets.

29 And he saith unto them, But whom say ye that I am? And Peter answereth and saith unto him, Thou art the Christ.

30 And he charged (instructed) them that they should tell no man of him.

Note: It would seem that this instruction to the apostles was temporary and for that particular time and circumstance. Perhaps they needed a bit of quiet time together for the Master to teach his disciples about his upcoming death (in about six months) and resurrection. Some manuscripts say "Don't go and tell anyone in the village."

31 And he began to teach them, that the Son of man (Christ; the "Son of Man" ["Man" is "Man of Holiness" or Heavenly Father-see Moses 6:57]) must suffer many things, and be rejected of the elders, and of the chief priests, and scribes (Jewish religious leaders), and be killed, and after three days rise again.

32 And he spake that saying openly. And Peter took him, and began to rebuke him (scold him for saying such things).

33 But when he had turned about and looked on his disciples (implying that all the disciples shared Peter's expressed feelings), he rebuked Peter, saying, Get thee behind me, Satan (don't stand in my way like Satan does): for thou savourest not (you are not considering) the things that be of God, but the things that be of men.

Note: Just a reminder that when you see a ¶, it means that there is now a change of topic.

34 And when he had called the people *unto him* with his disciples also, he said unto them, Whosoever will come after me, let him deny himself (put aside his personal interests), and take up his cross (sacrifice whatever is necessary), and follow me.

35 For whosoever will save his life (pursue his own selfish interests) shall lose it (shall lose the real richness of life); but whosoever shall lose his life (use his life) for my sake and the gospel's, the same shall save it.

Note: JST Mark 8:37-38 adds to verse 35 as follows:

37 For whosoever will save his life, shall lose it; or whosoever will save his life, shall be willing to lay it down for my sake; and if he is not willing to lay it down for my sake, he shall lose it.

38 But whosoever shall be willing to lose his life for my sake, and the gospel, the same shall save it.

36 For what shall it profit a man, if he shall gain the whole world, and lose his own soul?

37 Or what shall a man give in exchange for his soul?

Note: JST adds a verse here, namely "Therefore deny yourselves of these, and be not ashamed of me."

38 Whosoever (whoever) therefore shall be ashamed of me and of my words (will not accept me and my teachings) in this adulterous and sinful generation; of him also shall the Son of man (Christ) be ashamed (Christ will not accept them into his kingdom), when he cometh in the glory of his Father with the holy angels (the Second Coming).

MARK 9

1 AND he said unto them, Verily I say unto you, That there be some of them that stand here, which shall not taste of death, till they have seen the kingdom of God come with power (they will be alive until the Second Coming).

Note: The JST (Joseph Smith Translation) Places Mark 9:1 as the last verse of Mark, chapter 8 and gives it as follows: Mark 8:44 "And he said unto them again, Verily I say unto you, That there be some of them that stand here, which shall not taste of death, till they have seen the kingdom of God come with power." The Apostle John would be one of those to whom the Savior referred. We know that he was translated (see D&C 7:3) and is still alive.

Note: Next, Mark records the transfiguration of Christ, which occurred about six months before his crucifixion. For more detail about what happened upon the mountain, see the note after Matthew 17:8 in this book.

2 And after six days Jesus taketh *with him* Peter, and James, and John (the "First Presidency"), and leadeth them up into an high mountain apart by themselves: and he was transfigured (shined with glory) before them.

3 And his raiment (clothing) became shining, exceeding white as snow; so as no fuller (washer of clothes) on earth can white (bleach) them.

4 And there appeared unto them Elias (JST John the Baptist) with Moses: and they were talking with Jesus.

Note: JST Mark 9:4 informs us that John the Baptist, who had been killed (beheaded) by King Herod, also appeared on the Mount of Transfiguration. The "Elias" spoken of in Mark 9:4 was John the Baptist. The "Elias" spoken of in Matthew 17:3 was Elijah (see Matthew 17:3, footnote 3b). "Elias" is a title for one who is a forerunner, and can refer to any of several different prophets. See Bible Dictionary, page 663.

5 And Peter answered and said to Jesus, Master, it is good for us to be here (we are grateful to be here): and let us make three tabernacles (shelters); one for thee, and one for Moses, and one for Elias.

6 For he wist (knew) not what to say; for they were sore afraid (very frightened).

7 And there was a cloud that overshadowed them: and a voice (Heavenly Father's voice) came out of the cloud, saying, This is my beloved Son: hear him.

8 And suddenly, when they had looked round about, they saw no man any more, save (except) Jesus only with themselves.

Note: The enormous impact of this experience for these three apostles may be difficult for us to entirely comprehend. In the Jewish culture, Moses was **the** Prophet. You may have already noticed that the corrupt reli-gious leaders of the Jews have been constantly quoting the teachings of Moses against the Savior's doings and teachings. It was a great teaching moment for Peter, James and John to see Moses, as well as Elijah and John the Baptist, ministering to the Savior and acknowledging him as the Messiah.

Note: Both Moses and Elijah were translated (taken up into heaven without dying) and still had their physical, mortal, translated bodies when they appeared on the Mount of Transfiguration and ministered to Jesus. John the Baptist would have appeared there as a spirit. All three, Moses, Elijah and John the Baptist were resurrected with Christ (see D&C 133:54-55)

9 And as they came down from the mountain, he charged them that they should tell no man what things they had seen, till the Son of man (Christ; Son of Man) were risen (resurrected) from the dead.

10 And they kept that saying with themselves, questioning one with another what the rising from the dead should mean. (They didn't understand what resurrection meant or involved.)

11 And they asked him, saying, Why say the scribes that Elias must first come (what do the scribes mean when they say that Elias must come first)?

12 And he answered and told them, Elias verily cometh first (before Jesus), and restoreth all things; and how it is written of the Son of man (Christ; Son of Man), that he must suffer many things, and be set at

nought (set aside, crucified).

13 But I say unto you, That Elias (John the Baptist) is indeed come, and they have done unto him whatsoever they listed (whatever they wanted to do), as it is written (prophesied) of him. (JST adds "and he bore record of me, and they received him not. Verily this was Elias.")

Note: Matthew 17:13 tells us that the "Elias" referred to here was John the Baptist.

14 And when he came to *his* disciples, he saw a great multitude (big crowd) about them, and the scribes (Jewish religious leaders) questioning with them.

15 And straightway (immediately) all the people, when they beheld him (Jesus), were greatly amazed (surprised) and, running to *him* saluted (greeted) him.

16 And he asked the scribes, What question ye with them (what are you debating with my disciples about)?

17 And one of the multitude answered and said, Master, I have brought unto thee my son, which hath a dumb spirit (JST a devil);

18 And wheresoever he (the evil spirit) taketh him, he teareth him (throws him on the ground and he gets cut up): and he foameth, and gnasheth with his teeth, and pineth away: and I spake to (asked) thy disciples that they should cast him out; and they could not.

19 He answereth him, and saith, O faithless generation, how long shall I be with you? how long shall I suffer you? bring him unto me.

20 And they brought him unto him: and when he (the man possessed by the evil spirit) saw him (Jesus), straightway (immediately) the spirit tare him (caused him to fall and get cut more); and he fell on the ground, and wallowed foaming (at the mouth).

21 And he (Jesus) asked his father, How long is it ago since this came unto him? And he said, Of a child (when he was a child).

22 And ofttimes it hath cast him into the fire, and into the waters, to destroy him: but if thou canst do any thing, have compassion (mercy) on us, and help us.

23 Jesus said unto him, If thou canst believe, all things are possible to him that believeth.

24 And straightway (immediately) the father of the child cried out, and said with tears, Lord, I believe; help thou mine unbelief.

Note: Each of us, no doubt, at times have said or will say "I believe; help thou mine unbelief". It is a beautiful, humble, acknowledgment of our faith and yet our inadequacy to have as much faith as we would like to have.

25 When Jesus saw that the people came running together, he rebuked the foul (evil) spirit, saying unto him, *Thou* dumb and deaf spirit, I charge (command) thee, come out of him, and enter no more into him.

26 And *the spirit* cried (shrieked), and rent him sore (caused the man to flop around and get cut up more), and came out of him: and he (the man) was as one dead; insomuch (to the extent) that many said, He is dead.

27 But Jesus took him by the hand, and lifted him up; and he arose.

28 And when he was come into the house, his disciples asked him privately, Why could not we cast him (the evil spirit) out?

29 And he said unto them, This kind can come forth by nothing, but by prayer and fasting.

30 And they departed thence (left that place), and passed through Galilee; and he would not that any man should know it (wanted to have time alone with his apostles).

31 For he taught his disciples, and said unto them, The Son of man (Jesus; Son of Man; "Man" means "the Father"—see Moses 6:57) is delivered into the hands of men, and they shall kill him; and after that he is killed, he shall rise (be resurrected) the third day.

32 But they (the disciples) understood not that saying (what Jesus had said about his death and resurrection), and were afraid to ask him.

33 And he came to Capernaum (on the north end of the Sea of Galilee): and being in the house he asked them, What was it that ye disputed among yourselves by the way (what were you debating among yourselves as we were traveling)?

34 But they held their peace (didn't answer; obviously, they were embarrassed about it): for by the way (while traveling) they had disputed (argued) among themselves, who *should be* the greatest (JST who was the greatest among them).

35 And he sat down, and called the twelve, and saith unto them, If any man desire to be first (the greatest in God's kingdom), *the same* (he) shall be last of all (should consider himself to be least important of all), and servant of all.

36 And he took a child, and set him in the midst of them: and when he had taken him in his arms, he said unto them,

37 Whosoever shall receive one of such children in my name, receiveth me: and whosoever shall receive me, receiveth not me, but him that sent me. (JST "Whosoever shall humble himself like one of these children, and receiveth me, ye shall receive in my name. And whosoever shall receive me, receiveth not me only, but him that sent me, even the Father.")

38 And John answered him, saying, Master, we saw one casting out devils in thy name, and he followeth not us (is not one of us): and we forbad him (told him not to do it), because he followeth not us.

39 But Jesus said, Forbid him not: for there is no man which shall do a miracle in my name, that can lightly speak evil of me.

40 For he that is not against us is on our part (is on our side).

41 For whosoever shall give you a cup of water to drink in my name, because ye belong to Christ, verily I say unto you, he shall not lose his reward.

42 And whosoever shall offend (cause to stumble in their faithfulness-see Matthew 18:6, footnote 6a; many translations use "cause to commit sin" in place of "offend") one of *these* little ones that believe in me, it is better for him that a millstone (a large grinding stone) were hanged about his neck, and he were cast into the sea.

Note: In the next verses, there is much symbolism where parts of the body represent people. JST Mark 9:40-48 (in the back of your English LDS Bible) tells us what people are represented by hand, foot and eye. JST Matthew 18:9 gives additional interpretation which is included in the parentheses below.

43 And if thy hand (your brother; friend) offend thee (causes you to sin), cut it off (stay away from him): it is better for thee to enter into life maimed (crippled), than having two hands to go into hell (than following the sinful example of family members and going to hell with them), into the fire that never shall be quenched:

44 Where their worm dieth not (where they do not cease to exist), and the fire (their suffering) is not quenched (does not stop).

45 And if thy foot (friend; the person who is leading you) offend thee (leads you into sin), cut it off (quit associating with that person): it is better for thee to enter halt (crippled) into life, than having two feet (sticking with the friend) to be cast into hell, into the fire that never shall be quenched:

46 Where their worm dieth not (where they do not cease to exist), and the fire is not quenched (the suffering never ends).

47 And if thine eye (parents, family members who lead you) offend thee (cause you to stumble in the faith, commit sin etc.), pluck it out (leave them): it is better for thee to enter into the kingdom of God with one eye (alone), than having two eyes

(following parents' sinful example) to be cast into hell fire:

48 Where their worm dieth not, and the fire is not quenched.

49 For every one shall be salted (tested) with fire, and every sacrifice shall be salted with salt (every sacrifice we make for the gospel is part of our test).

Note: Apostle Bruce R. McConkie explains the phrase "salted with fire" as follows: "Every member of the Church shall be tested and tried in all things, to see whether he will abide in the covenant "even unto death" (D. & C. 98:14), regardless of the course taken by the other members of his family or of the Church. To gain salvation men must stand on their own feet in the gospel cause and be independent of the spiritual support of others. If some of the saints, who are themselves the salt of the earth, shall fall away, still all who inherit eternal life must remain true, having salt in themselves and enjoying peace one with another. *Doctrinal New Testament Commentary*, Vol. 1, page 421.)

50 Salt *is* good: but if the salt have lost his saltness, wherewith will ye season it? Have salt in yourselves, and have peace one with another.

MARK 10

1 AND he arose from thence (from where he was in Galilee), and cometh into the coasts (borders) of Judæa (the southern part of the country) by the farther (eastern) side of Jordan (river): and the people resort (came) unto him again; and, as he was wont (accus-

tomed to doing), he taught them again.

2 And the Pharisees (Jewish religious leaders) came to him, and asked him, Is it lawful (legal) for a man to put away (divorce) *his* wife? tempting him (trying to trap him).

3 And he answered and said unto them, What did Moses command you?

4 And they said, Moses suffered (allowed) to write a bill of divorcement (a legal divorce document), and to put *her* away (divorce her).

5 And Jesus answered and said unto them, For the (because of the) hardness of your heart he wrote you this precept (gave you this teaching).

6 But from the beginning of the creation God (Heavenly Father) made them male and female.

7 For this cause (for marriage) shall a man leave his father and mother, and cleave (be loyal) to his wife;

8 And they twain (the two of them) shall be one flesh (a family unit): so then they are no more twain (two), but one flesh.

9 What therefore God hath joined together, let not man put asunder (destroy).

10 And in the house his disciples asked him again of the same *matter* (to explain more of what he had said about divorce).

11 And he saith unto them, Whosoever shall put away (divorce) his wife, and marry another, committeth adultery against her.

12 And if a woman shall put away her husband, and be married to another, she committeth adultery.

Note: Refer to the note after Matthew 5:31 for more about divorce.

13 And they (the people) brought young children to him, that he should touch them: and *his* disciples rebuked those (scolded them) that brought *them*.

14 But when Jesus saw *it*, he was much displeased, and said unto them (his disciples, who are still learning), Suffer (allow) the little children to come unto me, and forbid them not: for of such is the kingdom of God.

15 Verily I say unto you, Whosoever (whoever) shall not receive the kingdom of God (accept the teachings of the gospel) as (like) a little child, he shall not enter therein.

16 And he took them (the children) up in his arms, put *his* hands upon them, and blessed them.

17 And when he was gone forth into the way (when he had gone on down the road), there came one (the rich young man in verse 22) running, and kneeled to him, and asked him, Good Master, what shall I do that I may inherit eternal life (exaltation)?

18 And Jesus said unto him, Why callest thou me good? *there is* none good but one, *that is*, God. (Jesus wants no glory for himself, rather gives all glory and credit to the Father.)

19 Thou knowest the commandments, Do not commit adultery, Do not kill, Do not steal, Do not bear false witness (lie; accuse someone falsely), Defraud (cheat) not, Honour thy father and mother.

20 And he answered and said unto him, Master, all these have I observed (done) from my youth.

21 Then Jesus beholding him loved

him (looked at him with kind, loving eyes), and said unto him, One thing thou lackest (there is one thing you haven't done yet): go thy way, sell whatsoever (everything) thou hast, and give to the poor, and thou shalt have treasure in heaven: and come, take up the cross (take up my cause), and follow me.

22 And he was sad at that saying, and went away grieved (troubled): for he had great possessions (he was very rich).

23 And Jesus looked round about, and saith unto his disciples, How hardly shall they that have riches enter into the kingdom of God (how hard it is for rich people to enter the kingdom of God)!

24 And the disciples were astonished (surprised, startled) at his words. But Jesus answereth again (continued), and saith unto them (explained what he meant), Children, how hard is it (it is very difficult) for them that trust in riches to enter into the kingdom of God!

Note: This is a very important point. Some people believe that to be rich is somehow evil and against the Savior's teachings. That is not what he taught here. To trust in wealth rather than God and to let wealth corrupt one's values and standards is the problem pointed out here by Jesus. See Jacob 2:16-20.

25 It is easier for a camel to go through the eye of a needle, than for a rich man to enter into the kingdom of God.

Note: There is a rumor going around

that the "eye of a needle" was a small gate in the walls of Jerusalem, used for entry into the city by night, after the main gates were closed. The rumor states that it was very difficult for a camel to get down and scrunch through the gate. Scholars indicate that this rumor has no truth to it. They indicate that the word "needle", as used in verse 25, refers to an ordinary sewing needle in the original Bible languages.

26 And they were astonished out of measure (could hardly believe what they had just heard), saying among themselves, Who then can be saved?

27 And Jesus looking upon them saith, With men it is impossible, but not with God: for with God all things are possible. (JST "And Jesus, looking upon them, said, With men that trust in riches, it is impossible; but not impossible with men who trust in God and leave all for my sake, for with such all these things are possible.")

28 Then Peter began to say unto him, Lo, we have left all, and have followed thee.

29 And Jesus answered and said, Verily (listen very carefully) I say unto you, There is no man that hath left house, or brethren, or sisters, or father, or mother, or wife, or children, or lands, for my sake, and the gospel's,

30 But he shall receive an hundredfold (a hundred times more) now in this time, houses, and brethren, and sisters, and mothers, and children, and lands, with persecutions; and in the world to come eternal life (eternal life).

31 But many *that are* first shall be last; and the last first. (JST "But there

are many who make themselves first, that shall be last, and the last first. This he said, rebuking Peter...")

32 And they were in the way (on the road) going up to Jerusalem; and Jesus went before (ahead of) them: and they were amazed; and as they followed, they were afraid. And he took again the twelve, and began to tell them what things should happen unto him,

33 *Saying*, Behold, we go up to Jerusalem; and the Son of man (Jesus, Son of Man) shall be delivered unto the chief priests (religious leaders of the Jews), and unto the scribes (Jewish religious leaders); and they shall condemn him to death, and shall deliver him to the Gentiles (the Romans):

34 And they (the Romans) shall mock him, and shall scourge (whip) him, and shall spit upon him, and shall kill him: and the third day he shall rise again (will be resurrected).

35 And James and John, the sons of Zebedee, come (came) unto him, saying, Master, we would that thou shouldest do for us whatsoever we shall desire.

36 And he said unto them, What would ye that I should do for you?

37 They said unto him, Grant unto us that we may sit, one on thy right hand, and the other on thy left hand, in thy glory (in heaven).

38 But Jesus said unto them, Ye know not what ye ask: can ye drink of the cup that I drink of (can you really follow me in everything)? and be baptized with the baptism that I am baptized with (go through what I have to go through)?

39 And they said unto him, We can.

And Jesus said unto them, Ye shall indeed drink of the cup that I drink of; and with the baptism that I am baptized withal shall ye be baptized:

40 But to sit on my right hand and on my left hand is not mine to give; but *it shall be given to them* for whom it is prepared. (In other words, it is not to be given as a matter of favoritism or mere request, rather it will be given to those who earn it according to the laws established by the Father.)

41 And when the ten (other apostles) heard *it*, they began to be much displeased with James and John.

Note: Watch now as the Savior, with kindness and skill calms the feelings of contention which have arisen among the twelve apostles here and uses the occasion to teach the principle of "servant leadership", which is that those who want to be greatest among the people of God must be those who humbly and sincerely serve the others.

42 But Jesus called them *to him*, and saith unto them, Ye know that they which are accounted to rule over the Gentiles (leaders among the gentiles) exercise lordship over them; and their great ones (most important leaders) exercise authority upon them.

43 But so shall it not be among you: but whosoever will be great among you, shall be your minister:

44 And whosoever of you will be the chiefest, shall be servant of all.

45 For even the Son of man (Jesus) came not to be ministered unto, but to minister, and to give his life a ransom (payment) for many.

46 And they came to Jericho (east

and down the mountain from Jerusalem, about 25 miles): and as he went out of Jericho with his disciples and a great number of people, blind Bartimæus, the son of Timæus, sat by the highway side begging.

47 And when he heard that it was Jesus of Nazareth, he began to cry out (yell), and say, Jesus, *thou* Son of David (the promised Messiah, prophesied to come through David), have mercy on me.

48 And many charged him that he should hold his peace (told him to be quiet): but he cried the more a great deal, *Thou* Son of David, have mercy on me.

49 And Jesus stood still, and commanded him to be called. And they call the blind man, saying unto him, Be of good comfort, rise; he calleth thee.

50 And he, casting away his garment (throwing down his cloak-wasting no time), rose, and came to Jesus.

51 And Jesus answered and said unto him, What wilt thou that I should do unto thee? The blind man said unto him, Lord, that I might receive my sight.

52 And Jesus said unto him, Go thy way; thy faith hath made thee whole (healed). And immediately he received his sight, and followed Jesus in the way (along the road).

MARK 11

Note: These next verses lead up to what is known as "the Triumphal Entry", the day when Jesus rode into Jerusalem accompanied by throngs of people shouting "Hosanna to the Son of David", in other words, celebrating and cheering Jesus as the promised Messiah who would save them and free them from their enemies. The Passover was underway and throngs of Jewish pilgrims had arrived in Jerusalem from many lands to join in Passover celebration and worship. This begins the last week of the Savior's mortal life.

1 AND when they came nigh (near) to Jerusalem, unto Bethphage and Bethany, at the mount of Olives (a few minutes' walk east of Jerusalem), he sendeth forth two of his disciples,

2 And saith unto them, Go your way into the village over against you (just ahead of you): and as soon as ye be entered into it, ye shall find a colt (a young male donkey) tied, whereon never man sat (that has never been ridden); loose (untie) him, and bring *him*.

3 And if any man say unto you, Why do ye this? say ye that the Lord hath need of him; and straightway (immediately) he will send him hither (here).

Note: Here is another miracle which is sometimes missed by people as they read. The young male donkey has never been ridden, yet when Jesus gets on him to ride into Jerusalem, the donkey does not object, rather, allows the Master to ride. This is another testimony of the Savior's power over all things.

4 And they (the two disciples) went their way, and found the colt tied by the door without (outside) in a place where two ways (roads) met; and they loose (untied) him.

5 And certain of them that stood

there (some people standing around) said unto them, What do ye, loosing the colt?

6 And they said (replied) unto them even as Jesus had commanded: and they let them go.

7 And they brought the colt to Jesus, and cast their garments (cloaks, robes) on him (the colt); and he (Jesus) sat upon him.

8 And many spread their garments in the way (on the road): and others cut down branches off the trees, and strawed (spread) *them* in the way (on the road in front of Jesus).

9 And they that went before (the people who went ahead), and they that followed, cried (shouted), saying, Hosanna ("Save us now." See Bible Dictionary, page 704); Blessed is he that cometh in the name of the Lord:

10 Blessed be the kingdom of our father David (JST "That bringeth the kingdom of our father David) , (JST "Blessed is he") that cometh in the name of the Lord: Hosanna in the highest.

11 And Jesus entered into Jerusalem, and into the temple: and when he had looked round about upon all things, and now the eventide was come, he went out unto Bethany with the twelve.

12 And on the morrow (the next day), when they were come from Bethany, he was hungry:

13 And seeing a fig tree afar off having leaves, he came, if haply (to see if) he might find any thing thereon: and when he came to it, he found nothing but leaves; for the time of figs was not yet (JST "for as yet the figs were not ripe").

14 And Jesus answered (spoke) and said unto it (the fig tree), No man eat fruit of thee hereafter for ever. And his disciples heard *it*. (See more about this in verses 20-21.)

15 And they come to (arrived at) Jerusalem: and Jesus went into the temple, and began to cast out them that sold and bought in the temple, and overthrew the tables of the money-changers, and the seats of them that sold doves;

Note: The temple had become a major marketplace for buying and selling birds and animals to be used for sacrifices. There was much of yelling and cheating etc. which typically go along with such dealings; therefore, Jesus cleansed the temple from these money-changers and their merchandise. John tells us (John 2:14-17) that Jesus cleansed the temple at the beginning of his ministry. Now, three years later, Jesus cleanses the temple again. This is the second time and the temple crowd obviously hadn't learned their lesson the first time.

16 And would not suffer (allow) that any man should carry *any* vessel (container) through the temple.

17 And he taught, saying unto them, Is it not written (in the scriptures), My house shall be called of all nations the house of prayer? but ye have made it a den of thieves.

18 And the scribes and chief priests (Jewish religious leaders, who wanted desperately to arrest Jesus and have him executed) heard it, and sought how they might destroy him: for they feared him, because all the people was

astonished at his doctrine (Jesus had become famous for his teachings).

19 And when even (evening) was come, he went out of the city.

20 And in the morning, as they passed by, they saw the fig tree dried up from the roots.

Note: The fig tree is symbolic of the hypocritical Jewish religious leaders who pretend to look official but do not produce the fruit of the gospel. It is also symbolic of the Jewish nation, the covenant people, who are "barren" as far as the gospel is concerned. See Talmage, *Jesus the Christ*, p. 443.

21 And Peter calling to remembrance saith unto him, Master, behold, the fig tree which thou cursedst is withered away (has dried up and died).

Note: Jesus will now use the fig tree incident to teach his disciples about the power of faith.

22 And Jesus answering saith unto them, Have faith in God.

23 For verily I say unto you, That whosoever shall say unto this mountain, Be thou removed, and be thou cast into the sea; and shall not doubt in his heart, but shall believe that those things which he saith shall come to pass; he shall have whatsoever he saith.

24 Therefore I say unto you, What things soever ye desire, when ye pray, believe that ye receive *them*, and ye shall have *them*.

Note: D&C 46:30 and 50:29-30 add to our understanding of this use of faith.

In these Doctrine and Covenants verses we are instructed that, in order to have this kind of faith, the Holy Ghost must inspire us as to what is ok for us to ask.

25 And when ye stand praying, forgive, if ye have ought (anything) against any: that your Father also which is in heaven may forgive you your trespasses. (In other words, if you want God to forgive your sins, you must forgive others.)

26 But if ye do not forgive, neither will your Father which is in heaven forgive your trespasses.

27 And they come (came) again to Jerusalem: and as he was walking in the temple, there come to him the chief priests, and the scribes, and the elders,

Note: These Jewish religious leaders are now working closely together to do away with Jesus. Keep in mind that there are large crowds of people standing near who are listening carefully to what now goes on.

28 And say (and the Jewish leaders said) unto him, By what authority doest thou these things? and who gave thee this authority to do these things?

29 And Jesus answered and said unto them, I will also ask of you one question, and answer me, and I will tell you by what authority I do these things. (If you will answer one question I ask you, then I will answer your question.)

30 (Here is my question to you:)The baptism of John, was *it* from heaven, or of men? answer me. (Was John the Baptist sent by heaven, or was he just a man who falsely claimed authority?)

31 And they reasoned with (talked it over among) themselves, saying, If we shall say, From heaven; he will say, Why then did ye not believe him?

32 But if we shall say, Of men; they feared the people (feared that the people would mob them): for all *men* counted John, that he was a prophet indeed.

33 And they answered and said unto Jesus, We cannot tell (we cannot answer your question). And Jesus answering saith unto them, Neither do I tell you by what authority I do these things (then I will not answer your question either).

MARK 12

Note: In this next parable, known as the Parable of the Wicked Husbandmen, the Savior clearly compares the wicked Jewish religious leaders to the wicked husbandmen (supervisors, foremen, stewards, those who run the business while the owner is away) who kill the owner's son in an attempt to take the kingdom from him. The notes in parentheses in the parable suggest one possible interpretation of symbolism in the parable.

1 AND he began to speak unto them (the Jewish leaders mentioned in Mark 11:27, who are trying to trap Jesus) by parables (stories which teach a lesson). A *certain* man (Heavenly Father) planted a vineyard (grape vines, symbolic of creating this earth and putting people on it)), and set an hedge (protection from danger [Satan, temptation etc]) about it, and digged *a place for* the winefat (built a place to harvest the grape juice, in other words,

planned for a good harvest of righteous people), and built a tower (so people could see enemies coming from far off and thus avoid being conquered, symbolic of prophets seeing dangers and warning their people), and let it out to husbandmen (placed supervisors over it), and went into a far country (heaven).

2 And at the season (at harvest time) he sent to the husbandmen (supervisors, stewards) a servant (prophets), that he might receive from the husbandmen of the fruit of the vineyard (the harvest).

3 And they caught *him*, (the prophets) and beat him, and sent *him* away empty (wouldn't listen to the prophets).

4 And again he sent unto them another servant (more prophets); and at him they cast stones, and wounded *him* in the head, and sent *him* away shamefully handled (badly abused).

5 And again he sent another (more prophets); and him they killed, and many others; beating some, and killing some.

6 Having yet therefore one son (Christ), his wellbeloved, he (the Father) sent him also last unto them, saying, They will reverence my son.

7 But those husbandmen said among themselves, This is the heir (the owner's son to whom all this will belong); come, let us kill him, and the inheritance shall be ours (let's kill Jesus so we can keep our positions of power and leadership over the people).

8 And they took him (Jesus), and killed (crucified) *him*, and cast *him* out of the vineyard (got rid of him from the earth).

9 What shall therefore the lord of the vineyard (Christ) do? he will come and destroy the husbandmen (at the Second Coming), and will give the vineyard unto others (to the righteous, who will inherit the earth).

10 And have ye not read this scripture; The stone (Christ) which the builders (the wicked husbandmen in verse two etc. and their people) rejected is become the head of the corner (the main part of the building):

11 This was the Lord's doing, and it is marvellous in our eyes?

Note: JST puts verses 10 and 11 together as follows:

"Again, have ye not read this Scripture; The stone which the builders rejected, is become the head of the corner; this was the Lord's doing, and it is marvelous in our eyes."

12 And they (the wicked Jewish religious leaders) sought to lay hold on him (tried to figure out a way to arrest him), but feared the people: for they knew that he had spoken the parable against them: and they left him, and went their way.

Note: Having failed to stop Jesus themselves, these wicked chief priests, scribes and elders now recruit others to help them trap Jesus and get him arrested. It is interesting to note that the Pharisees and Herodians (verse 13) normally are enemies. Now they have joined together to trap the Master. The Herodians were a political party among the Jews who supported the Herodian family as rulers (see Bible Dictionary, page 701) which was very

distasteful to the Pharisees.

13 And they send (sent) unto him certain of the Pharisees and of the Herodians, to catch him in his words (to get him to say something for which he could be arrested).

14 And when they were come (arrived), they say (said) unto him, Master, we know that thou art true (honest), and carest for no man (you are not afraid to say what you think): for thou regardest not the person of men (you don't care who you are talking to), but teachest the way of God in truth: (This is dripping with false flattery!) Is it lawful to give tribute (pay taxes) to Cæsar, or not?

15 Shall we give (pay), or shall we not give? But he, knowing their hypocrisy (trying to look righteous, but enjoying being evil), said unto them, Why tempt ye me? bring me a penny (a Roman coin equal to a normal day's pay-see Bible Dictionary, page 734), that I may see it.

16 And they brought it. And he saith unto them, Whose is this image and superscription (whose face and title are on the coin)? And they said unto him, Cæsar's.

17 And Jesus answering said unto them, Render (pay to) to Cæsar the things that are Cæsar's, and to God the things that are God's. And they marvelled at him (were surprised at how skillfully he got out of their trap).

Note: The Sadducees were another somewhat influential group of religious leaders among the Jews. They did not believe in the resurrection, and were normally enemies of the

Pharisees who did believe in resurrection. The Sadducees have now joined forces with the Pharisees in attempting to do away with Jesus

18 Then come (came) unto him the Sadducees, which say there is no resurrection (which didn't believe in resurrection); and they asked him, saying,

19 Master, Moses wrote unto us (gave us a law, saying), If a man's brother die, and leave *his* wife *behind him*, and leave no children, that his brother should take (marry) his wife, and raise up seed (children) unto (for) his brother.

20 Now there were seven brethren (brothers): and the first took a wife, and dying left no seed.

21 And the second took her, and died, neither left he any seed: and the third likewise.

22 And the seven had her (all seven brothers eventually married her), and left no seed (children): last of all the woman died also.

23 In the resurrection therefore, when they shall rise, whose wife shall she be of them? for the seven had her to wife.

24 And Jesus answering said unto them, Do ye not therefore err, because ye know not the scriptures, neither the power of God?

25 For when they shall rise from the dead, they neither marry, nor are given in marriage; but are as the angels which are in heaven. (After everyone on this earth has been resurrected, there will be no more marrying.)

Note: Here is a major doctrinal point.

Many religions use verse 25 to prove that there is no such thing as eternal marriage and family in the next life. On the contrary, the simple fact that the Sadducees asked the Savior the question "Whose wife shall she be of them?" (when they are all resurrected), is proof that the Savior had indeed preached marriage in the resurrection, in other words, eternal marriage. Otherwise, their question would not make any sense at all! The next point of correct doctrine which needs to be understood here is that after everyone from this earth is resurrected, there will be no more eternal marriages performed for them, because such marriages have to be done by mortals for themselves, or by mortals who serve as proxies for those who have died-see D&C 128:15 & 18. Brigham Young said: " And when the Millennium is over,...all the sons and daughters of Adam and Eve, *down to the last of their posterity* (bold added for emphasis), who come within the reach of the clemency of the Gospel,[will] have been redeemed in hundreds of temples through the administration of their children as proxies for them." *Discourses of Brigham Young*, p. 395. Since there will be no mortals left on earth after the resurrection is completed, there would be no one left to serve as proxies for eternal marriages.

26 And as touching the dead, that they rise (get resurrected): have ye not read in the book of Moses, how in the bush (the burning bush) God spake unto him, saying, I am the God of Abraham, and the God of Isaac, and

the God of Jacob (Exodus 3:6)?

27 He is not the God of the dead, but the God of the living: (JST "for he raiseth them up out of their graves.") ye therefore do greatly err (you Sadducees are making a big mistake in not believing in resurrection).

28 And one of the scribes (prominent Jewish religious leaders) came, and having heard them (the Sadducees) reasoning together, and perceiving that he (Christ) had answered them well (had answered their question about the seven brothers skillfully), asked him, Which is the first commandment of all?

29 And Jesus answered him, The first of all the commandments is, Hear, O Israel; The Lord our God is one Lord:

30 And thou shalt love the Lord thy God with all thy heart, and with all thy soul, and with all thy mind, and with all thy strength: this is the first commandment.

31 And the second *is* like, *namely* this, Thou shalt love thy neighbour as thyself. There is none other commandment greater than these.

32 And the scribe said unto him, Well, Master, thou hast said the truth: for there is one God; and there is none other but he:

33 And to love him with all the heart, and with all the understanding, and with all the soul, and with all the strength, and to love *his* neighbour as himself, is more than all whole burnt offerings and sacrifices (is more important than all the laws of animal sacrifice).

34 And when Jesus saw that he answered discreetly (carefully and wisely), he said unto him, Thou art not far from the kingdom of God. And no man after that durst (dared) ask him *any question*.

35 And Jesus answered (spoke) and said, while he taught in the temple, How say the scribes (the Jewish religious leaders who interpreted the scriptures for the people) that Christ is the Son of David (what do the scribes mean when they say that Christ is the Son of David)?

36 For David himself said (Psalm 110:1) by the Holy Ghost (by inspiration), The LORD (Heavenly Father) said to my Lord (Christ), Sit thou on my right hand, till I make thine enemies thy footstool (until you conquer all your enemies, including Satan).

37 David therefore himself calleth him Lord; and whence is he *then* his son (how can Christ be David's son if David himself calls him Lord)? And the common people heard him gladly (were pleased that Jesus was outsmarting their arrogant religious leaders).

38 And he said unto them (the people) in his doctrine, Beware of (watch out for) the scribes, which love to go in long clothing, and *love* salutations (to be greeted by the common people) in the marketplaces,

39 And the chief (the most important) seats in the synagogues, and the uppermost rooms at feasts:

40 Which devour widows' houses (take widow's houses away from them), and for a pretence (for show) make long prayers: these (wicked religious leaders) shall receive greater damnation (punishment).

41 And Jesus sat over against the treasury (across from where people contributed money in the temple), and beheld (watched) how the people cast money into the treasury: and many that were rich cast in much.

42 And there came a certain poor widow, and she threw in two mites, which make a farthing. (Bible Dictionary, page 734, tells us that one mite is equal to 1/64th of a days' pay.)

43 And he called *unto him* his disciples, and saith unto them, Verily I say unto you, That this poor widow hath cast more in, than all they which have cast into the treasury:

44 For all *they* did cast in of their abundance (they had plenty of money left over after they gave their contribution); but she of her want (in her poverty) did cast in all that she had, even all her living.

MARK 13

Note: JST Mark 13 and JST Matthew 24 are the same. Joseph Smith made many changes, added many words and phrases and rearranged some of the verses. See Matthew 24 in this book for these changes and additions.

1 AND as he went out of the temple, one of his disciples saith unto him, Master, see what manner of stones and what buildings *are here* (look at these magnificent temple buildings made of stones)!

2 And Jesus answering (responding) said unto him, Seest thou these great buildings (of the temple)? there shall not be left one stone upon another, that shall not be thrown down.

Note: The Savior's prophecy that the buildings of the temple would be torn down was fulfilled by about 70 to 73 AD as the Romans finally conquered the Jews and destroyed many of their cities.

3 And as he sat upon the mount of Olives over against (across from) the temple, Peter and James and John and Andrew asked him privately,

4 Tell us, when shall these things be (the things you have just prophesied)? and what *shall be* the sign when all these things shall be fulfilled (what are the signs before the Second Coming)?

5 And Jesus answering them began to say, Take heed (be careful) lest any *man* deceive you:

6 For many shall come in my name, saying, I am *Christ*; and shall deceive (fool) many.

7 And when ye shall hear of wars and rumours of wars, be ye not troubled (don't be too concerned): for *such things* must needs be; but the end (of the world) *shall* not *be* yet.

8 For nation shall rise against nation, and kingdom against kingdom (there will be lots of wars): and there shall be earthquakes in divers (various) places, and there shall be famines and troubles: these are the beginnings of sorrows.

9 But take heed to yourselves: for they shall deliver you up to councils (you will be arrested); and in the synagogues (Jewish church buildings) ye shall be beaten: and ye shall be brought before rulers and kings for my sake, for a testimony against them.

10 And the gospel must first be published among all nations.

11 But when they (your enemies) shall lead you, and deliver you up (arrest you), take no thought beforehand what ye shall speak, neither do ye premeditate: but whatsoever shall be given you in that hour, that speak ye: for it is not ye that speak, but the Holy Ghost (the Holy Ghost will help you know what to say).

12 Now the brother shall betray the brother to death, and the father the son; and children shall rise up against their parents, and shall cause them to be put to death (families will come apart and treat each other terribly).

13 And ye (disciples) shall be hated of all men for my name's sake (because of your loyalty to me): but he that shall endure unto the end, the same shall be saved.

14 But when ye shall see the abomination of desolation, spoken of by Daniel the prophet (Daniel 11:31 and 12:11), standing where it ought not, (let him that readeth understand,) then let them that be in Judæa flee to the mountains (to escape):

Note: "Abomination of desolation" means terrible things which will cause much destruction and misery. The abomination of desolation spoken of by Daniel was to have two fulfillments. The first occurred in 70 A.D. when Titus, with his Roman legions, surrounded Jerusalem and laid siege to conquer the Jews. This siege resulted in much destruction and terrible human misery and loss of life. In the last days, the abomination of desolation will occur again (see Joseph Smith–Matt. 1:31-32), meaning that Jerusalem will again be under siege.

See Bible Dictionary, p. 601.

15 And let him that is on the housetop not go down into the house, neither enter *therein*, to take any thing out of his house (just get away fast!):

16 And let him that is in the field not turn back again for to take up his garment (robe, cloak).

17 But woe to them that are with child (pregnant), and to them that give suck (are nursing babies and small children) in those days (when these things happen to Jerusalem)!

18 And pray ye that your flight be not in the winter (when it is more difficult to flee).

19 For *in* those days shall be affliction, such as was not from the beginning of the creation which God created unto this time, neither shall be.

20 And except that the Lord had shortened those days, no flesh should be saved (the Lord will intervene so that some Jews will be left): but for the elect's sake, whom he hath chosen, he hath shortened the days.

Note: Now the topic changes from the days when the Romans conquered and destroyed the Jewish nation, culminating in about 70 to 73 AD, to the last days and signs preceding the Savior's Second Coming.

21 And then if any man shall say to you, Lo, here *is* Christ; or, lo, *he is* there; believe *him* not (Christ will not come secretly or in just one place at the actual Second Coming, rather he will come and everyone will see him at once):

22 For false Christs and false

prophets shall rise, and shall shew signs and wonders, to seduce (fool), if *it were* possible, even the elect.

23 But take ye heed: behold, I have foretold you all things.

24 But in those days, after that tribulation, the sun shall be darkened, and the moon shall not give her light,

25 And the stars of heaven shall fall, and the powers that are in heaven shall be shaken. (There will be many signs of the times, that is, prophecies fulfilled in the last days showing that the Second Coming is near.)

26 And then shall they see the Son of man (Jesus, the Son of Man-see Moses 6:57) coming in the clouds with great power and glory.

27 And then shall he send his angels, and shall gather together his elect from the four winds, from the uttermost part of the earth to the uttermost part of heaven (the righteous will be gathered).

28 Now learn a parable (a story which teaches) of the fig tree; When her branch is yet tender (has new growth), and putteth forth leaves, ye know that summer is near:

29 So ye in like manner, when ye shall see these things (signs of the times) come to pass, know that it (the Second Coming) is nigh (near), *even* at the doors.

30 Verily I say unto you, that this generation (the dispensation of the fulness of times, the last dispensation) shall not pass, till all these things be done.

31 Heaven and earth shall pass away: but my words shall not pass away.

32 But of that day and *that* hour knoweth no man, no, not the angels which are in heaven, neither the Son, but the Father.

Note: Verse 32 is similar to Matthew 24:36, but adds that the Son, Jesus, won't know when the Second Coming will be, but only the Father.

33 Take ye heed (pay attention), watch and pray: for ye know not when the time is (when the Savior will come).

34 *For the Son of man* (the Savior) *is* as a man taking a far journey, who left his house (went to heaven), and gave authority to his servants (the Apostles, leaders of the Church), and to every man his work (to all members their responsibilities), and commanded the porter to watch.

35 Watch ye therefore: for ye know not when the master of the house cometh (symbolic of the Savior at his Second Coming), at even (evening), or at midnight, or at the cockcrowing, or in the morning:

36 Lest coming suddenly he find you sleeping (not living righteously).

37 And what I say unto you I say unto all, Watch.

MARK 14

Note: The Feast of the Passover, mentioned in verse 1, was celebrated in the springtime at about the same time as we celebrate Easter. It commemorated the destroying angel's passing over the houses of the children of Israel in Egypt, when the firstborn of the Egyptians were killed. The Israelites in Egypt at the time were instructed by Moses to sacrifice a lamb without blemish and to put blood from the lamb which was sacrificed on the doorposts of their houses. See Bible Dictionary, p. 672. Thus, through the blood of a lamb, the Israelites were protected from the anguish and punishment brought to the Egyptians by the destroying angel. The symbolism is clear. It is by the "blood of the Lamb" (the sacrifice of the Savior) that we are saved, after all we can do (2 Nephi 25:23). Now, at the time of Passover in Jerusalem, the "Lamb of God", Christ, will present himself to be sacrificed, that we might be saved. The Feast of the Passover brought large numbers of Jews from near and far to Jerusalem to join in the worship and celebration.

1 AFTER two days was *the feast of* the passover, and of unleavened bread: and the chief priests and the scribes (religious leaders of the Jews) sought how they might take him (Jesus) by craft (quietly), and put *him* to death.

2 But they said, Not on the feast day (not on Thursday, the day of the Feast of the Passover), lest there be an uproar of the people (for fear that the people will riot).

3 And being in Bethany (a village a short distance from Jerusalem, just over the Mount of Olives) in the house of Simon the leper, as he sat at meat (as Jesus ate dinner), there came a woman (Mary-see John 12:3) having an alabaster box of ointment of spikenard very precious (expensive); and she brake (broke) the box, and poured *it* on his head.

Note: The anointing of Jesus by Mary, in verse 3, contains much significant symbolism. Jesus is the Messiah.

"Messiah" means "the Anointed One" (Bible Dictionary, p. 731). It would seem that this Mary understood what the disciples did not yet fully understand, and symbolically "anointed" the Savior in preparation for his Atoning sacrifice. This sheds light on the divine nature and spiritual sensitivity of women.

4 And there were some that had indignation within themselves (who were angry), and said, Why was this waste of the ointment made?

5 For it might have been sold for more than three hundred pence (about a year's wages), and have been given to the poor. And they murmured against her.

6 And Jesus said, Let her alone; why trouble ye her? she hath wrought (done) a good work on me.

7 For ye have the poor with you always, and whensoever ye will ye may do them good: but me ye have not always.

8 She hath done what she could: she is come aforehand to anoint my body to the burying. (JST " She has done what she could, and this which she has done unto me, shall be had in remembrance in generations to come, wheresoever my gospel shall be preached; for verily she has come beforehand to anoint my body to the burying.")

9 Verily I say unto you, Wheresoever this gospel shall be preached throughout the whole world, *this* also that she hath done shall be spoken of for a memorial of her.

10 And Judas Iscariot, one of the twelve, went unto the chief priests

(main religious leaders of the Jews), to betray him unto them.

11 And when they heard *it*, they were glad, and promised to give him money. And he sought how he might conveniently betray him.

Note: Matthew 26:15 says they agreed to pay Judas thirty pieces of silver, which was the going price for a common slave. This devalued the Savior and was an insult to Judas.

12 And the first day of unleavened bread (Thursday), when they killed the passover (sacrificed the Passover lamb), his disciples said unto him, Where wilt thou that we go and prepare that thou mayest eat the passover (the Passover meal)?

13 And he sendeth forth two of his disciples, and saith unto them, Go ye into the city, and there shall meet you a man bearing (carrying) a pitcher of water: follow him.

14 And wheresoever he shall go in (whichever house he enters), say ye to the goodman (owner) of the house, The Master saith, Where is the guestchamber, where I shall eat the passover with my disciples?

15 And he will shew (show) you a large upper room furnished *and* prepared: there make ready for us.

16 And his disciples went forth, and came into the city, and found as he had said unto them: and they made ready the passover.

17 And in the evening he cometh (came) with the twelve.

18 And as they sat and did eat, Jesus said, Verily I say unto you, One of you which eateth with me shall betray me.

19 And they began to be sorrowful, and to say unto him one by one, *Is* it I? and another *said, Is* it I?

20 And he answered and said unto them, *It is* one of the twelve, that dippeth (that dips his bread) with me in the dish.

21 The Son of man (Jesus) indeed goeth (will be arrested, tried and crucified), as it is written of him (as it is prophesied in the scriptures): but woe to that man by whom the Son of man is betrayed! good were it for that man if he had never been born.

Note: The Savior now introduces the sacrament to his apostles. This is known as the "Last Supper". Jesus introduces the sacrament as a "new testament" (verse 24). The word "testament" often means "covenant" (see Bible Dictionary, page 651). Thus, the sacrament becomes a "new covenant" and replaces the "old covenant" of animal sacrifice as a means of making covenants and pointing our minds and hearts toward Christ and our commitments to him.

22 And as they did eat, Jesus took bread, and blessed, and brake *it*, and gave to them, and said, Take, eat: this is my body (this represents my body).

23 And he took the cup, and when he had given thanks, he gave *it* to them: and they all drank of it.

24 And he said unto them, This is my blood (this represents my blood) of the new testament (the new covenant, associated with the full gospel which Christ had restored), which is shed for many.

25 Verily I say unto you, I will drink

no more of the fruit of the vine, until that day that I drink it new in the kingdom of God (this is the last time I will partake of the sacrament with you during my mortal life).

26 And when they had sung an hymn, they went out into the mount of Olives.

27 And Jesus saith unto them, All ye shall be offended (stumble, leave, scatter, desert; see Strong's Concordance, #4624) because of me this night (all of you will scatter, desert me tonight because of what happens): for it is written (in Zachariah 13:7), I will smite the shepherd, and the sheep shall be scattered.

28 But after that I am risen (resurrected), I will go before you (ahead of you) into Galilee.

29 But Peter said unto him, Although all shall be offended (even if everyone else scatters and deserts you), yet *will* not I.

30 And Jesus saith unto him, Verily I say unto thee, That this day, *even* in this night, before the cock crow (a rooster crows) twice, thou shalt deny me thrice (you will deny knowing me three times before morning).

Note: Denying knowing Christ is forgivable and is not the same as denying the Holy Ghost. Peter was very disappointed by his behavior, as recorded in verses 66-72, but he went on to become a powerful apostle and the president of the church after the Savior was resurrected and taken up into heaven. Perhaps Peter's example here can be a lesson to us. We think we are strong in the gospel and claim to be willing to live it at all costs. Yet, some-times we falter and give in to temptation which disappoints us and makes us all the more determined to be stronger in the faith.

31 But he (Peter) spake the more vehemently (strongly, emphatically), If I should die with thee, I will not deny thee in any wise (in any way). Likewise also said they all (all the other apostles said the same thing Peter said).

32 And they came to a place which was named Gethsemane (the Garden of Gethsemane): and he saith to his disciples, Sit ye here, while I shall pray.

Note: "Gethsemane" means "oil press". There is significant symbolism here. The Jews put olives into bags made of mesh fabric and placed them in a press to squeeze olive oil out of them. The first pressings yielded pure olive oil which was prized for many uses, including healing and giving light in lanterns. In fact, we consecrate it and use it to administer to the sick. The last pressing of the olives, under the tremendous pressure of additional weights added to the press, yielded a bitter, red liquid which can remind us of the "bitter cup" which the Savior partook of. Symbolically, the Savior is going into the "oil press" (Gethsemane) to submit to the "pressure" of all our sins which will "squeeze" his blood out in order that we might have the healing "oil" of the Atonement to heal us from our sins.

33 And he taketh with him Peter and James and John (the "First

Presidency"), and began to be sore amazed (astonished), and to be very heavy (with depression and anguish-see Mark 14:33, footnote b);

34 And saith unto them, My soul is exceeding sorrowful unto death: tarry ye here, and watch.

Note: JST gives verses 32-34 as follows:

" And they came to a place which was named Gethsemane, which was a garden; and the disciples began to be sore amazed, and to be very heavy, and to complain in their hearts, wondering if this be the Messiah. And Jesus knowing their hearts, said to his disciples, Sit ye here, while I shall pray. And he taketh with him, Peter, and James, and John, and rebuked them, and said unto them, My soul is exceeding sorrowful, even unto death; tarry ye here and watch."

35 And he went forward a little, and fell on the ground, and prayed that, if it were possible, the hour might pass from him.

36 And he said, Abba (an intimate, personal, tender term; "Daddy" in the Aramaic language of New Testament times-see Bible Dictionary, page 600), Father, all things are possible unto thee; take away this cup from me: nevertheless not what I will, but what thou wilt.

Note: Apostle James E. Talmage describes the suffering of the Savior in Gethsemane as follows:

"Christ's agony in the garden is unfathomable by the finite mind, both as to intensity and cause. The thought

that He suffered through fear of death is untenable. Death to Him was preliminary to resurrection and triumphal return to the Father from whom He had come, and to a state of glory even beyond what He had before possessed; and, moreover, it was within His power to lay down His life voluntarily. He struggled and groaned under a burden such as no other being who has lived on earth might even conceive as possible. It was not physical pain, nor mental anguish alone, that caused Him to suffer such torture as to produce an extrusion of blood from every pore; but a spiritual agony of soul such as only God was capable of experiencing. No other man, however great his powers of physical or mental endurance, could have suffered so; for his human organism would have succumbed, and syncope would have produced unconsciousness and welcome oblivion. In that hour of anguish Christ met and overcame all the horrors that Satan, 'the prince of this world' could inflict. The frightful struggle incident to the temptations immediately following the Lord's baptism was surpassed and overshadowed by this supreme contest with the powers of evil.

"In some manner, actual and terribly real though to man incomprehensible, the Savior took upon Himself the burden of the sins of mankind from Adam to the end of the world." *Jesus the Christ*, page 613.

37 And he cometh, and findeth them sleeping, and saith unto Peter, Simon, sleepest thou? couldest not thou watch one hour?

38 Watch ye and pray, lest ye enter into temptation. The spirit truly *is* ready, but the flesh *is* weak.

39 And again he went away, and prayed, and spake the same words.

40 And when he returned, he found them asleep again, (for their eyes were heavy,) neither wist (knew) they what to answer him.

Note: These humble apostles were very tired by this time of the week (Thursday night). It had been a difficult week for them, worrying about the Savior's safety and the plots to kill him. No doubt they had had little sleep. Thus, in verse 40, "their eyes were heavy", in other words, they were very sleepy.

41 And he cometh the third time, and saith unto them, Sleep on now, and take *your* rest: it is enough, the hour is come (the time for my arrest, trial and crucifixion is here); behold, the Son of man (Christ) is betrayed into the hands of sinners.

42 Rise up, let us go; lo, he (Judas Iscariot) that betrayeth me is at hand (is coming).

43 And immediately, while he yet spake, cometh Judas, one of the twelve, and with him a great multitude with swords and staves (sticks), from (sent by) the chief priests and the scribes and the elders (the Jewish religious leaders).

44 And he (Judas) that betrayed him had given them (the soldiers) a token (sign), saying, Whomsoever I shall kiss, that same is he (the person I kiss is Jesus); take him (arrest him), and lead *him* away safely (don't let anyone take him away from you).

45 And as soon as he (Judas) was come (arrived), he goeth straightway (immediately) to him (Jesus), and saith, Master, master; and kissed him.

46 And they laid their hands on him (grabbed him), and took him.

47 And one of them (Peter) that stood by drew a sword, and smote (struck) a servant of the high priest, and cut off his ear. (Jesus healed this man's ear; see Luke 22:51.)

48 And Jesus answered (responded) and said unto them, Are ye come out, as against a thief, with swords and *with* staves to take me?

49 I was daily with you in the temple teaching, and ye took me not (why didn't you arrest me during the daytime?): but the scriptures must be fulfilled.

50 And they (the apostles) all forsook him, and fled (as Jesus said they would in verse 27).

51 And there followed him (Jesus) a certain young man (JST a disciple), having a linen cloth cast about *his* naked *body*; and the young men (soldiers or members of the mob) laid hold on him (grabbed the young man):

52 And he left the linen cloth, and fled from them (the soldiers) naked (JST and saved himself out of their hands).

53 And they led Jesus away to the high priest: and with him (Caiaphas, the high priest) were assembled all the chief priests and the elders and the scribes.

54 And Peter followed him (Jesus) afar off, even into the palace of the high priest: and he sat with the servants, and warmed himself at the

fire.

55 And the chief priests and all the council sought for witness against Jesus to put him to death; and found none.

56 For many bare false witness against him, but their witness agreed not together (the false witnesses they did get contradicted each other).

57 And there arose certain, and bare false witness against him, saying,

58 We heard him say, I will destroy this temple that is made with hands, and within three days I will build another made without hands.

59 But neither so did their witness agree together (they contradicted each other also).

60 And the high priest stood up in the midst, and asked Jesus, saying, Answerest thou nothing (aren't you going to say anything)? what *is it which* these witness against thee?

61 But he (Jesus) held his peace, and answered nothing. Again the high priest asked him, and said unto him, Art thou the Christ, the Son of the Blessed (the Son of God)?

62 And Jesus said, I am: and ye shall see the Son of man (Jesus; the Son of Man, meaning the Son of Man of Holiness [the Father]; see Moses 6:57) sitting on the right hand of power, and coming in the clouds of heaven (the Second Coming).

63 Then the high priest rent (tore) his clothes, and saith, What need we any further witnesses?

Note: Tearing your clothing was a cultural way of expressing strongest emotion among the Jews.

64 Ye have heard the blasphemy (this man claims to be the Son of God, the Messiah; he is mocking God!): what think ye? And they all condemned him to be guilty of death.

Note: Blasphemy, showing blatant disrespect for God, mocking God etc., was a crime punishable by death according to Jewish law.

65 And some began to spit on him, and to cover his face (blindfolded him), and to buffet (hit) him, and to say unto him, Prophesy (tell us which one of us is hitting you; see Luke 22:64): and the servants did strike him with the palms of their hands.

66 And as Peter was beneath (in a lower room) in the palace (where the trial was taking place), there cometh one of the maids (servants) of the high priest:

67 And when she saw Peter warming himself, she looked upon him, and said, And thou also wast with Jesus of Nazareth (you are one of Jesus' followers).

68 But he denied, saying, I know not, neither understand I what thou sayest. And he went out into the porch; and the cock (rooster) crew (crowed).

69 And a maid saw him (Peter) again, and began to say to them that stood by (the bystanders), This is *one* of them (Christ's followers).

70 And he denied it again. And a little after (a while later), they that stood by said again to Peter, Surely thou art one of them (followers of Jesus): for thou art a Galilæan, and thy speech agreeth *thereto* (we can tell by your Galilean accent).

71 But he began to curse and to swear, *saying*, I know not this man of whom ye speak.

72 And the second time the cock crew (a rooster crowed again). And Peter called to mind (remembered) the word that Jesus said unto him (in verse 30), Before the cock crow twice, thou shalt deny me thrice (three times). And when he thought thereon, he wept. (See note following verse 30.)

MARK 15

1 AND straightway (first thing) in the morning the chief priests held a consultation (a meeting) with the elders and scribes and the whole council, and bound Jesus (had Jesus tied up), and carried *him* away, and delivered *him* (turned him over) to Pilate (the Roman governor of that area).

2 And Pilate asked him, Art thou the King of the Jews? And he answering said unto him, Thou sayest it (in other words, "Yes I am."; see John 18:37).

3 And the chief priests accused him of many things: but he answered nothing.

4 And Pilate asked him again, saying, Answerest thou nothing (aren't you going to speak in your own defense)? behold (look) how many things they witness (testify) against thee.

5 But Jesus yet answered nothing; so that Pilate marvelled (was surprised).

6 Now at *that* feast he released unto them one prisoner, whomsoever they desired. (It was customary for Pilate to release a prisoner of the peoples' choosing each year at this time.)

7 And there was *one* (criminal) named Barabbas, *which lay* bound (in prison) with them that had made insurrection with him (with those who had rebelled against the government with him), who had committed murder in the insurrection.

Note: The name "Barabbas" means "son of the father" (see Bible Dictionary, page 619). This may be symbolic in that the "imposter", Satan, stirred up the multitude to demand the release of an "imposter", Barabbas, while the true "Son of the Father" is punished for crimes which he did not commit.

8 And the multitude crying aloud began to desire *him to do* as he had ever done unto them (release a prisoner).

9 But Pilate answered them, saying, Will ye that I release unto you the King of the Jews (mocking Jesus)?

10 For he knew that the chief priests had delivered him for envy (had had Jesus arrested because they were jealous of his power and popularity among the people).

11 But the chief priests moved (influenced) the people, that he should rather (instead) release Barabbas unto them.

12 And Pilate answered (responded) and said again unto them, What will ye then that I shall do *unto him* (Jesus) whom ye call the King of the Jews?

13 And they cried out again, Crucify him.

14 Then Pilate said unto them, Why, what evil hath he done? And they cried out the more exceedingly (more loudly), Crucify him.

15 And *so* Pilate, willing to content (please) the people, released Barabbas unto them, and delivered Jesus, when he had scourged *him* (had him beaten, whipped, flogged), to be crucified.

Note: "Scourging" was a very severe punishment and many prisoners did not live through it. It consisted of being whipped with a whip which was composed of leather thongs with bits of metal, bone etc. secured to the ends of the thongs.

16 And the soldiers led him away into the hall, called Prætorium (a room in the governors' house); and they call together the whole band (about six hundred Roman soldiers with a leader over them; see McConkie, *Doctrinal New Testament Commentary*, Vol. 1, page 781).

17 And they clothed him with purple (in mockery of his claim to be "King of the Jews"), and platted (made, wove) a crown of thorns, and put it about his *head*,

18 And began to salute him (saying), Hail, King of the Jews!

19 And they smote (hit) him on the head with a reed (stick, mock scepter of kingly authority), and did spit upon him, and bowing *their* knees worshipped him (pretended to worship him).

20 And when they had mocked him, they took off the purple from him, and put his own clothes on him, and led him out to crucify him.

21 And they compel (forced) one Simon a Cyrenian, who passed by, coming out of the country (probably a foreigner [perhaps a Jew who had come for Passover] who came from Cyrene, a city in northern Africa), the father of Alexander and Rufus, to bear (carry) his cross. (After the suffering in the Garden of Gethsemane, the whipping etc., Jesus was too weak to carry his own cross, which was a part of the legally required punishment and torture which went along with crucifixion.)

22 And they bring (brought) him unto the place Golgotha, which is, being interpreted, The place of a skull.

23 And they gave him to drink wine mingled with myrrh: but he received it not (refused it).

Note: This mixture of wine and myrrh was designed to drug the victim of crucifixion to lessen the pain somewhat. See Talmage, *Jesus the Christ*, pages 654-655.

24 And when they had crucified him (hung him on the cross), they parted his garments (divided up his clothes), casting lots upon them, what every man should take (gambling to see who got what item of clothing).

25 And it was the third hour (about 9 AM), and they crucified him.

26 And the superscription (writing) of his accusation (what he was accused of) was written over (above him on the cross), THE KING OF THE JEWS. (A sign was placed above him on the cross, which said "THE KING OF THE JEWS".)

27 And with him they crucify two thieves; the one on his right hand, and the other on his left.

28 And the scripture was fulfilled, which saith, And he was numbered

with the transgressors (killed with criminals).

29 And they that passed by railed on him (shouted, mocked him), wagging (shaking) their heads, and saying, Ah, thou that destroyest the temple, and buildest it in three days,

Note: These people obviously misunderstood what Jesus said regarding the temple. What he said is in John 2:19-21. He said that if they destroyed his body (the "temple of his body"), he would raise it up in three days (be resurrected in three days). By the time Jesus is on the cross, his statement has been misquoted and spread so that the mockers claim that he said he would destroy their massive temple in Jerusalem and rebuild it in three days.

30 Save thyself, and come down from the cross.

31 Likewise also the chief priests mocking said among themselves with the scribes, He saved others; himself he cannot save.

32 Let Christ the King of Israel descend (come down) now from the cross, that we may see and believe. And they that were crucified with him reviled him (mocked him).

Note: One of the thieves seems to have softened his attitude a bit later. The Savior said to him "Today shalt thou be with me in paradise." We will do more with this in Luke 23:43.

33 And when the sixth hour (about noon) was come, there was darkness over the whole land until the ninth hour (about 3 PM).

34 And at the ninth hour Jesus cried with a loud voice, saying, Eloi, Eloi, lama sabachthani? which is, being interpreted, My God, my God, why hast thou forsaken me?

Note: This had to have been a most difficult time for the Savior. Apparently, as part of the Atonement, Jesus had to experience what sinners do when they sin so much that the Spirit leaves them. At this point on the cross, we understand that all available help from the Father withdrew in order that the Savior might experience all things, including the withdrawal of the Spirit which sinners experience.

35 And some of them that stood by, when they heard it, said, Behold, he calleth Elias (Elijah).

36 And one ran and filled a spunge full of vinegar, and put it on a reed, and gave him to drink, saying, Let alone; let us see whether Elias will come to take him down.

37 And Jesus cried with a loud voice, and gave up the ghost (left his body, died).

38 And the veil of the temple was rent in twain (torn in two) from the top to the bottom.

39 And when the centurion (Roman soldier), which stood over against him (across from Jesus), saw that he so cried out (had so much strength when he cried out), and gave up the ghost, he said, Truly this man was the Son of God.

Note: It was common for victims of crucifixion to live two or three days before dying. The soldier was startled because he was experienced in crucifying people and it appeared to him that Jesus, who was still relatively strong, and after only six hours on the cross, had decided to leave his body and did so. That is exactly what happened and the Roman soldier apparently received a witness of Christ at that moment.

40 There were also women looking on afar off: among whom was Mary Magdalene, and Mary (possibly the Savior's mother; see Mark 6:3) the mother of James the less and of Joses, and Salome;

41 (Who also, when he was in Galilee, followed him, and ministered unto him;) and many other women which came up with him unto Jerusalem.

42 And now when the even (evening) was come, because it was the preparation, that is, the day before the sabbath,

43 Joseph of Arimathaea, an honourable counsellor, which also waited for the kingdom of God (who also was a believer), came, and went in boldly unto Pilate, and craved (requested) the body of Jesus.

44 And Pilate marvelled if he were already dead (was surprised that Jesus was already dead): and calling *unto him* the centurion, he asked him whether he (Jesus) had been any while dead (had been dead very long).

45 And when he knew *it* of the centurion (when the Roman soldier verified that Jesus was indeed dead), he gave the body to Joseph.

46 And he (Joseph of Arimathaea) bought fine linen, and took him down (from the cross), and wrapped him in the linen, and laid him in a sepulchre (tomb) which was hewn (carved) out of a rock, and rolled a stone unto the door of the sepulchre.

47 And Mary Magdalene and Mary *the mother* of Joses beheld (watched to see) where he was laid.

MARK 16

1 AND when the sabbath (Saturday for the Jews) was past, Mary Magdalene, and Mary the *mother* of James, and Salome, had bought sweet spices, that they might come and anoint him (finish preparing Jesus' body for burial).

2 And very early in the morning the first *day* of the week (Sunday), they came unto the sepulchre (tomb) at the rising of the sun.

3 And they said among themselves, Who shall roll us away the stone from the door of the sepulchre (so we can get into the tomb)?

4 And when they looked, they saw that the stone was rolled away: for it was very great (large).

5 And entering into the sepulchre, they saw a young man (JST two angels) sitting on the right side, clothed in a long white garment; and they were affrighted (afraid).

6 And he (JST the angels) saith unto them, Be not affrighted: Ye seek Jesus of Nazareth, which was crucified: he is risen (resurrected); he is not here: behold (look at) the place where they laid him.

7 But go your way, tell his disciples and Peter that he (Jesus) goeth before you (ahead of you) into Galilee: there shall ye see him, as he said unto you (in Mark 14:28).

8 And they went out quickly, and fled from the sepulchre; for they trembled and were amazed: neither said they any thing to any *man*; for they were afraid.

9 Now when *Jesus* was risen (resurrected) early the first *day* of the week, he appeared first to Mary Magdalene, out of whom he had cast seven devils (Luke 8:2).

10 *And* she went and told them that had been with him (his disciples), as they mourned and wept.

11 And they, when they had heard that he was alive, and had been seen of (by) her, believed not.

12 After that he appeared in another form unto two of them (two other disciples), as they walked (on the road to Emmaus; see Luke 24:13-35), and went into the country.

13 And they went and told it unto the residue (rest of the group): neither believed they them.

14 Afterward he appeared unto the eleven (apostles) as they sat at meat (as they were eating), and upbraided (scolded) them with their unbelief and hardness of heart, because they believed not them which had seen him after he was risen.

15 And he said unto them (the apostles), Go ye into all the world, and preach the gospel to every creature (person).

16 He that believeth and is baptized shall be saved; but he that believeth not shall be damned (will be stopped in their progress).

17 And these signs shall follow them that believe; In my name shall they cast out devils (evil spirits); they shall speak with new tongues (foreign languages);

18 They shall take up serpents (the Apostle Paul had an experience with this in Acts 28:3-6); and if they drink any deadly thing, it shall not hurt them: they shall lay hands on the sick, and they shall recover. (In other words, the apostles will have divine protection as they carry out the work of the Lord.)

19 So then after the Lord had spoken unto them, he was received up into heaven, and sat on the right hand of God.

20 And they went forth, and preached every where, the Lord working with *them*, and confirming the word with signs following. Amen.

THE GOSPEL OF LUKE

Luke was a physician according to Colossians 4:14 and was a missionary companion to Paul. Most Bible scholars believe that he was of gentile birth. He is also the author of Acts. His sensitivity to people and their needs shows in his writing. He gives emphasis to the role women played in the life and ministry of the Savior. Perhaps, because he is a physician, he alone of the gospel writers tells of Christ's bleeding during his agony in the Garden of Gethsemane. Luke was not an eyewitness to the Savior's ministry, rather learned from Paul and others about Jesus. It appears that he was writing to the Gentiles, especially the Greeks, to teach them of Jesus and his divine mission as our Savior and Redeemer.

LUKE 1

1 FORASMUCH as (since) many have taken in hand (have undertaken) to set forth in order a declaration of (to write about) those things which are most surely believed among us, (JST "As I am a messenger of Jesus Christ, and knowing that many have taken in hand to set forth in order a declaration of those things which are most surely believed among us;")

2 Even as they delivered them unto us, which from the beginning were eyewitnesses (not all were eyewitnesses of Christ, but were eyewitnesses to the gospel and the growth of the church), and ministers of the word;

3 It seemed good to me (Luke) also, having had perfect understanding of all things from the very first (I have been taught and understand all things from the birth of John the Baptist and from the birth of Jesus up to and including the crucifixion and resurrection of the Savior), to write unto thee in order, most excellent Theophilus ("friend of God", probably a Greek official of high rank),

4 That thou mightest know the certainty (that you might have a testimony) of those things, wherein thou hast been instructed.

5 THERE was in the days of Herod, the king of Judæa, a certain priest (in the Aaronic Priesthood) named Zacharias, of the course of Abia (a descendant of Aaron through Abijah): and his wife *was* of the daughters of Aaron (was a descendant of Aaron), and her name was Elisabeth.

Note: The priests who served in the temple at the time of Christ were members of the Aaronic Priesthood. Zacharias was a righteous holder of this priesthood. Those men who fulfilled priestly duties at the temple at Jerusalem were divided into 24 groups or "courses", each group assigned to serve for one week at a time. Zacharias was a member of the eighth "course" or group. Each group had upwards of 1400 men, so the privilege of officiating at the burning of incense in the temple might come once or never in the lifetime of a priest. (See Talmage, *Jesus the Christ*, pages 75-76.)

6 And they were both righteous before God, walking in all the commandments and ordinances of the Lord blameless.

7 And they had no child, because that Elisabeth was barren (had not been able to have children), and they both were *now* well stricken in years (were quite old and had given up on having children).

8 And it came to pass, that while he (Zacharias) executed the priest's office (carried out his duties in the temple) before God in the order of his course (JST his priesthood),

9 According to the custom of the priest's office, his lot was (he had been selected) to burn incense when he went into the temple of the Lord.

Note: Since it was generally a once-in-a-lifetime opportunity for an Aaronic Priesthood priest to have the privilege of burning incense in the temple, as mentioned in the note above, this would have been a very humbling and important day for Zacharias.

10 And the whole multitude of the people were praying without (outside of the temple, watching for the cloud of smoke from the incense to rise from the temple, and waiting for Zacharias to come back out in a few minutes) at the time of incense.

11 And there appeared unto him (Zacharias) an angel of the Lord standing on the right side of the altar of incense.

Note: This angel was Gabriel. He will also appear to Mary in a few months to tell her that she will be the mother of the Son of God. We are told that Gabriel is Noah. See Bible Dictionary, page 676.

12 And when Zacharias saw *him*, he was troubled, and fear fell upon him.

13 But the angel said unto him, Fear not, Zacharias: for thy prayer is heard; and thy wife Elisabeth shall bear thee a son, and thou shalt call his name John.

Note: The instruction by the angel to call their son "John" was very definite. Otherwise, they would very likely have named him Zacharias, after his father.

14 And thou shalt have joy and gladness; and many shall rejoice at his birth.

15 For he shall be great in the sight of the Lord, and shall drink neither wine nor strong drink (a sign that he was dedicated to a special calling); and he shall be filled with the Holy Ghost (see D&C 84:27), even from his mother's womb (before he is born).

16 And many of the children of Israel shall he turn to the Lord their God.

17 And he (John the Baptist) shall go before him (go ahead of Christ) in the spirit and power of Elias (one who prepares the way for even more important things; see *Teachings of the Prophet Joseph Smith*, pages 335-336; also see Bible Dictionary, page 663), to turn the hearts of the fathers to the children, and the disobedient to the wisdom of the just (righteous); to make ready a people prepared for the Lord (Jesus).

18 And Zacharias said unto the angel, Whereby (how) shall I know this? for I am an old man, and my wife well stricken in years (we are beyond the years when we can have children).

19 And the angel answering said

159

unto him, I am Gabriel (Noah; see note after verse 11 above), that stand in the presence of God; and am sent to speak unto thee, and to shew thee these glad tidings.

20 And, behold, thou shalt be dumb (unable to talk), and not able to speak, until the day that these things shall be performed (until John is born), because thou believest not my words, which shall be fulfilled in their season.

21 And the people waited for Zacharias, and marvelled that he tarried so long in the temple (were wondering what was taking him so long).

22 And when he came out, he could not speak unto them: and they perceived (understood) that he had seen a vision in the temple: for he beckoned unto them (described with his hands that he had seen a vision), and remained speechless.

23 And it came to pass, that, as soon as the days of his ministration were accomplished (after his week of temple duties was over; see note after verse five above), he departed to his own house.

24 And after those days his wife Elisabeth conceived, and hid herself five months, saying,

25 Thus hath the Lord dealt with me in the days wherein he looked on *me*, to take away my reproach among men (to take away the social stigma of being childless).

26 And in the sixth month the angel Gabriel (Noah; see note after verse 11 above) was sent from God unto a city of Galilee, named Nazareth,

27 To a virgin espoused (engaged, promised) to a man whose name was Joseph, of the house of David (who was a descendant of David); and the virgin's name was Mary.

Note: Being "espoused" (verse 27) was a much stronger commitment than engagement is in our day. An espoused couple was bound by covenants to each other even before their marriage and the espousal could not be broken off except through formal action similar to divorce.

28 And the angel came in unto her, and said, Hail, *thou that art* highly favoured, the Lord is with thee: blessed *art* thou among women.

29 And when she saw *him*, she was troubled at his saying, and cast in her mind what manner of salutation this should be (wondered what kind of a greeting this was).

30 And the angel said unto her, Fear not, Mary: for thou hast found favour with God.

31 And, behold, thou shalt conceive in thy womb, and bring forth a son, and shalt call his name JESUS.

32 He shall be great, and shall be called the Son of the Highest (the son of Heavenly Father): and the Lord God (Heavenly Father) shall give unto him the throne of his father (ancestor) David:

33 And he shall reign over the house of Jacob (house of Israel; descendents of Jacob) for ever; and of his kingdom there shall be no end.

34 Then said Mary unto the angel, How shall this be, seeing I know not a man (I am a virgin)?

35 And the angel answered and said unto her, The Holy Ghost shall come

upon thee, and the power of the Highest (the Father) shall overshadow thee: therefore also that holy thing (holy child) which shall be born of thee shall be called the Son of God.

36 And, behold, thy cousin Elisabeth, she hath also conceived a son in her old age: and this is the sixth month with her, who was called barren (childless; Elizabeth is six months pregnant).

37 For with God nothing shall be impossible.

38 And Mary said, Behold the handmaid of the Lord; be it unto me according to thy word. And the angel departed from her.

Note: There is probably not a greater example anywhere in scripture of humble faith and submission to the will of the Lord than the response given by Mary to the angel's announcement.

39 And Mary arose in those days, and went into the hill country with haste (hurried), into a city of Juda;

40 And entered into the house of Zacharias, and saluted (greeted) Elisabeth.

41 And it came to pass, that, when Elisabeth heard the salutation (greeting) of Mary, the babe leaped in her womb (little John the Baptist jumped inside of Elizabeth); and Elisabeth was filled with the Holy Ghost:

Note: Apostle Bruce R. McConkie teaches some comforting doctrine regarding stillborn children based on verse 41 above. It is as follows:

"[The babe leaped in her womb]. In this miraculous event the pattern is seen which a spirit follows in passing from his pre-existent first estate into mortality. The spirit enters the body at the time of quickening, months prior to the actual normal birth. The value and comfort attending a knowledge of this eternal truth is seen in connection with stillborn children. Since the spirit entered the body before birth, stillborn children will be resurrected and righteous parents shall enjoy their association in immortal glory." *Doctrinal New Testament Commentary*, Vol. 1, pages 84-85.

42 And she (Elizabeth) spake out with a loud voice, and said (note that Elizabeth will now exercise the gift of prophesy; see D&C 46:22), Blessed *art* thou (Mary) among women, and blessed is the fruit of thy womb (the child who will be born to you).

43 And whence is this to me, that the mother of my Lord should come to me (how do I rate the privilege of having the mother of the Son of God come visit me)?

44 For, lo, as soon as the voice of thy salutation (greeting) sounded in mine ears, the babe (John) leaped in my womb for joy.

45 And blessed is she that believed: for there shall be a performance of those things which were told her from the Lord (everything promised to you will be fulfilled).

Note: Just as Elizabeth was filled with the Spirit of prophecy, now Mary is given the gift of prophecy (see D&C 46:22) also. Her beautiful prophecies are recorded in verses 48-55.

46 And Mary said, My soul doth magnify (praise) the Lord,

47 And my spirit hath rejoiced (JST rejoiceth) in God my Saviour. (Her baby will be her Savior too.)

48 For he hath regarded (seen, considered) the low estate (humble condition) of his handmaiden (servant): for, behold, from henceforth all generations shall call me blessed (from now on, all people will know me and know how blessed I am).

49 For he that is mighty (God) hath done to me great things; and holy *is* his name.

50 And his mercy is on them that fear (respect and obey) him from generation to generation.

51 He hath shewed (demonstrated) strength with his arm (has shown his power); he hath scattered (punished) the proud in the imagination of their hearts (because of their pride).

52 He hath put down (humbled) the mighty from *their* seats (positions of power), and exalted them of low degree (blessed and lifted up the humble).

53 He hath filled the hungry (those who "hunger and thirst after righteousness"; see Matthew 5:6) with good things; and the rich (the rich who are prideful) he hath sent empty away.

54 He hath holpen (helped) his servant Israel (the covenant people), in remembrance of *his* mercy;

55 As he spake to our fathers (ancestors), to Abraham, and to his seed (posterity) for ever.

56 And Mary abode with her (stayed with Elizabeth) about three months, and returned to her own house.

57 Now Elisabeth's full time came that she should be delivered (the time came for her to have her baby); and she brought forth a son.

58 And her neighbours and her cousins heard how the Lord had shewed (showed) great mercy upon her; and they rejoiced with her.

59 And it came to pass, that on the eighth day they came to circumcise the child (John); and they called him Zacharias, after the name of his father.

60 And his mother answered (responded) and said, Not so; but he shall be called John (his name is not Zacharias; it is John!).

61 And they said unto her, There is none of thy kindred that is called by this name. (Why name him John? You have no relatives named John.)

62 And they made signs to his father, how he would have him called (asked Zacharias what the baby's name should be).

63 And he asked for a writing table, and wrote, saying, His name is John. And they marvelled all (were all surprised).

64 And his (Zacharias') mouth was opened immediately, and his tongue *loosed*, and he spake, and praised God.

65 And fear (awe) came on all that dwelt round about them: and all these sayings were noised abroad (were spread) throughout all the hill country of Judæa.

66 And all they that heard *them* laid *them* up in their hearts, saying, What manner of child shall this be (what kind of special child is John)! And the hand of the Lord was with him.

67 And his father Zacharias was filled with the Holy Ghost, and prophesied, saying,

68 Blessed *be* the Lord God of Israel (we are grateful to God); for he hath visited (come; helped) and redeemed his people,

Note: Zacharias is prophesying about the future as if it had already taken place. This is a common form of prophecy in the Bible.

69 And hath raised up an horn ("horn" was symbolic of safety, strength, and protection in Jewish culture) of salvation for us in the house of his servant David (among us descendants of David);

70 As he spake by the mouth of his holy prophets, which have been since the world began:

71 That we should be saved from our enemies, and from the hand of all that hate us;

72 To perform the mercy *promised* to our fathers (ancestors), and to remember (fulfil) his holy covenant;

73 The oath (promise) which he sware (promised) to our father (ancestor) Abraham,

74 That he would grant unto us, that we being delivered out of the hand of our enemies might serve him without fear (without fear of being persecuted),

75 In holiness and righteousness before him, all the days of our life.

76 And thou, child (little John the Baptist), shalt be called the prophet of the Highest (God): for thou shalt go before the face of (ahead of) the Lord (Jesus) to prepare his ways;

77 To give knowledge of salvation unto his people by the remission of their sins,

78 Through the tender mercy of our

God; whereby the dayspring (rising sun, dawn) from on high hath visited us (this is the dawn of a new day for us),

79 To give light to them that sit in darkness (spiritual darkness) and *in* the shadow of death, to guide our feet into the way of peace.

80 And the child (John) grew, and waxed strong (gained strength) in spirit, and was in (lived in) the deserts till the day of his shewing (beginning of his mission) unto Israel.

LUKE 2

1 AND it came to pass in those days, that there went out a decree from Caesar Augustus (the ruler over the Roman Empire from 31 BC to 14 AD), that all the world (everyone in the Roman Empire) should be taxed.

2 (*And* this taxing was first made when Cyrenius was governor of Syria.)

3 And all went to be taxed, every one into his own city.

Note: This was actually a process of registration or taking a census of all the people who were subject to the Roman government. Based on this census and registration, taxes were later assessed and then collected. The Roman government allowed people to register in the towns where they currently lived, but Jewish custom required that the Jews go to their home towns to register and be counted. Thus, Joseph and Mary had to travel from Nazareth to Bethlehem, a distance of some one hundred plus miles. See Talmage, *Jesus the Christ*, pages 91-92.)

4 And Joseph also went up from Galilee, out of the city of Nazareth, into Judæa, unto the city of David, which is called Bethlehem (thus fulfilling the prophecy in Micah 5:2 that Christ would be born in Bethlehem); (because he was of the house and lineage of David:)

5 To be taxed with Mary his espoused (married; see Matthew 1:24) wife, being great with child.

Note: Mary was indeed "great with child", for the Savior was born while she and Joseph were in Bethlehem. It is highly likely that Mary was in labor during the long journey from Nazareth to Bethlehem.

6 And so it was, that, while they were there, the days were accomplished that she should be delivered (the time came for her to have her baby).

7 And she brought forth her firstborn son, and wrapped him in swaddling clothes, and laid him in a manger; because there was no room for them in the inn (JST inns).

Note: "Swaddling clothes" were bands of cloth in which a new born baby was wrapped. The baby was placed diagonally upon a square piece of cloth. The bottom corner of the square cloth was folded up to cover the baby's feet, and the side corners were folded in to cover the baby's sides. Then bands of cloth were wound around the baby to make a warm, comfortable bundle.

8 And there were in the same country (in the Bethlehem area) shepherds abiding (staying) in the field, keeping watch over their flock by night.

9 And, lo, the angel of the Lord came upon them, and the glory of the Lord shone round about them: and they were sore (very) afraid.

10 And the angel said unto them, Fear not: for, behold, I bring you good tidings of great joy, which shall be to all people.

11 For unto you is born this day in the city of David (Bethlehem) a Saviour, which is Christ the Lord.

12 And this *shall be* a sign unto you; Ye shall find the babe wrapped in swaddling clothes, lying in a manger.

13 And suddenly there was with the angel a multitude of the heavenly host praising God, and saying,

14 Glory to God in the highest, and on earth peace, good will toward men.

15 And it came to pass, as the angels were gone away from them into heaven, the shepherds said one to another, Let us now go even unto Bethlehem, and see this thing which is come to pass (which has happened), which the Lord hath made known unto us.

16 And they came with haste (they hurried), and found Mary, and Joseph, and the babe lying in a manger.

17 And when they had seen *it*, they made known abroad the saying which was told them concerning this child (they told many others what the angel had told them about the birth of the Christ child).

18 And all they that heard *it* wondered (marveled and rejoiced) at those things which were told them by the shepherds.

19 But Mary kept all these things, and pondered *them* in her heart.

Note: It is hard to imagine the flood of tender feelings which must have been in Mary's heart, as she looked at her new born baby, realizing that this was the Son of God, the Promised Messiah, the Savior of the world. Yet, for the moment, it was her tiny, helpless baby boy, to hold and snuggle, to comfort and take care of, for her and Joseph to raise.

20 And the shepherds returned, glorifying and praising God for all the things that they had heard and seen, as it was told unto them.

21 And when eight days were accomplished (were up) for the circumcising (see Bible Dictionary, page 646) of the child, his name was called JESUS, which (who) was so named of (by) the angel before he was conceived in the womb.

Note: Both Joseph (Matthew 1:21) and Mary (Luke 1:31) were told by the angel Gabriel to name the baby "Jesus". Jesus the Greek form of Joshua or Jeshua, which means "God is help" or "savior". See Bible Dictionary, page 713.

22 And when the days of her purification (forty days; see Leviticus 12:1-4) according to the law of Moses were accomplished (over), they brought him (Jesus) to Jerusalem, to present *him* to the Lord (at the temple);

23 (As it is written in the law of the Lord [Exodus 13:2], Every male that openeth the womb shall be called holy [shall be dedicated] to the Lord;)

24 And to offer a sacrifice according to that which is said in the law of the Lord (Leviticus 12:6-8, A pair of turtledoves, or two young pigeons.

25 And, behold, there was a man in Jerusalem, whose name was Simeon; and the same man was just (very exact in living the gospel) and devout (very faithful), waiting for the consolation (redemption; see verse 38) of Israel: and the Holy Ghost was upon him.

26 And it was revealed unto him by the Holy Ghost, that he should not see death (die), before he had seen the Lord's Christ.

27 And he came by the Spirit (was prompted by the Holy Ghost to come) into the temple: and when the parents brought in the child Jesus, to do for him after the custom of the law (to present him in the temple as required),

28 Then took he him up in his arms (Simeon picked Jesus up), and blessed (praised) God, and said,

29 Lord, now lettest thou thy servant depart in peace, according to thy word (let me die in peace now, as you promised):

30 For mine eyes have seen thy salvation (I have seen the Savior who will bring salvation to us),

31 Which thou hast prepared before the face of all people (for everyone);

32 A light to lighten the Gentiles (non-israelites), and the glory of thy people Israel.

33 And Joseph and his mother marvelled at those things which were spoken of him (Jesus).

34 And Simeon blessed them, and said unto Mary his mother, Behold, this *child* is set (appointed) for the fall and rising again of many in Israel; and for a sign which shall be spoken

against (he will run into much opposition);

35 (Yea, a sword shall pierce through thy own soul also,) (JST "Yea, a spear shall pierce through him to the wounding of thine own soul also;")that the thoughts of many hearts may be revealed.

36 And there was one Anna, a prophetess, the daughter of Phanuel, of the tribe of Aser (Asher, one of the Twelve Tribes): she was of a great age, and had lived with an husband seven years from her virginity (for seven years, then he died);

37 And she *was* a widow of about fourscore and four years (was now about 84 years old), which departed not from the temple, but served *God* with fastings and prayers night and day.

38 And she coming in that instant (seeing Joseph and Mary with baby Jesus) gave thanks likewise unto the Lord, and spake of him (bore witness of Christ) to all them that looked for redemption in Jerusalem.

39 And when they had performed all things according to the law of the Lord (when they had performed all the required rituals in the temple, in conjunction with the birth of Jesus), they returned into Galilee, to their own city Nazareth.

40 And the child grew, and waxed strong in spirit, filled with wisdom: and the grace of God was upon him.

Note: In JST (the Joseph Smith Translation of the Bible) Matthew 2:24-26, we are given additional insight into the Savior's youth as follows: "And it came to pass that Jesus grew up with his brethren, and waxed strong, and waited upon the Lord for the time of his ministry to come. And he served under his father, and he spake not as other men, neither could he be taught; for he needed not that any man should teach him. And after many years, the hour of his ministry drew nigh."

41 Now his parents went to Jerusalem every year at the feast of the passover. (The Feast of the Passover, celebrated each year by the Jews in March or April, to commemorate the "passing over" of the angel of death over the Israelite homes in Egypt, when the firstborn of the Egyptians were killed. See Bible Dictionary, page 672.)

42 And when he was twelve years old, they went up to Jerusalem after the custom of the feast (as was the custom, to celebrate the Passover feast).

43 And when they had fulfilled the days (when they were finished), as they returned (to their home), the child Jesus tarried (stayed) behind in Jerusalem; and Joseph and his mother knew not *of it*.

44 But they, supposing him to have been in the company (they thought he was with friends or relatives in their traveling group), went a day's journey; and they sought (looked for) him among *their* kinsfolk (relatives) and acquaintance.

45 And when they found him not, they turned back again to Jerusalem, seeking him.

46 And it came to pass, that after three days they found him in the

temple, sitting in the midst of the doctors (teachers, men of high education), both hearing them, and asking them questions (JST changes this significantly: "and they were hearing him, and asking him questions".)

47 And all that heard him were astonished at his understanding and answers.

48 And when they (Joseph and Mary) saw him, they were amazed: and his mother said unto him, Son, why hast thou thus dealt with us (why did you give us such a scare)? behold, thy father and I have sought thee sorrowing (we have been looking for you, very worried!).

49 And he said unto them, How is it that ye sought me (why were you looking for me)? wist ye not (don't you know) that I must be about (be doing) my Father's (Heavenly Father's) business?

50 And they understood not the saying which he spake unto them. (Joseph and Mary didn't understand his explanation.)

51 And he went down (home) with them, and came to Nazareth, and was subject (obedient) unto them: but (JST "and") his mother kept all these sayings in her heart.

52 And Jesus increased in wisdom and stature, and in favour with God and man.

Note: When he was born, Jesus had the veil over his memory of the premortal life, just as all do. See Talmage, *Jesus the Christ*, page 111. President Joseph F. Smith said that Jesus did not know who he was as he lay in the cradle. See April 1901 General Conference. As

stated in verse 52, above, he gained wisdom as he grew. No doubt the veil was gone before he reached age twelve, for he knew who he was and felt the urgency of being about his Father's business, as expressed to Joseph and Mary in verse 49 above.

LUKE 3

1 NOW in the fifteenth year of the reign of Tiberius Cæsar (about 29 AD), Pontius Pilate being governor of Judæa, and Herod (Herod Antipas, son of Herod the Great) being tetrarch (ruler) of Galilee, and his brother Philip (another son of Herod the Great) tetrarch of Ituræa and of the region of Trachonitis, and Lysanias the tetrarch of Abilene,

2 Annas and Caiaphas being the high priests (the highest Jewish religious leaders), the word of God came unto John (the Baptist) the son of Zacharias in the wilderness (where he had been living since he was a small child).

3 And he came into all the country about (around) Jordan, preaching the baptism of repentance for the remission of sins;

4 As it is written in the book of the words of Esaias (Isaiah) the prophet, saying, The voice of one crying in the wilderness, Prepare ye the way of the Lord, make his paths straight.

Note: The JST adds a little over five verses here, which are left out of the Bible. They are as follows:

JST Luke 3:5-10.

5 For behold, and lo, he shall come, as it is written in the book of the prophets, to take away the sins of the world, and to bring salvation unto the

heathen nations, to gather together those who are lost, who are of the sheepfold of Israel;

6 Yea, even the dispersed and afflicted; and also to prepare the way, and make possible the preaching of the gospel unto the Gentiles;

7 And to be a light unto all who sit in darkness, unto the uttermost parts of the earth; to bring to pass the resurrection from the dead, and to ascend up on high, to dwell on the right hand of the Father,

8 Until the fullness of time, and the law and the testimony shall be sealed, and the keys of the kingdom shall be delivered up again unto the Father;

9 To administer justice unto all; to come down in judgment upon all, and to convince all the ungodly of their ungodly deeds, which they have committed; and all this in the day that he shall come;

10 For it is a day of power;

5 Every valley shall be filled, and every mountain and hill shall be brought low; and the crooked shall be made straight, and the rough ways *shall be* made smooth; (These things will happen at the Second Coming. See Isaiah 40:4, D&C 109:74.)

6 And all flesh shall see the salvation of God.

7 Then said he (John the Baptist) to the multitude that came forth to be baptized of him, O generation of vipers (offspring of poisonous snakes), who hath warned you to flee from the wrath to come (the punishments of God)?

Note: It can be puzzling why John scolds everyone in the crowd. But Matthew indicates that John's scolding was not directed at everyone, rather to some wicked Jewish religious leaders among the crowd. Matthew 3:7 tells us that John was speaking to the Pharisees and Sadducees among the people who had come out to listen to him. They were hypocritical religious leaders and insincere and deserved his scathing rebuke in verse 7 above. See note in this book after Matthew 3:7.

8 Bring forth therefore fruits (lives, deeds) worthy of repentance, and begin not to say within yourselves, We have Abraham to *our* father (we are related to Abraham, so we are automatically saved) JST "Abraham is our father; we have kept the commandments of God, and none can inherit the promises but the children of Abraham"): for I say unto you, That God is able of these stones to raise up children unto Abraham. (God could turn these rocks into descendants of Abraham. The message: You have to earn salvation yourselves. You will not get into heaven because Abraham was righteous and you descend from him.)

Note: It was strongly believed and taught among the Jews at this time that, because they were descendants of Abraham, they were automatically favored by God above all other people. In fact, they felt that they would be in the highest position in heaven, above any gentile even though the gentile converted to God and lived a righteous life.

9 And now also the axe (symbolic of the punishments from God) is laid unto

the root of the trees (symbolic of wicked people): every tree (person) therefore which bringeth not forth good fruit (does not live righteously) is hewn (cut) down, and cast into the fire (destroyed).

10 And the people asked him, saying, What shall we do then?

11 He answereth and saith unto them, He that hath two coats, let him impart (give) to him that hath none; and he that hath meat (food), let him do likewise.

12 Then came also publicans (tax collectors) to be baptized, and said unto him, Master, what shall we do?

13 And he said unto them, Exact no more (collect no more taxes) than that which is appointed you (than is legal; in other words, be honest with people).

14 And the soldiers likewise demanded of (asked) him, saying, And what shall we do? And he said unto them, Do violence to no man (don't make anyone bribe you to keep you from hurting them), neither accuse any falsely (if they won't pay you "protection money"); and be content with your wages.

Note: The explanations in parentheses in verse 14 above are taken from several other versions of the Bible which agree that Jesus is telling the soldiers to be satisfied with their wages and not to go around intimidating people and making them pay money to keep the soldiers from hurting them.

15 And as the people were in expectation (suspense), and all men mused in their hearts of John (were wondering about John), whether he were the Christ, or not;

16 John answered, saying unto *them* all, I indeed baptize you with water; but one mightier than I cometh (Christ), the latchet of whose shoes I am not worthy to unloose: he shall baptize you with the Holy Ghost and with fire:

Note: In the scriptures, the Holy Ghost is often compared to fire. The symbolism comes from the use of fire to purify gold. The gold ore is put in a container and fire is used to heat the container. The ore melts, the impurities float to the top, and the pure gold settles to the bottom. The impurities are then discarded and pure gold remains. Thus, the gold is purified by fire. Similarly, the Holy Ghost purifies us, if we allow it. Example: We commit sin. The Holy Ghost points it out and causes our conscience to burn within us. We respond by repenting. Thus we are purified, bit by bit.

17 Whose fan is in his hand (who is getting ready to harvest the earth), and he will throughly purge (cleanse) his floor (the threshing floor, symbolic of the earth), and will gather the wheat (the righteous) into his garner (barn, symbolic of heaven); but the chaff (the wicked) he will burn with fire unquenchable (and they won't be able to put the fire [punishment] out).

18 And many other things in his exhortation (warnings and teachings) preached he unto the people.

19 But Herod the tetrarch (Roman ruler for that part of Palestine), being reproved by him (scolded by John) for

(because of) Herodias his brother Philip's wife, and for all the evils which Herod had done,

20 Added yet this above all (added another huge sin to his collection), that he shut up (put) John in prison.

21 Now when all the people were baptized, it came to pass, that Jesus also being baptized (Matthew 3:13-17), and praying, the heaven was opened,

22 And the Holy Ghost descended in a bodily shape like a dove upon him (Jesus; John the Baptist saw the Holy Ghost come upon Christ-see Matthew 3:16 in this book), and a voice (the Father's voice) came from heaven, which said, Thou art my beloved Son; in thee I am well pleased.

Note: Next, in verses 23-38, Luke gives the genealogy of Jesus. Matthew gives a genealogy of Jesus in Matthew 1:1-17. Some people, who read these carefully, are confused because the two genealogies don't seem to agree completely. Matthew's account seems to be the royal lineage which would make Joseph, Mary's husband, the legal successor to the throne. He would have been king in Jerusalem if the Romans had not been in power. Thus, Jesus would be in line to be king of the Jews literally. According to Apostle James E. Talmage, Luke's genealogy of Christ seems to be the pedigree of Mary. For more on this, see Talmage, *Jesus the Christ*, pages 83-90.

23 And Jesus himself began to be about thirty years of age, being (as was supposed) the son of Joseph, which was *the son* of Heli,

24 Which was *the son* of Matthat, which was *the son* of Levi, which was *the son* of Melchi, which was *the son* of Janna, which was *the son* of Joseph,

25 Which was *the son* of Mattathias, which was *the son* of Amos, which was *the son* of Naum, which was *the son* of Esli, which was *the son* of Nagge,

26 Which was *the son* of Maath, which was *the son* of Mattathias, which was *the son* of Semei, which was *the son* of Joseph, which was *the son* of Juda,

27 Which was *the son* of Joanna, which was *the son* of Rhesa, which was *the son* of Zorobabel, which was *the son* of Salathiel, which was *the son* of Neri,

28 Which was *the son* of Melchi, which was *the son* of Addi, which was *the son* of Cosam, which was *the son* of Elmodam, which was *the son* of Er,

29 Which was *the son* of Jose, which was *the son* of Eliezer, which was *the son* of Jorim, which was *the son* of Matthat, which was *the son* of Levi,

30 Which was *the son* of Simeon, which was *the son* of Juda, which was *the son* of Joseph, which was *the son* of Jonan, which was *the son* of Eliakim,

31 Which was *the son* of Melea, which was *the son* of Menan, which was *the son* of Mattatha, which was *the son* of Nathan, which was *the son* of David,

32 Which was *the son* of Jesse, which was *the son* of Obed, which was *the son* of Booz (Boaz), which was *the son* of Salmon, which was *the son* of Naasson,

33 Which was *the son* of Aminadab, which was *the son* of Aram, which was *the son* of Esrom, which was *the son* of Phares, which was *the son* of Juda,

34 Which was *the son* of Jacob, which was *the son* of Isaac, which was *the son* of Abraham, which was *the son* of Thara, which was *the son* of Nachor,

35 Which was *the son* of Saruch, which was *the son* of Ragau, which was *the son* of Phalec, which was *the son* of Heber, which was *the son* of Sala,

36 Which was *the son* of Cainan, which was *the son* of Arphaxad, which was *the son* of Sem, which was *the son* of Noe (Noah), which was *the son* of Lamech,

37 Which was *the son* of Mathusala, which was *the son* of Enoch, which was *the son* of Jared, which was *the son* of Maleleel, which was *the son* of Cainan,

38 Which was *the son* of Enos, which was *the son* of Seth, which was *the son* of Adam, which was *the son* of God (JST "who was formed of God, and the first man on earth".)

LUKE 4

Note: Sometimes the question is asked as to whether or not the Holy Ghost was functioning during the time of the Savior's mortal mission. Based on Luke 4:1, next, the answer is definitely yes. For more on this subject, see Bible Dictionary, page 704. See also Acts 10:38.

1 AND Jesus being full of the Holy Ghost (after his baptism; see Matthew 3:13-17) returned from Jordan (the Jordan River east of Jerusalem), and was led by the Spirit into the wilderness,

Note: The Eighth Article of Faith states: "We believe the Bible to be the word of God as far as it is translated correctly;..." Verse 2, next, is an example of a place where the Bible is not correct. Jesus did not go into the wilderness to be tempted by Satan, rather he went into the wilderness, after his baptism, "to be with God" (JST Matthew 4:1).

2 Being forty days tempted of the devil (JST "And after forty days (after he had communed with God; see JST Matthew 4:2), the devil came unto him, to tempt him"). And in those days he did eat nothing: and when they (the forty days of fasting) were ended, he afterward hungered (was hungry).

3 And the devil said unto him, If thou be the Son of God, command this stone that it be made bread. (In other words, show me a miracle to prove you are Christ.)

4 And Jesus answered (responded to) him, saying, It is written (Deut. 8:3), That man shall not live by bread alone, but by every word of God.

5 And the devil, taking him up into an high mountain, shewed (showed) unto him all the kingdoms of the world in a moment of time. (Another place where the Bible is incorrect. The JST reads "And the Spirit taketh him up into a high mountain, and he beheld all the kingdoms of the world, in a moment of time.")

6 And the devil said unto him (JST "And the devil came unto him, and said unto him"), All this power will I

give thee, and the glory of them (the kingdoms of the world): for that is (JST "they are") delivered unto me (they are mine; see Revelation 13 heading); and to whomsoever I will I give it.

7 If thou therefore wilt worship me, all shall be thine.

8 And Jesus answered and said unto him, Get thee behind me, Satan: for it is written, Thou shalt worship the Lord thy God, and him only shalt thou serve.

9 And he brought him to Jerusalem (JST "And the Spirit brought him to Jerusalem"), and set him on a pinnacle of the temple, (JST "and the devil came unto him,") and said unto him, If thou be the Son of God, cast thyself down from hence (here):

10 For it is written, He shall give his angels charge (responsibility) over thee, to keep thee:

11 And in *their* hands they shall bear thee up, lest at any time thou dash (strike) thy foot against a stone.

12 And Jesus answering (responding) said unto him, It is said, Thou shalt not tempt the Lord thy God.

13 And when the devil had ended all the temptation, he departed from him for a season.

Note: We see three major forms of temptations plus a fourth in the verses above. First, temptation to gratify physical appetites as tempted by Satan. Second, the temptation for worldly power and glory. Third, the temptation to challenge God to make good on his promises, as if there were some doubt about how good his word is. Fourth, the phrase "If thou are the Son of God". This, for some of us, could be the most difficult temptation of all. Giving in to the challenge to inappropriately attempt to defend our own ego or position, would be giving in to pride.

14 And Jesus returned in the power of the Spirit into Galilee (an area in northern Israel): and there went out a fame of him (he became famous) through all the region round about.

15 And he taught in their synagogues (Jewish church buildings), being glorified of all (everybody said he was great!).

16 And he came to Nazareth, where he had been brought up (his home town): and, as his custom was, he went into the synagogue on the sabbath day, and stood up for to read.

17 And there was delivered unto him (brought to him at his request) the book of the prophet Esaias (Isaiah). And when he had opened the book, he found the place where it was written (Isaiah 61:1),

18 The Spirit of the Lord *is* upon me (Christ), because he hath anointed (called) me to preach the gospel to the poor; he hath sent me to heal the brokenhearted, to preach deliverance (remission of sins) to the captives (those under the bondage of sin), and recovering of sight to the blind (spiritually as well as physically), to set at liberty (redeem) them that are bruised (by sins),

19 To preach the acceptable year of the Lord (the time designated by the Father for Jesus to perform his mission on earth, as a mortal; see McConkie, *Doctrinal   New   Testament*

Commentary, Vol. 1, page 161).

20 And he closed the book, and he gave it again to the minister, and sat down. And the eyes of all them that were in the synagogue were fastened on him.

21 And he began to say unto them, This day is this scripture fulfilled in your ears. (In other words, I am the fulfillment of this prophecy of Isaiah.)

22 And all bare him witness (spoke well of him [for a few minutes]), and wondered (marveled) at the gracious words which proceeded out of his mouth. And they said (to each other), Is not this Joseph's son?

Note: The men of the synagogue, who heard Jesus claim to be the Messiah, after reading the passage from Isaiah, now begin to have doubts. They have heard of the many miracles and things a man named Jesus has been doing throughout the country. Now, when they see that he is the Jesus who grew up in their town, they say, in effect, "Now wait a minute. Isn't this Jesus who is Joseph the carpenter's son? We know his family. He grew up here. He is just a common man, one of us. How can he possibly think he is the Messiah?"

23 And he said unto them, Ye will surely say unto me this proverb (old saying), Physician, heal thyself: whatsoever we have heard done in Capernaum, do also here in thy country. (Prove that you are something special by doing the same miracles you have done elsewhere.)

24 And he said, Verily I say unto you, No prophet is accepted in his own country.

25 But I tell you of a truth, many widows were in Israel in the days of Elias (Elijah), when the heaven was shut up three years and six months, when great famine was throughout all the land;

26 But unto none of them was Elias (Elijah) sent, save (except) unto Sarepta, *a city* of Sidon, unto a woman *that* was a widow.

27 And many lepers (people with leprosy) were in Israel in the time of Eliseus (Elisha) the prophet; and none of them was cleansed, saving (except) Naaman the Syrian (2 Kings 5:14).

Note: The point Jesus is making to these men of his hometown seems to be that it wasn't necessary for prophets such as Elijah and Elisha to heal every person in the land or perform the same miracles for everyone in order to be accepted as a prophet sent from God. So why should it be different with Jesus? Why should he be required to perform the same miracles for the people of Nazareth as for others, in order to be accepted by them. Couldn't they exercise faith in what had been done elsewhere?

28 And all they in the synagogue, when they heard these things, were filled with wrath (were very angry),

29 And rose up, and thrust him out of the city, and led him unto the brow (cliff) of the hill whereon their city was built, that they might cast him down headlong (headfirst).

30 But he passing through the midst of them went his way,

Note: It will be interesting to get the rest of the details as to what happened here. This was a great miracle, if these wicked and hardhearted men would pay attention to it.

31 And came down to Capernaum, a city of Galilee, and taught them on the sabbath days.

32 And they were astonished at his doctrine: for his word was with power (he taught with power and authority).

33 And in the synagogue there was a man, which had a spirit of an unclean devil (was possessed by evil spirits), and cried out with a loud voice,

34 Saying, Let us alone; what have we to do with thee, *thou* Jesus of Nazareth? art thou come to destroy us? I know thee who thou art; the Holy One of God. (One of the evil spirits bears witness of Christ.)

35 And Jesus rebuked (sharply scolded) him, saying, Hold thy peace (be quiet), and come out of him. And when the devil had thrown him (tossed him around) in the midst, he came out of him, and hurt him not (no more).

36 And they were all amazed, and spake (spoke) among themselves, saying, What a word is this! for with authority and power he commandeth the unclean spirits, and they come out.

37 And the fame of him went out into every place of the country round about.

38 And he arose out of (left) the synagogue, and entered into Simon's (Peter's) house. And Simon's wife's mother (Peter's mother-in-law) was taken (sick) with a great fever; and they besought him for her (asked Jesus to heal her).

39 And he stood over her, and rebuked the fever (commanded the fever to leave); and it left her: and immediately she arose and ministered unto them.

Note: The fact that Peter was married is significant. Some religions believe that celibacy (intentionally not getting married) is the highest form of dedication to God. This is not true. Living worthily of exaltation in a family unit forever is the highest form of dedication to God.

40 Now when the sun was setting, all they that had any sick with divers (various) diseases brought them unto him; and he laid his hands on every one of them, and healed them.

41 And devils (evil spirits) also came out of many, crying out, and saying, Thou art Christ the Son of God. And he rebuking *them* suffered them not to speak (commanded them not to bear witness of him): for they knew that he was Christ.

Note: The veil, which erases our memory of our premortal life, is not upon Satan and the one third of premortal spirits who were cast out of heaven (Revelation 12:4) and down to the earth. They knew Christ in premortality and still recognize him here.

42 And when it was day (the next day), he departed and went into a desert place: and the people sought (found) him, and came unto him, and stayed him (stopped him), that he should not depart from them.

43 And he said unto them, I must preach the kingdom of God (the gospel) to other cities also: for there-

fore (that is the reason) am I sent.

44 And he preached in the synagogues (Jewish church buildings) of Galilee.

LUKE 5

1 AND it came to pass, that, as the people pressed upon him (crowded and pushed against him) to hear the word of God, he stood by the lake of Gennesaret (the Sea of Galilee),

2 And saw two ships standing by the lake: but the fishermen were gone out of them, and were washing *their* nets.

3 And he entered into one of the ships, which was Simon's (which belonged to Peter), and prayed (asked) him that he would thrust out a little from the land. And he sat down, and taught the people out of the ship.

4 Now when he had left speaking, he said unto Simon (Peter), Launch out into the deep, and let down your nets for a draught (a catch of fish).

5 And Simon answering (in response) said unto him, Master, we have toiled (worked hard fishing) all the night, and have taken nothing: nevertheless at thy word I will let down the net.

6 And when they had this done, they inclosed a great multitude of fishes: and their net brake (started to break; see Luke 5:6, footnote 6a).

7 And they beckoned (waved) unto *their* partners, which were in the other ship, that they should come and help them. And they came, and filled both the ships, so that they began to sink.

Note: There is beautiful symbolism here. As Peter and others follow the Savior's instructions, in faith, they have great success in catching fish. Symbolically, as Peter and the others follow Christ, he will make them "fishers of men", and they will have a large "catch" of converts. See end of verse 10 below.

8 When Simon Peter saw *it*, he fell down at Jesus' knees (very humble), saying, Depart from me; for I am a sinful man, O Lord. (I am not worthy to be in thy presence.)

9 For he was astonished, and all that were with him, at the draught (catch) of the fishes which they had taken:

10 And so *was* (were) also James, and John, the sons of Zebedee, which were partners with Simon (Peter). And Jesus said unto Simon, Fear not; from henceforth (from now on) thou shalt catch men.

11 And when they had brought their ships to land, they forsook all (left everything behind), and followed him.

12 And it came to pass, when he was in a certain city, behold a man full of leprosy: who seeing Jesus fell on *his* face (a cultural way of showing great humility), and besought (begged) him, saying, Lord, if thou wilt (if you are willing), thou canst make me clean. (This sick man has great faith in Christ.)

Note: Leprosy was one of the most dreaded diseases of the time. It was greatly feared by others, and a person who had the disease was required by law to warn others to stay clear so they would not accidently touch the leper and risk catching the disease. Lepers were social outcasts. The disease often caused fingers and toes to rot away.

See "Leper" and "Leprosy" in Bible Dictionary, pages 723-724.

13 And he (Jesus) put forth his hand, and touched him, saying, I will: be thou clean. And immediately the leprosy departed from him.

14 And he charged (instructed) him to tell no man: but go, and shew thyself to the priest (as commanded in Leviticus 14:2), and offer for thy cleansing, according as Moses commanded, for a testimony unto them.

15 But so much the more went there a fame abroad of him (this healing caused Jesus to become even more famous): and great multitudes came together to hear, and to be healed by him of their infirmities (sicknesses).

16 And he withdrew himself into the wilderness, and prayed.

17 And it came to pass on a certain day, as he was teaching, that there were Pharisees (religious leaders of the Jews) and doctors of the law (scribes [see verse 21], religious leaders who interpreted how to live the religious laws of the Jews) sitting by (watching), which were come out of every town of Galilee, and Judæa, and Jerusalem (who had come from all over, worried about Jesus and his growing popularity): and the power of the Lord was present to heal them (the people from the area who had come to be healed or brought their sick to be healed).

18 And, behold, men brought in a bed a man (carried a man on a bed) which was taken (sick) with a palsy: and they sought *means* to (tried to figure out how to) bring him in, and to lay *him* before (in front of) him (Jesus).

19 And when they could not find by what way they might bring him in (when they couldn't figure out a way) because of the multitude (the crowd), they went upon the housetop, and let him (the sick man in the bed) down through the tiling (roof) with *his* couch into the midst before (in front of) Jesus.

20 And when he (Jesus) saw their faith, he said unto him, Man, thy sins are forgiven thee.

21 And the scribes and the Pharisees (religious leaders who were trying to trap Jesus) began to reason (discuss among themselves), saying, Who is this which speaketh blasphemies? Who can forgive sins, but God alone?

Note: "Blasphemy", showing disrespect for God, mocking God etc. was a violation of law among the Jews which was punishable by death.

22 But when Jesus perceived (read) their thoughts, he answering said (responded, saying) unto them, What reason ye in your hearts (why are such thoughts in your hearts)?

23 Whether (which) is easier, to say, Thy sins be forgiven thee; or to say, Rise up and walk?

Note: The Savior is saying, in effect, "If I am a fraud, and imposter, as you say I am, which would be safer for me to say, 'Your sins are forgiven.' or 'Rise up and walk.'? Which would be less likely to expose me as a fake?" The obvious answer is "Your sins are forgiven." since there is no immediate way of telling whether or not that happens to the sick man. But as Jesus says "Rise up and walk.", there will be immediate evidence as to whether or not he is an imposter. This creates a very tense situation. The JST adds to verse 23 as follows: "Does it require more power to forgive sins than to make the sick rise up and walk?"

24 But that ye may know that the Son of man (I, the Son of Man, the Son of God; the Son of Man of Holiness [the Father]-see Moses 6:57) hath power upon earth to forgive sins, (he said unto the sick of the palsy,) I say unto thee, Arise, and take up thy couch (bed), and go into thine house.

25 And immediately he rose up before them, and took up that whereon he lay (his bed), and departed to his own house, glorifying (praising) God.

26 And they were all amazed, and they glorified God, and were filled with fear, saying, We have seen strange things to day.

27 And after these things he (Jesus) went forth, and saw a publican (tax collector), named Levi (Matthew), sitting at the receipt of custom (where they collected taxes): and he (Jesus) said unto him, Follow me.

28 And he left all, rose up, and followed him.

29 And Levi (Matthew) made him (Jesus) a great feast in his own house: and there was a great company of publicans (tax collectors) and of others that sat down with them.

30 But their scribes and Pharisees (the Jewish religious leaders who are trying to trap Jesus) murmured (grumbled) against his disciples (didn't come directly to Jesus), saying, Why do ye eat and drink with publicans and sinners?

Note: These hypocritical Jewish religious leaders had strict rules for themselves to avoid associating with publicans and sinners. They considered it a matter of personal righteousness not to do so, and considered that Jesus and his disciples were exposing their sinful natures by eating and associating with such people.

31 And Jesus answering (responding) said unto them (the Pharisees and scribes), They that are whole (well) need not a physician; but they that are sick. (If I am going to help people, I must associate with them.)

32 I (the Son of God) came not to call the righteous, but sinners to repentance.

Note: Above, Jesus claims very openly to be the Son of God, with power to call sinners to repentance and to forgive sins. This had to be very frustrating to the Pharisees and scribes!

33 And they (the Pharisees and scribes)said unto him (Jesus), Why do the disciples of John (followers of John the Baptist) fast often, and make prayers, and likewise *the disciples* of the Pharisees; but thine eat and drink? (In other words, why don't you and your disciples follow the rules we do?)

Note: John the Baptist is in prison at this time and is soon to be beheaded at Herod's command.

34 And he said unto them, Can ye make the children of the bridechamber fast, while the bridegroom is with them?

35 But the days will come, when the bridegroom shall be taken away from them, and then shall they fast in those days.

Note: Understanding a bit of Jewish culture will help with the last verse. Wedding imagery is involved. Jesus is the bridegroom, or groom, as we would say it. Faithful followers are the bride. "Bridechamber" would be the place where the wedding feast is held and, symbolically, would be the land of Israel where the Savior was performing His mortal mission. While the groom and the bride are together, much celebrating and feasting–hearing and understanding the Savior's teach-ings–would take place. It would not make sense to mourn and fast at this time. But, when the Savior is crucified and taken from them, the "children of the bridechamber", the faithful saints, will mourn and fast.

Note: Next, Jesus will teach that people who are set in their ways do not usually accept new ideas, in this case, the true gospel.

36 And he spake also a parable unto them; No man putteth (attaches) a piece of a new garment (cloth) upon an old (symbolic of putting the true gospel into old lifestyles); if otherwise, then both the new maketh a rent (tear), and the piece that was *taken* out of the new agreeth not with the old (is not compatible with the old piece).

37 And no man putteth new wine (new gospel) into old bottles (scribes and Pharisees, who are set in their evil ways); else the new wine will burst the bottles, and be spilled, and the bottles shall perish.

38 But new wine must be put into new bottles; and both are preserved.

Note: Leather bottles were used to store wine. Over time, the leather became hard and inflexible. If new wine were put in old leather bottles, the bottles would break because they could not stretch with the pressure generated by fermentation processes in the new wine.

39 No man also having drunk old *wine* straightway (immediately) desireth new: for he saith, The old is better. (People who are set in their ways, don't like new gospel, the true gospel.)

LUKE 6

1 AND it came to pass on the second sabbath after the first, that he went through the corn (grain) fields; and his disciples plucked the ears of corn (grain), and did eat, rubbing them in their hands.

Note: The Jews had developed thou-sands of laws over the years for observing the Sabbath. One of these laws was that it was forbidden to rub heads of wheat, barley or whatever grain together on the Sabbath because it was considered to be threshing grain (separating the grain kernels from the chaff) which violated the Sabbath.

2 And certain of the Pharisees (religious leaders of the Jews) said unto them, Why do ye that which is not lawful (legal) to do on the sabbath days?

3 And Jesus answering them said, Have ye not read so much as this, what David did, when himself was an hungred (hungry), and they (his soldiers) which were with him;

4 How he went into the house of God, and did take and eat the shewbread (sacred bread used in the tabernacle and temple), and gave also to them that were with him; which it is not lawful to eat but for the priests alone? (Only the priests were allowed to eat the shewbread.)

5 And he (Jesus) said unto them (the Pharisees), That the Son of man (Jesus; Son of Man-see Moses 6:57)is Lord also of the sabbath. (I am the God of the Sabbath.)

6 And it came to pass also on another sabbath, that he entered into the synagogue (Jewish church building) and taught: and there was a man whose right hand was withered (crippled).

7 And the scribes and Pharisees (religious leaders) watched him, whether (to see if) he would heal on the sabbath day; that they might find an accusation against him (that they might get him arrested).

8 But he knew their thoughts, and said to the man which had the withered hand, Rise up, and stand forth in the midst (of the synagogue). And he arose and stood forth.

9 Then said Jesus unto them (the scribes and Pharisees in verse 7), I will ask you one thing; Is it lawful (legal) on the sabbath days to do good, or to do evil? to save life, or to destroy *it*?

10 And looking round about upon them all, he said unto the man, Stretch forth thy hand. And he did so: and his hand was restored whole as the other.

Note: This must have been an intense scene. Just imagine how quiet it must have become, as Jesus slowly looked around at all of these wicked religious leaders and hypocrites who had gathered to trap him, then said to the man with the crippled hand "Stretch forth thy hand." And then the hand was healed.

11 And they (the scribes and Pharisees) were filled with madness (anger); and communed (discussed) one with another what they might do to Jesus.

12 And it came to pass in those days, that he went out into a mountain to pray, and continued all night in prayer to God.

Note: Next, Jesus will choose twelve of his disciples (followers) and call them to be the Twelve Apostles.

13 And when it was day, he called *unto him* his disciples: and of them he chose twelve, whom also he named apostles;

14 Simon, (whom he also named Peter,) and Andrew his brother, James and John, Philip and Bartholomew,

15 Matthew and Thomas, James the *son* of Alphæus, and Simon called Zelotes,

16 And Judas *the brother* of James, and Judas Iscariot, which also was the traitor (who would betray Jesus).

17 And he came down (from the mountain) with them, and stood in the plain, and the company of his disciples, and a great multitude of people out of all Judæa and Jerusalem, and from the sea coast of Tyre and Sidon, which came to hear him, and to be healed of their diseases;

18 And they that were vexed (troubled, possessed) with unclean spirits: and they were healed.

19 And the whole multitude sought to (tried to) touch him: for there went virtue (power) out of him, and healed *them* all.

Note: Luke next records what is often referred to as "the Sermon on the Plain". Scholars do not agree as to whether or not the Sermon on the Plain is the same as the Sermon on the Mount (Matthew 5, 6 and 7). Either way, we are given much help in understanding these teachings of the Savior by reading Third Nephi, chapters 12-14. In 3 Nephi 12:1-2, it is clear that the Sermon on the Mount was given to members of the Church and was designed to help them obtain the kingdom of heaven, in other words, celestial glory. The notes in parentheses in the next few verses demonstrate one possible way in which this sermon teaches members how to obtain celestial glory.

20 And he lifted up his eyes on his disciples, and said, Blessed *be ye* poor (you poor in spirituality, who repent): for yours is (you will obtain) the kingdom of God (celestial glory).

21 Blessed *are ye* that hunger (for personal righteousness) now: for ye shall be filled (with the Holy Ghost). Blessed *are ye* that weep now (for your sins, then repent): for ye shall laugh.

22 Blessed are ye, when men shall hate you (because you are doing what is right), and when they shall separate you (reject you) *from their company*, and shall reproach (insult, criticize) *you*, and cast out your name as evil (ruin your reputation), for the Son of man's (the Savior's) sake.

23 Rejoice ye (be happy) in that day (when such things happen to you), and leap for joy: for, behold, your reward *is* great in heaven (it will all be worth it when you get to celestial glory): for in the like manner (in the same way) did their fathers unto the prophets (their ancestors persecuted the prophets).

24 But woe unto you that are rich (the wicked who are rich)! for ye have received your consolation (your reward is your money here on earth, but it won't get you to celestial glory).

25 Woe unto you that are full (think you don't need the gospel)! for ye shall hunger (wish you had repented). Woe unto you that laugh now (at righteous people, and at the gospel)! for ye shall mourn and weep (in the next life).

26 Woe unto you (the wicked in verses 24-25), when all (wicked) men shall speak well of you (because you fit right in with them and their wicked lifestyle)! for so did their fathers (their ancestors) to the false prophets.

27 But I say unto you which hear (pay attention to my teachings), Love your enemies, do good to them which hate you,

28 Bless them that curse you, and pray for them which despitefully use (abuse) you.

29 And unto him that smiteth thee (hits you) on the *one* cheek offer also the other; and him that taketh away thy cloke forbid not *to take thy* coat also. (JST "And unto him who smiteth thee on the cheek, offer also the other; or, in other words, it is better to offer the other, than to revile again. And him who taketh away thy cloak, forbid not to take thy coat also. For it is better that thou suffer thine enemy to take these things, than to contend with him. Verily I say unto you, Your heavenly Father who seeth in secret, shall bring that wicked one into judgment.")

30 Give to every man that asketh of thee; and of him that taketh away thy goods ask *them* not again.

Note: A major message taught in verses 27-30 is that we must develop self control, character strength etc. to the point that our personalities and dispositions are not dependent upon how others are treating us.

31 And as ye would that men should do to you, do ye also to them likewise. (In other words, treat others the way you would like them to treat you. This is known as "the Golden Rule".)

32 For if ye love them (JST "them only") which love you, what thank have ye (JST "what reward have you")? for sinners also love those that love them.

33 And if ye do good to them which do good to you, what thank have ye? for sinners also do even the same.

Note: One important message we can get from verses 32-33 above is that if we love "only" (see JST in verse 32)

people who love us and are mean to everyone else and if we only do good to people who are nice to us, that makes us like most everybody else and does not build Christlike qualities in us.

34 And if ye lend *to them* of whom ye hope to receive, what thank (JST "reward") have ye? for sinners also lend to sinners, to receive as much again. (In other words, you are not truly generous if you only lend things to people in situations where you will profit by it.)

35 But love ye your enemies, and do good, and lend, hoping for nothing again; and your reward shall be great (because you are then truly loving and truly generous), and ye shall be the children of the Highest (you will obtain celestial glory and live in the presence of the Father): for he is kind unto the unthankful and to the evil.

Note: Remember, as mentioned in the note following verse 19 above, that this sermon is directed to baptized members of the Church who want to be forgiven of their sins (see 3 Nephi 12:2). The next verses contain more teachings about how to become Christlike and obtain celestial glory.

36 Be ye therefore merciful, as your Father also is merciful.

37 Judge not (JST Matthew 7:2 "judge not unrighteously"), and ye shall not be judged: condemn not (judge someone worthy of being damned by God and hoping they don't get a second chance), and ye shall not be condemned: forgive, and ye shall be

forgiven:

38 Give (be generous, kind and forgiving), and it (your reward) shall be given unto you; good measure, pressed down, and shaken together, and running over (overflowing), shall men give into your bosom. For with the same measure that ye mete (give out) withal (how you treat others) it shall be measured to you again (given back to you by God).

Note: The phrase "pressed down, and shaken together, and running over" in verse 38 above, calls to mind someone cooking a delicious meal, who takes ingredients and packs them tightly in the measuring cup, shakes it to make sure there is no dead space, and then adds more ingredients until the cup runs over. Symbolically, the Lord will pack all kinds of rewards in the "cup" of the righteous so that their "cup runneth over" (Psalm 23:5) with blessings and eternal rewards.

39 And he spake a parable (a story designed to teach a specific point) unto them, Can the blind lead the blind? shall they not both fall into the ditch? (Can the spiritually blind lead other spiritually blind people successfully?)

40 The disciple (follower; student) is not above (better than) his master (teacher): but every one that is perfect (has been perfectly prepared) shall be (become) as his master.

41 And why beholdest thou (why do you look at) the mote (speck; symbolical of a little imperfection) that is in thy brother's eye, but perceivest not (don't notice) the beam (huge roof beam) that is in thine own eye? (Why

are you so critical of little imperfections in others but can't see your own huge imperfections?)

42 Either (or else) how canst thou say to thy brother, Brother, let me pull out the mote that is in thine eye (let me fix your imperfections), when thou thyself beholdest not the beam that is in thine own eye (when you are so imperfect yourself)? Thou hypocrite, cast out first the beam out of thine own eye (straighten out your own life first), and then shalt thou see clearly to pull out the mote that is in thy brother's eye (then you will be able to help others effectively).

Note: The imagery of a small chip of wood and a huge beam of wood is intentional exaggeration by the Master to help us see the importance of not criticizing others when we are so imperfect outselves.

43 For a good tree (symbolic of good people) bringeth not forth corrupt fruit (a wicked life); neither doth a corrupt tree (a wicked person) bring forth good fruit (a good life).

44 For every tree (person) is known by his own fruit (the kind of life he or she leads). For of thorns (from thorn bushes) men do not gather (harvest) figs, nor of a bramble bush gather they (harvest) grapes. (In other words, you can't expect a righteous reward on Judgment Day if you have lived a wicked life, including the hypocrisy of continuously judging others harshly.)

45 A good man out of the good treasure of his heart bringeth forth that which is good; and an evil man out of the evil treasure of his heart bringeth

forth that which is evil: for of the abundance of the heart his mouth speaketh. (The true feelings and attitudes of our heart show up in the things we say about others.)

46 And why call ye me, Lord, Lord, and do not the things which I say? (Why do you pretend to follow me when you don't do what I say?)

47 Whosoever cometh to me, and heareth my sayings, and doeth them, I will shew (show) you to whom he is like:

48 He is like a man which built an house, and digged deep, and laid the foundation on a rock: and when the flood arose, the stream beat vehemently (fiercely) upon that house, and could not shake it: for it was founded upon a rock. (Symbolic of a life built upon Christ and his teachings, which cannot be destroyed by life's troubles.)

49 But he that heareth (the Savior's teachings), and doeth not (does not obey them), is like a man that without a foundation built an house upon the earth; against which the stream did beat vehemently (violently), and immediately it fell; and the ruin of that house was great. (Much spiritual destruction came upon that person.)

LUKE 7

1 NOW when he had ended all his sayings in the audience of the people, he entered into Capernaum.

2 And a certain centurion's servant, who was dear unto him, was sick, and ready to die. (A centurion was a Roman soldier in charge of one hundred soldiers.)

3 And when he heard of Jesus, he sent unto him the elders of the Jews, beseeching (asking) him that he would come and heal his servant.

4 And when they came to Jesus, they besought him instantly (asked Jesus right away to heal the centurion's servant), saying, That he (the Roman centurion) was worthy for whom he (Jesus) should do this:

5 For he (the centurion) loveth our nation, and he hath built us a synagogue (a church).

6 Then Jesus went with them. And when he was now not far from the house, the centurion sent friends to him, saying unto him, Lord, trouble not thyself: for I am not worthy that thou shouldest enter under my roof (enter into my house):

7 Wherefore neither thought I myself worthy to come unto thee (I didn't consider myself worthy to come to you so I sent friends): but say in a word (give the word), and my servant shall be healed.

8 For I also (like you) am a man set under authority (who has authority) , having under me soldiers, and I say unto one, Go, and he goeth; and to another, Come, and he cometh; and to my servant, Do this, and he doeth it.

9 When Jesus heard these things, he marvelled at him, and turned him about (turned around), and said unto the people that followed him, I say unto you, I have not found so great faith, no, not in Israel.

10 And they (the centurion's friends) that were sent (to Jesus), returning to the house, found the servant whole (healed) that had been sick.

11 And it came to pass the day after, that he (Jesus) went into a city called Nain (a city in Galilee); and many of

his disciples went with him, and much people (large crowds of people).

12 Now when he came nigh (near) to the gate of the city, behold, there was a dead man carried out, the only son of his mother, and she was a widow: and much people of the city was with her.

13 And when the Lord saw her, he had compassion on her, and said unto her, Weep not.

14 And he came and touched the bier (the board being used to carry the dead man): and they (the pallbearers) that bare (carried) *him* stood still. And he said, Young man, I say unto thee, Arise.

15 And he that was dead sat up, and began to speak. And he delivered him (turned him over) to his mother.

16 And there came a fear on all: and they glorified (praised) God, saying, That a great prophet (Jesus) is risen up among us; and, That God hath visited (blessed) his people.

17 And this rumour (news) of him (Jesus) went forth throughout all Judæa (the southern area of the Holy Land), and throughout all the region round about.

18 And the disciples of John (John the Baptist) shewed (showed) him (told him) of all these things (about Jesus).

19 And John (the Baptist) calling *unto him* two of his disciples sent *them* to Jesus, saying, Art thou he that should come (are you the Messiah)? or look we for another?

20 When the men (John the Baptist's disciples) were come unto him (Jesus), they said, John Baptist hath sent us unto thee, saying, Art thou he that should come? or look we for another?

21 And in that same hour he cured many of *their* (The people around Jesus at the time) infirmities and plagues (diseases), and of evil spirits; and unto many *that were* blind he gave sight.

Note: In verse 21, as well as in many verses of the King James version of the Bible (the one our Church uses), you will see words written in *italics*. Italics means that the scholars who prepared this version of the Bible didn't know the exact word or phrase that should be used in the translation. They wanted the reader to know that they didn't know, so they had the questionable words and phrases printed in italics. They were being very honest with us. This version of the Bible was prepared under the sponsorship of King James of England and was published in 1611 AD.

22 Then Jesus answering (answering the question John the Baptist's disciples asked in verse 20 above) said unto them, Go your way, and tell John what things ye have seen and heard; how that the blind see, the lame walk, the lepers are cleansed, the deaf hear, the dead are raised, to the poor the gospel is preached.

Note: Every time you read of the miraculous healings performed by the Savior, you may wish to consider them symbolic of his ability to heal all our spiritual "diseases", including spiritual blindness, failure to walk forward into the light of the gospel, grievous sins, spiritual deafness, spiritual death etc.

23 And blessed is he, whosoever shall not be offended in me (ashamed to accept Christ and his teachings).

24 And when the messengers of John were departed (to report back to John the Baptist), he (Christ) began to speak unto the people concerning John (the Baptist), What went ye out into the wilderness for to see? A reed shaken with the wind (a timid fellow, worried about what people think)?

25 But what went ye out for to see? A man clothed in soft raiment (high fashion clothing)? Behold, they which are gorgeously apparelled (dressed in expensive clothes), and live delicately (an easy life), are in kings' courts.

26 But what went ye out for to see? A prophet? Yea, I say unto you, and much more than a prophet.

27 This is he, of whom it is written (prophesied), Behold, I send my messenger before thy face, which shall prepare thy way before thee (Christ).

28 For I say unto you, Among those that are born of women there is not a greater prophet than John the Baptist: but he (Christ) that is least in the kingdom of God is greater than he (John the Baptist).

Note: Verse 28, above, can be a bit confusing, but the Prophet Joseph Smith explains it to us. He tells us that John the Baptist is the greatest prophet, born of woman, but that He, Christ, who is considered by the Jews to be the least in the kingdom, is above John the Baptist. See *Teachings of the Prophet Joseph Smith*, pages 275-276.

29 And all the people that heard him, and the publicans (even the tax collec-

tors), justified God (said that God's way is right), being baptized with the baptism of John (having been baptized by John).

30 But the Pharisees and lawyers (religious leaders among the Jews) rejected the counsel of God against (for) themselves, being not baptized of him (refused to be baptized by John).

31 And the Lord (Jesus) said, Whereunto then shall I liken the men of this generation? and to what are they like? (To what shall I compare the wicked of this day?)

32 They are like unto children sitting in the marketplace, and calling one to another, and saying, We have piped unto you (played the flute for you), and ye have not danced; we have mourned (sung a sad song) to you, and ye have not wept.

33 For John the Baptist came neither eating bread nor drinking wine; and ye say, He hath a devil.

34 The Son of man (Jesus) is come eating and drinking; and ye say, Behold a gluttonous man, and a winebibber (one who drinks too much wine), a friend of publicans and sinners!

Note: The main point of verses 31-34 is this: Jesus is telling them (the Pharisees and lawyers in verse 30) that they are like children who are never satisfied. Just as the children who wouldn't dance to happy flute music, neither would they be affected by a sad song, so also are the Pharisees and lawyers. They criticize John the Baptist and won't be affected by his teachings. They criticize Jesus and won't go along with his teachings.

They are never satisfied. The righteous can never win, in the eyes of the wicked. No matter what the righteous do, the wicked still criticize them.

35 But wisdom is justified of all her children. (All things will work out the way they should, whether you like it or not.)

36 And one of the Pharisees desired him that he (Jesus) would eat with him. And he went into the Pharisee's house, and sat down to meat (to eat).

37 And, behold, a woman in the city, which was a sinner (was a known sinner), when she knew (found out) that *Jesus* sat at meat (was eating a meal) in the Pharisee's house, brought an alabaster box (an expensive box) of ointment,

38 And stood at his feet behind *him* weeping, and began to wash his feet with tears, and did wipe *them* with the hairs of her head, and kissed his feet, and anointed *them* with the ointment (put the ointment on Christ's feet).

39 Now when the Pharisee which had bidden (invited Jesus to eat with him) him saw *it*, he spake within himself, saying (he said to himself), This man, if he were a prophet, would have known who and what manner of woman *this is* that toucheth him: for she is a sinner.

Note: The Pharisees were very strict about not even touching a known sinner. They considered it a matter of personal righteousness to avoid contact with sinners.

40 And Jesus answering (responding) said unto him, Simon (the Pharisee's name), I have somewhat to say unto thee. And he saith, Master, say on (go ahead).

41 There was a certain creditor (banker) which had two debtors (two people who owed him money) : the one owed five hundred pence, and the other fifty.

Note: A pence would be about a day's wages.

42 And when they had nothing to pay (couldn't pay), he frankly forgave them both. Tell me therefore, which of them will love him most?

43 Simon answered and said, I suppose that he, to whom he forgave most. And he said unto him, Thou hast rightly judged.

44 And he turned to the woman, and said unto Simon, Seest thou this woman? I entered into thine house, thou gavest me no water for my feet (you didn't wash my feet [a proper Jewish custom when entertaining guests]): but she hath washed my feet with tears, and wiped *them* with the hairs of her head.

45 Thou gavest me no kiss: but this woman since the time I came in hath not ceased to kiss my feet.

46 My head with oil thou didst not anoint: but this woman hath anointed my feet with ointment.

47 Wherefore (Therefore) I say unto thee, Her sins, which are many, are forgiven; for she loved much (she showed much love and service to me because she has much to be forgiven of and she knows it): but to whom little is forgiven, *the same* loveth little.

48 And he said unto her, Thy sins are

forgiven.

49 And they that sat at meat (dinner) with him began to say within themselves, Who is this that forgiveth sins also?

50 And he said to the woman, Thy faith hath saved thee; go in peace.

Note: It is logical to assume that this woman had heard Christ's teachings earlier and had already repented deeply. Her humble service to the Master, serving him to demonstrate her love for him because of his ability to cleanse and save her from her sins, can be symbolic of our serving the Savior in appreciation for the effects of his Atonement in our lives. Her willingness to appear in public, in spite of the embarrassment of having others gossip about her because of her reputation as a sinner, shows humility and resolve to serve the Savior at all costs.

LUKE 8

1 AND it came to pass afterward, that he went throughout every city and village, preaching and shewing (showing) the glad tidings of the kingdom of God: and the twelve (apostles) *were* with him,

2 And certain women, which had been healed of evil spirits and infirmities, Mary called Magdalene, out of whom went seven devils,

Note: The Savior had apparently cast seven evil spirits out of Mary Magdalene on an earlier occasion which is not recorded.

3 And Joanna the wife of Chuza Herod's steward (manager of his household), and Susanna, and many others, which ministered unto him of their substance (helped to support Jesus, using their own supplies).

4 And when much people were gathered together, and were come to him out of every city, he spake by a parable (a story told to teach a specific lesson):

5 A sower (farmer) went out to sow (plant) his seed: and as he sowed (planted), some fell by the way side (the pathway); and it was trodden down (walked on), and the fowls of the air (birds) devoured (ate)it.

6 And some fell upon a rock; and as soon as it was sprung up (started growing), it withered away (dried up and died), because it lacked moisture.

7 And some fell among thorns; and the thorns sprang (grew)up with it, and choked it.

8 And other fell on good ground, and sprang up (grew), and bare fruit (produced a crop) an hundredfold. And when he had said these things, he cried, He that hath ears to hear, let him hear (he that is spiritually in tune will understand what I am saying).

Note: Jesus will explain this parable to his disciples, beginning in verse 11.

9 And his disciples asked him, saying, What might this parable be (what does this story mean)?

10 And he said, Unto you it is given to know the mysteries (the basic teachings, principles etc.) of the kingdom of God: but to others (I teach) in parables; that seeing they might not see, and hearing they might not understand. (The spiritually deaf and blind don't want to understand the basics of the

gospel.)

11 Now the parable is this (I will now explain the parable): The seed is the word of God.

12 Those by the way side (the seeds that fall on the pathway in the field) are they (people) that hear; then cometh the devil, and taketh away the word out of their hearts, lest they should believe and be saved.

Note: Missionaries see application of verse 12 all the time in their teaching. For instance, they are invited into a home. The people listen to the gospel message and are excited. They make an appointment with the missionaries to return. But when the missionaries return for the next appointment, the family is cold and asks them to leave and not return. Satan has quickly quenched the flame of desire to hear the gospel.

13 They on the rock *are they* (people), which, when they hear, receive the word with joy; and these have no root, which for a while believe (stay active for a little while), and in time of temptation fall away.

14 And that (the seeds) which fell among thorns are they (people), which, when they have heard (the gospel), go forth, and are choked with cares and riches and pleasures of *this* life, and bring no fruit (fruit is symbolic of their lives) to perfection.

15 But that (seed) on the good ground are they (people), which in an honest and good heart, having heard the word, keep *it*, and bring forth fruit with patience (patiently remain faithful and produce righteous lives).

Note: The Prophet Joseph Smith gave additional insights into the Parable of the Sower, above. See note following Matthew 13:23 in this book.

16 No man, when he hath lighted a candle, covereth it with a vessel (container), or putteth it under a bed; but setteth *it* on a candlestick, that they which enter in may see the light. (In other words, let your good example of living the gospel be seen by others so that they can come unto Christ also.)

17 For nothing is secret, that shall not be made manifest; neither *any thing* hid, that shall not be known and come abroad. (God knows all things and all wickedness will eventually be exposed.)

18 Take heed therefore how ye hear (how you respond to the gospel when you hear it): for whosoever hath (whoever lives the gospel), to him shall be given (more knowledge, testimony etc.); and whosoever hath not (does not remain faithful), from him shall be taken even that which he seemeth to have (see D&C 1:33).

19 Then came to him *his* mother and his brethren (his family; see Luke 8:19, footnote a), and could not come at him for the press (couldn't get through the crowd to talk to Jesus).

20 And it was told him *by certain* (people) which said, Thy mother and thy brethren stand without (outside), desiring to see thee.

21 And he answered and said unto them, My mother and my brethren (in other words, my "family") are these which hear the word of God, and do it (see Mosiah 5:7).

Note: JST Matthew 12:44 adds important information to this situation. It says "And he gave them charge concerning her [asked them to take good care of his mother while he continued on his mission], saying, I go my way, for my Father hath sent me. And whosoever shall do the will of my Father which is in heaven, the same is my brother, and sister, and mother."

22 Now it came to pass on a certain day, that he went into a ship with his disciples: and he said unto them, Let us go over unto the other side of the lake (Sea of Galilee). And they launched forth.

23 But as they sailed he fell asleep: and there came down a storm of wind on the lake; and they were filled *with water* (JST "filled with fear"), and were in jeopardy (in danger of sinking).

24 And they (the disciples) came to him (Jesus), and awoke him, saying, Master, master, we perish. Then he arose, and rebuked (commanded) the wind and the raging of the water: and they ceased, and there was a calm.

25 And he said unto them, Where is your faith? And they being afraid wondered, saying one to another, What manner of (what kind of) man is this! for he commandeth even the winds and water, and they obey him.

26 And they arrived at the country of the Gadarenes, which is over against Galilee (southeast of the Sea of Galilee).

27 And when he went forth to land, there met him out of the city a certain man, which had devils long time (had been possessed by evil spirits for a long time), and ware (wore) no clothes, neither abode (lived) in *any* house, but in the tombs (lived among the graves).

28 When he saw Jesus, he cried out, and fell down before (in front of) him, and with a loud voice said, What have I to do with thee, Jesus, *thou* Son of God most high? I beseech (beg) thee, torment me not.

Note: The evil spirit seems to be speaking through the man who is possessed here.

29 (For he [Christ] had commanded the unclean spirit to come out of the man. For oftentimes it [the evil spirit] had caught [seized] him: and he was kept bound with chains and in fetters [leg irons]; and he brake [broke] the bands, and was driven of [by] the devil [evil spirit] into the wilderness.)

30 And Jesus asked him (the evil spirit), saying, What is thy name? And he said, Legion: because many devils were entered into him (many evil spirits were in the man).

31 And they (the evil spirits) besought (pleaded with) him that he would not command them to go out into the deep.

32 And there was there an herd of many swine (pigs) feeding on the mountain: and they besought (begged) him that he would suffer (allow) them to enter into them (the pigs). And he suffered them (allowed them to do so).

33 Then went the devils out of the man, and entered into the swine: and the herd ran violently down a steep place into the lake, and were choked (drowned).

34 When they that fed *them* (the

people whose job it was to take care of the pigs) saw what was done, they fled (ran), and went and told *it* (spread the news) in the city and in the country.

35 Then they (the city officials and owners of the pigs) went out to see what was done; and came to Jesus, and found the man, out of whom the devils were departed (had been cast out), sitting at the feet of Jesus, clothed, and in his right mind: and they were afraid.

36 They also which saw it (eyewitnesses) told them by what means he that was possessed of the devils was healed.

37 Then the whole multitude of the country of the Gadarenes round about besought (asked) him (Jesus) to depart from them (to leave their part of the country); for they were taken with great fear: and he went up into the ship, and returned back again.

Note: It is sad that these men, rather than asking the Savior to stay and teach them, after having performed such a beautiful healing for the man (symbolic of the fact that Christ can heal us from the effects of Satan's influence), instead asked him to leave their city and go elsewhere. It was no doubt a major economic disaster to lose about 2000 pigs (mark 5:13). But being materialistic, worrying more about wealth and possessions than spiritual, eternal things, can blind us to the value of the Savior and his Atonement.

38 Now the man out of whom the devils were departed besought him (asked Jesus) that he might be with him (if he could stay with Jesus): but Jesus sent him away, saying,

39 Return to thine own house, and shew how great things God hath done unto thee (stay here and be a witness of the fact that God healed you). And he went his way, and published throughout the whole city how great things Jesus had done unto him.

40 And it came to pass, that, when Jesus was returned, the people *gladly* received him: for they were all waiting for him.

41 And, behold, there came a man named Jairus, and he was a ruler of the synagogue: and he fell down at Jesus' feet, and besought him that he would (asked him to) come into his house:

42 For he had one only daughter, about twelve years of age, and she lay a dying. But as he went the people thronged him (crowded and bumped against him).

43 And a woman having an issue of blood twelve years (who had been bleeding for twelve years), which had spent all her living upon physicians (she had spent all her money to pay doctors), neither could be healed of any (no doctors had successfully treated her illness),

44 Came behind *him*, and touched the border of his garment (robe, cloak): and immediately her issue of blood stanched (the bleeding stopped).

45 And Jesus said, Who touched me? When all denied (nobody admitted touching him), Peter and they that were with him said, Master, the multitude throng thee and press *thee* (people in this crowd are bumping you and pressing against you constantly), and sayest thou, Who touched me?

46 And Jesus said, Somebody hath

touched me: for I perceive that virtue (power) is gone out of me.

47 And when the woman saw that she was not hid (that she had been discovered), she came trembling, and falling down before him, she declared unto him before (in front of) all the people for what cause (the reason why) she had touched him and how she was healed immediately.

48 And he said unto her, Daughter, be of good comfort: thy faith hath made thee whole (healed); go in peace.

49 While he yet spake, there cometh one from the ruler (Jairus; see verse 41) of the synagogue's *house*, saying to him, Thy daughter is dead; trouble not the Master (it is too late; don't bother Jesus).

50 But when Jesus heard it, he answered (responded to) him, saying, Fear not: believe only (just have faith), and she shall be made whole (will be healed).

51 And when he came into the house, he suffered (allowed) no man to go in, save (except) Peter, and James, and John, and the father and the mother of the maiden (the dead girl).

52 And all wept, and bewailed her: but he said, Weep not; she is not dead, but sleepeth.

53 And they (the mourners) laughed him to scorn (mocked and ridiculed Jesus), knowing that she was dead.

54 And he put them all out (sent the mourners out of the room), and took her by the hand, and called, saying, Maid, arise.

55 And her spirit came again, and she arose straightway (immediately): and he commanded to give her meat (food).

Note: In the language of our Bible, "meat" means any type of food. "Flesh" means meat, as in beef, lamb, chicken etc.

56 And her parents were astonished: but he charged (instructed) them that they should tell no man what was done.

Note: Some experiences with God are very private and personal and are to be kept to ourselves. Perhaps this is the reason the parents were so instructed by Jesus.

LUKE 9

1 THEN he called his twelve disciples together, and gave them power and authority over all devils, and to cure diseases.

2 And he sent them to preach the kingdom of God, and to heal the sick.

Note: This is an important part of the apostles' ongoing training.

3 And he said unto them, Take nothing for *your* journey, neither staves (staffs), nor scrip (a bag in which to carry food; see Bible Dictionary, page 770), neither bread, neither money; neither have two coats apiece.

4 And whatsoever house ye enter into, there abide, and thence depart.

5 And whosoever will not receive you, when ye go out of that city, shake off the very dust from your feet for a testimony against them (as a witness that you tried to teach them the gospel; see D&C 60:15).

6 And they departed, and went

through the towns, preaching the gospel, and healing every where.

Note: Just a reminder that the symbol, ¶ at the beginning of verse 7 and many other places in our Bible, means the beginning of a new topic.

7 ¶ Now Herod the tetrarch (Roman ruler) heard of all that was done by him (by Jesus): and he was perplexed (worried), because that it was said of some, that John was risen from the dead; (Some people were saying that Jesus was John the Baptist, whom Herod had killed [beheaded], come back to life.)

8 And of some, that Elias had appeared (some said that Jesus was Elijah the Prophet); and of others, that one of the old prophets was risen again (had come back to life).

9 And Herod said, John (the Baptist) have I beheaded: but who is this, of whom I hear such things? And he desired to see him (wanted to see Jesus).

10 And the apostles, when they were returned (from their missions as mentioned in verses 2-6), told him all that they had done (reported back to him). And he took them, and went aside privately into a desert place belonging to the city called Bethsaida. (Jesus wanted to have some private time with his apostles.)

11 And the people, when they knew it (when they found out where Jesus was), followed him: and he received them, and spake unto them of the kingdom of God, and healed them that had need of healing.

Note: Jesus demonstrated his compassion and kindness time and time again, putting aside his needs for rest and privacy, as in verse 11 above, to minister to the people.

12 And when the day began to wear away (was about gone), then came the twelve, and said unto him, Send the multitude away, that they may go into the towns and country round about, and lodge, and get victuals (food): for we are here in a desert place. (There is nowhere here to buy food.)

13 But he said unto them, Give ye them to eat. (This must have startled the apostles!) And they said, We have no more but five loaves and two fishes; except we should go and buy meat (food) for all this people.

14 For they were about five thousand men. (Matthew 14:21 says there were about 5000 men plus women and children.) And he said to his disciples, Make them sit down by fifties in a company (in groups of fifty).

15 And they did so, and made them all sit down.

16 Then he (Jesus) took the five loaves and the two fishes, and looking up to heaven, he blessed them, and brake, and gave to the disciples to set before the multitude.

17 And they (all the people) did eat, and were all filled: and there was taken up of fragments that remained to them twelve baskets (they gathered up twelve basketfuls of leftovers).

18 And it came to pass, as he was alone praying, his disciples were with him: and he asked them, saying, Whom say the people that I am?

19 They answering said, John the

Baptist; but some say, Elias (Elijah); and others say, that one of the old prophets is risen again (has come back to life).

20 He said unto them, But whom say ye that I am? Peter answering said, The Christ of God.

21 And he straitly (strictly) charged (told) them, and commanded *them* to tell no man that thing;

Note: It would seem that this instruction to the apostles was temporary and for that particular time and circumstance. Perhaps they needed a bit of quiet time together for the Master to teach his disciples about his upcoming death (in about six months) and resurrection. Some manuscripts say "Don't go and tell anyone in the village."

22 Saying, The Son of man (Jesus) must suffer many things, and be rejected of (by) the elders and chief priests and scribes (religious leaders of the Jews), and be slain, and be raised (resurrected) the third day.

23 And he said to *them* all, If any *man* will come after me, let him deny himself (put aside his own needs), and take up his cross (sacrifice whatever is necessary) daily, and follow me.

24 For whosoever will save his life (preserve his own worldly lifestyle rather than following me) shall lose it (will ultimately lose that way of life): but whosoever will lose his life for my sake (will change his lifestyle and follow me), the same shall save it (will keep the rich blessings of a righteous life forever).

25 For what is a man advantaged, if he gain the whole world, and lose himself (lose his soul), or be cast away (be cast away from heaven on Judgment Day)?

26 For whosoever shall be ashamed of me (will reject me) and of my words, of him shall the Son of man be ashamed (he will be rejected by Jesus), when he shall come in his own glory (at the Second Coming), and *in his* Father's, and of the holy angels.

27 But I tell you of a truth, there be some standing here, which shall not taste of death, till they see the kingdom of God.

Note: We know that John, the apostle, was one in this group around the Savior who would "not taste of death" (has not yet died). He was translated and allowed to stay on earth to minister to people until the Second Coming. See D&C 7:3. We don't know who any of the others are, standing by the Savior at this moment in verse 27, who would be translated. We do know that the Three Nephites were translated as described in 3 Nephi 28.

28 And it came to pass about an eight days after these sayings, he took Peter and John and James, and went up into a mountain to pray.

Note: It is now near October, and the Savior will be crucified the following April, thus ending his mortal ministry. Three of his apostles, Peter, James, and John are already taking on the role of First Presidency. They will experience tremendous additional training now as the Master takes them with him up on the mountain which is referred to as the Mount of Transfiguration. There, they will see Christ transfigured (shine with brilliant light) before their eyes, will hear the Father's voice, and will see, among others, the great prophets Moses and Elijah, who will minister to Jesus, and from whom they will receive additional priesthood keys. From JST Mark 9:3, we learn that John the Baptist was also there.

29 And as he prayed, the fashion of his countenance was altered, and his raiment (clothing) was white and glistering (shining).

30 And, behold, there talked with him two men, which were Moses and Elias (Elijah):

31 Who appeared in glory, and spake of his decease (death) which he (Jesus) should accomplish at Jerusalem.

32 But Peter and they that were with him (James and John) were heavy with sleep: and when they were awake, they saw his glory, and the two men that stood with him.

33 And it came to pass, as they (Moses and Elijah) departed from him (Christ), Peter said unto Jesus, Master, it is good for us to be here: and let us make three tabernacles (small booths, typically used among the Jews for private worship during the annual Feast of Tabernacles); one for thee, and one for Moses, and one for Elias (Elijah): not knowing what he said (not understanding the situation).

34 While he thus spake, there came a cloud, and overshadowed them: and they feared as they entered into the cloud.

35 And there came a voice (the Father's voice) out of the cloud, saying, This is my beloved Son: hear him.

36 And when the voice was past, Jesus was found alone. And they kept *it* close, and told no man in those days any of those things which they had seen.

Note: For additional information about what took place on the Mount of Transfiguration, see the note after Matthew 17:8 in this book.

37 And it came to pass, that on the next day, when they were come down from the hill (from the Mount of Transfiguration), much (many) people met him.

38 And, behold, a man of the company (in the crowd) cried out, saying, Master, I beseech (beg of) thee, look upon my son: for he is mine only child.

39 And, lo, a spirit (an evil spirit) taketh (possesses) him, and he suddenly crieth out; and it teareth him that he foameth again (it throws him around and makes him foam at the mouth), and bruising him (causes him to get bruised as he tosses around on the ground) hardly departeth from him (it hardly ever leaves him so he can have peace).

40 And I besought (begged) thy disciples to cast him out; and they could not.

41 And Jesus answering said, O faithless and perverse (wicked) generation (people), how long shall I be with you, and suffer you (put up with your lack of righteousness and faith)? Bring thy son hither (here).

42 And as he (the man's son) was yet a coming, the devil (evil spirit) threw

him down, and tare *him* (threw him around some more). And Jesus rebuked the unclean spirit (commanded the evil spirit to leave), and healed the child, and delivered him again to his father.

43 And they were all amazed at the mighty power of God. But while they wondered every one at all things which Jesus did, he said unto his disciples,

44 Let these sayings sink down into your ears: for the Son of man (Jesus) shall be delivered into the hands of men (arrested and turned over to wicked men).

45 But they understood not this saying (didn't understand what he was saying), and it was hid from them, that they perceived (understood) it not: and they feared to ask him of that saying (were afraid to ask him to explain what he meant).

46 Then there arose a reasoning (a debate) among them, which of them should be greatest.

47 And Jesus, perceiving the thought of their heart, took a child, and set him by him,

48 And said unto them, Whosoever shall receive this child in my name receiveth (accepts) me: and whosoever shall receive me receiveth him (the Father) that sent me: for he that is least (humbly considers himself to be the least) among you all, the same shall be great.

49 And John answered and said, Master, we saw one (a person) casting out devils in thy name; and we forbad him (told him not to), because he followeth not with us (he is not one of us).

50 And Jesus said unto him, Forbid him not (don't tell him not to): for he that is not against us is for us.

51 And it came to pass, when the time was come that he should be received up (perform the Atonement, be crucified, resurrected and taken up into heaven), he stedfastly (with determination) set his face to go to Jerusalem,

Note: Jesus and his apostles have been serving in the Galilee area, in northern Israel. Now, Jesus has told them that they must go south to Jerusalem. Normally, the Jews avoided going straight south from Galilee, because that would require traveling through the province of Samaria. The Jews despised the Samaritans (people of Samaria) and the Samaritans despised the Jews. Thus, the Jews normally traveled around Samaria, to the east, and then south to Jerusalem. But this time, Jesus is heading straight south, right through Samaria, which would no doubt cause his apostles some extra anxiety.

52 And sent messengers before his face (ahead of him): and they (the messengers) went, and entered into a village of the Samaritans, to make ready for him (to prepare things for him to rest, eat etc.).

53 And they (the Samaritans in the village) did not receive him (were rude to Jesus and would not allow him and his followers to buy provisions), because his face was as though he would go to Jerusalem (because they knew he was a Jew).

54 And when his disciples James and John saw *this*, they said, Lord, wilt

thou that we command fire to come down from heaven, and consume them (these Samaritans), even as Elias did (is it OK with you if we command fire to come down from heaven and destroy them like Elijah did to the fifty soldiers and their captain who were rude to him; see 2 Kings 1:10)?

55 But he turned, and rebuked (scolded) them, and said, Ye know not what manner of spirit ye are of (you don't realize how awful your attitude is).

56 For the Son of man (Jesus) is not come to destroy men's lives, but to save *them*. And they went to another village.

57 And it came to pass, that, as they went in the way (along the road), a certain man said unto him, Lord, I will follow thee whithersoever thou goest.

58 And Jesus said unto him, Foxes have holes, and birds of the air *have* nests; but the Son of man (I, Christ) hath not where (anywhere) to lay *his* head.

59 And he said unto another, Follow me. But he said, Lord, suffer (allow) me first to go and bury my father.

60 Jesus said unto him, Let the dead bury their dead: but go thou and preach the kingdom of God.

Note: There is probably more to the story than is recorded here. Perhaps "let the dead bury their dead" includes a message that following the Savior requires real commitment and sometimes requires one to leave the comforts of home and family and follow Jesus at all costs.

61 And another also said, Lord, I will follow thee; but let me first go bid them farewell, which are at home at my house.

62 And Jesus said unto him, No man, having put his hand to the plough (plow), and looking back, is fit for the kingdom of God. (Ultimately, we have to be committed to follow the Savior at all costs. If we achieve this level of commitment, all other things of eternal value, including family, will be ours forever.)

LUKE 10

Note: Jesus continues to organize the priesthood officers of his church by calling the seventy and sending them out two by two.

1 AFTER these things the Lord appointed other seventy also, and sent them two and two before his face (in advance of him) into every city and place, whither he himself would come.

2 Therefore said he unto them, The harvest truly is great (the potential for converts is large), but the labourers *are* few (there are relatively few missionaries etc.): pray ye therefore the Lord of the harvest, that he would send forth labourers into his harvest.

3 Go your ways: behold, I send you forth as lambs among wolves (you will be in danger at times).

4 Carry neither purse (money), nor scrip (food; see Bible Dictionary, page 70), nor shoes (wear sandals instead): and salute no man by the way (don't stop to visit or delay the work you are assigned; see McConkie, *Doctrinal New Testament Commentary*, Vol. 1, page 433).

5 And into whatsoever house ye

enter, first say, Peace be to this house.

6 And if the son of peace (a peaceful person) be there, your peace shall rest upon it: if not, it shall turn to you again.

7 And in the same house remain, eating and drinking such things as they give: for the labourer is worthy of his hire (it is worthwhile for people to support you). Go not from house to house. (Don't go mechanically from house to house. Go where the Spirit directs.)

8 And into whatsoever city ye enter, and they receive you, eat such things as are set before you:

9 And heal the sick that are therein, and say unto them, The kingdom of God is come nigh unto you (the true gospel is now available to you).

10 But into whatsoever city ye enter, and they receive you not, go your ways out into the streets of the same, and say,

11 Even the very dust of your city, which cleaveth on (sticks to) us, we do wipe off against you (as a witness that we tried to teach you; see D&C 60:15): notwithstanding (even though you have rejected us) be ye sure of this, that the kingdom of God is come nigh unto you (the true gospel of Christ is here for you).

12 But I say unto you, that it shall be more tolerable in that day (Judgment Day) for Sodom, than for that city (it is a very serious thing to reject the gospel, knowingly).

13 Woe unto thee, Chorazin! woe unto thee, Bethsaida (cities where Jesus had preached and done many miracles)! for if the mighty works had been done in Tyre and Sidon (non-Jewish cities), which have been done in you, they had (would have) a great while ago repented, sitting in sackcloth and ashes (would have humbled themselves).

14 But it shall be more tolerable for Tyre and Sidon at the judgment, than for you (because you have had great opportunities to know the gospel and they haven't).

15 And thou, Capernaum, which art exalted to heaven (whose inhabitants are prideful, cocky), shalt be thrust down to hell.

16 (JST "And he said unto his disciples") He that heareth you (pays attention to you) heareth me; and he that despiseth you despiseth me; and he that despiseth me despiseth him that sent me (the Father).

17 And the seventy returned again with joy, saying, Lord, even the devils are subject unto us through thy name (when we do it in the name of Jesus Christ).

18 And he said unto them, I beheld (saw) Satan as lightning fall from heaven. (I have authority over Satan.)

19 Behold, I give unto you power to tread on serpents and scorpions, and over all the power of the enemy (Satan and all who work with him in opposing the work of the Lord): and nothing shall by any means hurt you.

20 Notwithstanding (nevertheless) in this rejoice not (don't get cocky or boastful), that the spirits are subject unto you; but rather rejoice, because your names are written in heaven (you will go to celestial glory).

21 In that hour Jesus rejoiced in spirit, and said, I thank thee, O Father, Lord of heaven and earth, that thou

hast hid these things from the wise and prudent (JST "from them who think they are wise and prudent"), and hast revealed them unto babes (humble people who have childlike faith): even so, Father; for so it seemed good in thy sight.

22 All things are delivered to me of my Father: and no man knoweth who the Son is, but the Father; and who the Father is, but the Son, and *he* to whom the Son will reveal *him* (JST 'it').

23 And he turned him unto *his* disciples, and said privately, Blessed *are* the eyes which see the things that ye see:

24 For I tell you, that many prophets and kings have desired to see those things which ye see, and have not seen *them*; and to hear those things which ye hear, and have not heard *them*.

25 And, behold, a certain lawyer stood up, and tempted him (tried to trick Jesus), saying, Master, what shall I do to inherit eternal life (to get to heaven)?

26 He said unto him, What is written in the law (the scriptures, particularly Genesis, Exodus, Leviticus, Numbers and Deuteronomy)? how readest thou (what do you understand the scriptures to say on this matter)?

27 And he answering said, Thou shalt love the Lord thy God with all thy heart, and with all thy soul, and with all thy strength, and with all thy mind; and thy neighbour as thyself.

28 And he (Jesus) said unto him (the lawyer), Thou hast answered right: this do, and thou shalt live (get to heaven).

29 But he, willing to justify himself (wanting to make himself look good in front of the people who were standing around; see Luke 10:29, footnote a), said unto Jesus, And who is my neighbour?

Note: Jesus will now give the Parable of the Good Samaritan. It is helpful to know that the Jews despised the Samaritans and the Samaritans generally despised and made fun of the Jews. Samaria (the land of the Samaritans) was between Judea (in southern Israel) and Galilee (in northern Israel). When the Ten Tribes of Israel (Who lived in Samaria) were taken into captivity (about 721 BC) by the Assyrians, some Israelites were left behind and intermarried with the Assyrian soldiers who occupied Samaria. This intermarrying over the years led the Jews to despise the Samaritans for breaking the Law of Moses in which marrying outside of covenant Israel was forbidden.

30 And Jesus answering said, A certain man went down from Jerusalem to Jericho, and fell among thieves (was attacked by robbers), which stripped him of his raiment (clothing), and wounded *him*, and departed, leaving *him* half dead.

31 And by chance there came down a certain priest (Jewish priest) that way: and when he saw him, he passed by on the other side.

32 And likewise a Levite (another Jewish priesthood holder), when he was at the place, came and looked *on him*, and passed by on the other side.

33 But a certain Samaritan (a man from Samaria; Samaritans were despised by the Jews), as he journeyed, came where he was: and when he saw him,

he had compassion *on him,*

34 And went *to him,* and bound up his wounds, pouring in oil and wine (gave him first aid), and set him on his own beast, and brought him to an inn, and took care of him.

35 And on the morrow when he departed, he took out two pence (money representing two days' wages), and gave *them* to the host (the innkeeper), and said unto him, Take care of him; and whatsoever thou spendest more (beyond what I have paid you), when I come again, I will repay thee.

36 Which now of these three, thinkest thou, was neighbour unto him that fell among the thieves?

37 And he (the lawyer) said, He that shewed (showed) mercy on him. Then said Jesus unto him, Go, and do thou likewise.

38 Now it came to pass, as they went, that he entered into a certain village (Bethany, near the Mount of Olives, just outside Jerusalem): and a certain woman named Martha received him into her house.

39 And she had a sister called Mary, which also sat at Jesus' feet, and heard his word.

40 But Martha was cumbered about much serving (very busy with all the details that needed attention in order to feed the Savior), and came to him, and said (complained), Lord, dost thou not care that my sister hath left me to serve alone (doesn't it bother you that Mary is not helping me)? bid her therefore that she help me (tell her to help me).

41 And Jesus answered and said unto her, Martha, Martha, thou art careful and troubled about many things (you are meticulous and always fuss over the tiniest details):

42 But one thing is needful: and Mary hath chosen that good part (has chosen to listen to me and my teachings), which shall not be taken away from her (which is a wise thing for her to be doing with her agency).

LUKE 11

1 AND it came to pass, that, as he was praying in a certain place, when he ceased, one of his disciples said unto him, Lord, teach us to pray, as John (the Baptist) also taught his disciples.

Note: Jesus now gives what is commonly known as "The Lord's Prayer". It is an example of how to pray and of things which can be included in our prayers.

2 And he said unto them, When ye pray, say, Our Father which art in heaven, Hallowed be (holy is) thy name. Thy kingdom come. Thy will be done, as in heaven, so in earth.

3 Give us day by day our daily bread.

4 And forgive us our sins; for we also forgive every one that is indebted to us. And lead us not into temptation (JST "let us not be led unto temptation"); but deliver us from evil. (JST adds "for thine is the kingdom and power. Amen".)

Note: Next, Jesus will encourage his disciples to ask Heavenly Father for whatever they need. He reminds them that Heavenly Father is a Father with tender feelings toward his children and who likes to bless and help them. He also encourages them to continue praying for things they need, even if at first they don't get them.

5 And he said unto them (his disciples), (JST adds "Your heavenly Father will not fail to give unto you whatsoever ye ask of him. And he spake a parable, saying") Which of you shall have a friend, and shall go unto him at midnight, and say unto him, Friend, lend me three loaves (of bread);

6 For a friend of mine in his journey is come to me, and I have nothing to set before him (nothing to feed him)?

7 And he (the friend in verse 5) from within (inside his house) shall answer and say, Trouble me not: the door is now shut, and my children are with me in bed; I cannot rise and give thee.

8 I say unto you, Though he will not rise and give him, because he is his friend, yet because of his importunity (because he stays there and keeps knocking at the door and asking for help) he (the friend who has bread) will rise and give him as many as he needeth.

9 And I say unto you, Ask, and it shall be given you; seek, and ye shall find; knock, and it shall be opened unto you.

10 For every one that asketh receiveth; and he that seeketh findeth; and to him that knocketh it shall be opened.

11 If a son shall ask bread of any of you that is a father, will he give him a stone? or if *he ask* a fish, will he for a fish give him a serpent?

12 Or if he shall ask an egg, will he offer him a scorpion?

13 If ye then, being evil (being human, imperfect), know how to give good gifts unto your children: how much more shall *your* heavenly Father give the Holy Spirit to them that ask him?

14 And he was casting out a devil (an evil spirit), and it (the man) was dumb (couldn't talk; JST "And he was casting a devil out of a man, and he was dumb"). And it came to pass, when the devil was gone out, the dumb spake (the man who had been possessed by the evil spirit was able to talk); and the people wondered (the crowd was amazed)

15 But some of them said, He casteth out devils through Beelzebub the chief of the devils (Jesus is using Satan's power to cast out evil spirits).

16 And others, tempting (testing him) *him*, sought of him a sign from heaven.

17 But he, knowing their thoughts, said unto them, Every kingdom divided against itself is brought to desolation (is eventually destroyed); and a house *divided* against a house falleth.

18 If Satan also be divided against himself (if Satan is casting his own evil spirits out), how shall his kingdom stand (survive)? because ye say that I cast out devils through Beelzebub (Satan).

19 And if I by Beelzebub (by the power of Satan) cast out devils, by whom do your sons cast *them out*? therefore shall they be your judges.

Note: From JST Matt. 12:22-23, we learn the correct interpretation of verse 19 above:

22 And if I by Beelzebub cast out

devils, by whom do *your children* cast our devils? Therefore *they* shall be your judges.

23 But if I cast out devils by the Spirit of God, then the kingdom of God is come unto you. For *they also cast out devils by the Spirit of God, for unto them is given power over devils, that they may cast them out*."

(Bold italics added for emphasis) From the words in bold italics, we find that there were righteous Jews, obviously baptized and faithful, who were enabled by the Spirit of God to cast out evil spirits. See McConkie, *Doctrinal New Testament Commentary*, Vol. 1, p. 269.

20 But if I with the finger (power) of God cast out devils, no doubt the kingdom of God is come upon you (you are seeing the true kingdom of God in action and you had better pay attention).

21 When a strong man armed keepeth (guards) his palace, his goods are in peace (his possessions are safe):

22 But when a stronger than he shall come upon him, and overcome him, he taketh from him all his armour (protection) wherein he trusted, and divideth his spoils (takes his possessions).

23 He that is not with me is against me: and he that gathereth not with me scattereth.

24 When the unclean spirit is gone out of a man, he walketh through dry places, seeking rest; and finding none, he saith, I will return unto my house whence I came out.

25 And when he cometh, he findeth *it* swept and garnished.

26 Then goeth he, and taketh *to him*

seven other spirits more wicked than himself; and they enter in, and dwell there: and the last *state* of that man is worse than the first.

Note: Verses 24-26 above are especially difficult to understand without help. Matthew 12:43-45 is similar to Luke 11:24-26, and there is a note following Matthew 12:45 which explains these verses in Luke.

27 And it came to pass, as he spake these things, a certain woman of the company lifted up her voice, and said unto him, Blessed *is* the womb that bare thee, and the paps which thou hast sucked (blessed is the woman to whom you were born and nursed you; praising Mary, the mother of Jesus, as prophesied by Mary in Luke 1:48).

28 But he said, Yea rather (that is true, but even more important), blessed *are* they that hear the word of God, and keep (obey) it.

29 And when the people were gathered thick (in a tight crowd) together, he began to say, This is an evil generation: they seek a sign (always are wanting proof that I am the Messiah); and there shall no sign be given it (them), but the sign of Jonas (Jonah) the prophet (the signs they get will be miserable for them, like being swallowed by a whale was for Jonah, when he tried to reject God's call).

30 For as Jonas was a sign unto the Ninevites (the people to whom Jonah preached), so shall also the Son of man (Jesus; Son of Man-see Moses 6:57) be to this generation.

31 The queen of the south (the queen of Sheba) shall rise up in the judgment

with the men of this generation, and condemn them: for she came from the utmost parts of the earth to hear the wisdom of Solomon; and, behold, a greater than Solomon (in other words, the Son of God) is here.

Note: The point in verse 31 above seems to be that the Jews will be condemned (damned) by the good example of the Queen of Sheba, who came from far away to learn about God from Solomon, whereas the Jews have the Son of God in their midst, teaching them, and they ignore him.

32 The men of Nineve (Nineveh) shall rise up in the judgment with this generation (the Jews), and shall condemn it (by their good example): for they repented at the preaching of Jonas (Jonah); and, behold, a greater than Jonas is here.

33 No man, when he hath lighted a candle, putteth it in a secret place, neither under a bushel, but on a candle-stick, that they which come in may see the light.

34 The light of the body is the eye (the eye takes in light so you can see where you are going) : therefore when thine eye (your spiritual eye) is single (focused on God's light) thy whole body also is full of light; but when *thine eye* is evil (you look for evil, to participate in), thy body also *is* full of darkness.

35 Take heed therefore that the light which is in thee be not darkness.

36 If thy whole body therefore *be* full of light (full of gospel light), having no part dark (avoiding evil), the whole (your whole life) shall be full of

light, as when the bright shining of a candle doth give thee light.

37 And as he spake, a certain Pharisee besought (requested) him to dine with him: and he went in, and sat down to meat (to the meal).

38 And when the Pharisee saw *it*, he marvelled (was surprised) that he had not first washed before dinner.

Note: The Pharisees were very strict about washing before eating and had made it a very exact part of their religious rituals which made them look righteous in the eyes of others.

39 And the Lord said unto him, Now do ye Pharisees make clean (wash) the outside of the cup and the platter (plate); but your inward part is full of ravening (greed, seeking to rob and plunder the people) and wickedness.

40 *Ye* fools, did not he (God) that made that which is without (outside) make that which is within (inside) also? (God knows that you try to look clean on the outside but that you are filthy with wickedness on the inside.)

41 But rather give alms of such things as ye have; and, behold, all things are clean unto you. (The JST gives this verse as follows: "But if ye would rather give alms of such things as ye have; and observe to do all things which I have commanded you, then would your inward parts be clean also." In other words, if you would keep my commandments, you could be just as clean on the inside as you are on the outside.)

42 But woe unto you (you are in much trouble), Pharisees! for ye tithe (pay exact tithing on) mint and rue

(herbs) and all manner of herbs, and pass over (ignore) judgment (being fair to others) and the love of God: these (Christlike things) ought ye to have done, and not to leave the other (paying tithing exactly) undone. (In other words, you go through the motions of being religious but you are not!)

43 Woe unto you, Pharisees! for ye love the uppermost seats (the highest, most respected and prestigious seats) in the synagogues (Jewish meeting houses), and greetings in the markets. (You love to have people notice how important you are.)

44 Woe unto you, scribes and Pharisees, hypocrites (people who want to appear to others to be righteous, but in their hearts, they love to be wicked)! for ye are as graves which appear not (don't look like graves), and the men that walk over *them* are not aware *of them* (don't realize that there is rot and corruption just under the surface).

45 Then answered one of the lawyers, and said unto him, Master, thus saying thou reproachest us also. (By speaking so disrespectfully to the scribes and Pharisees, you are insulting us lawyers also!)

46 And he said, Woe unto you also, ye lawyers! for ye lade men (load people down) with burdens grievous to be borne (difficult to carry), and ye yourselves touch not the burdens with one of your fingers (you won't lift a finger to help).

47 Woe unto you! for ye build the sepulchres of the prophets (build big monuments to dead prophets), and your fathers (ancestors) killed them.

(You pretend to be righteous and honor past prophets, but if you had lived back then, you would have joined your ancestors in killing them!)

48 Truly ye bear witness (through your wicked lives) that ye allow (agree with) the deeds of your fathers: for they indeed killed them (past prophets), and ye build their sepulchres (you build big monuments upon past prophets' grave sites to honor them).

49 Therefore also said the wisdom of God (God, in his wisdom, said), I will send them (the Jews) prophets and apostles, and *some* of them they shall slay and persecute:

50 That the blood of all the prophets, which was shed from the foundation (the earliest days) of the world, may be required of this generation; (Since you have murder in your hearts for the prophets and apostles now, you are as good as guilty of participating in killing all the prophets whose blood has been spilt by the wicked since the beginning of time.)

51 From the blood of Abel unto the blood of Zacharias (John the Baptist's father), which perished (whom you had killed) between the altar and the temple: verily I say unto you, It shall be required of this generation. (You wicked people will answer for all this.)

52 Woe unto you, lawyers! for ye have taken away the key of knowledge (JST "the fulness of the scriptures"): ye entered not in yourselves (JST "ye enter not in yourselves into the kingdom"), and them that were entering in ye hindered (stopped). (In other words, you won't get to heaven yourselves and you prevent others

from going there too!)

53 And as he said these things unto them, the scribes and the Pharisees (Jewish religious leaders) began to urge *him* vehemently (strongly and angrily oppose him), and to provoke him to speak of many things (and bombarded him with many angry questions):

54 Laying wait for him (trying to trap him), and seeking to catch something out of his mouth, that they might accuse him (hoping Jesus would say something for which they could have him arrested).

LUKE 12

1 IN the mean time, when there were gathered together an innumerable multitude (a huge group) of people, insomuch that they trode (were stepping) one upon another, he began to say unto his disciples first of all, Beware ye of (watch out for) the leaven (yeast) of the Pharisees, which is hypocrisy.

Note: Here the Master Teacher warns his disciples against the evil doctrines of the Pharisees (Jewish religious leaders). He compares these doctrines to leaven (yeast) which is put in bread dough to make it rise. As the leaven works its way through the entire lump of dough, it influences everything. So also with these hypocritical Jewish leaders, who are influencing everything in Jewish society. (See also Matthew 16:6.)

2 For there is nothing covered, that shall not be revealed; neither hid, that shall not be known. (God knows all things.)

3 Therefore whatsoever ye have spoken in darkness shall be heard in the light; and that which ye have spoken in the ear in closets (spoken secretly) shall be proclaimed upon the housetops (broadcast to everyone).

4 And I say unto you my friends, Be not afraid of them that kill the body, and after that have no more that they can do (that is all they can do to you).

5 But I will forewarn you whom ye shall fear: Fear him, which after he hath killed hath power to cast into hell; yea, I say unto you, Fear him (fear Satan and spiritual death).

6 Are not five sparrows sold for two farthings, and not one of them is forgotten before God? (God knows the little birds, so you can be assured that he knows and cares about you.)

7 But even the very hairs of your head are all numbered. Fear not therefore: ye are of more value than many sparrows.

8 Also I say unto you, Whosoever (whoever) shall confess (be faithful to) me before men (in the presence of others), him shall the Son of man (Christ) also confess (accept) before the angels of God: (In other words, he will be invited to live in heaven.)

9 But he that denieth (rejects) me before men shall be denied (rejected) before the angels of God.

Note: The JST adds two verses here. They are as follows:

10 Now his disciples knew that he said this, because they had spoken evil against him before the people; for they were afraid to confess him before men.

11 And they reasoned among themselves, saying, He knoweth our hearts,

and he speaketh to our condemnation, and we shall not be forgiven. But he answered them, and said unto them,

10 And whosoever shall speak a word against the Son of man (Jesus), it shall be forgiven him: but unto him that blasphemeth against the Holy Ghost (denies the Holy Ghost) it shall not be forgiven.

11 And when they (arrest you, and) bring you unto the synagogues, and *unto* magistrates (public officials), and powers (the courts etc.), take ye no thought how or what thing ye shall answer, or what ye shall say:

12 For the Holy Ghost shall teach you in the same hour what ye ought to say.

13 And one of the company (a person in the crowd) said unto him, Master, speak to my brother, that he divide the inheritance with me (tell my brother to share his inheritance with me).

14 And he (Jesus) said unto him, Man, who made me a judge or a divider (arbitrator) over you?

15 And he said unto them, Take heed, and beware of covetousness (greed): for a man's life consisteth not in the abundance of the things which he possesseth (worldly possessions are not what makes life worthwhile).

Note: Next, Jesus will give what is known as "The Parable of the Foolish Rich Man". It is given in Perea during the winter of 31 AD. The main message is "You can't take it with you." The point is that we must avoid allowing our worldly possessions take the place of God in our lives.

16 And he spake a parable (a story which teaches a certain lesson) unto them, saying, The ground of a certain rich man brought forth plentifully (grew very good crops):

17 And he thought within himself, saying, What shall I do, because I have no room where to bestow (store) my fruits (crops)?

18 And he said, This will I do: I will pull down (tear down) my barns, and build greater (bigger ones); and there will I bestow (store) all my fruits and my goods.

19 And I will say to my soul (to myself), Soul (Self), thou hast much goods laid up for many years (you have enough to last for several years); take thine ease (relax, take it easy), eat, drink, *and* be merry.

20 But God said unto him, *Thou* fool, this night thy soul shall be required of thee (tonight you will die): then whose shall those things be, which thou hast provided (then who will all your stuff belong to)?

21 So *is* he that layeth up treasure for himself, and is not rich toward God. (So it is with people who allow their possessions to take the place of God in their lives.)

22 And he said unto his disciples, Therefore I say unto you, Take no thought for your life, what ye shall eat; neither for the body, what ye shall put on.

Note: This counsel applies to the apostles and those involved in full-time service of God, such as missionaries. JST Matthew 6:25-27 makes this very clear as follows: "(25) And, again, I say unto you, Go ye into the world, and care not for the world; for the world will hate you, and will persecute you, and will turn you out of their synagogues. (26) Nevertheless, ye shall go forth from house to house, teaching the people; and I will go before you. (27) And your heavenly Father will provide for you, whatsoever things ye need for food, what ye shall eat; and for raiment, what ye shall wear or put on." It does not apply to everyone. Occasionally, individuals or groups take this literally as applying to them and the results are tragic and disastrous. The Savior continues this counsel to his apostles in the next verses.

23 The life is more than meat (food), and the body *is more* than raiment (clothing).

24 Consider the ravens: for they neither sow (plant) nor reap (harvest); which neither have storehouse nor barn; and God feedeth them: how much more are ye better than the fowls? (God takes good care of birds and you are much more important than they are.)

25 And which of you with taking thought can add to his stature one cubit? (Which of you could think and thus add inches to your height?)

26 If ye then be not able to do that thing which is least, why take ye thought for the rest? (Since you can't do such an unimportant thing, why worry about the rest of your needs?)

27 Consider the lilies (flowers) how they grow: they toil not (they don't work), they spin not (they don't weave cloth for clothing); and yet I say unto you, that Solomon in all his glory was not arrayed (dressed) like one of these.

28 If then God so clothe the grass (makes the grass beautiful), which is to day in the field, and to morrow is cast into the oven (is gone); how much more *will he clothe* you, O ye of little faith (JST "...how much more will he provide for you, if ye are not of little faith")?

29 And seek not ye what ye shall eat, or what ye shall drink, neither be ye of doubtful mind (don't doubt that the Lord will do this for you).

30 For all these things (the things you need daily to take care of your physical needs) do the nations of the world seek after: and your Father knoweth that ye have need of these things.

31 But rather seek ye the kingdom of God (JST "Therefore seek ye to bring forth the kingdom of God"); and all these things shall be added unto you.

32 Fear not, little flock; for it is your Father's good pleasure to give you the kingdom.

33 Sell that (what) ye have, and give alms (pay your offerings to God); provide yourselves (JST "not") bags which wax not (the JST deletes "not") old (leather bags to carry food in), a treasure in the heavens that faileth not (doesn't ever run out), where no thief approacheth, neither moth corrupteth (ruins). (JST "This he spake unto his disciples, saying, Sell that ye have and give alms; provide not for yourselves bags which wax old, but rather provide a treasure in the heavens, that faileth not; where no thief approacheth, neither moth corrupteth.")

34 For where your treasure is, there will your heart be also.

35 Let your loins be girded about (be dressed and ready), and *your* lights burning (have your lamps burning, as in the Parable of the Ten Virgins, Matthew 25:1-13);

36 And ye yourselves like unto men that wait (are prepared) for their lord, when he will return from the wedding; that when he cometh and knocketh, they may open unto him immediately.

Note: The counsel and imagery here deal with our being prepared for the Second Coming. When the Savior actually does come, there will be no time for further preparation to meet him. As indicated at the end of verse 36 above, we must be prepared to "immediately" open the door for him when he comes. In other words, those who are prepared and worthy will "immediately" be taken up to meet him at his coming. See D&C 88:96.

37 Blessed are those servants, whom the lord when he cometh shall find watching: verily I say unto you, that (JST "for") he (Christ) shall gird (prepare) himself, and make them to sit down to meat (eat, symbolic of partaking of the blessings of the gospel), and will come forth and serve them.

Note: The Joseph Smith Translation (JST) adds much for verses 38-48 here. As we continue, we will put a few notes in these verses as they stand in Luke. Then, at the end of verse 48, we will include JST Luke 12:41-57 in its entirety, which covers Luke 12:38-48.

38 And if he shall come in the second watch (in the middle of the night), or come in the third watch (the early morning hours before sunrise; see Bible Dictionary, page 788), and find *them* so (watching and prepared), blessed are those servants.

Note: The scriptures are very clear that no one knows the exact timing of the Second Coming. See Matthew 24:36 and Mark 13:32.

39 And this know, that if the goodman (owner) of the house had known what hour the thief would come, he would have watched (would not have been caught off guard), and not have suffered (allowed) his house to be broken through (into).

40 Be ye therefore ready also: for the Son of man (Christ) cometh at an hour when ye think not.

41 Then Peter said unto him, Lord, speakest thou this parable unto us, or even to all?

42 And the Lord said, (I speak to those who are faithful) Who then is that faithful and wise steward, whom his lord shall make ruler over *his* household (who will attain exaltation), to give *them their* portion of meat (their reward) in due season (when it is time)?

43 Blessed is that servant, whom his lord when he cometh shall find so doing (living righteously).

44 Of a truth I say unto you, that he will make him ruler over all that he hath (exaltation; see D&C 84:37-38).

45 But and if that servant say in his heart, My lord delayeth his coming; and shall begin to beat the menservants and maidens, and to eat and drink, and

to be drunken; (In other words, if people live wickedly because they either don't believe the Lord will come, or think that they have plenty of time to repent after they have "enjoyed" wickedness...)

46 The lord (Christ) of that servant will come in a day when he looketh not for *him* (when he is not prepared), and at an hour when he is not aware, and will cut him in sunder (he will be destroyed at the Second Coming), and will appoint him his portion (punishment) with the unbelievers.

47 And that servant, which knew his lord's will (was accountable), and prepared not *himself* (those who knew the gospel but didn't live it), neither did according to his will, shall be beaten with many *stripes* (will be severely punished; in ancient times, each time a person was hit with a whip, it was called a "stripe").

Note: This may sound harsh, but we are governed by eternal laws. The Savior has taught us over and over again in the scriptures, that mercy cannot rob justice, "Nay; not one whit." (Alma 42:25.) He constantly extends him mercy to us (Jacob 6:4), and through his Atonement allows us to repent, be healed of the aftermath of sin, and become righteous, clean, new people. However, if we ignore the gospel and do not live as we know we should, then the Law of Justice must take over and we have to suffer for our own sins, which suffering is beyond our ability to comprehend. (See D&C 19:15-19.)

48 But he that knew not (did not know the gospel, therefore was not as accountable), and did commit things worthy of stripes, shall be beaten with few stripes. (All people are born with a conscience, and therefore have some degree of accountability, whether they know the gospel or not.) For unto whomsoever much is given, of him shall be much required (see D&C 82:3): and to whom men have committed much (JST "and to whom the Lord has committed much"), of him they will ask the more. (More is expected of them.)

Note: As indicated in the note at the end of verse 37 above, JST 12:41-57, which covers verses 38-48, is included here and reads as follows:

41 For, behold, he cometh in the first watch of the night, and he shall also come in the second watch, and again he shall come in the third watch.

42 And verily I say unto you, He hath already come, as it is written of him; and again when he shall come in the second watch, or come in the third watch, blessed are those servants when he cometh, that he shall find so doing;

43 For the Lord of those servants shall gird himself, and make them to sit down to meat, and will come forth and serve them.

44 And now, verily I say these things unto you, that ye may know this, that the coming of the Lord is as a thief in the night.

45 And it is like unto a man who is an householder, who, if he watcheth not his goods, the thief cometh in an hour of which he is not aware, and taketh his goods, and divideth them among his fellows.

46 And they said among themselves,

If the good man of the house had known what hour the thief would come, he would have watched, and not have suffered his house to be broken through and the loss of his goods.

47 And he said unto them, Verily I say unto you, be ye therefore ready also; for the Son of man cometh at an hour when ye think not.

48 Then Peter said unto him, Lord, speakest thou this parable unto us, or unto all?

49 And the Lord said, I speak unto those whom the Lord shall make rulers over his household, to give his children their portion of meat in due season.

50 And they said, Who then is that faithful and wise servant?

51 And the Lord said unto them, It is that servant who watcheth, to impart his portion of meat in due season.

52 Blessed be that servant whom his Lord shall find, when he cometh, so doing.

53 Of a truth I say unto you, that he will make him ruler over all that he hath.

54 But the evil servant is he who is not found watching. And if that servant is not found watching, he will say in his heart, My Lord delayeth his coming; and shall begin to beat the menservants, and the maidens, and to eat, and drink, and to be drunken.

55 The Lord of that servant will come in a day he looketh not for, and at an hour when he is not aware, and will cut him down, and will appoint him his portion with the unbelievers.

56 And that servant who knew his Lord's will, and prepared not for his Lord's coming, neither did according to his will, shall be beaten with many stripes.

57 But he that knew not his Lord's will, and did commit things worthy of stripes, shall be beaten with few. For unto whomsoever much is given, of him shall much be required; and to whom the Lord has committed much, of him will men ask the more. (End of JST quote.)

49 (JST adds "For they are not well pleased with the Lord's doings; therefore") I am come to send fire on the earth (because people do not keep the commandments, they will be burned at his coming) ; and what will I, if it be already kindled?

50 But I have a baptism to be baptized with (I have a "baptism of fire", a most difficult task of my own, namely, to perform the Atonement.); and how am I (JST "I am") straitened (confined, can't go on to other things) till it be accomplished (I must not deviate at all from my assigned course, until I have accomplished it)!

51 Suppose ye (do you suppose) that I am come (have come) to give peace on earth? I tell you, Nay; but rather division (to divide the righteous from the wicked):

52 For from henceforth (from now on) there shall be five in one house divided, three against two, and two against three. (In other words, some members of a family will accept the gospel and others will not. As a result, they will be divided against each other.)

53 The father shall be divided against the son, and the son against the father; the mother against the daughter,

and the daughter against the mother; the mother in law against her daughter in law, and the daughter in law against her mother in law.

54 And he said also to the people, When ye see a cloud rise out of the west, straightway (right away) ye say, There cometh a shower; and so it is. (You predict the weather by looking at the signs in the sky.)

55 And when *ye see* the south wind blow, ye say, There will be heat (it will be hot); and it cometh to pass (it happens).

56 *Ye* hypocrites, ye can discern the face of the sky (you can predict the weather by looking at the signs in the sky) and of the earth; but how is it that ye do not discern this time (why are you so blind to the signs about the coming of Christ, which are all around you)?

57 Yea, and why even of yourselves judge ye not what is right? (These signs are so obvious that you should be able to tell what's going on without help!)

Note: Next, the Savior gives counsel for us to be peacemakers. He counsels us to work things out quickly with those with whom we have a disagreement, rather than letting it fester and drag on. If we have bad feelings, bitterness, hatred etc. toward others, and do not quickly work it out, it is like being thrown into prison. The longer it drags on, the more difficult it is to work through. We pay a much heavier price by allowing such things to go unresolved than if we would quickly and humbly work things out.

58 When thou goest with thine adversary to the magistrate (when someone takes you to court; symbolic of when you have a disagreement with someone), *as thou art* in the way (as you are on your way to the courthouse), give diligence (try hard) that thou mayest be delivered from him (to make peace and work things out with him before you go to court); lest he hale thee to the judge (for fear that he will take you in front of the Judge), and the judge deliver thee (turns you over) to the officer, and the officer cast thee (puts you) into prison.

59 I tell thee, thou shalt not depart thence (you will not get out of the prison you allowed yourself to be put in), till thou hast paid the very last mite (until you have paid dearly every last bit of the punishment).

LUKE 13

1 THERE were present at that season (JST "At that time") some that told him (Jesus) of the Galilæans, whose blood Pilate had mingled with their sacrifices (who had been killed by Pontius Pilate, the Roman governor).

2 And Jesus answering (responding) said unto them, Suppose ye that these Galilæans were sinners above all the Galilæans, because they suffered such things? (Do you suppose that they were more wicked than other Galileans, and that's why they were killed?)

3 I tell you, Nay: but, except ye repent, ye shall all likewise perish (if you don't repent, you will all be killed off by enemies).

4 Or those eighteen, upon whom the tower in Siloam fell, and slew (killed)

them, think ye that they were sinners above all men that dwelt in Jerusalem (worse sinners than anyone else in Jerusalem)?

5 I tell you, Nay: but, except ye repent, ye shall all likewise perish.

Note: This next parable is known as "The Parable of the Barren Fig Tree". The main point is that it is what you actually do that counts, not what you say you will do. If you claim to be spiritual and righteous, but your deeds are evil, you will end up being destroyed by your enemies (symbolic of Satan and his evil hosts). It was given in the winter of 32 AD. The notes in parentheses give one possible interpretation out of many possibilities.

6 He spake also this parable (a story that teaches a particular point); A certain *man* (the Father) had a fig tree (the Jews) planted in his vineyard (on earth); and he came and sought fruit (looked for righteous lives) thereon (among the Jews), and found none.

7 Then said he unto the dresser of his vineyard (symbolic of Christ; see Talmage, *Jesus the Christ*, page 443), Behold, these three years (the three years of Christ's mission) I come seeking fruit (righteousness) on this fig tree (among the Jews), and find none: cut it down (John the Baptist said "now...the axe is laid unto the root of the trees"; Luke 3:9; in other words, destruction is almost here for the wicked Jews); why cumbereth it the ground (why let it keep cluttering the earth)?

8 And he (Jesus) answering said unto him, Lord, let it alone this year also,

till I shall dig about it (cultivate it), and dung it (nourish it; in other words, let's give the Jews one more chance to repent):

9 And if it bear fruit, *well* (if they do, wonderful!): and if not, *then* after that (this one more chance) thou shalt cut it down (destroy their nation).

Note: The Jews did not take advantage of this last opportunity, at that time, to repent. They crucified Christ and persecuted his followers. The Romans completed the destruction of Jerusalem and the Jews about 70-73 AD.

10 And he was teaching in one of the synagogues on the sabbath.

11 And, behold, there was a woman which had a spirit of infirmity (had been weak and sickly) eighteen years, and was bowed together (was bent over), and could in no wise lift up *herself* (could not straighten herself out at all).

12 And when Jesus saw her, he called *her to him*, and said unto her, Woman, thou art loosed from thine infirmity (you are set free from being crippled).

13 And he laid *his* hands on her: and immediately she was made straight, and glorified (praised) God.

14 And the ruler of the synagogue answered (responded) with indignation (anger), because that Jesus had healed on the sabbath day, and said unto the people, There are six days in which men ought to work: in them therefore come and be healed, and not on the sabbath day. (If you want to be healed in my synagogue, come on any

of the six days of the week when work is permitted. But don't come to be healed on the Sabbath.)

15 The Lord then answered him, and said, *Thou* hypocrite, doth not each one of you on the sabbath loose (untie) his ox or *his* ass from the stall, and lead him away to watering?

16 And ought not this woman, being a daughter of Abraham, whom Satan hath bound, lo, these eighteen years, be loosed (freed) from this bond (the bondage of being crippled) on the sabbath day? (You treat your beasts of burden better that you treat this woman.)

17 And when he had said these things, all his adversaries (opponents) were ashamed: and all the people rejoiced for all the glorious things that were done by him.

18 Then said he, Unto what is the kingdom of God like? and whereunto shall I resemble it (unto what shall I compare it)?

19 It is like a grain of mustard seed (a very tiny seed; symbolic of very small beginnings for the Church), which a man (God) took, and cast into his garden (the earth); and it grew, and waxed a great tree (became a large tree); and the fowls of the air lodged in the branches of it.

Note: Joseph Smith explained this parable. " And again, another parable put He forth unto them, having an allusion to the Kingdom that should be set up, just previous to or at the time of the harvest, which reads as follows—'The Kingdom of Heaven is like a grain of mustard seed, which a man took and sowed in his field: which indeed is the least of all seeds: but, when it is grown, it is the greatest among herbs, and becometh a tree, so that the birds of the air come and lodge in the branches thereof.' Now we can discover plainly that this figure is given to represent the Church as it shall come forth in the last days." For more of the Prophet's explanation, see *Teachings of the Prophet Joseph Smith*, pages 98-99 and page 159.

20 And again he said, Whereunto shall I liken the kingdom of God?

21 It is like leaven (yeast), which a woman took and hid in three measures of meal, till the whole was leavened. (The Church will start out small but will expand into the whole world; see *Teachings of the Prophet Joseph Smith*, pages 100 and 102.)

22 And he went through the cities and villages, teaching, and journeying toward Jerusalem.

23 Then said one unto him, Lord, are there few that be saved (will just a few be saved)? And he said unto them,

24 Strive to enter in at the strait (narrow) gate: for many, I say unto you, will seek to enter in (into heaven), and shall not be able.

25 When once the master of the house (the Lord) is risen up, and hath shut to the door (once your opportunities to repent and join Christ are over), and ye begin to stand without (outside), and to knock at the door, saying, Lord, Lord, open unto us; and he shall answer and say unto you, I know you not whence ye are (you don't belong to me; you haven't made covenants with me):

26 Then shall ye begin to say, We

have eaten and drunk in thy presence, and thou hast taught in our streets.

27 But he shall say, I tell you, I know you not whence ye are (you do not belong to me); depart from me, all ye workers of iniquity (wickedness).

28 There shall be weeping and gnashing of teeth (grinding teeth together in agony), when ye shall see Abraham, and Isaac, and Jacob, and all the prophets, in the kingdom of God, and you *yourselves* thrust out.

29 And they (righteous people who have made and kept covenants with me) shall come from the east, and from the west, and from the north, and *from* the south (in other words, from all nations of the world), and shall sit down in the kingdom of God.

30 And, behold, there are last (the humble, righteous who are considered by the wicked to be the lowest) which shall be first (exalted), and there are first (the wicked who considered themselves to be superior to the righteous) which shall be last (will receive the lowest rewards on Judgment Day).

31 The same day there came certain of the Pharisees (Jewish religious leaders), saying unto him (Jesus), Get thee out, and depart hence (leave!): for Herod will (desires to) kill thee.

32 And he said unto them, Go ye, and tell that fox (King Herod), Behold, I cast out devils, and I do cures to day and to morrow, and the third *day* (the day I am resurrected) I shall be perfected.

33 Nevertheless I must walk to day, and to morrow, and the *day* following (I will not leave; my work requires that I stay here to complete it): for it cannot be that a prophet perish out of Jerusalem. (It is prophesied that I will be killed in Jerusalem, and so it must be.)

Note: The JST adds a verse here. It is: "This he spake, signifying of his death. And in this very hour he began to weep over Jerusalem,"

34 (JST "Saying") O Jerusalem, Jerusalem, which killest the prophets, and stonest them that are sent unto thee; how often would I have gathered thy children (your people) together, as a hen *doth gather* her brood (chicks) under *her* wings, and ye would not (you would not come)!

Note: There is beautiful symbolism here. The Savior compares himself to a mother hen, with warm, soft feathers under her wings, where her chicks can be gathered to comfortable safety when danger comes. His invitation to the Jews has been to come to the warm, pleasant peace and safety of the gospel, but they have rejected his offer.

35 Behold, your house is left unto you desolate: and verily I say unto you, Ye shall not see me (JST "Ye shall not know me, until ye have received from the hand of the Lord a just recompense for all your sins;"), until *the time* come when ye shall say, Blessed *is* he that cometh in the name of the Lord.

LUKE 14

1 AND it came to pass, as he (Jesus) went into the house of one of the chief Pharisees (a man very high up in religious leadership) to eat bread on the

sabbath day, that they (the Jewish religious leaders who are trying desperately to find a way to get rid of him) watched him.

2 And, behold, there was a certain man before him (in front of him) which had the dropsy (probably edema accompanied by severe swelling).

3 And Jesus answering (responding) spake unto the lawyers and Pharisees, saying, Is it lawful (legal) to heal on the sabbath day?

4 And they held their peace (didn't reply). And he took *him* (the man with dropsy), and healed him, and let him go;

5 And answered them (asked the lawyers and Pharisees), saying, Which of you shall have an ass or an ox fallen into a pit, and will not straightway (immediately) pull him out on the sabbath day?

6 And they could not answer him again to these things (they couldn't come up with a good answer).

7 And he put forth a parable to those which were bidden (to the guests at the dinner), when he marked (noticed) how they chose out the chief (most prestigious) rooms; saying unto them,

8 When thou art bidden of (invited by) any *man* to a wedding, sit not down in the highest room (the room reserved for the guests who were highest in authority in the community); lest a more honourable man than thou (one higher in authority than you) be bidden of (invited by) him;

9 And he that bade thee (the host) and him (the man higher in authority than you) come and say to thee, Give this man place (let this guest sit where you are sitting); and thou begin with

shame (with embarrassment) to take the lowest room.

10 But when thou art bidden (invited), go and sit down in the lowest room; that when he that bade thee (the host) cometh, he may say unto thee, Friend, go up higher: then shalt thou have worship (respect) in the presence of them that sit at meat (at dinner) with thee.

11 For whosoever exalteth himself (pridefully presents himself to others as being important) shall be abased (put down, humbled); and he that humbleth himself shall be exalted.

12 Then said he (Jesus) also to him that bade him (who invited him to this dinner), When thou makest a dinner or a supper, call not (don't invite) thy friends, nor thy brethren (family members), neither thy kinsmen (relatives), nor *thy* rich neighbours; lest they also bid thee again (return the favor by inviting you to their place), and a recompence be made thee (you are thus repaid).

Note: Jesus is teaching here that true charity and generosity are demonstrated when you do kind things for others with no thought or chance for reward.

13 But when thou makest a feast, call the poor, the maimed (crippled), the lame, the blind:

14 And thou shalt be blessed (by God); for they cannot recompense thee (pay you back): for thou shalt be recompensed at the resurrection of the just (your payment will be that you are resurrected with the righteous and enter celestial glory).

15 And when one of them that sat at meat (dinner) with him heard these things, he said unto him, Blessed is he that shall eat bread in the kingdom of God (is with God in heaven).

Note: This next parable given by the Master is known as the Parable of the Great Supper. The main point is that people who are indifferent to the invitation to participate in the Church and Kingdom of God will lose out and eventually suffer the consequences. The notes in parentheses represent one possible interpretation. See Talmage, *Jesus the Christ*, pages 450-452 for additional information. We understand that this parable was given in Perea in the winter of 33 AD.

16 Then said he unto him, A certain man (God) made a great supper (a great feast of gospel, covenants etc.), and bade (invited) many (the people of covenant Israel, including the Jews):

17 And sent his servant (Jesus, the prophets, missionaries etc.) at supper time to say to them that were bidden (invited), Come; for all things are now ready (the gospel is here for you).

18 And they all with one *consent* began to make excuse. The first said unto him, I have bought a piece of ground, and I must needs go and see it: I pray thee have me excused (please excuse me).

19 And another said, I have bought five yoke of oxen, and I go to prove them (see how they perform): I pray thee have me excused.

20 And another said, I have married a wife, and therefore I cannot come.

21 So that servant came, and shewed (showed) his lord these things (the excuses). Then the master of the house (God) being angry said to his servant, Go out quickly into the streets and lanes of the city, and bring in hither the poor, and the maimed (crippled), and the halt (lame), and the blind (since the covenant people will not come, go into all the world and invite the Gentiles, who are looked upon by the covenant people as spiritually poor, maimed, halt and blind).

22 And the servant said, Lord, it is done as thou hast commanded, and yet there is room (we still have more room, symbolic of the fact that there is plenty of room in the celestial kingdom for everyone who wants to qualify to come).

23 And the lord (the Father) said unto the servant (Christ), Go out into the highways and hedges, and compel (urge, encourage) *them* to come in, that my house may be filled.

Note: The symbolism in the above verses is that the Savior, in his mercy, keeps trying to bring us to the feast of rich blessings prepared by the Father.

24 For I say unto you, That none of those men which were bidden (invited) shall taste of my supper. (None of those of covenant Israel, who refuse to come unto Christ, will partake of the "feast" of gospel blessings.)

25 And there went great multitudes (large crowds) with him: and he turned, and said unto them,

26 If any *man* come to me, and hate not his father, and mother, and wife, and children, and brethren, and sisters, yea, and his own life also, (JST "or in

other words, is afraid to lay down his life for my sake;") he cannot be my disciple.

27 And whosoever doth not bear his cross, and come after me (whoever is not willing to sacrifice whatever is necessary to follow me), cannot be my disciple.

Note: The JST adds a verse here, as follows: "Wherefore, settle this in your hearts, that ye will do the things which I shall teach, and command you." The whole point here is that if you are half-hearted about following the Savior, you will be unsuccessful.

28 For which of you, intending to build a tower, sitteth not down first, and counteth the cost, whether (to see if) he have *sufficient* (enough money) to finish *it*?

29 Lest haply (JST "unhappily"), after he hath laid the foundation, and is not able to finish it, all that behold it begin to mock him,

30 Saying, This man began to build, and was not able to finish. (The JST adds "And this he said, signifying there should not any man follow him, unless he was able to continue; saying,")

31 Or what king, going to make war against another king, sitteth not down first, and consulteth (looks the situation over) whether (to see if) he be able with ten thousand to meet him (the enemy) that cometh against him with twenty thousand?

32 Or else, while the other is yet a great way off, he sendeth an ambassage (ambassador, negotiator), and desireth conditions of peace.

33 So likewise, whosoever he be of

you that forsaketh not all that he hath (is not willing to sacrifice everything for the gospel), he cannot be my disciple.

Note: The JST adds the following before verse 34:

"Then certain of them came to him, saying, Good Master, we have Moses and the prophets, and whosoever shall live by them, shall he not have life? And Jesus answered, saying, Ye know not Moses, neither the prophets; for if ye had known them, ye would have believed on me; for to this intent they were written. For I am sent that ye might have life. Therefore I will liken it unto salt which is good;"

34 Salt *is* good: but if the salt have lost his savour, wherewith shall it be seasoned?

35 It is neither fit for the land, nor yet for the dunghill; *but* men cast it out. He that hath ears to hear, let him hear. (JST here adds "He who hath ears to hear, let him hear. These things he said, signifying that which was written, verily must all be fulfilled."

LUKE 15

1 THEN drew near unto him all the publicans (tax collectors) and sinners for to hear him.

2 And the Pharisees and scribes murmured (grumbled), saying, This man receiveth (accepts) sinners, and eateth with them.

Note: The Pharisees and scribes were very strict about not associating with sinners, as a matter of religion. The following parable which the Savior gives is generally known as the

Parable of the Lost Sheep. Joseph Smith tells us that it is directed to the Pharisees and scribes in verse 2 who are complaining that Jesus is associating with sinners. See *Teachings of the Prophet Joseph Smith*, page 277.

3 And he spake this parable unto them (the grumbling Pharisees and scribes in verse 2), saying,

4 What man of you, having an hundred sheep, if he lose one of them, doth not leave the ninety and nine in the wilderness, and go after that which is lost, until he find it?

5 And when he hath found *it*, he layeth *it* on his shoulders, rejoicing.

6 And when he cometh home, he calleth together *his* friends and neighbours, saying unto them, Rejoice with me; for I have found my sheep which was lost.

7 I say unto you, that likewise joy shall be in heaven over one sinner that repenteth, more than over ninety and nine just persons, which need no repentance.

Note: Reading verse 7 above could make a person feel bad that a repentant sinner makes heaven happier than a righteous person. One could almost be tempted to commit an occasional sin so as to bring more joy to heaven when he or she repents. But wait! That is not at all what verse 7 is saying. Using the Prophet Joseph Smith's explanation that the ninety nine "just persons" represent the Sadducees and Pharisees "that are so righteous; they will be damned anyhow;" (*Teachings of the Prophet Joseph Smith*, page 277-278), we can then understand verse 7 as follows: "There is more joy in heaven over one humble sinner who repents, than over ninety nine self-righteous hypocrites like you Pharisees and Sadducees who claim to be just men who need no repentance!" This verse, then, is actually a scathing rebuke of these evil religious leaders of the Jews, whom the Savior called "whited sepulchres" (Matthew 23:27), in other words, whitewashed coffins which look clean on the outside, but inside are full of rot and filth.

Note: This next parable is usually referred to as the Parable of the Lost Coin. Again, it is in response to the criticism of the Pharisees and scribes in verse 2, and reminds us that it is worth whatever effort is necessary to save one lost soul.

8 Either (another example:) what woman having ten pieces of silver, if she lose one piece, doth not light a candle, and sweep the house, and seek diligently till she find *it*?

9 And when she hath found *it*, she calleth *her* friends and her neighbours together, saying, Rejoice with me; for I have found the piece which I had lost.

10 Likewise, I say unto you, there is joy in the presence of the angels of God over one sinner that repenteth.

Note: Next comes the Parable of the Prodigal Son.

11 And he said, A certain man (symbolic of God) had two sons (symbolic or different types of people):

12 And the younger of them said to *his* father, Father, give me the portion of goods that falleth *to me* (give me my

inheritance now, instead of waiting until you die; symbolism: I am not interested in future exaltation, but rather want to enjoy the ways of the world now). And he (the father) divided unto them *his* living (divided up his property between his two sons; symbolism: our Father respects our agency).

13 And not many days after the younger son gathered all together (put all his financial resources together), and took his journey into a far country (symbolism: he fell away from the church), and there wasted his substance (financial resources) with riotous (wild) living (symbolism: he wasted his potential for joy and happiness in celestial glory for temporary worldly, sinful pleasures).

14 And when he had spent all (symbolism: when he was wasted away by his wicked lifestyle), there arose a mighty famine in that land (symbolism: Satan left him with no support, as taught in Alma 30:60); and he began to be in want (in need, poverty, desperation).

15 And he went and joined himself to (got a job with) a citizen of that country (symbolism: he didn't yet turn to God for help); and he sent him into his fields to feed swine. (Feeding pigs was about the lowest, most humiliating job a person could have; symbolism: he was totally humbled.)

16 And he would fain have filled his belly with the husks that the swine did eat (he got so hungry that even the carob tree pods he was feeding the pigs started to look good to him): and no man gave unto him (no one gave him anything to help him in his poverty;

symbolism: there was no worldly source of effective help for him).

17 And when he came to himself (came to his senses; symbolism: he started repenting), he said, How many hired servants of my father's have bread enough and to spare, and I perish with hunger (I am starving)!

18 I will arise and go to my father, and will say unto him, Father, I have sinned against heaven, and before thee (I have been wicked; symbolic of sincere confession),

19 And am no more worthy to be called thy son (symbolism: I am not worthy of exaltation): make me as (let me be) one of thy hired servants (symbolism: let me go into one of the other degrees of glory).

20 And he arose, and came to his father. But when he was yet a great way off (still a long distance off), his father saw him (had been watching for him), and had compassion, and ran, and fell on his neck (hugged him), and kissed him (symbolism: the Father is merciful and kind and is anxious to "run" to us to help us return to him).

21 And the son said unto him, Father, I have sinned against heaven, and in thy sight, and am no more worthy to be called thy son (symbolism: the son, thoroughly humbled by his wickedness, acknowledges his unworthiness to live with the Father in celestial exaltation).

22 But the father said to his servants, Bring forth the best robe, and put *it* on him; and put a ring on his hand, and shoes on *his* feet:

Note: A question sometimes arises among members of the Church as to whether or not the returning prodigal son could ever repent sufficiently to gain exaltation, especially in view of his intentional wickedness. There is much symbolism in this verse which can help answer that question:

The "robe" is symbolic of royalty and status. It is also symbolic of acceptance by God, as in 2 Nephi 4:33 where Nephi says "O Lord, wilt thou encircle me around in the robe of thy righteousness! O Lord, wilt thou make a way for mine escape before mine enemies!" See also Isaiah 61:10. In Revelation 7:9, white robes are given to those who live in the presence of God (celestial glory). The "best robe" would be symbolic of potential for highest status, in other words, exaltation.

The "ring" is symbolic of authority to rule. Example: a signet ring which a king would use to stamp official documents and make them legal and binding.

"Shoes on his feet": Shoes were very expensive in the days of the Savior's ministry and were only worn by the wealthy and the rulers. Thus, shoes would be symbolic of wealth, power and authority to rule.

Summary: The cultural symbolism in this verse would lead us to believe that the father was not only welcoming his wayward son back with open arms, but also that he was inviting him to repent and reestablish himself as a ruler in his household, symbolic of potential for exaltation. President David O McKay, in April Conference, 1956, speaking of the prodigal son, said "The Spirit of forgiveness will be operative" when the prodigal son comes to himself and repents. Elder Richard G. Scott, in October Conference 2002, speaking of Alma the Younger and the four sons of Mosiah, who he said "were tragically wicked", said that there are no "second-class" citizens after true repentance. Said he, "If you have repented from serious transgression and mistakenly believe that you will always be a second-class citizen in the kingdom of God, learn that is not true." Thus, the prodigal son does not have to remain a "second-class citizen" in the Father's kingdom. However, the older brother may have to change his attitude if he plans to retain his status in the Father's kingdom.

23 And bring hither the fatted calf, and kill *it*; and let us eat, and be merry (symbolic of joy and rejoicing on earth and in heaven when a sinner repents and returns):

24 For this my son was dead (symbolic of being spiritually dead), and is alive again (symbolic of rebirth, through the Atonement); he was lost, and is found. And they began to be merry (to celebrate).

25 Now his elder son (symbolic of a member who has been active all his life) was in the field: and as he came and drew nigh (near) to the house, he heard musick and dancing.

26 And he called one of the servants, and asked what these things meant (what is going on?).

27 And he said unto him, Thy brother is come; and thy father hath killed the fatted calf, because he hath received him safe and sound.

28 And he was angry, and would not go in: (This is hardly appropriate behavior for one who is supposed to be a faithful son.) therefore came his father out, and intreated (pleaded with) him.

29 And he answering said to *his* father, Lo (now see here!), these many years do I serve thee, neither transgressed I at any time thy commandment: and yet thou never gavest me a kid, that I might make merry with my friends: (you never killed even so much as a young goat for me to have a party with my friends!)

30 But as soon as this thy son (implies "thy son", not my brother anymore) was come (came home), which hath devoured thy living with harlots (wasted his inheritance with prostitutes), thou hast killed for him the fatted calf.

31 And he said unto him, Son, thou art ever with me, and all that I have is thine. (This presupposes that the older son rethinks his attitude about his returning younger brother, repents and helps him to get reestablished in his father's household.)

32 It was meet (needful, good) that we should make merry (celebrate), and be glad: for this thy brother (emphasizing that he is "your brother", not just "my son") was dead (spiritually), and is alive again (has repented, is a new person); and was lost, and is found.

LUKE 16

Note: This next parable is known as the Parable of the Unjust Steward.

1 AND he said also unto his disciples, There was a certain rich man, which had a steward (a man in charge of all his business dealings); and the same was accused unto him (someone complained to the rich man) that he (the steward) had wasted his goods (was mismanaging the business).

2 And he called him, and said unto him, How is it that I hear this of thee (what's this I hear about you)? give an account of thy stewardship (give me a report on how the business is doing); for thou mayest be no longer steward (I am going to fire you).

3 Then the steward said within himself, What shall I do? for my lord taketh away from me the stewardship: I cannot dig (I can't do manual labor); to beg I am ashamed (I would be embarrassed to be a beggar).

4 I am resolved what to do, that, when I am put out of the stewardship, they may receive me into their houses (I have a plan, so that, after I am fired, I will have friends who will take care of me).

5 So he called every one of his lord's debtors (people who owed the owner money) *unto him*, and said unto the first, How much owest thou unto my lord?

6 And he said, An hundred measures of oil. And he said unto him, Take thy bill, and sit down quickly, and write fifty.

7 Then said he to another, And how much owest thou? And he said, An hundred measures of wheat. And he said unto him, Take thy bill, and write fourscore (eighty).

8 And the lord commended (congratulated) the unjust steward, because he

had done wisely: for the children of this world are in their generation wiser than the children of light (often, people in business worry more about their future security on earth than members of the church worry about their future security in heaven; see Talmage, *Jesus the Christ*, page 463).

9 And I say unto you, Make to yourselves friends of the mammon of unrighteousness; that, when ye fail (when your life is over), they may receive you into everlasting habitations. (Elder Talmage [see reference above in verse 8] suggests that this verse basically means that we should make "friends" in heaven by using money wisely and honestly, so that you can enter heaven. Money is often used dishonestly by others, and is thus referred to as "the mammon of unrighteousness".)

10 He that is faithful in that which is least (in small responsibilities) is faithful also in much: and he that is unjust (dishonest) in the least is unjust also in much.

11 If therefore ye have not been faithful in the unrighteous mammon (if you are not honest in your dealings with people), who will commit to your trust the true *riches* (how can you be trusted with the true riches of eternity, the gospel, covenants etc.)?

12 And if ye have not been faithful in that which is another man's (in the daily world of business), who shall give you that which is your own (how do you expect to earn a place in heaven)?

13 No servant can serve two masters: for either he will hate the one, and love the other; or else he will hold to the one, and despise the other. Ye cannot serve God and mammon (you cannot be righteous and worldly at the same time).

14 And the Pharisees also, who were covetous (greedy), heard all these things: and they derided (mocked) him.

15 And he said unto them, Ye are they which justify yourselves before men (make yourselves look righteous in public); but God knoweth your hearts: for that which is highly esteemed among men is abomination in the sight of God (even though people respect you and think you are righteous, God knows that you are full of evil and wickedness).

16 The law and the prophets (the Old Testament books) were until John: since that time the kingdom of God is preached, and every man presseth (strives to get) into it (JST "every man who seeketh truth presseth into it").

17 And it is easier for heaven and earth to pass, than one tittle of the law to fail.

Note: Verses 16 and 17 are very fragmentary. Much got left out of the Bible here. The JST adds the following:

"16 And they said unto him, We have the law, and the prophets (the Old Testament); but as for this man (Jesus) we will not receive him to be our ruler; for he maketh himself to be a judge over us.

17 Then said Jesus unto them, The law and the prophets (the books of the Old Testament) testify of me; yea, and all the prophets who have written, even until John (up to and including John the Baptist), have foretold of

these days.

18 Since that time, the kingdom of God is preached, and every man who seeketh truth presseth (seeks to get) into it.

19 And it is easier for heaven and earth to pass, than for one tittle (tiny bit) of the law (the words of God in the Old Testament) to fail (not be fulfilled).

20 And why teach ye the law (the Old Testament), and deny that which is written (that which is prophesied about me; see verse 17); and condemn him (Jesus) whom the Father hath sent to fulfill the law (to fulfill the prophesies about him given in the Old Testament), that ye might all be redeemed?

21 O fools! for you have said in your hearts, There is no God (you secretly believe that there is no God). And you pervert (pollute) the right way; and the kingdom of heaven suffereth violence of you (the kingdom of God is badly damaged by you); and you persecute the meek; and in your violence you seek to destroy the kingdom; and ye take the children of the kingdom (righteous saints) by force (you use force to stop righteous people from living their religion). Woe unto you (you are in deep trouble!), ye adulterers!

22 And they reviled (angrily responded to) him again, being angry for the saying (what Jesus had just said), that they were adulterers.

23 But he continued, saying, Whosoever putteth away his wife, and marrieth another, committeth adultery; and whosoever marrieth her who is put away from her husband, committeth adultery. Verily I say unto you, I will

liken you unto the rich man."

This is the end of the JST verses. We will now continue with the Bible version as it stands.

18 (JST "But he continued, saying,"; in other words, he continued scolding the Pharisees who had attempted to ridicule him in verse 14) Whosoever putteth away his wife, and marrieth another, committeth adultery: and whosoever marrieth her that is put away from *her* husband committeth adultery. (JST adds "Verily I say unto you, I will liken you unto the rich man.)

Note: The JST additions in the above verses give very important insight to verse 18. When taken alone, as it stands in Luke 16:18, and applied to everyone, it becomes a real problem. It would then mean that anyone who is divorced and remarries is guilty of adultery. Divorce is a very serious problem today and in most cases is not justified. Yet, when things are in proper order and the individuals involved are worthy, the Lord through our prophets today allows people who have been divorced to remarry and be sealed in the temple. Certainly this would not be the case if the very ordinance of marrying immediately made them adulterers. The JST shows us that Jesus was addressing the hypocritical Pharisees, who verbally attacked him in verse 14. Thus, we understand that, among other evil practices, the Pharisees were secretly involved in marrying and divorcing to make their sexual conquests seem legal. The Savior said they were adulterers and strongly condemned them for this evil at the end of JST Luke 12:21, which unfortunately was left out of the Bible.

19 There was a certain rich man (remember that the Savior is comparing the Pharisees with this rich man; see verse 18 above), which was clothed in purple and fine linen, and fared sumptuously (lived in luxury) every day:

20 And there was a certain beggar named Lazarus, which (who) was laid at his gate, full of (covered with)sores,

21 And desiring to be fed with the crumbs which fell from the rich man's table: moreover the dogs came and licked his sores. (Symbolizing that dogs take better care of beggars and people in need than the Pharisees do.)

22 And it came to pass, that the beggar died, and was carried by the angels into Abraham's bosom (was taken to paradise): the rich man also died, and was buried;

23 And in hell he lift up his eyes, being in torments, and seeth Abraham afar off, and Lazarus in his bosom (with Abraham in paradise).

24 And he cried and said, Father Abraham, have mercy on me, and send Lazarus, that he may dip the tip of his finger in water, and cool my tongue; for I am tormented in this flame (it is miserable here in hell).

25 But Abraham said, Son, remember that thou in thy lifetime receivedst thy good things, and likewise Lazarus evil things: but now he is comforted, and thou art tormented.

26 And beside all this, between us and you there is a great gulf fixed: so that they which would pass from hence to you cannot; neither can they pass to us, that *would come* from thence.

Note: This "gulf" or barrier between spirit prison and paradise was bridged by the Savior during the time that his body lay in the tomb and his spirit visited the righteous in paradise. There, in paradise, he set up missionary work and authorized the righteous spirits in paradise to go to spirit prison and teach the gospel there. See D&C, section 138, 1 Peter 3:18 and 4:6.

27 Then he said, I pray thee therefore, father (Abraham), that thou wouldest send him to my father's house (to warn them about what has happened to me):

28 For I have five brethren (brothers); that he (Lazarus) may testify unto them, lest they also come into this place of torment (hell, spirit prison).

29 Abraham saith unto him, They have Moses and the prophets; let them hear them. (They have already been given that message through the writings of the prophets in the scriptures.)

30 And he said, Nay, father Abraham (they don't pay much attention to the scriptures): but if one went unto them from the dead, they will repent. (That would scare them enough to repent.)

31 And he said unto him, If they hear not (pay no attention to) Moses and the prophets, neither will they be persuaded (converted), though one rose from the dead (even if one came back from the dead to them).

LUKE 17

1 THEN said he unto the disciples, It is impossible but (unavoidable, inevitable) that offences will come (things will come along that cause people to sin): but woe *unto him*, through whom they come!

2 It were better for him that a millstone were hanged about his neck, and he cast into the sea, than that he should offend (cause to commit sin; cause to stumble in the gospel; see Matthew 17;6, footnote a) one of these little ones (children or righteous adult members who are childlike in their faith).

3 Take heed to yourselves (be careful): If thy brother trespass (sins) against thee, rebuke (tell) him; and if he repent, forgive him.

4 And if he trespass against thee seven times in a day, and seven times in a day turn again to thee, saying, I repent; thou shalt forgive him. (Be forgiving.)

5 And the apostles said unto the Lord, Increase our faith.

Note: Verses 6-10 seem to be instruction from the Lord on strengthening our faith. First he tells them the power of faith. Then he explains that they must avoid thinking that God owes them because they keep the commandments (see Mosiah 2:22-24). This counsel appears to be designed to keep them humble to enable them to better exercise faith.

6 And the Lord said, If ye had faith as a grain of mustard seed, ye might say unto this sycamine tree (mulberry tree), Be thou plucked up by the root, and be thou planted in the sea; and it should obey you.

7 But which of you, having a servant plowing or feeding cattle, will say unto him by and by (immediately; see Luke 17:7, footnote b), when he is come from the field, Go and sit down to meat (sit down and eat your dinner)?

8 And will not rather (instead) say unto him, Make ready wherewith I may sup (prepare my dinner), and gird thyself (clean up), and serve me, till I have eaten and drunken; and afterward thou shalt eat and drink?

9 Doth he thank that servant because he did the things that were commanded him? I trow (think) not.

10 So likewise ye, when ye shall have done all those things which are commanded you, say, We are unprofitable servants: we have done that which was our duty to do.

11 And it came to pass, as he went to Jerusalem, that he passed through the midst of Samaria and Galilee.

12 And as he entered into a certain village, there met him ten men that were lepers (had leprosy), which stood afar off:

13 And they lifted up *their* voices (spoke loudly), and said, Jesus, Master, have mercy on us.

14 And when he saw *them*, he said unto them, Go shew yourselves unto the priests (as required by the Law of Moses; see Leviticus 14:2). And it came to pass, that, as they went, they were cleansed (healed).

15 And one of them, when he saw that he was healed, turned back, and with a loud voice glorified (praised) God,

16 And fell down on *his* face at his

feet (humbly laid down at Jesus' feet-a sign of deep humility in Jewish culture), giving him thanks: and he was a Samaritan.

Note: Samaritans were despised by Jews and Jews were despised by Samaritans (inhabitants of Samaria). Originally, about 700 years before Christ, the ancestors of the Samaritans were members of the tribes of Israel, especially Ephraim. When the Assyrians conquered the Ten Tribes and took them away into captivity about 722 BC, Israelites who were permitted to remain ended up inter-marrying with the occupational armies. This led to their being shunned by the Jews and developed into the long-standing ethnic dislike and hatred prevalent at the time of Christ's mortal ministry.

17 And Jesus answering said, Were there not ten cleansed (healed)? but where *are* the nine?

18 There are not found that returned to give glory to God, save this stranger (foreigner, non Israelite; this may imply that the other nine lepers were Jews) .

19 And he said unto him, Arise, go thy way: thy faith hath made thee whole.

20 And when he was demanded of (asked by) the Pharisees, when the kingdom of God should come, he answered them and said, The kingdom of God cometh not with observation:

21 Neither shall they say, Lo here! or, lo there! for, behold, the kingdom of God is within you (JST "has already come unto you").

22 And he said unto the disciples, The days will come, when ye shall desire to see one of the days of the Son of man (Jesus), and ye shall not see *it*. (Perhaps meaning that there will be days when the disciples will long for a day with the Savior, or perhaps meaning that they will long for his Second Coming.)

23 And they (people) shall say to you, See here (Christ is here); or, see there (Christ is there): go not after *them,* nor follow *them* (don't believe them).

24 For as the lightning, that light-eneth out of the one *part* under heaven, shineth unto the other *part* under heaven; so shall also the Son of man be in his day (at the Second Coming). (In other words, when the Savior comes again, it won't be a low key event, with his appearing to a small group here or a little group there. Rather, when he comes, everyone will see him at once, just like everyone, from horizon to horizon, sees a large light-ning strike.)

25 But first (before his Second Coming) must he suffer many things, and be rejected of this generation (he must suffer, be rejected and crucified).

26 And as it was in the days of Noe (Noah), so shall it be also in the days of the Son of man (at the time of the Second Coming). (At the time of the Second Coming, people will be ignoring the gospel just like they did in the days of Noah.)

27 They did eat, they drank, they married wives, they were given in marriage, until the day that Noe (Noah) entered into the ark, and the flood came, and destroyed them all.

28 Likewise also as it was in the days of Lot (Abraham's nephew, who chose to live in Sodom; see Genesis 19:1); they did eat, they drank, they bought, they sold, they planted, they builded;

29 But the same day that Lot went out of Sodom it rained fire and brimstone from heaven, and destroyed *them* all. (All the wicked in Sodom and Gomorrah were destroyed [Genesis 19:24], just like the wicked will be at the Second Coming.)

30 Even thus shall it be in the day when the Son of man is revealed (at the Second Coming).

31 In that day, he which shall be upon the housetop, and his stuff in the house, let him not come down to take it away: and he that is in the field, let him likewise not return back.

32 Remember Lot's wife (who looked back, in disobedience to very simple instructions from God; see Genesis 19:17 and 26).

33 Whosoever shall seek to save his life (by making his own rules) shall lose it (will lose salvation); and whosoever shall lose his life (follow God's laws) shall preserve it (will gain salvation).

34 I tell you, in that night (when the Savior actually comes) there shall be two *men* in one bed; the one shall be taken (taken up to meet him; see D&C 88:96), and the other shall be left (to be burned).

35 Two *women* shall be grinding together; the one shall be taken, and the other left.

36 Two *men* shall be in the field; the one shall be taken, and the other left.

37 And they answered and said unto him, Where, Lord (JST "Where, Lord, shall they be taken")? And he said unto them, Wheresoever the body is, thither will the eagles be gathered together.

Note: The JST clarifies verse 37 above, then adds three more verses 38-40. They are as follows:

"37 And he said unto them, Wheresoever the body is gathered; or, in other words, whithersoever the saints are gathered, thither (to that place) will the eagles be gathered together; or, thither will the remainder be gathered together.

38 This he spake, signifying the gathering of his saints; and of angels descending and gathering the remainder unto them; the one from the bed, the other from the grinding, and the other from the field, whithersoever he listeth (chooses).

39 For verily there shall be new heavens, and a new earth, wherein dwelleth righteousness. (The Millennium.)

40 And there shall be no unclean thing (remaining on earth); for the earth becoming old, even as a garment, having waxed in corruption (grown in wickedness), wherefore it (the wickedness) vanisheth away, and the footstool (earth) remaineth sanctified (made holy), cleansed from all sin. (Prepared for the Millennium.)

LUKE 18

Note: This next parable is usually known as the Parable of the Unjust Judge. The main point (see verse 1) seems to be that some situations in life require that we continue to pray for desired blessings over a long period of time and we ought not to give up.

1 AND he spake a parable unto them *to this end* (with this purpose in mind), that men ought always to pray, and not to faint (give up);

2 Saying, There was in a city a judge, which feared not God, neither regarded man:

3 And there was a widow in that city; and she came unto him, saying, Avenge me of mine adversary (I have been wronged; please render judgment against my enemy).

4 And he would not for a while: but afterward he said within himself, Though I fear not God, nor regard man (even though I'm not afraid of God or man);

5 Yet because this widow troubleth me (keeps asking me for help), I will avenge her (grant her request), lest (for fear that) by her continual coming she weary me.

6 And the Lord (Jesus) said, Hear (pay attention to) what the unjust judge saith.

7 And shall not God avenge his own elect (will answer the prayers of his saints for justice) , which cry (pray) day and night unto him, though he bear long with them (even if it takes a long time before he grants their request)?

8 I tell you that he will avenge them speedily (JST "I tell you that he will come [Second Coming] and when he does come, he will avenge his saints [take care of their enemies] speedily"). Nevertheless when the Son of man (Jesus) cometh, shall he find faith on the earth?

Note: This next parable is known as the Parable of the Pharisee and the Publican. Remember that the Pharisees

claim to be important religious leaders of the Jews, live in luxury, are secretly wicked and love to look righteous to others. On the other hand, the publicans are tax collectors and are despised by the Pharisees. This parable was given in Galilee, early in the spring in 33 AD. It warns us against thinking that we are better than others and thus despising people.

9 And he spake this parable unto certain which trusted in themselves that they were righteous, and despised others:

10 Two men went up into the temple to pray; the one a Pharisee, and the other a publican.

11 The Pharisee stood and prayed thus with himself (like this, bragging about himself to God), God, I thank thee, that I am not as other men *are*, extortioners (thieves), unjust (unrighteous), adulterers, or even as this publican.

12 I fast twice in the week, I give tithes of all that I possess (I pay tithing on all I have).

13 And the publican, standing afar off, would not lift up so much as *his* eyes unto heaven, but smote upon his breast (a cultural sign of deep sorrow), saying, God be merciful to me a sinner.

14 I tell you, this man (the publican) went down to his house justified (in harmony with God) *rather* than the other (the Pharisee): for every one that exalteth himself (is lifted up in pride) shall be abased (brought down, humbled); and he that humbleth himself shall be exalted.

15 And they (the people) brought unto him also infants, that he would

touch them: but when *his* disciples saw *it*, they rebuked them (scolded those people).

16 But Jesus called them (his disciples) *unto him*, and said, Suffer (allow) little children to come unto me, and forbid them not: for of such is the kingdom of God.

17 Verily I say unto you, Whosoever shall not receive the kingdom of God as a little child shall in no wise (shall not) enter therein.

18 And a certain ruler asked him, saying, Good Master, what shall I do to inherit eternal life?

19 And Jesus said unto him, Why callest thou me good? none is good, save (except) one, *that is*, God.

Note: There is no agreement among scholars as to the reason Jesus scolded the ruler for calling him "good". Perhaps there was a root word for "good" that, among the Jews, was reserved only for the Father. We will have to leave this alone until we are taught more.

20 Thou knowest the commandments, Do not commit adultery, Do not kill, Do not steal, Do not bear false witness, Honour thy father and thy mother.

21 And he said, All these have I kept from my youth up.

22 Now when Jesus heard these things, he said unto him, Yet lackest thou one thing (there is one thing missing in your life): sell all that thou hast, and distribute unto the poor, and thou shalt have treasure in heaven: and come, follow me.

23 And when he heard this, he was very sorrowful: for he was very rich.

24 And when Jesus saw that he was very sorrowful, he said, How hardly shall they that have riches enter into the kingdom of God (how hard it is for the rich to enter heaven)!

25 For it is easier for a camel to go through a needle's eye, than for a rich man to enter into the kingdom of God.

Note: There is a rumor going around that the "eye of a needle" was a small gate in the walls of Jerusalem, used for entry into the city by night, after the main gates were closed. The rumor states that it was very difficult for a camel to get down and scrunch through the gate. Scholars indicate that this rumor has no truth to it. They indicate that the word "needle", as used in verse 25, refers to an ordinary sewing needle in the original Bible languages.

26 And they that heard it said, Who then can be saved?

27 And he said, The things which are impossible with men are possible with God. (JST "And he said unto them, It is impossible for them who trust in riches, to enter into the kingdom of God; but he who forsaketh the things which are of this world, it is possible with God, that he should enter in.")

28 Then Peter said, Lo, we have left all, and followed thee. (This implies "We have forsaken all to follow you, so, are we going to get into heaven?")

29 And he said unto them, Verily I say unto you, There is no man that hath left house, or parents, or brethren, or wife, or children, for the kingdom of God's sake,

30 Who shall not receive manifold

(much) more in this present time, and in the world to come life everlasting (exaltation).

31 Then he took *unto him* the twelve, and said unto them, Behold, we go up to Jerusalem, and all things that are written by the prophets concerning the Son of man (Christ) shall be accomplished.

32 For he shall be delivered unto (turned over to) the Gentiles (the Romans), and shall be mocked, and spitefully entreated (insulted), and spitted on:

33 And they shall scourge (whip, flog) *him*, and put him to death: and the third day he shall rise again (shall be resurrected).

34 And they understood none of these things: and this saying was hid from them, neither knew they the things which were spoken. (They could not comprehend what Jesus was saying.)

35 And it came to pass, that as he was come nigh (near) unto Jericho, a certain blind man sat by the way (road) side begging:

36 And hearing the multitude pass by, he asked what it meant (what was happening).

37 And they told him, that Jesus of Nazareth passeth by.

38 And he cried, saying, Jesus, *thou* Son of David (thou descendent of King David, in other words, thou Promised Messiah), have mercy on me.

39 And they which went before (ahead of Jesus) rebuked (scolded) him, that he should hold his peace (told him to keep quiet): but he cried so much the more (even louder), Thou Son of David, have mercy on me.

40 And Jesus stood (stopped), and commanded him to be brought unto him: and when he was come near, he asked him,

41 Saying, What wilt thou that I shall do unto thee? And he said, Lord, that I may receive my sight.

42 And Jesus said unto him, Receive thy sight: thy faith hath saved thee.

43 And immediately he received his sight, and followed him, glorifying (praising, thanking) God: and all the people, when they saw *it*, gave praise unto God.

LUKE 19

1 AND *Jesus* entered and passed through Jericho.

2 And, behold, *there was* a man named Zacchæus, which was the chief among the publicans (the chief of the tax collectors), and he was rich.

3 And he sought to see Jesus who he was (tried to get where he could get a view of Jesus); and could not for the press (because of the crowd), because he was little of stature (he was a little, short man).

4 And he ran before (so he ran ahead), and climbed up into a sycomore tree to see him: for he (Jesus) was to pass that *way*.

5 And when Jesus came to the place, he looked up, and saw him, and said unto him, Zacchæus, make haste (hurry), and come down; for to day I must abide (stay) at thy house.

Note: This is a rather tender scene. The people hated tax collectors, considering them to be sinners, and Zacchaeus was the head tax collector. Jesus says "I must stay at your house", implying that he himself, the Creator of heaven and earth, had a very strong desire to stay with this humble man and reassure him of his worth to God.

6 And he made haste, and came down (out of the tree), and received him (Christ) joyfully.

7 And when they saw *it*, they all murmured (criticized), saying, That he was gone to be guest with a man that is a sinner.

8 And Zacchæus stood, and said unto the Lord (Jesus); Behold, Lord, the half of my goods I give to the poor; and if I have taken any thing from any man by false accusation (if I have mistakenly collected more taxes than I should from anyone), I restore *him* fourfold (I pay him back four times what I took).

9 And Jesus said unto him, This day is salvation come to this house (I have come to this house), forsomuch as (because) he also is a son of (descendant of) Abraham (is of the House of Israel).

10 For the Son of man (I, Christ) is (has) come to seek and to save that which was lost (those who are lost).

11 And as they heard these things, he added and spake a parable, because he was nigh (near) to Jerusalem, and because they thought that the kingdom of God should immediately appear. (Apparently, the disciples think that the kingdom of God is soon to be established with power and glory. Such is not the case. The Second Coming is still a long way off, and part of the next parable will explain this to the disciples.)

Note: This next parable is known as the Parable of the Pounds. In addition to telling the disciples that the Second Coming is still a long way off, the parable seems to have a major message to the effect that each of us is given an equal opportunity to labor diligently in the work of the Lord, and ultimately become gods. Even though we have this equal opportunity, the results of our efforts will vary because of differences in our talents and abilities. Nevertheless, each of us who tries and produces according to our abilities, will be given a stewardship to rule over others, in other words, will become gods. On the other hand, those of us who do nothing to further the work of God with our talents and abilities, will not become gods.

12 He said therefore, A certain nobleman (symbolic of Christ) went into a far country to receive for himself a kingdom, and to return.

13 And he called his ten servants (symbolic of all people), and delivered them ten pounds (each got the same amount of money, one pound; symbolic of the fact that each of us will ultimately have an equal opportunity to serve God and become gods), and said unto them, Occupy till I come (put your pound to good use until I return).

14 But his citizens (symbolic of rebellious people on earth) hated him, and sent a message after him, saying, We will not have this *man* (Christ) to reign over us.

15 And it came to pass, that when he was returned (symbolic of the Second Coming), having received the

kingdom, then he commanded these servants to be called unto him, to whom he had given the money, that he might know how much every man had gained by trading (symbolic of Judgment Day).

16 Then came the first (the first man), saying, Lord, thy pound hath gained ten pounds.

17 And he said unto him, Well, thou good servant: because thou hast been faithful in a very little, have thou authority over ten cities (you can be a god).

18 And the second came, saying, Lord, thy pound hath gained five pounds.

19 And he said likewise to him, Be thou also over five cities (you can be a god).

20 And another came, saying, Lord, behold, *here is* thy pound, which I have kept laid up in a napkin:

21 For I feared thee, because thou art an austere (very strict) man: thou takest up that thou layedst not down, and reapest that thou didst not sow. (In other words, you don't miss a thing!)

22 And he saith unto him, Out of thine own mouth will I judge thee, *thou* wicked servant. Thou knewest that I was an austere man, taking up that I laid not down, and reaping that I did not sow:

23 Wherefore then gavest not thou my money into the bank (why didn't you invest my money; symbolically, why didn't you use the talents and abilities I gave you, to do good?), that at my coming I might have required mine own with usury (interest)?

24 And he said unto them that stood by, Take from him the pound (the

opportunity to become a god), and give it to him that hath ten pounds.

25 (And they said unto him, Lord, he hath ten pounds.) (He has ten pounds already. He doesn't need more.)

26 For I say unto you, That unto every one which hath shall be given; and from him that hath not, even that he hath shall be taken away from him. (Those who become gods will continue to increase in the number of worlds they have, whereas, those who prove unworthy of exaltation will lose the opportunity for exaltation.)

27 But those mine enemies, which would not that I should reign over them (who didn't want me to be their ruler; see verse 14), bring hither (here), and slay *them* before me (symbolic of the wicked who will be destroyed at the Second Coming).

28 And when he had thus spoken, he went before (ahead), ascending (climbing) up to Jerusalem.

29 And it came to pass, when he was come nigh (near) to Bethphage and Bethany, at the mount called *the mount of Olives* (just outside Jerusalem), he sent two of his disciples,

30 Saying, Go ye into the village over against you (across from you); in the which at your entering ye shall find a colt (a young, male donkey) tied, whereon yet never man sat (which has not been broken to ride): loose (untie) him, and bring *him hither*.

31 And if any man ask you, Why do ye loose *him*? thus shall ye say unto him, Because the Lord hath need of him.

32 And they (the two disciples) that were sent went their way, and found even as he had said unto them.

33 And as they were loosing the colt (untying the donkey), the owners thereof said unto them, Why loose ye the colt?

34 And they said, The Lord hath need of him.

35 And they brought him (the donkey) to Jesus: and they cast their garments upon the colt, and they set Jesus thereon.

Note: This is what is referred to as the "Triumphal Entry", when Jesus rode into Jerusalem to the cheers and praises of multitudes who welcomed him as the promised one who would free them from their enemies. It is early spring, Passover time, when Jews from all over throng into Jerusalem to celebrate and worship. As Christ rides into Jerusalem, they spread their clothing and palm leaves (John 12:13) on the path in front of him, "thus carpeting the way as for the passing of a king". (Talmage, *Jesus the Christ*, page 514.) Many scholars believe that the Triumphal Entry took place on Sunday. This is the first day of the last week of the Savior's mortal life. He will be crucified on Friday.

36 And as he went, they spread their clothes in the way (on the path in front of him).

37 And when he was come nigh (near Jerusalem), even now at the descent of the mount of Olives, the whole multitude of the disciples began to rejoice and praise God with a loud voice for all the mighty works that they had seen;

38 Saying, Blessed *be* the King that cometh in the name of the Lord: peace in heaven, and glory in the highest.

39 And some of the Pharisees from among the multitude (in the crowd) said unto him, Master, rebuke thy disciples (tell your disciples not to say such things about you).

40 And he answered and said unto them, I tell you that, if these should hold their peace, the stones would immediately cry out.

41 And when he was come near, he beheld the city (Jerusalem), and wept over it,

42 Saying, If thou hadst known, even thou, at least in this thy day, the things *which belong* unto thy peace (if only your inhabitants had been righteous and had done things which would have brought you peace)! but now they are hid from thine eyes (peace is no longer available).

43 For the days shall come upon thee, that thine enemies shall cast a trench about thee, and compass thee round, and keep thee in on every side (you will be attacked by enemy armies who will lay siege against you, dig trenches around you, and surround you),

44 And shall lay thee (Jerusalem) even with the ground (will tear you down to the ground), and thy children (inhabitants) within thee; and they (enemy armies) shall not leave in thee one stone upon another; because thou knewest not the time of thy visitation (because you would not acknowledge that your day of punishment would come).

Note: Next, Jesus cleanses the temple again. Brother Talmage suggests that this takes place on Monday. See *Jesus the Christ*, pages 524-529. John tells us (John 2:14-17) that Jesus cleansed the temple at the beginning of his ministry. Now, three years later, Jesus cleanses it again. This is the second time and the money changers obviously hadn't learned their lesson the first time. This cleansing of the temple would involve clearing the outer courtyard of the temple grounds of those involved in making these sacred grounds a "den of thieves". Money changers, who exchanged temple coins for foreign currency, and merchants who sold animals for sacrifices had reduced the temple grounds to anything but a sacred place.

45 And he (Jesus) went into the temple, and began to cast out them that sold therein, and them that bought;

46 Saying unto them, It is written (in the scriptures; see Jeremiah 7:11), My house is the house of prayer: but ye have made it a den of thieves.

47 And he taught daily in the temple. (This must have been very frustrating to the religious leaders of the Jews, especially after Jesus had cleansed the temple.) But the chief priests and the scribes and the chief of the people sought to destroy him,

48 And could not find what they might do: for all the people were very attentive to hear him. (They couldn't figure out a way to destroy Jesus without causing a riot among the people.)

LUKE 20

Note: The religious rulers of the Jews are getting desperate. Jesus' popularity is increasing. The huge crowds,

including Jewish pilgrims from many countries, are very excited about Jesus, and are no doubt talking enthusiastically about his cleansing of the temple yesterday. These hypocritical religious leaders have lost every public debate with Jesus in the past. They are losing face with the people. Three groups of leaders, the chief priests, the scribes and the elders now have joined together to confront the Master.

1 AND it came to pass, *that* on one of those days (probably Tuesday; see Talmage, *Jesus the Christ*, page 530), as he taught the people in the temple, and preached the gospel, the chief priests and the scribes came upon *him* with the elders,

2 And spake unto him, saying, Tell us, by what authority doest thou these things (including cleansing the temple yesterday)? or who is he that gave thee this authority?

3 And he answered and said unto them, I will also ask you one thing; and answer me: (I will ask you one question. If you answer mine, I will answer yours; see Matthew 21:24.)

4 The baptism of John, was it from heaven, or of men (did John the Baptist have authority from heaven, or was he just an ordinary man)?

5 And they reasoned with themselves (talked it over among themselves), saying, If we shall say, From heaven; he will say, Why then believed ye him not?

6 But and if we say, Of men; all the people will stone us: for they be persuaded (the people believe) that John was a prophet.

7 And they answered, that they could

not tell whence *it was* (they could not answer his question).

8 And Jesus said unto them, Neither tell I you by what authority I do these things.

Note: In this next parable, known as the Parable of the Wicked Husbandmen, the Savior clearly compares the wicked Jewish religious leaders to the wicked husbandmen who kill the owner's son in an attempt to take the kingdom from him. The notes in parentheses in the parable represent one possible interpretation.

9 Then began he to speak to the people this parable; A certain man (symbolic of Heavenly Father) planted a vineyard (planted grape vines; symbolic of establishing Israel, especially the Jews [see Isaiah 5:7] in the Holy Land), and let it forth (turned them over) to husbandmen (farmers in charge of the vineyard; symbolic of the religious leaders of the Jews), and went into a far country (heaven) for a long time.

10 And at the season (at harvest time) he sent a servant (symbolic of prophets) to the husbandmen, that they should give him of the fruit of the vineyard (the harvest; symbolizing that the leaders were to have taught righteousness and brought people to God): but the husbandmen beat him, and sent *him* away empty (rejected the prophets).

11 And again he sent another servant (more prophets): and they beat him also, and entreated (treated) him shamefully, and sent *him* away empty (rejected them too).

12 And again he sent a third: and they wounded him also, and cast him out.

13 Then said the lord of the vineyard (the owner; symbolic of the Father), What shall I do? I will send my beloved son (symbolic of Christ): it may be they will reverence *him* (respect and honor him) when they see him.

14 But when the husbandmen (symbolic of the religious leaders of the Jews) saw him, they reasoned among themselves, saying, This is the heir (everything will belong to him): come, let us kill him, that the inheritance may be ours (let's kill Jesus so we can keep our power, authority and position over the people).

15 So they cast him (the son of the owner; symbolic of the Savior) out of the vineyard, and killed *him*. What therefore shall the lord of the vineyard (symbolic of Christ) do unto them?

16 He shall come (Second Coming) and destroy these husbandmen, and shall give the vineyard to others (righteous religious leaders; symbolic of the restoration of the gospel through Joseph Smith etc.). And when they heard it, they said, God forbid.

17 And he beheld them (looked at them), and said, What is this then that is written (in the scriptures; see Psalm 118:22), The stone (symbolic of Christ, the "Rock of our salvation") which the builders (the Jews) rejected, the same is become the head of the corner (cornerstone; capstone)?

Note: "Capstone" could symbolize "the finisher of our salvation". Strong's Concordance, numbers 1137 and 1119, suggest a possible association of words to imply "kneeling". This could tie in with the fact that "all shall bow the knee, and every tongue shall confess" that Jesus is the Christ. See D&C 76:110 and Philippians 2:10-11.)

18 Whosoever shall fall upon that stone (Christ) shall be broken; but on whomsoever it shall fall (the wicked), it will grind him to powder.

19 And the chief priests and the scribes the same hour sought to lay hands on him; and they feared the people (they tried to figure out a safe way to arrest him immediately, without causing a riot): for they perceived (they understood) that he had spoken this parable against them. (In other words, they understood full well that they were the "Wicked husbandmen" in the parable Jesus had just told them in verses 9-16 above.)

20 And they (the scribes, Pharisees and elders) watched him, and sent forth spies, which should feign (pretend) themselves just (righteous, sincere) men, that they might take hold of his words (catch Jesus saying something for which he could be arrested), that so they might deliver him unto the power and authority of the governor (the Roman governor, Pontius Pilate).

21 And they (the spies in verse 20) asked him, saying, Master, we know that thou sayest and teachest rightly, neither acceptest thou the person *of any* (you don't change your teachings because of peer pressure), but teachest the way of God truly: (They were indeed pretending to be "just men", as instructed by their evil bosses in verse 20.)

22 Is it lawful (legal) for us to give tribute (pay taxes) unto Cæsar (the Roman emperor), or no?

23 But he perceived their craftiness (Jesus understood their sly intentions), and said unto them, Why tempt ye me (why are you trying to trick me)?

24 Shew (show) me a penny (a Roman penny representing about a day's wage). Whose image (picture) and superscription (writing on the coin) hath it? They answered and said, Cæsar's.

25 And he said unto them, Render (pay) therefore unto Cæsar the things which be Cæsar's, and unto God the things which be God's.

26 And they could not take hold of his words before the people (their plot didn't work): and they marvelled (were stunned) at his answer, and held their peace (kept quiet).

27 Then came to *him* certain of the Sadducees (another influential group of Jewish religious leaders, who did not believe in resurrection), which deny that there is any resurrection; and they asked him,

28 Saying, Master, Moses wrote unto us (taught us), If any man's brother die, having a wife, and he die without children, that his brother should take (marry) his wife, and raise up seed unto his brother (produce children for his dead brother).

29 There were therefore seven brethren (brothers): and the first took a wife, and died without children.

30 And the second took her to wife (married her), and he died childless.

31 And the third took her; and in like manner the seven also: and they left no children, and died. (Ultimately, all

seven brothers married her in turn, remained childless, and died. This must have been a rather frightening trend for the last three or four brothers to see.)

32 Last of all the woman died also.

33 Therefore in the resurrection whose wife of them is she? for seven had her to wife.

Note: Here is a major doctrinal point. Many religions use these next three verses to prove that there is no such thing as eternal marriage and family in the next life. On the contrary, the simple fact that the Sadducees asked the Savior whose wife she would be when they are all resurrected (verse 33 above), is proof that the Savior had indeed preached marriage in the resurrection, in other words, eternal marriage. Otherwise, their question would not make any sense at all!

34 And Jesus answering said unto them, The children of this world marry, and are given in marriage:

35 But they which shall be accounted worthy to obtain that world, and the resurrection from the dead (JST "through the resurrection from the dead"), neither marry, nor are given in marriage:

36 Neither can they die any more: for they are equal unto the angels; and are the children of God, being the children of the resurrection.

Note: The above three verses can be confusing. Perhaps these verses are not translated correctly. Perhaps there are some things left out. Whatever the case, we have been given correct doctrine regarding eternal marriage (D&C 132:19-20). We have also been taught that, after everyone from this earth is resurrected, there will be no more eternal marriages performed for former residents of this earth, because such marriages have to be done by mortals for themselves, or by mortals who serve as proxies for those who have died-see D&C 128:15 & 18. Brigham Young said: " And when the Millennium is over,...all the sons and daughters of Adam and Eve, *down to the last of their posterity* (bold added for emphasis), who come within the reach of the clemency of the Gospel,[will] have been redeemed in hundreds of temples through the administration of their children as proxies for them." *Discourses of Brigham Young*, p. 395. Since there will be no mortals left on earth after the resurrection is completed, there would be no one left to serve as proxies for eternal marriages.

37 Now that the dead are raised (the fact that the dead are resurrected; remember that Jesus is talking here to Sadducees, who do not believe in resurrection-see verse 27), even Moses shewed (showed; proved) at the bush (when he talked to God at the burning bush), when he calleth the Lord the God of Abraham, and the God of Isaac, and the God of Jacob.

38 For he is not a God of the dead, but of the living: for all live unto him (everyone will be resurrected).

39 Then certain of the scribes answering said, Master, thou hast well said.

40 And after that they (the spies,

mentioned in verse 20 above, and perhaps others also in the crowd) durst not (didn't dare) ask him any *question at all.*

41 And he said unto them, How say they that Christ is David's son (what do people mean when they say Christ is King David's son)?

42 And David himself saith in the book of Psalms (110:1), The LORD (the Father; see McConkie, *Doctrinal New Testament Commentary*, Vol. 1, page 612) said unto my Lord (Christ), Sit thou on my right hand,

43 Till I make thine enemies thy footstool (until all your enemies have been subdued under your feet).

44 David therefore calleth him Lord (God), how is he then his son (how can he be David's son)?

45 Then in the audience (withing hearing) of all the people he said unto his disciples,

46 Beware of (watch out for) the scribes (religious rulers among the Jews), which (who) desire to walk in long robes, and love greetings in the markets, and the highest seats in the synagogues, and the chief rooms at feasts (they love to appear very important in public);

47 Which devour widows' houses (take widow's houses from them), and for a shew (for show) make long prayers: the same (the scribes) shall receive greater damnation.

LUKE 21

1 AND he looked up, and saw the rich men casting their gifts into the treasury (depositing their donations at the temple in Jerusalem).

2 And he saw also a certain poor widow casting in thither two mites (one mite was about one sixty-fourth of a day's pay; see Bible Dictionary, page 734).

3 And he said, Of a truth (certainly) I say unto you, that this poor widow hath cast in more than they all:

4 For all these (rich men) have of their abundance (plenty) cast in unto the offerings of God: but she of her penury (poverty) hath cast in all the living that she had. (She has given everything she has to live on.)

5 And as some spake of the temple, how it was adorned (decorated) with goodly (beautiful) stones and gifts, he said,

6 *As for* these things (the huge stones used to build the temple) which ye behold (see), the days will come, in the which there shall not be left one stone upon another, that shall not be thrown down (the temple in Jerusalem will be destroyed).

7 And they asked him, saying, Master, but when shall these things be? and what sign *will there be* when these things shall come to pass?

Note: The Savior has just told his disciples about the coming destruction of Jerusalem by the Romans, which will be essentially complete by 73 AD. Next, he will teach them many of the "signs of the times", meaning prophecies which will be fulfilled before the Second Coming. For more complete notes, see Matthew 24 in this book.

8 And he said, Take heed (be careful) that ye be not deceived: for many shall come in my name, saying, I am *Christ*; and the time draweth near: go ye not

therefore after them. (There will be many false christs in the last days. Don't follow them.)

9 But when ye shall hear of wars and commotions, be not terrified (don't panic when you see the signs of the times being fulfilled): for these things must first come to pass (must happen before the Second Coming); but the end is not by and by (right away).

10 Then said he unto them, Nation shall rise against nation, and kingdom against kingdom (in the last days):

11 And great earthquakes shall be in divers (various) places, and famines, and pestilences; and fearful sights and great signs shall there be from heaven.

12 But before all these (things which will happen in the last days), they shall lay their hands on you (the disciples), and persecute *you*, delivering you up to the synagogues (arresting you), and into prisons, being brought before kings and rulers for my name's sake (because of your service to me).

13 And it shall turn to you for a testimony (it will work out so that you can bear testimony of me).

14 Settle *it* therefore (determine) in your hearts, not to meditate before (think in advance) what ye shall answer:

15 For I will give you a mouth and wisdom, which all your adversaries shall not be able to gainsay (oppose, put down) nor resist.

16 And ye shall be betrayed both by parents, and brethren, and kinsfolks (relatives), and friends; and *some* of you shall they cause to be put to death (they will kill some of you).

17 And ye shall be hated of all *men* for my name's sake (because of your loyalty to me).

18 But there shall not an hair of your head perish (unnoticed by God).

19 In your patience (loyal service at all costs) possess ye your souls (you will earn exaltation; the highest degree of glory in the celestial kingdom).

20 And when ye shall see Jerusalem compassed (surrounded) with armies, then know that the desolation thereof is nigh (the "desolation of abomination" spoken of by Daniel; see notes for Matthew 24:15 in this book).

21 Then let them which are in Judæa flee to the mountains; and let them which are in the midst of it depart out; and let not them that are in the countries enter thereinto (come into Judea and Jerusalem).

Note: Many faithful saints at the time of the Roman attacks followed the prophetic counsel in verse 21 above. They fled to Pella, east of Samaria, and thus escaped the Romans.

22 For these be the days of vengeance, that all things (all the prophecies) which are written may be fulfilled.

23 But woe unto them that are with child (are pregnant, so they can't run fast), and to them that give suck (are nursing, thus have small children and can't run away fast with them in tow), in those days! for there shall be great distress in the land, and wrath upon this people (the Jews).

24 And they (the Jews) shall fall (be killed) by the edge of the sword, and shall be led away captive into all nations: and Jerusalem shall be trodden down of (by) the Gentiles,

until the times of the Gentiles be fulfilled. (JST adds "Now these things he spake unto them, concerning the destruction of Jerusalem. And then his disciples asked him, saying, Master, tell us concerning thy coming (the Second Coming)?"

25 And there shall be signs (in the last days) in the sun, and in the moon, and in the stars; and upon the earth distress of nations (much trouble between nations), with perplexity; the sea and the waves roaring (much trouble upon the oceans and waters); (The JST gives verse 25 as follows: "And he answered them, and said, In the generation in which the times of the Gentiles shall be fulfilled, there shall be signs in the sun, and in the moon, and in the stars; and upon the earth distress of nations with perplexity, like the sea and the waves roaring. The earth also shall be troubled, and the waters of the great deep;")

26 Men's hearts failing them for fear (people will be depressed, giving up hope), and for looking after those things (because of seeing the terrible things) which are coming on the earth: for the powers of heaven shall be shaken.

27 And then shall they see the Son of man (Jesus) coming in a cloud with power and great glory (the Second Coming).

Note: Every one will see the Savior, when he comes in glory at the time of his Second Coming, including those who caused his crucifixion. See Revelation 1:7

.

28 And when these things (prophecies) begin to come to pass (begin to happen), then look up, and lift up your heads; for your redemption draweth nigh. (The righteous can rejoice at the Second Coming, because their troubles, persecutions etc. are over.)

Note: Next, Jesus gives the Parable of the Fig Tree. The main point is that, just as a farmer can tell when a fruit tree is about to start growing leaves, so also wise saints will be familiar with the signs of the times so that they will recognize that the Second Coming is near.

29 And he spake to them a parable; Behold the fig tree, and all the trees;

30 When they now shoot forth (start putting on leaves and blossoms), ye see and know of your own selves that summer is now nigh at hand (close at hand).

31 So likewise ye, when ye see these things come to pass (the signs of the times), know ye that the kingdom of God (Second Coming) is nigh at hand (is getting close).

32 Verily I say unto you, This generation shall not pass away (JST "This generation, the generation when the times of the Gentiles be fulfilled, shall not pass away"), till all be fulfilled (until all the signs of the times have been fulfilled).

Note: The "times of the Gentiles" refers to the period of time in the last days when the gospel is being taken to everyone but the Jews. In the days of the Savior's mortal ministry, he and his apostles took the gospel message only to the Jews. Then, after his resurrection, he instructed his apostles to go into all the world (Mark 16:15.) Thus, the Jews were the "first" to get the gospel in the days of the Savior, and the Gentiles (everyone else) were "last". In the last days it will be just the opposite. First, the gospel will be taken to the Gentiles, then it will go to the Jews. Thus, the "last" (Gentiles) will be first (in the last days) and the "first" (Jews) will be last to get it in the last days.

33 Heaven and earth shall pass away: but my words shall not pass away (what I say is absolutely reliable).

34 And take heed to yourselves (watch out), lest at any time your hearts be overcharged with surfeiting (wicked, lustful living), and drunkenness, and cares of this life, and so that day (the Second Coming) come upon you unawares (catches you off guard).

35 For as a snare (a trap which catches an unsuspecting animal totally by surprise) shall it come on all them (the wicked or foolish) that dwell on the face of the whole earth.

Note: D&C 106:4-5 differentiates between the "world" and the "children of light" as far as being caught off guard at the Savior's coming is concerned. The "world", meaning the wicked, will be caught off guard, similar to one who is caught unexpectedly by a "thief in the night" (D&C 106:4.) On the other hand, the "children of light" (D&C 106:5), meaning the saints who are familiar with the signs of the times, are not caught off guard.

36 Watch ye therefore, and pray always, that ye may be accounted worthy to escape all these things that shall come to pass, and to stand (worthily) before the Son of man (Christ).

Note: We understand that, at this point, it is most likely Tuesday evening of the last week of the Savior's life. See Talmage, *Jesus the Christ*, page 563 and 586.

37 And in the day time he was teaching in the temple; and at night he went out, and abode (spent time teaching) in the mount that is called *the mount* of Olives.

38 And all the people came early in the morning to him in the temple, for to hear him.

LUKE 22

1 NOW the feast of unleavened bread drew nigh (near), which is called the Passover.

Note: The Feast of the Passover was celebrated in the springtime at about the same time as we celebrate Easter. It commemorated the destroying angel's passing over the houses of the children of Israel in Egypt, when the firstborn of the Egyptians were killed. The Israelites in Egypt at the time were instructed by Moses to sacrifice a lamb without blemish and to put blood from the lamb which was sacrificed on the doorposts of their houses. See Bible Dictionary, p. 672. Thus, through the blood of a lamb, the Israelites were protected from the anguish and punishment brought to the Egyptians by the destroying angel. The symbolism is clear. It is by the "blood of the Lamb" (the sacrifice of the Savior) that we are saved, after all we can do (2 Nephi 25:23). Now, at the time of Passover in Jerusalem, the "Lamb of God", Christ, will present himself to be sacrificed, that we might be saved. The Feast of the Passover brought large numbers of Jews from near and far to Jerusalem to join in the worship and celebration.

2 And the chief priests and scribes sought how they might kill him; for they feared the people (were afraid of causing a riot by arresting Jesus).

3 Then entered Satan into Judas surnamed Iscariot, being of the number of the twelve.

4 And he (Judas) went his way, and communed (plotted) with the chief priests and captains, how he might betray him (Jesus) unto them.

5 And they were glad, and covenanted to give him money (thirty pieces of silver).

6 And he (Judas) promised (agreed to the terms), and sought opportunity to betray him (Jesus) unto them in the absence of the multitude. (Judas looked for opportunities to betray Jesus quietly, out of sight of the public. We understand this to be taking place at the end of the third day of the last week of the Savior's life, probably Tuesday.)

7 Then came the day of unleavened bread, when the passover must be killed. (This is Thursday, the fifth day of the week, when the actual feast of the Passover was eaten.)

8 And he (Jesus) sent Peter and John, saying, Go and prepare us the passover, that we may eat (find a place for us to eat the Passover meal).

9 And they said unto him, Where wilt thou that we prepare?

10 And he said unto them, Behold, when ye are entered into the city, there shall a man meet you, bearing a pitcher of water; follow him into the house where he entereth in.

11 And ye shall say unto the goodman (owner) of the house, The Master saith unto thee, Where is the guestchamber (room), where I shall eat the passover with my disciples?

12 And he shall shew (show) you a large upper room furnished: there make ready.

13 And they went, and found as he had said unto them: and they made ready the passover.

14 And when the hour was come, he sat down, and the twelve apostles with him.

15 And he said unto them, With desire (deep emotion) I have desired to eat this passover with you before I suffer:

16 For I say unto you, I will not any more eat thereof, until it be fulfilled in the kingdom of God.

Note: Jesus now introduces the sacrament to his apostles. This final Passover meal, partaken of with them, is known as the "Last Supper".

17 And he took the cup, and gave thanks, and said, Take this, and divide it among yourselves:

18 For I say unto you, I will not drink of the fruit of the vine, until the kingdom of God shall come (this is the last time I will partake of the sacra-

ment with you during my mortal life; see Matthew 26:29).

19 And he took bread, and gave thanks, and brake it, and gave unto them, saying, This is my body (this represents my body) which is given for you: this do in remembrance of me.

20 Likewise also the cup after supper, saying, This cup is the new testament (the new covenant) in my blood (represents my blood), which is shed for you.

21 But, behold, the hand of him (Judas Iscariot) that betrayeth me is with me on the table.

22 And truly the Son of man (Christ) goeth (dies), as it was determined (planned): but woe unto that man by whom he is betrayed!

23 And they began to enquire among themselves, which of them it was that should do this thing (betray the Savior).

24 And there was also a strife (an argument) among them, which of them should be accounted the greatest (which of them was the most important).

25 And he said unto them, The kings of the Gentiles exercise lordship (power, authority) over them; and they that exercise authority upon them are called benefactors.

26 But ye *shall* not *be* so: but he that is greatest among you, let him be as the younger; and he that is chief, as he that doth serve. (If you want to be the greatest, you must consider yourself to be the lowest and serve the others.)

27 For whether is greater (who is commonly considered to be the most important), he that sitteth at meat (is eating the meal), or he that serveth

(who serves the meal)? *is* not he that sitteth at meat (answer: the person eating the meal)? but I am among you as he that serveth (I am among you as your servant).

28 Ye are they which have continued with me in my temptations (you are my loyal followers).

29 And I appoint unto you a kingdom (you will be exalted), as my Father hath appointed unto me;

30 That ye may eat and drink at my table in my kingdom, and sit on thrones judging the twelve tribes of Israel.

Note: We understand from JST Mark 14:30 that Judas Iscariot has already left the scene to betray the Master. Thus, Christ's statement to the apostles that they are appointed a kingdom, verses 29-30 above, would apply to the eleven remaining apostles, not to Judas.

31 And the Lord said, Simon (Peter), Simon (Peter), behold, Satan hath desired *to have* you, that he may sift *you* as wheat (JST "And the Lord said, Simon, Simon, behold Satan hath desired you, that he may sift the children of the kingdom as wheat."): (Satan would like to destroy Peter's effectiveness, so that the members of the Church would be without his leadership.)

32 But I have prayed for thee, that thy faith fail not (so that Satan will not be successful): and when thou art converted, strengthen thy brethren.

Note: It is significant that the Savior says to Peter, "...when thou art converted, strengthen thy brethren." Peter feels that he is already completely converted and strong in the faith. Yet, this will be a most difficult night for him, as he denies knowing the Savior on three different occasions. Afterwards, he will be much stronger as we see in Acts, chapter 4 and elsewhere.

33 And he said unto him, Lord, I am ready to go with thee, both into prison, and to death.

34 And he said, I tell thee, Peter, the cock (rooster) shall not crow this day, before that thou shalt thrice deny that thou knowest me.

Note: Denying knowing the Savior is not the same as denying the Holy Ghost. Denying the Holy Ghost, as described in D&C 76:31-35, is an unforgivable sin. Peter's denying that he knows the Savior and has been one of his followers for three years is not unforgivable, though so doing brought Peter deep anguish and tears.

35 And he said unto them, When I sent you (on your first missions; see Matthew 10:9-10) without purse (money), and scrip (a bag to carry food in; see Bible Dictionary, page 70), and shoes (a sign of wealth and power), lacked ye any thing (were any of your needs not taken care of)? And they said, Nothing.

36 Then said he unto them, But now, he that hath a purse, let him take *it*, and likewise *his* scrip: and he that hath no sword, let him sell his garment, and buy one. (Things have changed, so from now on, equip yourselves as well as you can.)

37 For I say unto you, that this that is written must yet be accomplished in me (the prophecies about my death, burial and resurrection must now take place), And he was reckoned among the transgressors (including the prophecy that I will be killed between two thieves): for the things concerning me have an end. (The things that are going to happen to me have a purpose, namely, they will lead up to my accomplishing the Atonement.)

38 And they said, Lord, behold, here *are* two swords. And he said unto them, It is enough. (The apostles still don't seem to grasp the significance of what Jesus just told them, that he must go through with the Atonement. Otherwise, they would not have mentioned the swords for defending him against the coming dangers.)

39 And he came out, and went, as he was wont (as was his custom), to the mount of Olives; and his disciples also followed him.

40 And when he was at the place (the Garden of Gethsemane), he said unto them, Pray that ye enter not into temptation.

Note: "Gethsemane" means "oil press". There is significant symbolism here. The Jews put olives into bags made of mesh fabric and placed them in a press to squeeze olive oil out of them. The first pressings yielded pure olive oil which was prized for many uses, including healing and giving light in lanterns. In fact, we consecrate it and use it to administer to the sick. The last pressing of the olives, under the tremendous pressure of additional weights added to the press, yielded a bitter, red liquid which can remind us of the "bitter cup" which the Savior partook of. Symbolically, the Savior is going into the "oil press" (Gethsemane) to submit to the "pressure" of all our sins which will "squeeze" his blood out in order that we might have the healing "oil" of the Atonement to heal us from our sins.

41 And he was withdrawn from them about a stone's cast, and kneeled down, and prayed,

42 Saying, Father, if thou be willing, remove this cup from me: nevertheless not my will, but thine, be done.

43 And there appeared an angel unto him from heaven, strengthening him. (Apostle Bruce R. McConkie suggested that this angel might be Michael [Adam]; see April 1985 General Conference).

44 And being in an agony he prayed more earnestly: and his sweat was as it were great drops of blood falling down to the ground. (JST "...and he sweat as it were great drops of blood".)

Note: Some Christians wonder whether or not Jesus actually did sweat drops of blood, or if it was figurative, because of the wording in Luke. Mosiah 3:7 and D&C 19:18 clear up any doubt. He did bleed from every pore.

45 And when he rose up from prayer, and was come to (returned to) his disciples, he found them sleeping for sorrow (exhausted by their worrying about Jesus and his safety),

46 And said unto them, Why sleep ye? rise and pray, lest ye enter into temptation.

47 And while he yet spake, behold a multitude (a group of soldiers and others, with swords and sticks, sent by and accompanied by the chief priests and elders; see Matthew 26:47, Luke 22:52), and he that was called Judas, one of the twelve, went before them (Judas led them), and drew near unto Jesus to kiss him.

48 But Jesus said unto him, Judas, betrayest thou the Son of man (Son of God) with a kiss?

49 When they which were about him (Jesus' apostles) saw what would follow (what was about to happen), they said unto him, Lord, shall we smite with the sword?

50 And one of them (Peter) smote (struck) the servant of the high priest, and cut off his right ear.

51 And Jesus answered and said, Suffer ye thus far (let them arrest me). And he touched his ear (the servant's ear), and healed him.

52 Then Jesus said unto the chief priests, and captains of the temple, and the elders, which were come to him, Be ye come out, as against a thief (as if I were a thief, trying to hide from you), with swords and staves?

53 When I was daily with you in the temple, ye stretched forth no hands against me (why didn't you arrest me in broad daylight, when I was in the temple): but this is your hour, and the power of darkness (this is the evil hour you've planned, so go ahead with your plot).

54 Then took they him (they arrested him), and led *him*, and brought him into the high priest's house (palace). And Peter followed afar off (at a

distance).

55 And when they (the rowdy crowd who had come to help arrest Jesus) had kindled a fire in the midst of the hall (courtyard), and were set down together, Peter sat down among them.

56 But a certain maid (young lady) beheld (saw) him as he sat by the fire, and earnestly looked upon him (and stared at him), and said, This man was also with him (Jesus).

57 And he denied him (denied knowing Jesus), saying, Woman, I know him not.

58 And after a little while another saw him, and said, Thou art also of them (you are one of Jesus' followers). And Peter said, Man, I am not.

59 And about the space of one hour after another (person in the crowd) confidently affirmed (spoke with confidence), saying, Of a truth (for sure) this *fellow* also was with him: for he is a Galilæan.

60 And Peter said, Man, I know not what thou sayest. And immediately, while he yet spake (while he was speaking), the cock crew (the rooster crowed).

61 And the Lord (Jesus) turned, and looked upon Peter. And Peter remembered the word of the Lord, how he had said unto him, Before the cock crow, thou shalt deny me thrice (three times).

62 And Peter went out, and wept bitterly.

63 And the men that held Jesus mocked him, and smote (hit) *him*.

64 And when they had blindfolded him, they struck him on the face, and asked him, saying, Prophesy, who is it that smote thee? (Use your power to tell us who hits you.)

65 And many other things blasphemously (mockingly) spake they against him.

66 And as soon as it was day, the elders of the people and the chief priests and the scribes came together, and led him into their council (this council was known as the Sanhedrin and was the highest court run by the Jewish religious leaders; see Bible Dictionary, page 769), saying,

67 Art thou the Christ? tell us. And he said unto them, If I tell you (if I say "Yes."), ye will not believe:

68 And if I also ask you, ye will not answer me, nor let *me* go.

69 Hereafter shall the Son of man sit on the right hand of the power of God (after you are finished with me, I will sit on the right side of the Father up in heaven).

70 Then said they all, Art thou then the Son of God? And he said unto them, Ye say that I am ("I am."; see Mark 14:62).

71 And they said, What need we any further witness (why do we need any more evidence)? for we ourselves have heard of his own mouth (we heard from his own mouth that he claims to be the Son of God).

LUKE 23

1 AND the whole multitude of them (the Sanhedrin, verse 66 above) arose, and led him unto Pilate (the Roman governor).

2 And they began to accuse him, saying, We found this *fellow* perverting (undermining) the nation (the Roman Empire), and forbidding to give tribute to Cæsar, saying that he

himself is Christ a King.

Note: In saying that Jesus told people not to pay taxes (tribute) to Caesar, these religious leaders show their true colors as liars. Christ had specifically taught "Render therefore unto Caesar the things which be Caesar's,..." (Luke 20:25).

3 And Pilate asked him, saying, Art thou the King of the Jews? And he answered him and said, Thou sayest it. (John 18:37 records the Master's response as "To this end was I born, and for this cause came I into the world..."; in other words, "Yes, I am.")

4 Then said Pilate to the chief priests and to the people, I find no fault in this man.

5 And they were the more fierce, saying, He stirreth up the people, teaching throughout all Jewry, beginning from Galilee to this place (from Galilee in the north to Jerusalem in the south).

6 When Pilate heard of Galilee, he asked whether the man were a Galilæan (whether or not Jesus was a citizen of Galilee).

Note: What Pontius Pilate is trying to do here is avoid the responsibility of handling the case of Jesus by sending him to the Roman governor of Galilee, who at that time was Herod, and happened to be visiting Jerusalem.

7 And as soon as he knew that he belonged unto Herod's jurisdiction, he sent him to Herod, who himself also was at Jerusalem at that time.

8 And when Herod saw Jesus, he was exceeding (very) glad: for he was desirous to see him of a long season (he had wanted to meet Jesus for a long time), because he had heard many things of him; and he hoped to have seen some miracle done by him.

9 Then he questioned with him in many words; but he answered him nothing (Jesus refused to answer Herod at all).

10 And the chief priests and scribes stood and vehemently (angrily) accused him (presented their case against Jesus to Herod).

11 And Herod with his men of war set him at nought (ridiculed him), and mocked *him*, and arrayed (dressed) him in a gorgeous robe, and sent him again to Pilate.

12 And the same day Pilate and Herod were made friends together: for before they were at enmity between themselves (they were enemies before this).

13 And Pilate, when he had called together the chief priests and the rulers and the people,

14 Said unto them, Ye have brought this man unto me, as one that perverteth the people (undermines the nation): and, behold, I, having examined *him* before you (in front of you), have found no fault in this man touching those things whereof ye accuse him (I find no truth in the things you accuse Jesus of):

15 No, nor yet Herod: for I sent you to him; and, lo, nothing worthy of death is done unto him (Jesus has done nothing worthy of death).

16 I will therefore chastise (lightly punish) him, and release *him*.

17 (For of necessity [according to

custom; see Matthew 27:15 in this book] he must release one [a prisoner] unto them at the feast.)

18 And they cried out all at once, saying, Away with this *man*, and release unto us Barabbas:

19 (Who for a certain sedition [undermining the government] made in the city, and for murder, was cast into prison.)

Note: The name "Barabbas" means "son of the father" (see Bible Dictionary, page 619). This may be symbolic in that the "imposter", Satan, stirred up the multitude to demand the release of an "imposter", Barabbas, while the true "Son of the Father" is punished for crimes which he did not commit.

20 Pilate therefore, willing to release Jesus, spake again to them.

21 But they cried, saying, Crucify *him*, crucify him.

22 And he said unto them the third time, Why, what evil hath he done? I have found no cause of death in him: I will therefore chastise him, and let *him* go.

23 And they were instant (insistant) with loud voices, requiring (demanding) that he might be crucified. And the voices of them and of the chief priests prevailed (won out, meaning that Pilate gave in).

24 And Pilate gave (passed) sentence that it should be as they required (demanded).

Note: Pilate was a weak leader, an embarrassment to the Roman Empire. About three years after this public show of weakness on his part, he was removed from office by the Roman Empire, and tradition has it that he was banished and later committed suicide. See Smith's Bible Dictionary, pages 519-520.

25 And he released unto them him (Barabbas) that for sedition and murder was cast into prison, whom they had desired; but he (Pilate) delivered Jesus to their will (turned him over to the people, as they had requested).

26 And as they led him away, they laid hold upon (siezed) one Simon, a Cyrenian, coming out of the country (a foreigner; probably a Jew from the city of Cyrene, in northern Africa, likely in Jerusalem for the Passover), and on him they laid the cross (made him carry Jesus' cross), that he might bear it after (carry it behind) Jesus.

Note: The Savior would have been very weak, physically, by now, having suffered in Gethsemane, having been mocked and hit by the soldiers, Luke 22:64, and scourged (whipped), Matthew 27:26. Thus, he was too weak physically to carry his own cross, which was a normal part of the punishment of crucifixion.

27 And there followed him a great company of people, and of women, which also bewailed (cried) and lamented (mourned for) him.

28 But Jesus turning unto them said, Daughters of Jerusalem, weep not for me, but weep for yourselves, and for your children.

29 For, behold, the days are coming,

in the which they shall say, Blessed are the barren, and the wombs that never bare, and the paps which never gave suck. (In other words, women who never had children are the fortunate ones. This would be exactly opposite of Jewish culture of the day, in which women who had no children were considered to be the unfortunate ones and were looked down upon.)

30 Then shall they begin to say to the mountains, Fall on us; and to the hills, Cover us. (Conditions will get so bad in Jerusalem that people will desire death rather than face the persecutions and difficulties which will come.)

31 For if they do these things in a green tree, what shall be done in the dry? (If they do such wicked things in good times, what will they do when bad times come?)

Note: The JST adds another verse here. It is: "This he spake, signifying the scattering of Israel, and the desolation of the heathen, or in other words, the Gentiles."

32 And there were also two other, malefactors (criminals), led with him to be put to death.

33 And when they were come to the place, which is called Calvary, there they crucified him, and the malefactors (thieves), one on the right hand, and the other on the left.

34 Then said Jesus, Father, forgive them; for they know not what they do (JST adds "Meaning the soldiers who crucified him"). And they parted his raiment, and cast lots.

Note: The statement, verse 34 above, which Jesus uttered from the cross, shows his compassion for those who were crucifying him. As noted in the JST, verse 34 above, Joseph Smith taught that it applied to the Roman soldiers, rather than to the Jewish religious leaders who arranged his crucifixion and did know what they were doing. Jesus uttered a total of seven recorded statements from the cross. The references for these statements and the statements themselves follow, and are in chronological order:

1. Luke 23:34 "Father, forgive them; for they know not what they do."

2. Luke 23:43 "Today shalt thou be with me in paradise."

3. John 19:26-27 "Woman, behold thy son!" Behold thy mother!"

4. Matthew 27:46 "My God, my God, why hast thou forsaken me?"

5. John 19:28 "I thirst."

6. John 19:30 "It is finished."

7. Luke 23:46 "Father, into thy hands I commend my spirit."

35 And the people stood beholding (staring). And the rulers (religious leaders of the Jews) also with them derided (mocked) *him*, saying, He saved others; let him save himself, if he be Christ, the chosen of God (the Messiah).

36 And the soldiers also mocked him, coming to him, and offering him vinegar,

37 And saying, If thou be the king of the Jews, save thyself.

38 And a superscription also was written over him (a sign was put above him on the cross) in letters of Greek, and Latin, and Hebrew, THIS IS THE KING OF THE JEWS.

39 And one of the malefactors (thieves) which were hanged (being crucified) railed on him (angrily yelled insults at him), saying, If thou be Christ, save thyself and us.

40 But the other (thief) answering (responding) rebuked him (scolded the other thief), saying, Dost not thou fear God, seeing thou art in the same condemnation?

41 And we indeed justly; for we receive the due reward of our deeds (we are getting what we deserve): but this man hath done nothing amiss (wrong).

42 And he said unto Jesus, Lord, remember me when thou comest into thy kingdom.

43 And Jesus said unto him, Verily I say unto thee, To day shalt thou be with me in paradise.

Note: It is a common belief that the thief on the cross went to paradise. This is not the case. Our Bible Dictionary explains this. It says: "The Bible rendering is incorrect. The statement would more accurately read, 'Today shalt thou be with me in the world of spirits' since the thief was not ready for paradise". See Bible Dictionary, page 742. No doubt, with his humble attitude, this thief accepted the gospel as taught by missionaries in Spirit Prison.

44 And it was about the sixth hour (about noon), and there was a darkness over all the earth until the ninth hour (about 3 PM).

Note: In the Jewish time system, the "sixth hour" would be about noon, the "ninth hour" would be about 3 PM in our time system. We understand that Jesus was nailed onto the cross at the "third hour" which would be about 9 AM.

45 And the sun was darkened, and the veil of the temple was rent in the midst (torn in two).

46 And when Jesus had cried with a loud voice, he said, Father, into thy hands I commend my spirit: and having said thus, he gave up the ghost (left his body).

47 Now when the centurion (Roman soldier in command of one hundred soldiers) saw what was done, he glorified God, saying, Certainly this was a righteous man.

Note: It apparently startled the Centurion that Jesus had so much strength that he could speak so loudly. Usually it took two to three days for victims of crucifixion to die, and near the end they were so exhausted they would not be able to speak loudly at all. To this soldier, experienced at crucifying people, it was as if Jesus had voluntarily left his body when he so chose, which indeed he did!

48 And all the people that came together to that sight, beholding the things which were done, smote their breasts, and returned.

Note: Pounding on one's chest, "smote their breasts" in verse 48 above, was a cultural way of expressing deep fear and a feeling of impending doom, destruction etc. It had gotten extremely dark and foreboding over the last three hours. And that, plus Christ's loud voice when he left must have terrified them. Thus they beat their chests, with a feeling of doom hanging over them as they left for home.

49 And all his acquaintance, and the women that followed him from Galilee, stood afar off, beholding these things (watching these things).

50 And, behold, there *was* a man named Joseph, a counsellor (a member of the council of the Jews); *and he was* a good man, and a just:

51 (The same had not consented to the counsel and deed of them;) (Joseph had opposed the decision of the Jewish religious leaders to execute Jesus) he was of Arimathæa, a city of the Jews: who also himself waited for the kingdom of God.

52 This *man* went unto Pilate, and begged (requested) the body of Jesus.

53 And he took it down (from the cross), and wrapped it in linen, and laid it in a sepulchre (a tomb) that was hewn (cut) in stone, wherein never man before was laid.

54 And that day was the preparation, and the sabbath drew on. (It was getting very late on Friday and the Sabbath was about to begin. The Jewish Sabbath was held on Saturday.)

55 And the women also, which came with him (Jesus) from Galilee, followed after (followed Joseph of Arimathea), and beheld (saw) the sepulchre, and how his body was laid.

56 And they returned, and prepared spices and ointments; and rested the sabbath day according to the commandment. (It was too late for them to anoint Jesus' body with spices

and ointments, because such work was forbidden on the Sabbath. So they went home and kept the Sabbath holy, and planned on coming back to the tomb early Sunday morning to finish final preparations for the Savior's burial.)

LUKE 24

1 NOW upon the first *day* of the week (Sunday), very early in the morning, they (the women named in verse 10) came unto the sepulchre (tomb), bringing the spices which they had prepared, and certain *others* with them.

2 And they found the stone rolled away from the sepulchre.

3 And they entered in, and found not the body of the Lord Jesus.

4 And it came to pass, as they were much perplexed thereabout (they were very concerned about this), behold, two men (angels) stood by them (JST says the angels were standing by the stone) in shining garments:

5 And as they (the women) were afraid, and bowed down *their* faces to the earth, they (the angels) said unto them, Why seek ye the living among the dead?

6 He is not here, but is risen (has been resurrected): remember how he spake unto you when he was yet in Galilee,

7 Saying, The Son of man (The Son of God) must be delivered into the hands of sinful men, and be crucified, and the third day rise again.

8 And they remembered his words,

9 And returned from the sepulchre, and told all these things unto the eleven (the apostles), and to all the

rest.

10 It was Mary Magdalene, and Joanna, and Mary *the mother* of James, and other *women that were* with them, which told these things unto the apostles.

11 And their words seemed to them (the apostles) as idle tales (nonsense), and they believed them not.

12 Then arose Peter, and ran unto the sepulchre; and stooping down, he beheld the linen clothes (Jesus' burial clothing) laid by themselves, and departed, wondering in himself at that which was come to pass (wondering what had happened).

13 And, behold, two of them (two of Christ's disciples, not apostles) went that same day to a village called Emmaus, which was from Jerusalem *about* threescore furlongs (about 7 miles from Jerusalem).

14 And they talked together of all these things which had happened.

15 And it came to pass, that, while they communed *together* and reasoned, Jesus himself drew near, and went (started walking) with them.

16 But their eyes were holden that they should not know him. (Jesus kept them from recognizing him.)

17 And he said unto them, What manner of communications *are* these that ye have one to another, as ye walk, and are sad (what are you talking about that makes you so sad)?

18 And the one of them, whose name was Cleopas, answering said unto him, Art thou only a stranger in Jerusalem, and hast not known the things which are come to pass therein these days? (You must have just arrived or you would know the tragic things which

have happened here in recent days.)

19 And he said unto them, What things? And they said unto him, Concerning Jesus of Nazareth, which (who) was a prophet mighty in deed and word (powerful in actions and teaching) before God and all the people:

20 And how the chief priests and our rulers delivered him (turned him over) to be condemned to death, and have crucified him.

21 But we trusted that it had been he which should have redeemed Israel (we were hoping that he would turn out to be the promised Messiah who would free us from our enemies): and beside all this, to day is the third day since these things were done (and besides that, it has been three days now since he was crucified).

22 Yea, and certain women also of our company (of our group of followers of Jesus) made us astonished (told us an amazing story), which were early at the sepulchre (who went to the tomb early this morning);

23 And when they found not his body, they came, saying, that they had also seen a vision of angels, which (who) said that he was alive.

24 And certain of them (Peter and John) which were with us went to the sepulchre, and found it even so as the women had said (found the tomb empty, just like the women said): but him they saw not (but Peter and John didn't see Christ). (The implication here is that, since Peter and John didn't see Jesus, and the women's account couldn't be trusted, because of the emotional state they were in, the whole thing about Jesus has turned out to be

a big disappointment!)

25 Then he said unto them, O fools, and slow of heart to believe all that the prophets have spoken:

26 Ought not Christ to have suffered these things, and to enter into his glory? (In other words, why is it so hard to believe that Jesus was the Christ, that he suffered, died, was resurrected and has entered into his glory in heaven?)

27 And beginning at Moses and all the prophets (starting with the writings of Moses [Genesis, Exodus, Leviticus, Numbers and Deuteronomy] and continuing with the other Old Testament prophets, he expounded unto them (taught them) in all the scriptures the things concerning himself (prophesying of him).

28 And they drew nigh (near) unto the village (Emmaus), whither they went (which was their destination): and he made as though he would have gone further (kept going farther).

29 But they constrained him (stopped him), saying, Abide (stay) with us: for it is toward evening, and the day is far spent. And he went in to tarry (stay) with them.

30 And it came to pass, as he sat at meat (supper) with them, he took bread, and blessed it, and brake, and gave to them.

31 And their eyes were opened, and they knew him; and he vanished out of their sight.

32 And they said one to another, Did not our heart burn within us, while he talked with us by the way (along the way), and while he opened (explained) to us the scriptures?

33 And they rose up the same hour, and returned to Jerusalem, and found the eleven gathered together, and them (other members) that were with them,

34 Saying, The Lord is risen indeed, and hath appeared to Simon (Peter).

35 And they (the two disciples to whom Jesus had appeared on the way to Emmaus) told what things were done in the way (as they walked along the road), and how he was known of them in breaking of bread (how they finally recognized Jesus when he served them supper).

36 And as they thus spake, Jesus himself stood in the midst of them, and saith unto them, Peace be unto you.

37 But they were terrified and affrighted (frightened), and supposed that they had seen a spirit (thought they were seeing a ghost).

38 And he said unto them, Why are ye troubled? and why do thoughts arise in your hearts?

39 Behold (look at) my hands and my feet, that it is I myself: handle (feel) me, and see; for a spirit hath not flesh and bones, as ye see me have.

40 And when he had thus spoken, he shewed (showed) them his hands and his feet.

41 And while they yet believed not for joy (they were so happy they could hardly believe what was happening), and wondered (marvelled), he said unto them, Have ye here any meat (do you have any food)?

42 And they gave him a piece of a broiled fish, and of an honeycomb.

43 And he took it, and did eat before them (before their eyes).

44 And he said unto them, These are (this is what I meant by) the words which I spake unto you, while I was

yet with you, that all things must be fulfilled, which were written in the law of Moses, and *in* the prophets, and *in* the psalms (in other words, the Old Testament), concerning me.

45 Then opened he their understanding, that they might understand the scriptures, (then he taught them.)

46 And said unto them, Thus it is written, and thus it behoved Christ to suffer (Christ had to suffer), and to rise from the dead the third day:

47 And that repentance and remission of sins should be preached in his name among all nations, beginning at Jerusalem. (The Atonement had to be accomplished, in order that repentance and remission of sins could be made available to all people, beginning at Jerusalem.)

48 And ye are witnesses of these things.

49 And, behold, I send the promise of my Father upon you: but tarry ye (wait) in the city of Jerusalem, until ye be endued with (clothed with, endowed with) power from on high.

50 And he led them out as far as to Bethany, and he lifted up his hands, and blessed them.

51 And it came to pass, while he blessed them, he was parted (separated) from them, and carried up into heaven.

52 And they worshipped him, and returned to Jerusalem with great joy:

53 And were continually in the temple, praising and blessing God (expressing gratitude to God). Amen.

THE GOSPEL OF JOHN

John was one of the original twelve apostles. Before that, he was a disciple of John the Baptist, along with Peter, James, and Andrew. He was a fisherman by trade, in partnership with Peter, Andrew (Peter's brother) and James (John's brother). Whereas the Gospels (books) of Matthew, Mark and Luke cover essentially the same material, presenting a narrative of the Savior's mortal life and teachings, the Gospel of John emphasizes the Savior's role in the overall plan of salvation and presents many more doctrines taught by him. According to D&C 7:3, John was translated (has not died yet) and will continue to preach the gospel and help with the gathering of Israel until the Second Coming. In 1831, the Prophet Joseph Smith said that, at that time, John was working with the Lost Ten Tribes, preparing them for their return. See History of the Church, Vol. 1, page 176. John is the author of four other books in the Bible, 1 John, 2 John, 3 John and the Book of Revelation.

JOHN 1

Note: Joseph Smith made many additions and clarifications in verses 1-34. The JST (Joseph Smith Translation of the Bible) contains these changes. You can read JST John 1:1-34, in its entirety, in the back of your LDS Bible, pages 807-808. Many of the JST changes are included here.

1 IN the beginning was the Word, and the Word was with God, and the Word was God. (JST " In the beginning was the gospel preached through the Son. And the gospel was the word, and the word was with the Son, and the Son was with God, and the Son was of God.")

2 The same (Christ) was in the beginning with God.

3 All things were made by him; and without him was not any thing made that was made. (Christ is the creator.)

4 In him was life; and the life was the light of men. (JST " In him was the gospel, and the gospel was the life, and the life was the light of men;")

5 And the light shineth in darkness (in the spiritually dark world); and the darkness comprehended it not. (JST " And the light shineth in the world, and the world perceiveth it not")

6 There was a man sent from God, whose name was John (John the Baptist).

7 The same came for a witness, to bear witness of the Light, that all *men* through him might believe. (JST "The same came into the world for a witness, to bear witness of the light, to bear record of the gospel through the Son, unto all, that through him [Christ] men might believe.")

8 He (John the Baptist) was not that Light, but *was sent* to bear witness of that Light.

9 *That* was the true Light (Christ), which lighteth every man that cometh into the world (see D&C 93:2).

Note: The "Light of Christ" is often referred to as the "conscience" which is given to every person born into this world. This is true, and as a result, all people have a basic God-given ability to tell right from wrong, and thus are

254

accountable to God for their behaviors. A major purpose of the Light of Christ is to lead people to the true gospel, where they can be baptized and receive the Holy Ghost, which is a far more powerful "light".

10 He was in the world, and the world was made by him, and the world knew him not. (JST "Even the Son of God. He who was in the world, and the world was made by him, and the world knew him not.")

11 He came unto his own, and his own received him not (his own people rejected him).

12 But as many as received him, to them gave he power to become the sons of God (power to become exalted; see D&C 76:24), *even* (JST "only") to them that believe on his name:

Note: Just a reminder. The word "even", above, is printed in *italics*. In the King James Bible (the version our church uses), words or phrases in italics mean that the translators did not know for sure what words to use.

13 Which were born (JST "He was born"), not of blood, nor of the will of the flesh, nor of the will of man, but of God. (In other words, Jesus was literally the Son of God, not just a highly successful man born to mortal parents.)

14 And the Word (Christ) was made flesh (received a mortal body), and dwelt among us, (and we beheld his glory, the glory as of the only begotten of the Father,) full of grace (ability to help us) and truth.

Note: Sometimes confusion arises between Christ's being the "only begotten of the Father" and our being spirit sons and daughters of God. In other words, we are also begotten of the Father. So, how can we be begotten of the Father if Christ is the "only begotten" of the Father? The answer is simple. In premortality, all of us, including Jesus, were begotten and born as spirit children of our heavenly parents (see Proclamation on the Family, September 23, 1995, second paragraph). But Jesus was the only mortal whose father was Heavenly Father. Thus, Jesus is the "only begotten of the Father (as a mortal), and that is what the phrase "only begotten" means, wherever we find it in the scriptures.

15 John (the Baptist) bare (bore) witness of him (Christ), and cried (preached), saying, This was he of whom I spake, He that cometh after me is preferred before me (is higher in authority than I am): for he was before me.

16 And of his fulness have all we received, and grace for grace. (JST " For in the beginning was the Word, even the Son, who is made flesh, and sent unto us by the will of the Father. And as many as believe on his name shall receive of his fullness. And of his fullness have all we received, even immortality and eternal life, through his grace.") (We have been taught the fulness or the complete gospel by Christ, thus are in a position to proceed step by step until we gain exaltation.)

17 For the law was given by Moses, *but* grace (JST "life") and truth came

by Jesus Christ. (JST adds "For the law was after a carnal commandment, to the administration of death; but the gospel was after the power of an endless life, through Jesus Christ, the Only Begotten Son, who is in the bosom of the Father.")

Note: Verse 17 above is basically saying that the Law of Moses was a schoolmaster law to help prepare the Israelites for the higher law which the Savior restored to earth. No one could be saved in celestial exaltation through the Law of Moses. It is only through the full gospel, with all covenants and ordinances, that we can be exalted. By the way, this would not be a particularly popular thing for John the Baptist to say, because people of his day would look upon it as a "put down" for Moses, their most important prophet.

18 No man hath seen God at any time; the only begotten Son, which is in the bosom of the Father, he hath declared *him*. (JST "And no man hath seen God at any time, except he hath borne record of the Son; for except it is through him [Christ] no man can be saved.")

Note: Many Christians use verse 18 above, as it stands in the Bible, to argue that Joseph Smith could not have seen Heavenly Father. They, of course, won't accept the JST change, which clears up the matter. Therefore, it is sometimes helpful to invite them to turn to Acts 7:55-56, and show them that Stephen saw both the Father and the Son. If they are honest in heart, this will help them. You could then take

them back to John 1:18 and suggest that "man" can imply worldly, non spiritual, unworthy individuals, who, of course, would not be privileged to see God. An example of the word "man" or "men", used this way, would be Genesis 6:1-3, where "sons of God" (righteous men) married "daughters of men" (worldly women) and thus received the warning that destruction would come within a hundred and twenty years (the Flood) because of such wickedness. Solomon married many "strange women" which would be the equivalent of "daughters of men" and thus lost his testimony. See 1 Kings 11:1-4.

19 And this is the record of John (the Baptist), when the Jews (religious leaders of the Jews) sent priests and Levites from Jerusalem to ask him, Who art thou?

20 And he confessed, and denied not (JST "And he confessed, and denied not that he was Elias"; but confessed (told them plainly), I am not the Christ.

Note: The word "Elias", among other definitions, means "one who prepares the way". See Bible Dictionary, page 663. Obviously, the Jewish religious leaders were familiar with prophecies that said that an Elias would prepare the way before the Messiah (example: Isaiah 40:3), and thus, when they heard all the talk about John the Baptist, they sent some of their men to ask him some questions.

21 And they asked him, What then? Art thou Elias? And he saith, I am not. Art thou that prophet? And he

answered, No. (JST " And they asked him, saying; How then art thou Elias? And he said, I am not that Elias who was to restore all things. And they asked him, saying, Art thou that prophet? And he answered, No.")

Note: Verse 21 above may need a bit of clarification. First of all, Joseph Smith added "I am not that Elias who was to restore all things." This is very helpful, because it lets us know that we are dealing with two different definitions of "Elias" in these verses. One Elias is a "preparer". The other "Elias" is a "restorer". John the Baptist is the "preparer" while Jesus is the "restorer". See Bible Dictionary, page 663. So, what John the Baptist is emphatically saying to the questioners in verse 21 is "No, I am not the Messiah! Rather, I am the Elias who is preparing the way for him."

22 Then said they (the messengers sent from the Jewish religious leaders in verse 19 above) unto him, Who art thou? that we may give an answer to them that sent us. What sayest thou of thyself (tell us about you)?

23 He said, I *am* the voice of one crying in the wilderness, Make straight the way of the Lord, as said the prophet Esaias (Isaiah; see Isaiah 40:3).

24 And they which were sent were of the Pharisees. (Pharisees were religious leaders among the Jews.)

25 And they asked him, and said unto him, Why baptizest thou then, if thou be not that Christ, nor Elias (JST "nor Elias who was to restore all things,") neither that prophet? (In other words, why are you baptizing if you are not the promised Messiah?)

26 John answered them, saying, I baptize with water: but there standeth one among you, whom ye know not; (referring to Jesus, who is just preparing to begin his mortal ministry.)

27 He it is, who coming after me is preferred before me (is higher in authority than I), whose shoe's latchet (sandal buckle) I am not worthy to unloose. (JST " He it is of whom I bear record. He is that prophet, even Elias, who, coming after me, is preferred before me, whose shoe's latchet I am not worthy to unloose, or whose place I am not able to fill; for he shall baptize, not only with water, but with fire, and with the Holy Ghost.")

28 These things were done in Bethabara beyond Jordan, where John was baptizing.

29 The next day John seeth Jesus coming unto him, and saith, Behold the Lamb of God, which taketh away the sin of the world. (John the Baptist bears witness of Jesus to the crowd around him.)

30 This is he of whom I said, After me cometh a man which is preferred before me: for he was before me. (JST " And John bare record of him unto the people, saying, This is he of whom I said; After me cometh a man who is preferred before me; for he was before me,")

31 And I knew him not: but that he should be made manifest to Israel (JST "...and I knew him, and that he should be made manifest to Israel;"), therefore (this is the reason, in answer to the question in verse 25) am I come

baptizing with water.

32 And John bare record, saying, I saw the Spirit descending from heaven like a dove, and it abode upon him. (JST " And John bare record, saying; When he was baptized of me, I saw the Spirit descending from heaven like a dove, and it abode upon him.")

Note: Sometimes people ask whether or not the Holy Ghost, on occasions, changes into a dove. The answer is "No." See *Teachings of the Prophet Joseph Smith*, pages 275-276.

33 And I knew him not: but he that sent me to baptize with water (JST "And I knew him; for he who sent me to baptize with water"), the same said unto me, Upon whom thou shalt see the Spirit descending, and remaining on him, the same is he which baptizeth with the Holy Ghost.

34 And I saw, and bare record that this is the Son of God.

Note: Although John already was acquainted with Jesus (see JST in verses 31 and 32 above), the Holy Ghost bore strong witness of the Savior to John at the time he baptized Christ.

35 Again the next day after John stood, and two of his disciples (the day after he baptized Jesus, John the Baptist was standing there with two of his followers);

36 And looking upon Jesus as he walked (and seeing Jesus as he walked by), he (John) saith, Behold (look!) the Lamb of God!

37 And the two disciples (John's followers) heard him (John the Baptist) speak, and they followed Jesus.

38 Then Jesus turned, and saw them following, and saith unto them, What seek ye (what can I do for you?) They said unto him, Rabbi, (which is to say, being interpreted, Master,) where dwellest thou (where do you live)?

39 He saith unto them, Come and see. They came and saw where he dwelt (lived), and abode (stayed) with him that day: for it was about the tenth hour (about 4 PM).

40 One of the two which heard John *speak*, and followed him, was Andrew, Simon Peter's brother. (Andrew will become one of the Savior's original twelve apostles.)

41 He first findeth his own brother Simon (Peter), and saith unto him, We have found the Messias (the promised Messiah), which is, being interpreted, the Christ ("the Anointed One").

Note: Anointing is a very significant thing in the Bible. It means "being prepared for" a future event or blessing. David was "anointed" to become king some years before he became king. When we administer to the sick, we "anoint" him or her first, in preparation for the actual blessing. Christ was the "Anointed One", meaning he was prepared in advance to actually perform the Atonement when the time was right for his mortal mission.

42 And he (Andrew) brought him (Peter) to Jesus. And when Jesus beheld (saw) him, he said, Thou art Simon the son of Jona: thou shalt be

called Cephas, which is by interpretation, A stone.

Note: It is interesting to watch the Master at work, building Peter's self-image and confidence. Imagine Peter's saying to himself afterward, "Wow! He called me a rock. That means he thinks I am a "rock solid" person. Well, I'll just make sure I am!"

43 The day following Jesus would (wanted to) go forth into Galilee, and findeth Philip, and saith unto him, Follow me.

44 Now Philip was of Bethsaida, the city of Andrew and Peter (the same city where Andrew and Peter lived).

45 Philip findeth Nathanael, and saith unto him, We have found him (the Messiah), of whom Moses in the law (the first five books of the Old Testament), and the prophets (Old Testament prophets such as Isaiah and Jeremiah), did write, Jesus of Nazareth, the son of Joseph (the carpenter of Nazareth).

46 And Nathanael said unto him, Can there any good thing come out of Nazareth? Philip saith unto him, Come and see.

47 Jesus saw Nathanael coming to him, and saith of him, Behold an Israelite indeed, in whom is no guile!

48 Nathanael saith unto him, Whence knowest thou me (how do you know me)? Jesus answered and said unto him, Before that Philip called thee, when thou wast under the fig tree, I saw thee (I saw you sitting under a fig tree before Philip talked to you).

49 Nathanael answered and saith unto him, Rabbi, thou art the Son of God; thou art the King of Israel.

50 Jesus answered and said unto him, Because I said unto thee, I saw thee under the fig tree, believest thou? thou shalt see greater things than these.

51 And he saith unto him, Verily, verily, I say unto you, Hereafter ye shall see heaven open, and the angels of God ascending and descending upon the Son of man (Christ).

Note: Jesus is often referred to as "the Son of man" in the New Testament. Moses 6:57 in the Pearl of Great Price teaches us what it means and how it should be written. It says "...for, in the language of Adam, Man of Holiness is his name (Heavenly Father's name), and the name of his Only Begotten is the Son of Man, even Jesus Christ". Therefore, the full name of the Savior, in the language of Adam, would be "Son of Man of Holiness'. For whatever reason, the printers of the King James Bible neglected to capitalize "Man" and thus printed it "Son of man".

JOHN 2

Note: Next comes one of the most famous miracles performed by the Master. It is the turning of water into wine.

1 AND the third day (JST "the third day of the week") there was a marriage in Cana of Galilee; and the mother of Jesus was there:

2 And both Jesus was called (invited), and his disciples, to the marriage.

Note: Some have wondered if this

could be Jesus' marriage. Several factors combine to suggest that this would not be the case. For one thing, in the culture of the day, the marriage would be held at the groom's home town. If it were Jesus's wedding, it would have been held in Nazareth. Another thing against this notion is that Jesus and his disciples were invited to attend (verse 2). This would be a bit strange if he were the groom. Another factor is that, if it were Christ's wedding, one would expect the Gospel writers to mention it.

3 And when they wanted wine (they ran out of wine), the mother of Jesus saith unto him, They have no wine.

4 Jesus saith unto her, Woman, what have I to do with thee? (JST "Woman, what wilt thou have me to do for thee? That will I do;") mine hour is not yet come (I have time to help).

Note: The word "woman" was a term of high respect in the days of Jesus.

5 His mother saith unto the servants, Whatsoever he saith unto you, do *it* (do whatever he says).

6 And there were set there six waterpots of stone, after the manner of the purifying of the Jews, containing two or three firkins apiece.

Note: A "firkin" was a little more that 8 gallons. See Bible Dictionary, page789, under "bath" and "firkin". So, there were six containers, with a capacity of 16 to 24 gallons each. This would make a total of about 96 to 144 gallons of water which Jesus turned into wine. It is of interest to note that

wedding feasts lasted the better part of a week and there were apparently more guests than expected at this one.

7 Jesus saith unto them (the servants), Fill the waterpots with water. And they filled them up to the brim.

8 And he saith unto them, Draw out now, and bear unto the governor of the feast (take wine out of the containers and take some to the master of ceremonies). And they bare *it*. (The servants must have had a surprised look on their faces.)

9 When the ruler of the feast (host, master of ceremonies) had tasted the water that was made wine, and knew not whence it was (didn't know where it came from): (but the servants which drew the water knew;) the governor of the feast called the bridegroom (the groom),

10 And saith unto him, Every man at the beginning doth set forth good wine; and when men have well drunk, then that which is worse: *but* thou hast kept the good wine until now.

Note: Since wine was expensive, the common practice was to set good wine out at the beginning of the feast, then when the guests had drunk enough to become less discriminating, less expensive wine was served to save on expenses. The master of ceremonies was surprised that the groom was serving the best wine at this point of the feast.

11 This beginning of miracles (the first miracle) did Jesus in Cana of Galilee, and manifested forth his

glory; and his disciples believed on him. (This was a faith promoting miracle for his disciples.)

12 After this he went down to Capernaum, he, and his mother, and his brethren (probably his brothers; see John 2:12, footnote a), and his disciples: and they continued (stayed) there not many days.

13 And the Jews' passover was at hand, and Jesus went up to Jerusalem,

Note: This marks the beginning of the Savior's formal three year public ministry. The Feast of the Passover was celebrated in the springtime at about the same time as we celebrate Easter. It brought large numbers of Jews from near and far to Jerusalem to join in the worship and celebration. It commemorated the destroying angel's passing over the houses of the children of Israel in Egypt, when the firstborn of the Egyptians were killed. The Israelites in Egypt at the time were instructed by Moses to sacrifice a lamb without blemish and to put blood from the lamb which was sacrificed on the doorposts of their houses. See Bible Dictionary, p. 672. Thus, through the blood of a lamb, the Israelites were protected from the anguish and punishment brought to the Egyptians by the destroying angel. The symbolism is clear. It is by the "blood of the Lamb" (the sacrifice of the Savior) that we are saved, after all we can do (2 Nephi 25:23). This is the first Passover attended by Jesus after he began his three year ministry. Three years from now, at the time of Passover in Jerusalem, the "Lamb of God", Christ, will present himself to be sacrificed,

that we might be saved.

14 And found in the temple (the outer courtyard or "temple grounds") those that sold oxen and sheep and doves, and the changers of money sitting:

Note: Because Jews came from all over, including many other countries to worship at the temple in Jerusalem, it had become big business for merchants to sell sacrificial animals and to exchange foreign money for temple coin. It was a wild, boisterous scene of animal sounds, merchants yelling at patrons to buy from them etc., anything but reverent and worshipful, which met the Savior's eyes as he approached the temple. He will cleanse the temple again in three years, during the last week of his life.

15 And when he had made a scourge (whip) of small cords, he drove them all out of the temple, and the sheep, and the oxen; and poured out the changers' money, and overthrew the tables;

16 And said unto them that sold doves, Take these things hence (get these things out of here); make not my Father's house an house of merchandise (a common market place).

17 And his disciples remembered that it was written (in the scriptures), The zeal of thine house hath eaten me up (Psalm 69:9).

18 Then answered the Jews (the Jewish religious leaders responded) and said unto him, What sign shewest thou unto us, seeing that thou doest these things (where did you get

authority to cleanse the temple)?

19 Jesus answered and said unto them, Destroy this temple, and in three days I will raise it up. (In other words, I am the Messiah. That is where I get my authority. When you kill me, as prophesied, I will resurrect in three days.)

20 Then said the Jews (who missed the point completely), Forty and six years was this temple in building (it took forty six years to build this temple), and wilt thou rear it up (rebuild it) in three days?

21 But he spake of the temple of his body.

22 When therefore he was risen from the dead (resurrected), his disciples remembered (recalled) that he had said this unto them; and they believed the scripture, and the word which Jesus had said.

23 Now when he was in Jerusalem at the passover, in the feast *day* (on Thursday, the day of the actual Passover feast), many believed in his name, when they saw the miracles which he did.

24 But Jesus did not commit himself unto them (did not let down his guard), because he knew all *men* (JST "all things"),

25 And needed not that any should testify of man: for he knew what was in man (he knew their thoughts).

JOHN 3

1 THERE was a man of the Pharisees (who was a Pharisee), named Nicodemus, a ruler of the Jews:

Note: The Pharisees were prominent religious leaders among the Jews.

Jesus' popularity has begun to threaten their position of power and control over the Jews. They will play a prominent role in getting Jesus crucified. However, Nicodemus is a good man and will oppose the majority of the Pharisees. He now sincerely seeks Jesus out to ask him questions. He is probably many years older than Jesus. In about three years, he will help Joseph of Arimathea take Christ's crucified body, prepare it for burial and gently place it in the tomb. See John 19:38-42.

2 The same (Nicodemus) came to Jesus by night, and said unto him, Rabbi ("my master", a humble, respectful term for "my teacher"), we know that thou art a teacher come from God: for no man can do these miracles that thou doest, except God be with him.

3 Jesus answered and said unto him, Verily, verily, I say unto thee, Except a man be born again, he cannot see the kingdom of God.

Note: In effect, Jesus is saying to Nicodemus, "I want you to be my child, to be born again to me, and then let me be your parent and raise you in the right ways so that you can live with me in celestial glory."

4 Nicodemus saith unto him, How can a man be born when he is old? can he enter the second time into his mother's womb, and be born?

5 Jesus answered, Verily, verily (this is the main point; listen carefully), I say unto thee, Except a man be born of water (baptized) and *of* the Spirit

(receive the gift of the Holy Ghost), he cannot enter into the kingdom of God (he cannot be taught the things he must do to become celestial).

6 That which is born of the flesh is flesh; and that which is born of the Spirit is spirit (there is a difference between being a common person and being a spiritual person).

7 Marvel not that I said unto thee, Ye must be born again.

8 The wind bloweth where it listeth (where it will), and thou hearest the sound thereof, but canst not tell whence it cometh (where it comes from), and whither it goeth (where it is going): so is every one that is born of the Spirit. (Perhaps meaning that that is how it is with one who has the gift of the Holy Ghost. Promptings come and inspiration is given. We don't demand it or control it any more than we can control the wind, but it does come and it comes according to the will of the Lord.)

9 Nicodemus answered and said unto him, How can these things be?

10 Jesus answered and said unto him, Art thou a master (religious ruler) of Israel, and knowest not these things? (Nicodemus was a member of the Sanhedrin, the chief ruling body of religious leaders over the Jews; see Bible Dictionary, page 769.)

11 Verily, verily, I say unto thee, We speak that (of what) we do know, and testify that we have seen; and ye (the world) receive not our witness (do not accept our testimony).

Note: Verses 11-21 seem to be a direct quote which would be familiar to Nicodemus. See John 3:11, footnote b.

We don't know where it comes from, but the Savior used it to teach this good man.

12 If I have told you earthly things (simple basics such as faith, repentance, baptism etc), and ye believe not, how shall ye believe, if I tell you *of* heavenly things?

13 And no man hath ascended up to heaven, but he that came down from heaven, *even* the Son of man which is in heaven. (Christ bears witness that he is the Son of God.)

14 And as Moses lifted up the serpent in the wilderness (Numbers 21:8-9), even so must the Son of man (Christ) be lifted up: (Christ will be crucified as part of his Atonement.)

15 That whosoever believeth in him should not perish (spiritually), but have eternal life (exaltation).

Note: "Eternal life" always means exaltation.

16 For God so loved the world, that he gave his only begotten Son, that whosoever believeth in him should not perish, but have everlasting life (exaltation).

17 For God sent not his Son into the world to condemn the world; but that the world through him might be saved.

18 He that believeth on him is not condemned (stopped in progress): but he that believeth not is condemned already, because he hath not believed in the name of the only begotten Son of God. (JST adds "which before was preached by the mouth of the holy prophets; for they testified of me.")

Note: The JST addition, "testified of

me" is a most significant addition, because it tells us that Jesus was telling Nicodemus clearly that he, Jesus, is the Son of God.

19 And this is the condemnation (this is the reason people get condemned, damned, stopped), that light is come into the world (because the gospel is presented to them), and men loved darkness rather than light (and people choose wickedness rather than the gospel), because their deeds were evil.

20 For every one that doeth evil hateth the light (wickedness, by its very nature, makes you hate light and truth), neither cometh to the light, lest his deeds should be reproved. (People involved in wickedness won't come to the light because they don't want to face the consequences of their sins.)

21 But he that doeth truth (lives righteously) cometh to the light, that his deeds may be made manifest (made known), that they are wrought in God (accomplished through God's help).

22 After these things came Jesus and his disciples into the land of Judæa (the southern province in which Jerusalem was located); and there he tarried (remained) with them, and baptized.

Note: For a short period of time here, the missions of John the Baptist and Jesus overlapped.

23 And John (the Baptist) also was baptizing in Aenon near to Salim (about half way between the Sea of Galilee and the Dead Sea), because there was much water there: and they came, and were baptized.

Note: The fact that John the Baptist was baptizing in a place where there was "much water" is another reminder that he was baptizing by immersion. In fact, the word "baptize" means to immerse. See Bible Dictionary, page 618, under "Baptism".

24 For John was not yet cast into prison (the Baptist hadn't yet been put in prison).

25 Then there arose a question between some of John's disciples (John the Baptist's followers) and the Jews about purifying. (In other words, a debate as to whether or not direct descendants of Abraham, such as the Jews, even needed baptism in order to be "purified".)

Note: The "purifying", mentioned in verse 25 above, refers to the purifying power of baptism. A long-standing apostate Jewish tradition taught that only Gentile converts needed to be baptized, and that direct descendants of Abraham, such as the Jews, were exempted from baptism. In fact, they had substituted other washing and cleansing rites for themselves. See Mark 7:1-8. See McConkie, *Doctrinal New Testament Commentary*, Vol. 1, page 146.

26 And they (John's disciples) came unto John, and said unto him, Rabbi ("my master"; see Bible Dictionary, page759), he (Jesus) that was with thee beyond Jordan, to whom thou barest

witness (of whom your bore testimony), behold, the same baptizeth, and all men come to him (JST "...the same baptizeth, and he receiveth of all people who come unto him").

Note: Perhaps John's followers are a bit jealous or concerned that "all men come to him", in other words, they are saying "everybody is coming to Jesus". Perhaps they are worried that Jesus is taking away from John's popularity.

27 John answered and said, A man can receive nothing, except it be given him from heaven (each of us only does the work assigned to us by God).

28 Ye yourselves bear me witness (you are my witnesses), that I said, I am not the Christ, but that I am sent before him. (Jesus' mission is to be the Messiah. My mission is to prepare the way for him.)

29 He that hath the bride (to whom the Church belongs) is the bridegroom (Jesus): but the friend (John the Baptist) of the bridegroom, which standeth and heareth him, rejoiceth greatly because of the bridegroom's voice: this my joy therefore is fulfilled. (I am very happy just to be a friend of Jesus and to hear him preaching.)

30 He must increase, but I *must* decrease.

Note: Verse 30, above, is one of the sweetest, humblest statements ever uttered.

31 He (Jesus) that cometh from above (from heaven) is above all (is in charge of all things here): he that is of the earth is earthly (I am just an ordinary man), and speaketh of the earth: he that cometh from heaven is above all.

32 And what he hath seen and heard, that he testifieth; and no man receiveth his testimony (people will reject Christ).

33 He that hath received his testimony hath set to his seal that God is true. (Those who accept Christ's testimony certify that this is God's work.)

34 For he (Christ) whom God (the Father) hath sent speaketh the words of God: for God giveth not the Spirit by measure *unto him* (JST "...for God giveth him not the Spirit by measure, for he dwelleth in him, even the fulness"). (Jesus is not limited in how much of the Spirit of God he has, like we are.)

35 The Father loveth the Son, and hath given all things into his hand (has given Jesus full authority to accomplish his mission).

36 He that believeth on the Son hath everlasting life (will receive exaltation): and he that believeth not the Son shall not see life (will not be exalted); but the wrath (punishment) of God abideth on him (will come upon him).

JOHN 4

1 WHEN therefore the Lord knew how the Pharisees had heard that Jesus made and baptized more disciples than John,

2 (Though Jesus himself baptized not, but his disciples,)

Note: Verse 2 above is a mistake in the Bible. The JST for verses 1-2 is as follows:

"1 When therefore the Pharisees had heard that Jesus made and baptized more disciples than John,

2 They sought more diligently some means that they might put him to death; for many received John as a prophet, but they believed not on Jesus.

3 Now the Lord knew this, though he himself baptized not so many as his disciples;

4 For he suffered them for an example (Jesus set the example for them), preferring one another."

3 He left Judæa, and departed again into Galilee.

4 And he must needs go through Samaria.

Note: Normally, the Jews avoided going through Samaria. The Jews despised the Samaritans (people of Samaria) and the Samaritans despised the Jews. Thus, the Jews normally traveled around Samaria in order to get to Galilee. But this time, Jesus is heading straight north, right through Samaria, which would no doubt cause his apostles some extra anxiety.

5 Then cometh he to a city of Samaria, which is called Sychar, near to the parcel of ground that Jacob gave to his son Joseph (who was sold into Egypt).

6 Now Jacob's well was there. Jesus therefore, being wearied with *his* journey, sat thus on the well: *and* it was about the sixth hour (about noon).

7 There cometh a woman of Samaria to draw water (to get water from the well): Jesus saith unto her, Give me to drink (please give me a drink).

8 (For his disciples were [had] gone away unto the city to buy meat [food].)

Note: The following account of the Savior and the Samaritan woman is both delightful and profoundly moving. For our purposes, we will imagine her to be somewhat feisty and a bit sharp-tongued. We might imagine also a bit of a twinkle in the eyes of the Savior as he begins this conversation.

9 Then saith the woman of Samaria unto him (JST "Wherefore he being alone, the woman of Samaria said unto him"), How is it that thou, being a Jew, askest drink of me, which am a woman of Samaria? for the Jews have no dealings with the Samaritans. (In other words, why would a Jew like you ask a Samaritan woman like me for a drink. Don't you know that Jews don't have anything to do with us?)

Note: Watch, now, as the Savior gets her curiosity up.

10 Jesus answered and said unto her, If thou knewest the gift of God, and who it is that saith to thee, Give me to drink; thou wouldest have asked of him, and he would have given thee living water. (If you knew about the gift Father in Heaven has for you, and who I am, you would have ask me for a drink, and I would have given you "living water".)

11 The woman saith unto him, Sir, thou hast nothing to draw with, and the well is deep: from whence then hast thou that living water? (Sir, you don't even have anything to get water out of

the well. It is way too deep. So, just where do you think you are going to get me some of your so called "living water" from?)

12 Art thou greater than our father Jacob, which gave us the well, and drank thereof himself, and his children, and his cattle? (Do you think your "living water" is better than the water Jacob provided us here in this well? It was good enough for Jacob and his family and his animals. In other words, what makes you think your water is better than the Prophet Jacob's?)

13 Jesus answered and said unto her, Whosoever (whoever) drinketh of this water shall thirst again (will just get thirsty again):

14 But whosoever drinketh of the water that I shall give him shall never thirst (will never be thirsty again); but the water that I shall give him shall be in him a well of water springing up into everlasting life (eternal life).

15 The woman saith unto him, Sir, give me this water, that I thirst not, neither come hither to draw.

Note: The woman still doesn't get it. She thinks Jesus is talking about some kind of magical water that, when someone drinks it, they never get thirsty again. She wants some so that she doesn't ever have to come to the well again and do the hard work of getting water. Watch how the Savior really gets her attention by the next things he says to her. A wonderful teaching moment has been quickly generated by the Master Teacher!

16 Jesus saith unto her, Go, call thy

husband, and come hither (go get your husband and bring him back here).

17 The woman answered and said, I have no husband. Jesus said unto her, Thou hast well said, I have no husband (that is right; you have no husband):

18 For thou hast had five husbands; and he whom thou now hast is not thy husband (you are not married to the man you are living with now): in that saidst thou truly (you were certainly telling the truth when you said you have no husband!).

19 The woman saith unto him, Sir, I perceive that thou art a prophet. (Sir, it just dawned on me that you are a prophet.)

20 Our fathers (ancestors) worshipped in this mountain (worshiped here in Samaria, rather than in Jerusalem); and ye (you Jews) say, that in Jerusalem is the place where men ought to worship.

Note: After Solomon, the Twelve Tribes split into two nations, Israel (ten of the tribes) in the north, with headquarters in Samaria, and Judah (the tribe of Judah and part of Benjamin) in the south, with headquarters in Jerusalem. There was much animosity between the two nations. Consequently, the people of the northern kingdom, Israel, even refused to come to Jerusalem to worship. Instead, they set up an apostate temple and apostate priests in their own country of Samaria and worshiped there.

21 Jesus saith unto her, Woman, believe me, the hour cometh, when ye shall neither in this mountain (here in

Samaria), nor yet at Jerusalem, worship the Father. (In other words, there will be a complete apostasy such that no one will have correct knowledge of God, thus, no one can worship correctly.)

22 Ye worship ye know not what: (Because of apostasy and ignorance, you Samaritans don't really know who or what you worship.) we (Jews) know what we worship: for salvation is of the Jews (salvation comes from the Jews, through Christ).

23 But the hour cometh, and now is, when the true worshippers shall worship the Father in spirit and in truth (the time has arrived when I will restore the true gospel, so that sincere people can worship the Father by the power of the Holy Ghost with true doctrines): for the Father seeketh such to worship him.

Note: The next verse has often been used to discredit Joseph Smith's testimony that "the Father has a body of flesh and bones" (D&C 130:22). This is another place where the Bible was not translated correctly (8th Article of Faith). The JST straightens this out.

24 God *is* a Spirit: and they that worship *him* must worship him in spirit and in truth. (JST "For unto such hath God promised his Spirit. And they who worship him, must worship in spirit and in truth.")

25 The woman saith unto him, I know that Messias (Messiah) cometh, which is called Christ: when he is come, he will tell us all things. (This woman is familiar with the prophecies about the coming of the Messiah, who

will be known as Christ.)

26 Jesus saith unto her, I that speak unto thee am he (the Messiah, Christ; the Jehovah of the Old Testament; see John 4:26, footnote a).

27 And upon this (just as Jesus finished saying this to the woman) came his disciples, and marvelled (were surprised) that he talked with the woman (that he would talk with a Samaritan woman): yet no man said, What seekest thou? or, Why talkest thou with her? (But none of the disciples dared scold him for so doing.)

28 The woman then left her waterpot (left it at the well), and went her way into the city, and saith to the men,

29 Come, see a man, which told me all things that ever I did (who knows everything about me): is not this the Christ?

30 Then they went out of the city, and came unto him (Jesus).

31 In the mean while his disciples prayed him, saying, Master, eat (urged him to eat the food they had bought).

32 But he said unto them, I have meat (food) to eat that ye know not of.

Note: Here, the Master Teacher creates a teaching moment to help his disciples understand more about him and his mission. His disciples at first miss the point completely, thus are "off balance" and in a state of readiness to learn.

33 Therefore said the disciples one to another, Hath any man brought him *ought* (anything) to eat? (The Savior said he has food [verse 32], so the disciples assume someone else must have brought him something to eat

while they were gone buying food.)

34 Jesus saith unto them, My meat (food) is to do the will of him that sent me, and to finish his work.

Note: The implication here is that the "meat" or food, which the Savior has, is to partake of all the work and suffering necessary, as assigned him by the Father, to accomplish the Atonement.

35 Say not ye, There are yet four months, and *then* cometh harvest? behold, I say unto you, Lift up your eyes, and look on the fields; for they are white already to harvest. (You say that harvest is four months away. I say that harvest time is now. In other words, it is time to start "harvesting souls", gathering converts into my Church now.)

36 And he that reapeth (he who helps me gather converts) receiveth wages (receives a reward), and gathereth fruit unto life eternal (stores up blessings for himself in heaven, namely exaltation): that both he that soweth (the prophets of old, who laid the foundation by planting the gospel seeds; see JST verse 40, at the end of verse 38 below) and he that reapeth (he who harvests) may rejoice together. (Those who plant the gospel seed, but don't get to be around long enough to see it grow to maturity in the people, will rejoice together with the missionaries etc. who actually bring the people into the Church.)

37 And herein is that saying true, One soweth, and another reapeth (one person plants and another person harvests).

38 I sent you to reap that whereon ye bestowed no labour (I sent you to harvest where you did not do any of the work to grow and nourish the crop): other men laboured (prophets of old laid the foundation), and ye are entered into their labours (you finish what they started). (JST John 4:40. "I have sent you to reap that whereon ye bestowed no labor; the prophets have labored, and ye have entered into their labors.")

39 And many of the Samaritans of that city believed on him for (because of) the saying of the woman, which testified, He told me all that ever I did.

40 So when the Samaritans were come unto him, they besought him that he would tarry with them (they asked him to stay with them): and he abode (remained) there two days.

41 And many more believed because of his own word;

42 And said unto the woman, Now we believe, not because of thy saying: for we have heard *him* ourselves, and know that this is indeed the Christ, the Saviour of the world.

43 Now after two days he departed thence (he left there), and went into Galilee.

44 For Jesus himself testified, that a prophet hath no honour (is rejected) in his own country.

Note: Jesus' "own country" was his home town of Nazareth. Indeed, the people there rejected him. See Luke 4:16-30.)

45 Then when he was come into Galilee, the Galilæans received him, having seen all the things that he did at

Jerusalem at the feast (at the Passover feast): for they also went unto the feast.

46 So Jesus came again into Cana of Galilee, where he made the water wine (see John 2:1-11). And there was a certain nobleman, whose son was sick at Capernaum.

47 When he heard that Jesus was come out of Judæa into Galilee, he went unto him, and besought (begged) him that he would come down, and heal his son: for he was at the point of death.

48 Then said Jesus unto him, Except ye see signs and wonders, ye will not believe.

49 The nobleman saith unto him, Sir, come down ere my child die (please come before my child dies).

50 Jesus saith unto him, Go thy way; thy son liveth (has been healed). And the man believed the word that Jesus had spoken unto him, and he went his way (headed home).

51 And as he was now going down, his servants met him, and told *him*, saying, Thy son liveth.

52 Then enquired he of them the hour when he began to amend (the nobleman asked his servants when his son began to get better). And they said unto him, Yesterday at the seventh hour (about 1 PM) the fever left him.

53 So the father knew that *it was* at the same hour, in the which Jesus said unto him, Thy son liveth: and himself believed, and his whole house (he and his household were converted to Christ).

54 This is again the second miracle (the first one, according to John, was turning water into wine; see John 2:11)

that Jesus did, when he was come out of Judæa into Galilee.

JOHN 5

Note: This is the beginning of the second year of the Savior's mortal mission. He begins this year by traveling to Jerusalem for the feast of the Passover.

1 AFTER this there was a feast (Passover) of the Jews; and Jesus went up to Jerusalem.

2 Now there is at Jerusalem by the sheep *market* a pool, which is called in the Hebrew tongue Bethesda, having five porches.

3 In these (porches) lay a great multitude of impotent (crippled) folk, of blind, halt (lame), withered, waiting for the moving of the water.

4 For an angel went down at a certain season into the pool, and troubled the water: whosoever then first after the troubling of the water stepped in was made whole (healed) of whatsoever disease he had.

Note: Apparently there was a false belief which gave sick and crippled people hope that they would be healed if they were the first to get into the water after the water started being moved by an unseen angel. This is superstition and is not the way God works.

5 And a certain man was there, which had an infirmity thirty and eight years (had been an invalid for thirty eight years).

6 When Jesus saw him lie (laying there), and knew that he had been now

a long time *in that case* (in that situation), he saith unto him, Wilt thou be made whole (would you like to be healed)?

7 The impotent (crippled) man answered him, Sir, I have no man, when the water is troubled, to put me into the pool: but while I am coming, another steppeth down before me (when I try to get into the water first, someone else always beats me to it).

8 Jesus saith unto him, Rise, take up thy bed, and walk.

9 And immediately the man was made whole (was healed), and took up his bed, and walked: and on the same day was the sabbath (this all happened on the Sabbath).

10 The Jews (religious leaders of the Jews, Pharisees-see Matthew 12:2 and 10) therefore said unto him that was cured (the man who had been healed), It is the sabbath day: it is not lawful (legal) for thee to carry *thy* bed.

11 He answered them, He that made me whole (the man who healed me), the same said unto me, Take up thy bed, and walk.

12 Then asked they him, What man is that which said unto thee, Take up thy bed, and walk?

13 And he that was healed wist not who it was (didn't know the name of the man who had healed him): for Jesus had conveyed himself away, a multitude being in *that* place (Jesus had left right after healing him and was quickly lost in the crowd by the pool).

14 Afterward Jesus findeth him (the man he had healed) in the temple (in the temple courtyard), and said unto him, Behold, thou art made whole (you have been healed): sin no more, lest a worse thing come unto thee.

Note: This had to be a specific case in which future sinning on the part of the man who had been healed would cause physical punishment. We must avoid generalizing this situation to apply to all people. Otherwise, we would come to believe, as did the Jews, that all illness is caused by sin. Imagine the gossip which would go around about anyone who was sick if we believed this false notion!

15 The man departed, and told the Jews that it was Jesus, which had made him whole. (Now that the healed man had met Jesus on the grounds of the Temple, and thus knew his name, he apparently found the Pharisees and told them the name of the man who had healed him.)

16 And therefore did the Jews persecute Jesus, and sought to slay him, because he had done these things on the sabbath day.

Note: Over the centuries, the Jewish religious leaders had imposed thousands of rules and laws concerning Sabbath behavior upon the Jews. These became known as the "tradition of the elders". See Matthew 15:2, Mark 7:5. They were caught up in the "letter of the law" as opposed to the "spirit of the law" regarding the Sabbath. As evidenced in verse 16 above, it was against the law to heal on the Sabbath. A few additional examples of these "traditions of the elders" follow:

Things a faithful Jew was not allowed to do on the Sabbath (according to the Tradition of the Elders):

1. Scatter two seeds (it was considered to be planting).
2. Sweep or break a single clod of dirt (it was considered to be plowing).
3. Pluck one blade of grass.
4. Water fruit or remove a dead leaf.
5. Pick fruit or even lift it from the ground.
6. Cut a mushroom (it was a double sin, one of both harvesting and of planting, because a new one would grow in place of the old one).
7. Roll wheat together to take away the husks (guilty of sifting with a sieve.)
8. Rub the ends of wheat stalks (guilty of threshing).
9. Throw wheat stalks up in the air (guilty of winnowing).
10. Dip a radish in salt for too long a time (could be dipped into salt as long as it was not left too long which would make one guilty of pickling).
11. Rub mud off a dress (mud on a dress might be crushed in the hand and shaken off, but the dress must not be rubbed for fear of bruising the fabric).
12. Spit on the ground then rub it into the soil with the foot (it was considered irrigating because something might grow where you spit; however, it was legal to spit into a handkerchief, or spit upon rocks because nothing would grow).

13. Put a plaster on a sore.
14. Write a big letter, leaving room for two small ones (but it was ok to write one big letter occupying the space of two small letters).
15. Carry a burden that was heavier than a fig.
16. Carry a piece of food larger than the size of an olive.
17. Carry objects that could be put to practical use, for instance, two horse hairs (because they could be made into a bird trap), a scrap of clean paper (because it could be written on), a small piece of paper already written upon (because it could be made into a wrapper).
18. Carry enough ink to write two letters.
19. Carry enough wax to fill up a small hole.
20. Carry a pebble (because you might aim it at a little bird).
21. Carry a small piece of broken pottery (because you could stir coals of a fire with it).
22. Write two letters, either with the right or left hand (but you could write letters in sand, because they would not remain). It was also permitted to write letters with the hand turned upside down, or with the foot, or with the mouth or the elbow.
23. Save a house or its contents from fire (however, you could rescue the scriptures and phylacteries [tiny leather boxes with scripture scrolls in them which the Jews tied to their foreheads or left arms] and the cases that contained them, plus food and

drink needed for the Sabbath. Also, if food were in a basket, the whole basket could legally be carried out with everything in it. Only absolutely necessary clothing could be saved, however, a person might put on a dress, bring it out, take it off, go back in and put on another, save it and so on).

24. Carry a legal burden more than a Sabbath day's journey, which was 2,000 cubits [about 3,000 feet], (however, on Friday, a person could deposit food for two meals 2,000 cubits from his house, then, on the Sabbath, he could go the 2,000 cubits, sit down and eat, and then that would be considered to be his residence and so he could go another 2,000 cubits from that point).

25. Provide first aid, unless the persons life was in danger.

26. Set broken bones.

27. Perform a surgical operation.

28. Wear a plaster on a wound or sore (unless the purpose was to prevent the wound from getting worse rather than an attempt to heal it).

29. Wear false teeth or wear a gold plug in a tooth.

30. Replace wadding if it fell out of the ear.

31. Light a fire.

32. Keep an oven warm.

33. Eat an egg that had been laid on the Sabbath (unless the hen had been kept for eating rather than laying eggs, in which case the egg could be eaten because it was considered to be a part of the hen that had fallen off).

Adapted from McConkie, *The Mortal Messiah*, pages 199-212.

17 But Jesus answered them (in answer to the Jewish religious leaders' criticism of his healing on the Sabbath, verse 16), My Father worketh hitherto, and I work (my Father has done much of his work on the Sabbath, and I will continue to do so too).

18 Therefore (because of Jesus' reply) the Jews sought the more (even more) to kill him, because he not only had broken the sabbath, but said also that God was his Father (claims to be the Son of God), making himself equal with God.

19 Then answered Jesus and said unto them, Verily, verily, I say unto you, The Son can do nothing of himself, but what he seeth the Father do: for what things soever he (the Father) doeth, these also doeth the Son likewise. (In other words, the Son does nothing that is not in complete harmony with the Father's will. See McConkie, *Doctrinal New Testament Commentary*, Vol. 1, page 192.)

Note: Occasionally, members of the Church use verse 19 above to suggest that Heavenly Father was the Savior of the world upon which he grew up. Their reasoning is: since Jesus said that he does nothing but what he sees the Father do, and since Jesus is our Savior, the Father had to have been the Savior on his world. Of course it is possible that the Father was the Savior on his world, but to use this verse to "prove" it is not sound thinking.

Brigham Young said, "The Savior told his disciples as he saw the Father do, so does he, and as Joseph Smith saw Jesus do, so did Joseph do, and as I saw Joseph do, so do I also." (Taken from remarks which appear to have been given at the dedication of the Seventies Hall in Nauvoo, late December, 1844. See BYU Studies, Winter 1978, Volume 18, No. 2, pages 177-178.) Joseph Smith was not crucified. Brigham Young was not martyred in Carthage Jail. From that same volume of BYU Studies, page 176, Joseph Smith says, "For the Savior says, the work that my Father did, do I also,...He took himself...a body and then laid down his life that he might take it up again,...We then also took bodies to lay them down, to take them up again..." Again the point of verse 19 is that Jesus was, in all things, in perfect harmony with the Father's will.

20 For the Father loveth the Son, and sheweth (shows) him all things that himself doeth (that he himself does): and he will shew him greater (more) works than these, that ye may marvel.

21 For as the Father raiseth up the dead (resurrects people), and quickeneth *them* (causes them to become alive spiritually); even so the Son (Christ) quickeneth (gives eternal life to) whom he will.

Note: Since every person who has ever been born on earth will be resurrected (1 Corinthians 15:22), in other words, will be "quickened", the last phrase in verse 21 above cannot mean that Jesus will be selective as to whom he resurrects. Another scriptural use of the

word "quicken" is to be made alive spiritually, which, in turn, leads to eternal life (exaltation). Jesus will be our final judge, and as such will give exaltation to "whom he will".

22 For the Father judgeth no man, but hath committed all judgment unto the Son: (The Father has given all the responsibility for final judgment to Jesus.)

23 That all *men* should honour the Son, even as they honour the Father. He that honoureth not the Son honoureth not the Father which hath sent him.

24 Verily, verily, I say unto you, He that heareth my word, and believeth on him that sent me (Heavenly Father), hath everlasting life (exaltation in the highest degree of glory in the celestial kingdom), and shall not come into condemnation (will not be stopped from eternal progress); but is passed from death unto life.

25 Verily, verily, I say unto you, The hour is coming, and now is, when the dead (in spirit prison; 1 Peter 3:18-21, D&C 138) shall hear the voice of the Son of God: and they that hear (obey) shall live.

26 For as the Father hath life in himself (is "an immortal, resurrected, exalted being,", McConkie, *Doctrinal New Testament Commentary*, Vol. 1, page 194) ; so hath he given to the Son to have life in himself; (Jesus has power over death.)

27 And hath given him authority to execute judgment also, because he is the Son of man (the Son of God). (See Moses 6:57 for an explanation of why Jesus is called the Son of Man.)

28 Marvel not at this: for the hour is coming, in the which all that are in the graves shall hear his voice (everyone will be resurrected),

29 And shall come forth; they that have done good, unto the resurrection of life (eternal life, exaltation); and they that have done evil, unto the resurrection of damnation (those who will have limits placed on their progression; see D&C 76:112).

30 I can of mine own self do nothing (I follow the Father's commands exactly): as I hear, I judge: and my judgment is just (completely fair); because I seek not mine own will, but the will of the Father which hath sent me.

31 If I bear witness of myself, my witness is not true (valid). (The law of witnesses requires that there be at least two witnesses.)

32 There is another (the Father) that beareth witness of me; and I know that the witness which he witnesseth of me is true.

33 Ye sent unto John (the Baptist), and he bare witness unto the truth.

34 But I receive not testimony from man: but these things I say, that ye might be saved. (JST "And he received not his testimony of man, but of God, and ye yourselves say that he is a prophet, therefore ye ought to receive his testimony. These things I say that ye might be saved."

35 He (John the Baptist) was a burning and a shining light: and ye were willing for a season to rejoice in his light.

36 But I have greater witness than *that* of John (that which John the Baptist gave of me): for the works (restoring the gospel, performing the Atonement etc.) which the Father hath given me to finish, the same works that I do, bear witness of me, that the Father hath sent me.

37 And the Father himself, which hath sent me, hath borne witness of me. Ye (the Jews) have neither heard his voice at any time, nor seen his shape (meaning that the Father has "shape", a resurrected, physical body; see D&C 130:22).

38 And ye (the Jews) have not his word abiding in you (do not have the Father's gospel in your hearts): for whom he (the Father) hath sent, him ye believe not (you refuse to believe what I am teaching you).

39 Search the scriptures; for in them ye think ye have eternal life (since you won't listen to me, go ahead and keep studying your scriptures, the Law of Moses etc. without help, thus perpetuating your spiritual blindness; you think you can be saved that way; it won't work): and they are they which testify of me. (If you understood the scriptures correctly, you would see that they testify of me.)

40 And ye will not (refuse to) come to me, that ye might have life (eternal life).

41 I receive not honour from men. (I am not honored by men like you are.)

42 But I know you (the Jews who are angry because Jesus healed the invalid on the Sabbath, and now want to kill Christ; see verse 16 above), that ye have not the love of God in you (I know the evil which is in your hearts.)

43 I am come (have come) in my Father's name, and ye receive me not (you reject me): if another shall come

in his own name, him ye will receive. (You accept false leaders and false prophets who build themselves up in the eyes of the people for personal gain, who practice priestcraft; see Alma 1:12 and 16.)

44 How can ye believe, which receive honour one of another, and seek not the honour that *cometh* from God only? (How can you believe and trust those who join together to build themselves up, rather than seeking God?)

45 Do not think that I will accuse you (I will not even need to bear witness against you) to the Father: there is *one* that accuseth you, *even* Moses, in whom ye trust (because the teachings of Moses about me, which you blatantly misinterpret and refuse to believe, will bear witness against you).

46 For had ye believed Moses (if you believed Moses, who clearly taught about me), ye would have believed me: for he wrote of me.

47 But if ye believe not his writings, how shall ye believe my words? (If you won't believe Moses, how can you possibly believe me?)

Note: Moses was the most important prophet in Jewish culture. In fact, the Jews were constantly angered by the fact that Jesus did not do things the way Moses taught, forgetting that many of the things Moses gave them were "schoolmaster" laws (Galatians 3:24), to prepare them for the higher laws the Messiah would give them.

JOHN 6

Note: This is the beginning of the third year of the Savior's mortal ministry.

1 AFTER these things Jesus went over *the sea* of Galilee, which is the sea of Tiberias.

2 And a great multitude followed him, because they saw his miracles which he did on them that were diseased (sick).

3 And Jesus went up into a mountain, and there he sat with his disciples.

4 And the passover, a feast of the Jews, was nigh (near).

5 When Jesus then lifted up *his* eyes, and saw a great company (huge crowd) come unto him, he saith unto Philip, Whence (where) shall we buy bread, that these may eat (to feed all these people)?

6 And this he said to prove (test) him: for he himself knew what he would do.

7 Philip answered him, Two hundred pennyworth of bread is not sufficient for them, that every one of them may take a little. (Two hundred day's wages; see Mark 6:37, footnote a, [for an average worker or about $30,000] would only buy enough for each member of the crowd to have just a little to eat)

8 One of his disciples, Andrew, Simon Peter's brother, saith unto him,

9 There is a lad here, which hath five barley loaves, and two small fishes: but what are they among so many?

10 And Jesus said, Make the men sit down. Now there was much grass in the place. So the men sat down, in number about five thousand (plus women and children; see Matthew 14:21).

11 And Jesus took the loaves; and

when he had given thanks, he distributed to the disciples, and the disciples to them that were set down; and likewise of the fishes as much as they would (everyone ate as much as they wanted).

12 When they were filled (when the people in the crowd were full), he said unto his disciples, Gather up the fragments that remain, that nothing be lost (wasted).

13 Therefore they gathered *them* together, and filled twelve baskets with the fragments (leftovers) of the five barley loaves, which remained over and above unto them that had eaten.

14 Then those men, when they had seen the miracle that Jesus did, said, This is of a truth that prophet that should come into the world (this is definitely the Messiah).

15 When Jesus therefore perceived that they (the members of the multitude who had just been fed) would come and take him by force, to make him a king, he departed again into a mountain himself alone.

Note: Apparently, the multitude felt that if they could have Jesus for their king, he would feed them everyday and take care of all their needs so they wouldn't have to work. Therefore, they tried to force him to be their king. They missed the symbolism that Christ can indeed take care of all our spiritual needs by giving us the "bread of life" on a daily basis.

16 And when even (evening) was *now* come, his disciples went down unto the sea,

17 And entered into a ship, and went over the sea toward Capernaum (on the northwest side of the Sea of Galilee). And it was now dark, and Jesus was not come to them (had not joined them).

18 And the sea arose by reason of a great wind that blew (a terrible storm came up).

19 So when they had rowed about five and twenty or thirty furlongs (about three to four miles from shore), they see Jesus walking on the sea, and drawing nigh (getting close) unto the ship: and they were afraid.

20 But he saith unto them, It is I; be not afraid.

21 Then they willingly received him into the ship: and immediately the ship was at the land whither they went (the ship was suddenly at its destination, a miracle recorded only by John).

22 The day following (the day following the feeding of the 5,000), when the people which stood on the other side of the sea (near where they had been fed by the Master the day before) saw that (realized that) there was none other boat there, save (except) that one whereinto his disciples were entered, and that Jesus went not with his disciples into the boat, but *that* his disciples were gone away alone; (In other words, the next day the crowd came to see if Jesus was still there, so they could get him to feed them again. They knew that the disciples had gotten into the only boat the night before and had headed towards Capernaum without Jesus. At any rate, they saw that neither Jesus nor his disciples were there, so they determined to try to find them.)

23 (Howbeit [however] there came

other boats from Tiberias nigh unto the place where they did eat bread [some boats from Tiberias came that morning and came to shore near the site of the feeding of the 5,000], after that the Lord had given thanks:)

24 When the people therefore saw that Jesus was not there, neither his disciples, they also took shipping (got aboard the boats from Tiberias), and came to Capernaum, seeking for Jesus.

25 And when they had found him on the other side of the sea, they said unto him, Rabbi, when camest thou hither (when did you come here)?

26 Jesus answered them and said, Verily, verily (this is very important; listen carefully!), I say unto you, Ye seek me, not because ye saw the miracles, (JST "not because ye desire to keep my sayings, neither because ye saw the miracles"), but because ye did eat of the loaves, and were filled. (You are not looking for me because you want to obey my gospel, rather just to be fed again. In other words, you are looking for me for the wrong reasons.)

27 Labour not (don't spend all your effort working) for the meat (food, worldly things) which perisheth (which does not last), but for that meat (food, symbolic of spiritual priorities) which endureth (lasts) unto everlasting life (and bring exaltation), which the Son of man (Christ; Son of Man) shall give unto you: for him hath God the Father sealed (sent).

Note: Now begins a brief series of interesting questions and answers between the spiritually blind and insensitive crowd and the Master.

28 Then said they unto him, (Question:) What shall we do, that we might work the works of God? (What would it take to teach us how to multiply loaves and fishes?)

29 (Answer:) Jesus answered and said unto them, This is the work of God, that ye believe on him whom he hath sent. (You must develop faith in Jesus Christ.)

30 They said therefore unto him, (Question:) What sign shewest thou then, that we may see, and believe thee? what dost thou work? (They are getting a bit irritated that he is stalling and not teaching them how to multiply loaves and fishes. They challenge him to show them a sign to prove to them that he has not lost the power which he had yesterday when he fed them.)

31 Our fathers did eat manna in the desert; as it is written, He gave them bread from heaven to eat. (In other words they seem to be taunting Jesus, saying in effect, "Hint, hint. Moses gave our ancestors bread [manna] every day when he was their leader. What's the matter? Aren't you as capable as Moses?")

Note: What follows in verses 32-58 is known as the "Bread of Life" sermon. It is famous, and contains tremendous symbolism.

32 Then Jesus said unto them, (Answer:)Verily, verily, I say unto you, Moses gave you not that bread from heaven (Moses didn't give you that manna); but (furthermore) my Father giveth you the true bread (symbolic of Christ) from heaven.

33 For the bread of (from) God is he

(Christ) which cometh down from heaven, and giveth life (resurrection and the possibility of eternal life) unto the world.

34 Then said they unto him, Lord, evermore give us this bread (give us bread so we will never get hungry again). (They still don't get the point; see verse 52. They don't understand the symbolism that Christ and his gospel will nourish them spiritually forever in celestial glory.)

35 And Jesus said unto them, I am the bread of life: he that cometh to me shall never hunger (spiritually); and he that believeth on me shall never thirst (spiritually). (In other words, those who hunger and thirst after righteousness and eternal life and come unto me will be nourished eternally.)

36 But I said unto you, That ye also have seen me, and believe not.

37 All (all the righteous people) that the Father giveth me shall come to me; and him that cometh to me I will in no wise (never) cast out (of my kingdom).

38 For I came down from heaven, not to do mine own will, but the will of him (the Father) that sent me.

39 And this is the Father's will which hath sent me, that of all which he hath given me (all the righteous saints) I should lose nothing (none of them), but should raise it up again at the last day (resurrect them in the resurrection of the righteous).

40 And this is the will of him that sent me, that every one which seeth the Son, and believeth on him, may have everlasting life: and I will raise him up at the last day (JST "and I will raise him up in the resurrection of the just at the last day.").

41 The Jews then murmured (grumbled) at him, because he said, I am the bread which came down from heaven.

42 And they said, Is not this Jesus, the son of Joseph, whose father and mother we know? how is it then that he saith, I came down from heaven? (How can Jesus have come down from heaven? We know his parents. We've known him all his life.)

43 Jesus therefore answered and said unto them, Murmur not among yourselves (don't criticize me among yourselves for saying what I've said).

44 No man can come to me, except the Father which hath sent me draw him: and I will raise him up at the last day. (The JST makes major changes to this verse as follows: "No man can come unto me, except he doeth the will of my Father who hath sent me. And this is the will of him who hath sent me, that ye receive the Son; for the Father beareth record of him; and he who receiveth the testimony, and doeth the will of him who sent me, I will raise up in the resurrection of the just.")

45 It is written in the prophets (in the Old Testament; Isaiah 54:13), And they shall be all taught of God. Every man therefore that hath heard, and hath learned of the Father, cometh unto me. (Everyone who has properly understood Old Testament prophets will come unto me.)

46 Not that any man hath seen the Father, save he which is of God (except he who is worthy, such as Stephen in Acts 7:55-56), he hath seen the Father.

47 Verily, verily, I say unto you, He that believeth on me (Christ) hath

everlasting life (will be exalted, will be placed into the highest degree of glory in the celestial kingdom and will become a god).

48 I am that bread of life. (Symbolism: I am the spiritual "bread" sent to you by my Father, that, when you eat it, that is, when you internalize it and make it part of your lives, you are exalted.)

49 Your fathers (ancestors, mentioned in verse 31) did eat manna in the wilderness, and are dead (and still died spiritually).

50 This is the bread (symbolic of me, my gospel and my Atonement) which cometh down from heaven, that a man may eat thereof (internalize it), and not die (not die spiritually).

51 I am the living bread which came down from heaven: if any man eat of this bread, he shall live for ever (shall have eternal life): and the bread that I will give is my flesh, which I will give for the life of the world. (I will sacrifice my body through suffering in the Garden of Gethsemane and crucifixion in order to accomplish the Atonement and provide eternal life for those who qualify.)

52 The Jews therefore strove (argued) among themselves, saying, How can this man give us his flesh to eat? (They still don't get the point!)

Note: Just as the Savior repeated the message time and time again in the previous verses, so he will repeat it several times in the next verses. He is giving these spiritually insensitive people every chance to understand that they must accept his Atonement and his gospel in order to be saved. They

must symbolically eat him ("he that eateth me", verse 57), that is, eat or internalize everything he is and offers them and make it a part of their lives, in order to receive eternal life. Sadly, many of them will still not get the point, even after so much repetition, and will leave him (verse 66).

53 Then Jesus said unto them, Verily, verily, I say unto you, Except (unless) ye eat the flesh of the Son of man (Christ), and drink his blood, ye have no life in you. (Unless you take advantage of the Atonement and make it part of your lives, you will not have the life and light of the gospel here in mortality nor in the world to come.)

54 Whoso eateth my flesh, and drinketh my blood, hath eternal life; and I will raise him up (resurrect him in the resurrection of the righteous) at the last day (JST "...and I will raise him up in the resurrection of the just at the last day").

55 For my flesh is meat (symbolic of spiritual food) indeed, and my blood is drink (symbolic of spiritual drink) indeed. (This is sacrament symbolism.)

56 He that eateth my flesh, and drinketh my blood, dwelleth in me, and I in him. (He becomes one with me, united with me in the gospel.)

57 As the living Father hath sent me, and I live by the Father: so he that eateth me (internalizes my gospel), even he shall live by me (will be saved through living in accordance with my gospel).

58 This is that bread which came down from heaven: not as your fathers did eat manna (physical nourishment),

and are dead: he that eateth of this bread (spiritual nourishment) shall live for ever (will have eternal life, exaltation).

59 These things said he in the synagogue (Jewish church building), as he taught in Capernaum.

60 Many therefore of his disciples (followers), when they had heard *this* (the Bread of Life Sermon), said, This is an hard saying; who can hear it? (This is too deep for us. Nobody can understand what he is saying.)

61 When Jesus knew in himself that his disciples murmured at it, he said unto them, Doth this offend you (are you bothered, offended by what I have taught about the Bread of Life)?

62 *What* and if ye shall see the Son of man ascend up where he was before? (Would it offend you if you saw me go back up into heaven where I came from?) (Jesus will do exactly that after his resurrection.)

63 It is the spirit that quickeneth (it is the Holy Ghost that gives you understanding); the flesh profiteth nothing (you can't possibly understand what I've said from an intellectual, academic basis): the words that I speak unto you, *they* are spirit (spiritual), and *they* are life (they bring eternal life). (In summary, the things I have just taught about the Bread of Life can only be understood with the help of the Holy Ghost.)

64 But there are some of you that believe not. For Jesus knew from the beginning who they were that believed not, and who should betray him.

65 And he said, Therefore said I (this is the reason I said) unto you, that no man can come unto me, except it were given unto him of my Father.

66 From that *time* many of his disciples went back (left him), and walked no more with him.

67 Then said Jesus unto the twelve, Will ye also go away? (Is this doctrine of the Bread of Life so hard to accept that you, too, will leave me?)

68 Then Simon Peter answered him, Lord, to whom shall we go? thou hast the words of eternal life. (This is the right answer!)

69 And we believe and are sure that thou art that Christ, the Son of the living God.

70 Jesus answered them, Have not I chosen you twelve, and one of you is a devil?

71 He spake of Judas Iscariot *the son* of Simon (not Peter, the Apostle, rather, a different Simon): for he it was that should (would) betray him, being one of the twelve.

JOHN 7

1 AFTER these things Jesus walked in Galilee: for he would not walk in Jewry (in Judea, in the Jerusalem area), because the Jews sought to kill him.

2 Now the Jews' feast of tabernacles was at hand.

Note: The Feast of Tabernacles was held in the fall at harvest time in Jerusalem. See Bible Dictionary, page 673. It drew large crowds and was a week-long celebration of thanksgiving which included daily animal sacrifices, and a ceremony where people waved palm, myrtle, willow, and citrus branches toward the cardinal points of the compass (north, south, east and west), symbolizing the presence of God throughout the universe.

Note: Next, in verses 3-5, there may be a hint of sarcasm on the part of Jesus' close relatives, likely including his own half-brothers, who do not believe in him (verse 5), as they tell him he really ought to go to Jerusalem for the Feast of Tabernacles so he can make a spectacle of himself in front of his disciples as well as huge numbers of people. There is a hint that these family members and close relatives were embarrassed that Jesus was part of their family.

3 His brethren (close relatives, probably including his own brothers; see McConkie, *Doctrinal New Testament Commentary*, Vol. 1, page 437) therefore said unto him, Depart hence (leave), and go into Judæa, that thy disciples also may see the works that thou doest.

4 For *there is* no man *that* doeth any thing in secret, and he himself seeketh to be known openly (no man keeps to himself who wants everybody to know who he is). If thou do these things, shew thyself to the world (if you claim to be so great, get out in public and let them see you).

5 For neither did his brethren believe in him.

6 Then Jesus said unto them, My time is not yet come (it is not time for me to go to Jerusalem): but your time is alway ready (you go ahead and go to Jerusalem for the feast; I will come along later).

7 The world cannot hate you (the people of the world don't hate you because you are just normal people and most of them don't even know you); but me it hateth, because I testify of it, that the works thereof are evil (but they hate me because I tell them they are wicked).

8 Go ye up unto this feast (the Feast of Tabernacles in Jerusalem): I go not up yet unto this feast; for my time is not yet full come (it is not time for me to go).

9 When he had said these words unto them, he abode *still* (still remained) in Galilee.

10 But when his brethren were gone (had gone) up, then went he also up unto the feast, not openly, but as it were in secret. (The religious leaders of the Jews had already indicated that they wanted to kill him; see verse 1.)

11 Then the Jews sought him (looked for him) at the feast, and said, Where is he?

12 And there was much murmuring (much talk) among the people concerning him: for some said, He is a good man: others said, Nay; but he deceiveth the people (he is a fraud).

13 Howbeit (however) no man spake openly of him for fear of the Jews (for fear of the Jewish religious leaders).

14 Now about the midst of the feast (the middle of the week-long festivities) Jesus went up into the temple, and taught.

15 And the Jews marvelled, saying, How knoweth this man letters, having never learned (how does Jesus know so much; he hasn't had the formal training that our religious leaders have)?

16 Jesus answered them, and said,

My doctrine is not mine, but his that sent me. (My Father is my teacher.)

17 If any man will do his will, he shall know of the doctrine, whether it be of God, or *whether* I speak of myself. (If any one will live the gospel, he will find out that it is true.)

18 He that speaketh of himself (teaches his own, man-made doctrines) seeketh his own glory: but he (Christ) that seeketh his glory that sent him (the glory of the Father), the same is true (he is a true messenger, one you can trust), and no unrighteousness is in him.

19 Did not Moses give you the law (the first five books of the Old Testament), and *yet* none of you keepeth the law (none of you obey it)? Why go ye about to kill me?

20 The people answered and said, Thou hast a devil (you are crazy!): who goeth about to kill thee (what makes you think anybody is out to kill you)?

21 Jesus answered and said unto them, I have done one work (I healed the crippled man on the Sabbath), and ye all marvel.

22 Moses therefore gave unto you circumcision; (not because it is of Moses [not because it originated with Moses, rather with Abraham], but of the fathers;) and ye on the sabbath day circumcise a man.

23 If a man on the sabbath day receive circumcision, that the law of Moses should not be broken; are ye angry at me, because I have made a man every whit whole on the sabbath day? (You have your priorities mixed up. You allow a man to be circumcised on the Sabbath, but you get angry at

me for healing a man on the Sabbath.)

24 Judge not according to the appearance (JST "Judge not according to your traditions"), but judge righteous judgment.

25 Then said some of them of Jerusalem (who were from Jerusalem), Is not this he, whom they seek to kill?

26 But, lo, he speaketh boldly (look, he is speaking out boldly in public), and they (the Pharisees etc.) say nothing unto him. Do the rulers know indeed that this is the very Christ? (Maybe they think he actually is Christ and are afraid of him.)

27 Howbeit (regardless of what they think) we know this man whence he is (we know where Jesus comes from, namely Nazareth): but when Christ (the promised Messiah) cometh, no man knoweth whence he is (no one will know where he comes from).

Note: It was a false tradition among the Jews that no one would know where the true Christ came from.

28 Then cried Jesus in the temple (Jesus spoke loudly so everyone could hear) as he taught, saying, Ye both know me, and ye know whence I am: and I am not come of myself (I have not come on my own), but he that sent me is true, whom ye know not (rather, I have been sent by the True God, whom you do not know because of your wickedness) .

29 But I know him: for I am from him, and he hath sent me.

30 Then they sought to take him (wanted to arrest him): but no man laid hands on him, because his hour was not yet come. (No one was able to

seize him because it was not time yet for his trial and crucifixion.)

31 And many of the people believed on him, and said, When Christ cometh, will he do more miracles than these which this *man* hath done? (In other words, this has to be the Christ.)

32 The Pharisees heard that the people murmured (were saying) such things concerning him; and the Pharisees and the chief priests sent officers to take him (to arrest him).

33 Then said Jesus unto them, Yet a little while am I with you, and *then* I go unto him that sent me (then I will return to my Father in Heaven).

34 Ye shall seek me, and shall not find *me*: and where I am, *thither* (there) ye cannot come.

35 Then said the Jews among themselves, Whither (where) will he go, that we shall not find him? will he go unto the dispersed among the Gentiles, and teach the Gentiles (will he go to the Greeks and teach them; see John 7:35, footnote a)?

36 What *manner* of saying is this that he said (what does he mean by saying), Ye shall seek me, and shall not find *me*: and where I am, *thither* ye cannot come?

37 In the last day (the eighth day; see Bible Dictionary, pate 673), that great *day* (the culmination) of the feast, Jesus stood and cried, saying, If any man thirst, let him come unto me, and drink.

38 He that believeth on me, as the scripture (Isaiah 44:3, 55:1) hath said, out of his belly shall flow rivers of living water.

Note: Picture if you will, throngs of Jews crowding the grounds around the temple, watching in rapt attention as water from the stream of Siloam (symbolic of water drawn from the wells of salvation-Isaiah 12:3) was carried to the altar and then poured upon it, flowing down off it onto the ground, in a great ritual show symbolic of the living waters, including the Holy Ghost, which flow from the altar of God onto the earth to quench the spiritual thirst of the faithful-Isaiah 44:3, 55:1. Perhaps, at that very moment, Jesus stood and, with a loud voice, spoke to the onlookers saying, "If any man thirst, let him come unto me, and drink". There could not have been a more dramatic setting. Jesus was openly claiming to be the Messiah and to be the Jehovah of the Old Testament who had promised to give these "living waters" to the faithful.

39 (But this spake he of the Spirit, which they that believe on him should receive: for the Holy Ghost was not yet *given*; because that Jesus was not yet glorified [JST "for the Holy Ghost was promised unto them who believe, after that Jesus was glorified"] .)

Note: "...the Holy Ghost was not yet given" in verse 39 above, causes some to believe that the Holy Ghost was not here at all during the time Jesus was here. This is not the case. The Holy Ghost was obviously functioning and active on earth during the Savior's mortal ministry. He attended the Savior's baptism (Matthew 3:13-17. The Savior was "full of the Holy Ghost" in Luke 4:1. Thus, our understanding is that, while the Holy Ghost did function during Christ's mortal ministry, the full power of the Gift of the Holy Ghost was not here. See Bible Dictionary, page 704.

40 Many of the people therefore, when they heard this saying (what Jesus said in verses 37 and 38 above), said, Of a truth this is the Prophet (some prophet who was to come before Christ; see McConkie, *Doctrinal New Testament Commentary*, Vol. 1, page 448).

41 Others said, This is the Christ. But some said, Shall Christ come out of Galilee? (Referring no doubt to the prophecy that Christ was to be born in Bethlehem, and thus, they thought, should come from Bethlehem, not Nazareth in Galilee.)

42 Hath not the scripture said, That Christ cometh of the seed of David, and out of the town of Bethlehem, where David was?

43 So there was a division among the people because of him.

44 And some of them (the officers in verse 45) would have taken him (arrested him); but no man laid hands on him.

45 Then came the officers (soldiers) to the chief priests and Pharisees (Jewish religious leaders); and they (the Pharisees etc.) said unto them, Why have ye not brought him (why didn't you arrest Jesus)?

46 The officers answered, Never man spake like this man (nobody ever taught like he does).

47 Then answered them the Pharisees (then the Pharisees and chief priests said to the soldiers), Are ye also deceived (has Jesus got you fooled

also)?

48 Have any of the rulers or of the Pharisees believed on him (have any of us rulers been deceived by him)?

49 But this people who knoweth not the law are cursed. (The people don't understand the teachings of Moses. That's why they are subject to being deceived by Jesus.)

50 Nicodemus saith unto them, (he that came to Jesus by night [John 3:1-2], being one of them [Nicodemus was a member of the Pharisees],)

51 Doth our law judge *any* man, before it hear him, and know what he doeth? (Why are we violating our own laws? We haven't even given Jesus a fair trial and already we are judging him.)

52 They answered and said unto him, Art thou also of Galilee (has he converted you too)? Search, and look: for out of Galilee ariseth no prophet. (Check the scriptures. There is no mention of a Prophet who comes from Galilee.)

53 And every man went unto his own house.

JOHN 8

1 JESUS went unto the mount of Olives (just a few minutes' walk east of Jerusalem).

2 And early in the morning he came again into the temple (the courtyard of the temple), and all the people came unto him; and he sat down, and taught them.

3 And the scribes and Pharisees (hypocritical religious leaders of the Jews) brought unto him a woman taken in adultery; and when they had set her in the midst (when they had put

her in the middle of the crowd),

4 They say unto him, Master, this woman was taken in adultery, in the very act (we caught her right while she was doing it).

Note: One has to wonder why these Jewish leaders didn't also bring the man who was involved with this woman, to the Savior. Perhaps he was one of their own. In JST Luke 16:21, Jesus called these leaders "adulterers". We don't know if the man was a fellow Pharisee, but it is pure hypocrisy to single out the woman for embarrassment and humiliation.

5 Now Moses in the law commanded us, that such should be stoned: but what sayest thou?

Note: These evil men are still trying to trap Jesus by getting him to say something against Moses and his laws.

6 This they said, tempting him (trying to lure him into a trap), that they might have to accuse him (in order for them to build a legal case against him). But Jesus stooped down, and with his finger wrote on the ground, *as though he heard them not.* (Imagine how quiet the crowd was at this point. Imagine also how frightened the woman was.)

7 So when they continued (kept) asking him, he lifted up himself (stood up), and said unto them, He that is without sin among you (perhaps implying whoever has not committed the same sin; see McConkie, *Doctrinal New Testament Commentary*, Vol. 1, page 451), let him first cast a stone at her.

8 And again he stooped down, and wrote on the ground.

9 And they which heard it, being convicted by *their own* conscience, went out (left) one by one, beginning at the eldest, *even* unto the last: and Jesus was left alone, and the woman standing in the midst.

10 When Jesus had lifted up himself (had stood up), and saw none but the woman, he said unto her, Woman, where are those thine accusers? hath no man condemned thee? (Where did the men go who wanted to stone you? Didn't any of them condemn you to death?)

11 She said, No man, Lord. And Jesus said unto her, Neither do I condemn thee: go, and sin no more. (JST adds "And the woman glorified God from that hour, and believed on his name.")

Note: Jesus did not forgive the woman at this point. Obviously, she has some serious repenting to do. But he did not condemn her meaning that she still had time to repent. The Joseph Smith Translation, cited above at the end of verse 11, confirms that she began repenting.

12 Then spake Jesus again unto them, saying, I am the light of the world: he that followeth me shall not walk in darkness (spiritual darkness), but shall have the light of life (eternal life).

13 The Pharisees therefore said unto him, Thou bearest record of thyself; thy record is not true. (You are not following the law of witnesses.)

14 Jesus answered and said unto them, Though I bear record of myself, yet my record is true: for I know whence I came (where I am from), and whither I go (and where I am going); but ye cannot tell whence I come, and whither I go.

15 Ye judge after the flesh (you are judging me by worldly standards); I judge no man.

16 And yet if I judge, my judgment is true (valid): for I am not alone, but I and the Father that sent me. (I do have another witness of me, namely, the Father.)

17 It is also written in your law, that the testimony of two men is true. (This is the law of witnesses the Jews were referring to in verse 13.)

18 I am one that bear witness of myself, and the Father that sent me beareth witness of me.

19 Then said they unto him, Where is thy Father? Jesus answered, Ye neither know me, nor my Father: if ye had known me, ye should have (would have) known my Father also.

20 These words spake Jesus in the treasury (one of the temple buildings), as he taught in the temple: and no man laid hands on him; for his hour was not yet come.

21 Then said Jesus again unto them, I go my way, and ye shall seek me (to kill me), and shall die in your sins: whither I go, ye cannot come. (You can't come to heaven because you refuse to repent.)

22 Then said the Jews, Will he kill himself? because he saith, Whither I go, ye cannot come. (Does he mean that he is going to commit suicide, and that is how he will get away from us so that we can't follow him around?)

23 And he said unto them, Ye are from beneath; I am from above: ye are of this world; I am not of this world. (We are worlds apart.)

24 I said therefore unto you, that ye shall die in your sins: for if ye believe not that I am he (the Messiah), ye shall die in your sins.

25 Then said they unto him, Who art thou? And Jesus saith unto them, Even *the same* that I said unto you from the beginning. (I already told you.)

26 I have many things to say and to judge of you: but he (the Father) that sent me is true; and I speak to the world those things which I have heard of him.

27 They understood not that he spake to them of the Father.

28 Then said Jesus unto them, When ye have lifted up (crucified) the Son of man (me), then shall ye know that I am *he* (the Messiah), and *that* I do nothing of myself; but as my Father hath taught me, I speak these things. (You will know that I am God's Son and that I bring you his word.)

29 And he that sent me is with me: the Father hath not left me alone; for I do always those things that please him.

30 As he spake these words, many believed on him.

31 Then said Jesus to those Jews which believed on him, If ye continue in my word, *then* are ye my disciples indeed;

32 And ye shall know the truth, and the truth shall make you free.

Note: Verse 32 is one of the most profound verses in all the scriptures. The truth sets us free. For example, if people believe that a baby who dies without baptism is forever damned from returning to heaven, D&C 137:10 sets them free from the anguish and lingering guilt of having neglected this rite for the child. If one has lived a life of serious sin, and upon repenting and changing lifestyle, still believes that he or she will forever be a "second-class" citizen in the Church, Isaiah 1:18 will set him or her free from feelings of being permanently limited by past lifestyle. So will Elder Richard G. Scott's talk in October Conference, 2000, set such persons "free", wherein he said "If you have repented from serious transgression and mistakenly believe that you will always be a second-class citizen in the kingdom of God, learn that is not true."

33 They answered him, We be Abraham's seed (we are descendants of Abraham), and were never in bondage (slavery) to any man (we don't need to be set free): how sayest thou (what do you mean when you say), Ye shall be made free?

34 Jesus answered them, Verily, verily, I say unto you, Whosoever committeth sin is the servant of sin (is a slave to sin).

35 And the servant abideth not in the house for ever (slaves don't live in the master's house): *but* the Son abideth ever (but the Son lives in the Father's house).

36 If the Son therefore shall make you free, ye shall be free indeed. (If I make you free from sin, you are free indeed!)

37 I know that ye are Abraham's seed (descendants); but ye seek to kill

me, because my word hath no place in you (because you have rejected me).

38 I speak that which I have seen with my Father: and ye do that which ye have seen with your father (the devil; see verse 44).

39 They answered and said unto him, Abraham is our father (we live by Abraham's standards). Jesus saith unto them, If ye were Abraham's children (true followers), ye would do the works of Abraham.

40 But now ye seek to kill me, a man that hath told you the truth, which I have heard of God (from the Father): this did not Abraham (Abraham would not try to kill me).

41 Ye do the deeds of your father (the devil; see verse 44). Then said they to him, We be not born of fornication (we have not "stepped out" on God); we have one Father, even God. (We are completely loyal to God.)

Note: The words "fornication" and "adultery"are often used in the Bible to refer, symbolically, to complete disloyalty to God. Example: Revelation 14:8, Jeremiah 3:8-9. See Bible Dictionary, page 604, under "adultery".

42 Jesus said unto them, If God were your Father, ye would love me: for I proceeded forth and came from God; neither came I of myself, but he sent me.

43 Why do ye not understand my speech? even because ye cannot hear my word (JST "even because ye cannot bear my word.").

44 Ye are of *your* father the devil, and the lusts of your father ye will do

(you live the wicked lifestyle sponsored by your "father", the devil). He was a murderer from the beginning, and abode not in the truth, because there is no truth in him. When he speaketh a lie, he speaketh of his own: for he is a liar, and the father of it. (The devil is the father of lies.)

45 And because I tell you the truth, ye believe me not.

46 Which of you convinceth (convicts) me of sin? And if I say the truth, why do ye not believe me?

47 He that is of God (the righteous) heareth (JST "receiveth ") God's words: ye therefore hear (JST "receive") *them* not, because ye are not of God.

48 Then answered the Jews, and said unto him, Say we not well that thou art a Samaritan (you yourself are "born of fornication"; see verse 41), and hast a devil?

Note: The phrase "thou art a Samaritan" in verse 48 above is saying, in effect, that Jesus is "illegitimate", and God is not his father. The Samaritans came from remnants of the ten northern tribes of Israel, who intermarried with non-covenant people, mainly Assyrian occupational armies, beginning in about 722 BC. Thus, Samaritans were considered by the Jews to be former members of the House of Israel who had "stepped out on God" by marrying non-members and thereby had polluted the race. They were "illegitimate" children, therefore, were despised by the Jews.

49 Jesus answered, I have not a devil; but I honour my Father, and ye do dishonour me.

50 And I seek not mine own glory: there is one that seeketh and judgeth.

51 Verily, verily, I say unto you, If a man keep my saying, he shall never see death (spiritual death).

52 Then said the Jews unto him, Now we know that thou hast a devil (now we know that you are crazy!). Abraham is dead, and the prophets; and thou sayest, If a man keep my saying, he shall never taste of death (will never die).

53 Art thou greater than our father Abraham, which is dead? and the prophets are dead: whom makest thou thyself (who do you think you are)?

54 Jesus answered, If I honour myself, my honour is nothing: it is my Father that honoureth me; of whom ye say, that he is your God:

55 Yet ye have not known him (you don't follow him, you don't know him); but I know him: and if I should say, I know him not, I shall be a liar like unto you: but I know him, and keep his saying (follow his commandments).

56 Your father (ancestor) Abraham rejoiced to see my day (saw my day in vision): and he saw it, and was glad.

57 Then said the Jews unto him, Thou art not yet fifty years old, and hast thou seen Abraham? (They just keep missing the point!)

58 Jesus said unto them, Verily, verily, I say unto you, Before Abraham was, I am (I am the God who appeared to Abraham).

Note: "I am" in verse 58 above is usually written "I AM", and is another name for Jehovah, the God of the Old

Testament. See John 8:58, footnote 7. See also Exodus 3:14. Jesus has just told the Jews, in terms they do understand, that he is Jehovah, the God of the Old Testament, and that the reason he has seen Abraham (verses 56-57 above) is that he is the God of Abraham and appeared to him. Because the Jews finally understand clearly who Jesus is claiming to be, they are furious with him.

59 Then took they up stones to cast at him: but Jesus hid himself, and went out of the temple, going through the midst of them, and so passed by.

JOHN 9

1 AND as *Jesus* passed by, he saw a man which was blind from *his* birth.

2 And his disciples asked him, saying, Master, who did sin, this man, or his parents, that he was born blind?

Note: There was a false idea among the Jews that any physical illness was a result of sin.

3 Jesus answered, Neither hath this man sinned, nor his parents: but that the works of God should be made manifest (be shown) in him.

4 I must work the works of him that sent me, while it is day: the night cometh, when no man can work. (JST " I must work the works of him that sent me, while I am with you; the time cometh when I shall have finished my work, then I go unto the Father.")

5 As long as I am in the world, I am the light of the world.

6 When he had thus spoken, he spat on the ground, and made clay of the spittle, and he anointed the eyes of the blind man with the clay,

Note: There is symbolism in the use of "clay", in verse 6 above. "Clay" is symbolic of this earth as well as of our mortal bodies. Touching the blind man's eyes with the clay so he could see can symbolize the fact that, by our being sent to this earth, in mortal bodies, we learn things that enable us to "see" the spiritual things of eternity.

7 And said unto him, Go, wash in the pool of Siloam, (which is by interpretation, Sent.) He went his way therefore, and washed, and came seeing (could see).

8 The neighbours therefore, and they which before had seen him that he was blind, said, Is not this he that sat and begged (isn't this the blind man who used to be a beggar)?

9 Some said, This is he: others said, He is like him (he just looks like that blind man): but he (the blind man) *said*, I am *he* (I am the one who was healed).

10 Therefore said they unto him, How were thine eyes opened?

11 He answered and said, A man that is called Jesus made clay, and anointed mine eyes, and said unto me, Go to the pool of Siloam, and wash: and I went and washed, and I received sight.

12 Then said they unto him, Where is he? He said, I know not.

13 They brought to the Pharisees him that aforetime was blind. (Some Jews brought the formerly blind man to the Pharisees.)

14 And it was the sabbath day when Jesus made the clay, and opened his

eyes. (Jesus had healed the blind man on the Sabbath.)

15 Then again the Pharisees also asked him how he had received his sight. He said unto them, He (Jesus) put clay upon mine eyes, and I washed, and do see (and I can see).

16 Therefore said some of the Pharisees, This man is not of God, because he keepeth not the sabbath day (Jesus can't be sent by God, because he breaks the Sabbath by healing people on it). Others said, How can a man that is a sinner do such miracles? And there was a division among them.

17 They say unto the blind man again, What sayest thou of him, that he hath opened thine eyes (what's your opinion of Jesus)? He said, He is a prophet.

18 But the Jews did not believe concerning him, that he had been blind, and received his sight, until they called the parents of him (the blind man) that had received his sight.

Note: The Jewish religious leaders are trying desperately to discredit Jesus in the eyes of the people and it is not working. They now try to discredit the blind man's parents by suggesting that they don't really know for sure that their son was born blind.

19 And they asked them, saying, Is this your son, who ye say (claim) was born blind? how then doth he now see (if he was really blind, how could he see now)?

20 His parents answered them and said, We know that this is our son, and that he was born blind:

21 But by what means he now seeth, we know not (we don't understand what happened so that he can now see); or who hath opened his eyes, we know not: he is of age; ask him: he shall speak for himself. (Don't rely merely on what we say. Ask him. He is old enough to speak for himself.)

22 These *words* spake his parents, because they feared the Jews (the religious rulers of the Jews): for the Jews had agreed (plotted) already, that if any man did confess that he was Christ, he should be put out of the synagogue. (Anyone who says Jesus is the promised Messiah will be excommunicated.)

23 Therefore said his parents, He is of age; ask him. (The parents were afraid of getting excommunicated, so they told the Pharisees to ask their son what happened.)

24 Then again called they the man that was blind, and said unto him, Give God the praise: we know that this man (Jesus) is a sinner. (Give God the praise for your being healed, but don't give this imposter, Jesus, any credit.)

25 He answered and said, Whether he be a sinner or no, I know not (whether or not Jesus is a sinner, I don't know): one thing I know, that, whereas I was blind, now I see (but one thing I do know: I was blind and now I can see). (This formerly blind man is not intimidated by the Jewish rulers, which must have been frustrating for them.)

26 Then said they to him again, What did he (Jesus) to thee? how opened he thine eyes?

27 He answered them, I have told you already, and ye did not hear (what's the matter, are you dense?):

wherefore would ye hear it again (why do you want me to tell you again)? will ye also be his disciples (are you being converted to him too)?

28 Then they reviled him (insulted him), and said, Thou art his disciple (you are loyal to Jesus); but we are Moses' disciples.

29 We know that God spake unto Moses: *as for* this *fellow*, we know not from whence he is (we don't know where he comes from).

30 The man answered and said unto them, Why herein is a marvellous thing (well, this is getting more interesting all the time), that ye (the big religious leaders who are supposed to know these things) know not from whence he is, and yet he hath opened mine eyes.

31 Now we know that God heareth not sinners: but if any man be a worshipper of God, and doeth his will, him he heareth. (If Jesus were a sinner, God would not support him in such miracles.)

32 Since the world began was it not heard that any man opened the eyes of one that was born blind (JST adds "except he be of God"). (Only men of God have ever been able to heal the blind.)

33 If this man (Jesus) were not of God, he could do nothing.

34 They answered and said unto him, Thou wast altogether born in sins, and dost thou teach us (you, a complete sinner, have the gall to pretend to teach us)? And they cast him out. (They excommunicated him.)

35 Jesus heard that they had cast him out; and when he had found him, he said unto him, Dost thou believe on the Son of God?

36 He answered and said, Who is he, Lord, that I might believe on him?

37 And Jesus said unto him, Thou hast both seen him, and it is he that talketh with thee. (You are talking with him now.)

38 And he said, Lord, I believe. And he worshipped him.

39 And Jesus said, For judgment I am come into this world (I have come to the world in order that all people can receive a fair judgment), that (so that) they which see not might see (so that the spiritually blind, who repent, can see spiritual things); and that they which see (who claim to see, but are in spiritual darkness) might be made blind (can use their agency to remain spiritually blind).

40 And *some* of the Pharisees which were with him heard these words, and said unto him, Are we blind also?

41 Jesus said unto them, If ye were blind, ye should have no sin: but now ye say, We see; therefore your sin remaineth. (If you were ignorant of the truth, you would not be accountable, but it is as you say; you are sinning against light, therefore you remain accountable.)

JOHN 10
Note: Next, the Master uses the imagery of a shepherd leading his sheep to illustrate that he is the Good Shepherd, and other, unauthorized shepherds (Pharisees etc.) try to sneak in and lead the sheep astray. In the days of Jesus, it was a common practice for several shepherds to keep their sheep overnight in the same enclosure, so that only one guard would have to

be on duty through the night. The next morning, each shepherd would come to the enclosure, identify himself to the guard,and then literally call his own sheep to come out of the herd to him, often calling each of his own sheep by its own name. His sheep recognized his voice and came out of the herd and followed him throughout the day as he led them to pasture and water.

1 VERILY, verily, I say unto you, He that entereth not by the door into the sheepfold (is not authorized by God to lead the sheep), but climbeth up some other way, the same is a thief and a robber (symbolic of Satan, apostates etc. who try to lead us astray).

2 But he (Christ) that entereth in by the door (is authorized by God) is the shepherd of the sheep.

3 To him the porter (guard) openeth; and the sheep hear his voice: and he calleth his own sheep by name, and leadeth them out.

4 And when he putteth forth his own sheep, he goeth before them (leads them, rather than herding them), and the sheep follow him: for they know his voice.

5 And a stranger will they not follow, but will flee from him: for they know not the voice of strangers.

6 This parable spake Jesus unto them: but they understood not what things they were which he spake unto them.

7 (Jesus now explains the parable.) Then said Jesus unto them again, Verily, verily, I say unto you, I am the door of the sheep (symbolic of the door to heaven).

8 All that ever came before me are thieves and robbers (any others who claim to be the doorway to heaven are false): but the sheep did not hear them (my true followers don't come to them when they call).

9 I am the door: by me if any man enter in, he shall be saved, and shall go in and out, and find pasture (will be nourished by God).

10 The thief (symbolic of Satan, the wicked etc.) cometh not, but for to steal, and to kill, and to destroy: I am come that they might have life (to bring the saints eternal life), and that they might have it more abundantly.

11 I am the good shepherd: the good shepherd giveth his life for the sheep (I will give my life for you).

12 But he that is an hireling (a hired servant), and not the shepherd, whose own the sheep are not, seeth the wolf coming, and leaveth the sheep, and fleeth: and the wolf catcheth them, and scattereth the sheep.

13 The hireling fleeth (runs away when danger comes), because he is an hireling, and careth not for the sheep (he doesn't love the sheep like the owner does).

14 I am the good shepherd, and know my sheep, and am known of mine (my true followers know my voice and come when I call).

15 As the Father knoweth me, even so know I the Father: and I lay down my life for the sheep (I will give my life for my people as I perform the Atonement).

16 And other sheep I have, which are not of this fold (are not on this continent): them also I must bring, and they shall hear my voice; and there shall be one fold, *and* one shepherd (all of my

righteous followers will ultimately come together with me in celestial glory).

Note: We know from 3 Nephi 15:21 that Jesus was referring to the Nephites on the American continent, when he said "other sheep I have, which are not of this fold; them also I must bring, and they shall hear my voice;" (verse 16 above). We know also that there were yet other sheep besides the Nephites. To the Nephites, Jesus said, "I say unto you that I have other sheep, which are not of this land, neither of the land of Jerusalem,..." (3 Nephi 16:1). As we read 3 Nephi 17:4, we are told that Jesus was referring to the Lost Ten Tribes.

17 Therefore (for this reason) doth my Father love me, because I lay down my life, that I might take it again.

18 No man taketh it from me, but I lay it down of myself (no one can take my life from me, rather, I will give my life intentionally). I have power to lay it down (to leave my body), and I have power to take it again (I have power to resurrect). This commandment have I received of my Father. (This is what my Father asked me to do.)

19 There was a division therefore again among the Jews for (because of) these sayings (because Jesus said that no one could kill him, rather, he would give his life willingly, then resurrect himself).

20 And many of them said, He hath a devil (he is possessed by an evil spirit), and is mad (has lost his mind); why hear ye him (why do you even listen to him)?

21 Others said, These are not the words of him that hath a devil. Can a devil open the eyes of the blind?

22 And it was at Jerusalem the feast of the dedication (see Bible Dictionary, page 673), and it was winter.

23 And Jesus walked in the temple in Solomon's porch.

24 Then came the Jews round about him, and said unto him, How long dost thou make us to doubt (how long are you going to keep us wondering about who you really are)? If thou be the Christ, tell us plainly.

25 Jesus answered them, I told you, and ye believed not (I have told you many times and in many ways that I am Christ, but you won't believe me): the works (miracles and teaching) that I do in my Father's name, they bear witness of me (they tell you who I am).

26 But ye believe not, because ye are not of my sheep, as I said unto you. (You have been in apostasy so long that you no longer even recognize the voice of the Good Shepherd when he calls.)

27 My sheep hear my voice, and I know them, and they follow me:

28 And I give unto them eternal life; and they shall never perish (they will never suffer spiritual death), neither shall any *man* pluck them out of my hand (no one can take them away from me.).

29 My Father, which gave *them* me, is greater than all; and no *man* is able to pluck *them* out of my Father's hand.

30 I and *my* Father are one. (We are completely united in all things.)

31 Then the Jews took up stones again to stone him (to throw rocks at

him and kill him).

32 Jesus answered them, Many good works have I shewed (shown) you from my Father; for which of those works do ye stone me? (I have done many wonderful miracles and much good; for which of these things are you going to stone me?)

33 The Jews answered him, saying, For a good work we stone thee not; but for blasphemy; and because that thou, being a man, makest thyself God. (We are not stoning you for those things, rather because you have mocked God and claim that you are God.)

34 Jesus answered them, Is it not written in your law (Psalm 82:6), I said, Ye are gods (you can become gods)?

Note: This is a very important doctrinal point. Many Christians are very offended by our teaching that we can become gods (D&C 132:20). Here in the Bible itself is a statement, confirmed by the Savior himself, that we can become gods. He reaffirms what had already been given in Psalm 82:6

35 If he called them gods, unto whom the word of God came, and the scripture cannot be broken; (If your scriptures teach that you can become gods, why is it blasphemy [mocking God] for me to say I am a God?)

Note: Blasphemy, according to Jewish law, was a sin which would get a person executed.

36 Say ye of him (me), whom the Father hath sanctified (prepared), and

sent into the world, Thou blasphemest; because I said, I am the Son of God (are you saying that I mock God by claiming to be his Son)?

37 If I do not the works of my Father (if what I do doesn't remind you of the Father), believe me not (then don't believe me).

38 But if I do (remind you of the Father), though ye believe not me, believe the works: that ye may know, and believe, that the Father is in me, and I in him.

39 Therefore (because of what he said) they sought (tried) again to take (arrest) him: but he escaped out of their hand,

40 And went away again beyond Jordan into the place where John at first baptized; and there he abode (stayed).

41 And many resorted (went) unto him, and said, John did no miracle (John the Baptist didn't do miracles): but all things that John spake of this man (Jesus) were true (everything he said about Jesus turned out to be true).

42 And many believed on him there.

JOHN 11

1 NOW a certain *man* was sick, *named* Lazarus, of Bethany (about two miles outside of Jerusalem), the town of Mary and her sister Martha (the town where Mary and Martha lived).

2 (It was *that* Mary which anointed the Lord with ointment, and wiped his feet with her hair [Matthew 26:7], whose brother Lazarus was sick.)

3 Therefore his sisters sent unto him (Jesus), saying, Lord, behold, he (Lazarus) whom thou lovest is sick.

4 When Jesus heard *that*, he said,

This sickness is not unto death, but for the glory of God, that the Son of God might be glorified thereby. (He won't be dead very long. He will die, verses 13-14, and this situation will help many to believe in God and to be have a chance to be much more aware of who I am.)

5 Now Jesus loved Martha, and her sister, and Lazarus.

6 When he had heard therefore that he was sick, he abode (stayed) two days still in the same place where he was.

7 Then after that saith he to *his* disciples, Let us go into Judæa (to the Jerusalem area) again.

8 *His* disciples say unto him, Master, the Jews of late (just recently) sought to (tried to) stone thee; and goest thou thither (there) again?

Note: His disciples are very worried about his safety and don't want him going to Mary and Martha's house in Bethany, because it is only two miles from Jerusalem where the Jews are who have already tried to kill him.

9 Jesus answered, Are there not twelve hours in the day? If any man walk in the day, he stumbleth not, because he seeth the light of this world. (I must keep right on going with my work.)

10 But if a man walk in the night, he stumbleth, because there is no light in him.

11 These things said he: and after that he saith unto them, Our friend Lazarus sleepeth; but I go, that I may awake him out of sleep.

12 Then said his disciples, Lord, if he sleep, he shall do well (if he is just sleeping, he will be ok).

13 Howbeit (however) Jesus spake of his death: but they thought that he had spoken of taking of rest in sleep.

14 Then said Jesus unto them plainly, Lazarus is dead.

15 And I am glad for your sakes that I was not there, to the intent ye may believe (I am glad he is dead, because what is going to happen will strengthen your testimonies); nevertheless let us go unto him.

16 Then said Thomas, which is called Didymus (the twin), unto his fellow disciples, Let us also go, that we may die with him.

Note: This apostle of Christ, Thomas, is usually known mainly as "doubting Thomas", because he refused to believe that Jesus had been resurrected unless he could see him personally and feel the wounds in his hands and side. See John 20:25-28. Here we see Thomas in a much different light. He is a man of courage and conviction, and encourages the other disciples to join him in going to Jerusalem with Jesus so that they could all die with him.

17 Then when Jesus came (arrived in Bethany at Martha's house), he found that he (Lazarus) had *lain* in the grave four days already.

Note: Four days is very significant because of Jewish beliefs about death. They had a false belief that the spirit must remain by a dead person's body for three days. After that, the person is for sure dead. The fact that Lazarus had been dead for four days, and in fact, had already begun to stink (verse 39) left no doubt in the minds of the mourners that he was very dead.

18 Now Bethany was nigh (near) unto Jerusalem, about fifteen furlongs off (two miles away):

19 And many of the Jews came to Martha and Mary, to comfort them concerning their brother.

20 Then Martha, as soon as she heard that Jesus was coming, went and met him: but Mary sat *still* in the house.

21 Then said Martha unto Jesus, Lord, if thou hadst been here, my brother had not died (if you had come quickly, when I first sent word to you of Lazarus' illness, he would not have died).

22 But I know, that even now, whatsoever thou wilt ask of God, God will give *it* thee. (Martha has great faith, and hints that she believes that even now, Lazarus could be brought back to life.)

23 Jesus saith unto her, Thy brother shall rise again.

24 Martha saith unto him, I know that he shall rise again in the resurrection at the last day.

25 Jesus said unto her, I am the resurrection, and the life (I have power over death and can give eternal life): he that believeth in me, though he were dead, yet shall he live: (The righteous will be "made alive" in two ways. First, as is the case with all mortals, they will be resurrected. Second, they will receive eternal life, exaltation in celestial glory.)

26 And whosoever liveth (is spiritually alive) and believeth in me shall never die (spiritually). Believest thou this?

27 She saith unto him, Yea, Lord: I believe that thou art the Christ, the Son of God, which should come into the world. (I believe that you are the promised Messiah.)

28 And when she had so said, she went her way, and called Mary her sister secretly, saying, The Master is come, and calleth for thee.

29 As soon as she heard *that*, she arose quickly, and came unto him (Jesus).

30 Now Jesus was not yet (had not yet) come into the town, but was in that place where Martha met him.

31 The Jews then which were with her in the house, and comforted her, when they saw Mary, that she rose up hastily and went out, followed her, saying, She goeth unto the grave (to Lazarus' tomb) to weep there.

32 Then when Mary was come where Jesus was, and saw him, she fell down at his feet, saying unto him, Lord, if thou hadst been here, my brother had not (would not have) died.

33 When Jesus therefore saw her weeping, and the Jews also weeping which came with her, he groaned in the spirit, and was troubled, (This was a very emotional time for Jesus.)

34 And said, Where have ye laid him (where have you buried him)? They said unto him, Lord, come and see.

35 Jesus wept.

Note: Verse 35 is the shortest verse in the Bible. It is a reminder of the great kindness and compassion the Master has for us.

36 Then said the Jews, Behold how

he loved him!

37 And some of them said, Could not this man, which opened the eyes of the blind, have caused that even this man should not have died (couldn't Jesus have prevented Lazarus from dying if he had been here)?

38 Jesus therefore again groaning in himself cometh to the grave. It was a cave (tomb), and a stone lay upon it.

39 Jesus said, Take ye away the stone (open the tomb). Martha, the sister of him that was dead, saith unto him, Lord, by this time he stinketh: for he hath been *dead* four days.

40 Jesus saith unto her, Said I not unto thee, that, if thou wouldest believe, thou shouldest see the glory of God (you would see the power of God in action)?

41 Then they took away the stone *from the place* where the dead was laid. And Jesus lifted up his eyes, and said, Father, I thank thee that thou hast heard me.

42 And I knew that thou hearest me always: but because of the people which stand by I said it (I said it out loud for the benefit of the people who have gathered around), that they may believe that thou hast sent me.

43 And when he thus had spoken, he cried with a loud voice, Lazarus, come forth.

44 And he that was dead came forth, bound hand and foot with grave-clothes: and his face was bound about with a napkin. Jesus saith unto them, Loose him (unwrap him), and let him go.

45 Then many of the Jews which came to Mary, and had seen the things which Jesus did, believed on him.

46 But some of them went their ways to the Pharisees, and told them what things Jesus had done.

47 Then gathered the chief priests and the Pharisees a council (the chief religious leaders of the Jews called an emergency meeting), and said, What do we (what can we do about Jesus)? for this man doeth many miracles.

48 If we let him thus alone (if we don't do something), all *men* will believe on him: and the Romans shall come and take away both our place (our positions of authority) and nation. (They are concerned about their own power and prestige. They are an example of the fact that wickedness does not promote rational thought.)

49 And one of them, *named* Caiaphas (the highest religious leader among the Jews at that time), being the high priest that same year, said unto them, Ye know nothing at all (you are a pack of idiots!),

50 Nor consider that it is expedient for us, that one man should die for the people, and that the whole nation perish not. (The solution is clear. It is better that Jesus die, than our whole nation be disrupted and destroyed by the Romans.)

51 And this spake he not of himself: but being high priest that year, he prophesied that Jesus should die for that nation;

52 And not for that nation only, but that also he should gather together in one the children of God that were scattered abroad.

Note: Verses 51-52 present a problem. The way it is written, it sounds like the wicked high priest, Caiaphas, is actually prophesying that it is necesssary for Jesus to die in order to gather the righteous from all the world and save them, which is true. In verse 51, John says that Caiaphas spoke "not of himself", implying perhaps that, by virtue of his office, the Spirit came upon him and caused him to prophesy truth. Apostle James E. Talmage helps us understand this matter in *Jesus the Christ*, page 498.

53 Then from that day forth they (the council of the Pharisees, known as the Sanhedrin; see Bible Dictionary, page 769) took counsel together for to put him to death.

54 Jesus therefore walked no more openly among the Jews; but went thence (from there) unto a country near to the wilderness, into a city called Ephraim, and there continued (stayed) with his disciples.

55 And the Jews' passover was nigh (close) at hand: and many went out of the country up to Jerusalem before the passover, to purify themselves (to prepare themselves to properly observe Passover week).

Note: This is the final Passover for the Savior during his mortal life. He will spend the final week of his life teaching the people during the Passover week festivities and worship in Jerusalem. He will be crucified on Friday of that week. The religious rulers of the Jews will be watching for Jesus, knowing that he will come.

56 Then sought they (they watched) for Jesus, and spake (spoke) among themselves, as they stood in the temple, What think ye, that he will not come to the feast? (They were wondering whether or not Jesus would show up in Jerusalem, because of the danger to him.)

57 Now both the chief priests and the Pharisees had given a commandment, that, if any man knew where he were (if any one spotted Jesus), he should shew *it* (report it), that they might take (arrest) him.

JOHN 12

Note: This chapter begins the last week of the Savior's mortal life. It is Passover time in Jerusalem and Jews from many countries have joined the huge crowds in Jerusalem in preparation for the festivities and worship. The Passover feast itself will be held on Thursday. It is eaten in celebration of the passing of the destroying angel over the homes of the Children of Israel when the firstborn sons of all the families of the Egyptians were slain in order to persuade Pharaoh to let the Israelite slaves go free. There is much symbolism associated with the Passover. The Children of Israel were held in bondage (slavery) by the Egyptians, symbolizing the bondage of Satan. After repeated attempts by Moses to get Pharaoh to let the Israelite slaves go free, the Children of Israel were instructed by Moses (Exodus 12:5) to select and sacrifice a male lamb (symbolizing Christ), without blemish (symbolizing that Christ was perfect), of the first year (symbolizing that Christ was in the prime of life). They were to take hyssop (Exodus 12:22), a sponge-like plant, (associated with Christ on the

299

cross, see John 19:29), dip it in the blood of the lamb and then put the blood on the lintel (top of the door frame) and on the door posts of the front door of their dwelling (Exodus 12:7 and 22). This blood of the lamb provided protection for their household. The ensuing death of the firstborn of Pharaoh and all other Egyptian families caused the Israelite slaves to be set free. The death of the "firstborn" is symbolic of the death of the Savior, the "Firstborn" of the Father in the spirit world (Colossians 1:15). The Savior is referred to as "the Lamb of God". It is through the blood of the Lamb of God that we are set free from the bondage of sin. During the Passover, at the very time the Jews are celebrating being set free from Egyptian bondage by the blood of lambs, the Lamb (Christ) will present himself to be sacrificed in order that all of us might be set free from physical death and from the bondage of sin.

1 THEN Jesus six days before the passover (this would probably be on Saturday, since Passover was on Thursday) came to Bethany, where Lazarus was (lived) which (who) had been dead, whom he raised from the dead.

2 There they made him a supper; and Martha served: but Lazarus was one of them that sat at the table with him.

3 Then took Mary (Martha and Lazarus' sister) a pound of ointment of spikenard, very costly (very expensive; see note in verse 5), and anointed (poured it on) the feet of Jesus, and wiped his feet with her hair: and the house was filled with the odour of the ointment.

4 Then saith one of his disciples, Judas Iscariot, Simon's *son*, which should betray him (the one who would betray Christ),

5 Why was not this ointment sold for three hundred pence (about 300 day's wages), and given to the poor?

6 This he said, not that he cared for the poor; but because he was a thief, and had the bag (the money purse), and bare what was put therein. (Judas Iscariot was apparently the treasurer of the Twelve.)

7 Then said Jesus, Let her alone: against the day of my burying hath she kept this. (She has anointed my body in preparation for my death and burial.) (JST gives this verse as follows: "Then said Jesus, Let her alone; for she hath preserved this ointment until now, that she might anoint me in token of my burial.")

Note: It would appear here that Mary is more sensitive and aware of what is going to happen to Jesus, than most of the others at this time.

8 For the poor always ye have with you; but me ye have not always.

9 Much (many) people of the Jews therefore knew that he was there: and they came not for Jesus' sake only, but that they might see Lazarus also, whom he had raised from the dead. (People didn't come just to see Jesus, but they were also curious to see Lazarus who had been brought back to life after having been dead for four days.)

10 But the chief priests consulted (plotted) that they might put Lazarus

also to death;

11 Because that by reason of him many of the Jews went away, and believed on Jesus. (They wanted to get rid of Lazarus due to the fact that many Jews were being converted to Jesus because of his raising Lazarus from the dead.)

Note: Next comes what is known as the "Triumphal Entry" of Jesus into Jerusalem. Excitement about Jesus was making its way through the large crowds in Jerusalem, and when word came that Jesus was even now approaching the city, large numbers of people lined the streets and threw pieces of clothing along the way in front of the Master. They took palm branches and laid them in the path also. Symbolically, in Jewish culture, palm branches represent triumph and victory over enemies. In effect, the people were excitedly welcoming Jesus as a king.

12 On the next day (probably Sunday) much people that were come to the feast (of Passover), when they heard that Jesus was coming to Jerusalem,

13 Took branches of palm trees, and went forth to meet him, and cried, Hosanna: Blessed is the King of Israel that cometh in the name of the Lord.

Note: In conjunction with the dedication of our temples, we participate in what is known as the Hosanna Shout. See McConkie, *Mormon Doctrine*, page 368. "Hosanna" means "Lord, save us now", see Bible Dictionary, pages 704-705. Another translation of

Hosanna is "O, please, Jehovah, save (us) now, please!". During the dedication of the Kirtland Temple on March 27, 1836, Joseph Smith gave a dedicatory prayer. In the prayer (D&C 109), the Prophet plead with the Lord "that we may be clothed upon with robes of righteousness, with palms in our hands, and crowns of glory upon our heads, and reap eternal joy for all our sufferings." (D&C 109:76.) The prayer was followed by the Saints standing and participating in the Hosanna Shout. Afterward, they sang *The Spirit of God Like a Fire is Burning* which includes the phrase, "Hosanna, Hosanna to God and the Lamb!" (See *Mormon Doctrine*, by Bruce R. McConkie, page 368, for more about the Hosanna Shout). Today, worthy members are invited to bring clean, white handkerchiefs with them to temple dedications. These handkerchiefs are symbolic of palm fronds, and represent victory and triumph over our enemies of sin and weakness through the Atonement of Christ.

14 And Jesus, when he had found a young ass (a young, male donkey, which had never been ridden; see Luke 19:30), sat thereon; as it is written,

15 Fear not, daughter of Sion: behold, thy King cometh, sitting on an ass's colt.

16 These things understood not his disciples at the first: but when Jesus was glorified (had been resurrected), then remembered they that these things were written of him, and *that* they had done these things unto him.

17 The people therefore that was with him when he called Lazarus out

of his grave, and raised him from the dead, bare record. (The people who were with Jesus when he raised Lazarus from the dead, spread the word among the Passover crowds that Jesus was coming into Jerusalem.)

18 For this cause the people also met him (this is why the crowds came to meet him as he arrived), for that they heard that he had done this miracle (because they heard that he had raised a man from the dead).

19 The Pharisees therefore said among themselves, Perceive ye how ye prevail nothing (we can't seem to do anything about Jesus)? behold, the world is gone after him (everybody is starting to follow him).

20 And there were certain Greeks among them that came up to worship at the feast:

21 The same came therefore to Philip (an apostle; see John 1:44), which was of Bethsaida of Galilee, and desired him, saying, Sir, we would see Jesus (we would like to see Jesus).

22 Philip cometh and telleth Andrew (an apostle): and again Andrew and Philip tell (told) Jesus.

23 And Jesus answered them, saying, The hour is come, that the Son of man (Christ) should be glorified (the time has come for me to finish my mortal mission).

24 Verily, verily, I say unto you, Except a corn (kernel) of wheat fall into the ground and die, it abideth (remains) alone: but if it die, it bringeth forth much fruit (if it dies and is buried, it grows and produces much wheat).

25 He that loveth his life (selfishly lives according only to worldly desires) shall lose it; and he that hateth his life in this world (prioritizes on spiritual, eternal values) shall keep it unto life eternal.

26 If any man serve me, let him follow me; and where I am, there shall also my servant be (if you follow me, you will be with me in heaven): if any man serve me, him will *my* Father honour (honor with celestial glory and exaltation).

27 Now is my soul troubled (this is getting very difficult; see D&C 19:18); and what shall I say? Father, save me from this hour (should I ask my Father to save me from what I am now going to have to go suffer): but for this cause (the Atonement) came I unto this hour (to this point in my mortal life).

28 Father, glorify thy name. Then came there a voice (the Father's voice) from heaven, *saying*, I have both glorified *it*, and will glorify *it* again.

29 The people therefore, that stood by, and heard it, said that it thundered: others said, An angel spake (spoke) to him.

30 Jesus answered and said, This voice came not because of me, but for your sakes. (In other words, you were allowed to hear my Father's voice to strengthen you.)

31 Now is the judgment of this world (my accomplishing of the Atonement now will finish qualifying me to judge the world): now shall the prince of this world (Satan; see John 12:31, footnote a) be cast out. (In other words, my Atonement will pave the way for righteous people to overcome Satan and cast him out of their lives through repentance.)

32 And I, if I be lifted up from the

earth (crucified; see verse 33), will draw all *men* unto me. (Through the Atonement of Christ, he will have power to bring all people to himself, then on to the Father, if they will repent.)

33 This he said, signifying what death he should die.

34 The people answered him (responded to what he had just said, then asked), We have heard out of the law (the Old Testament) that Christ abideth (will remain) for ever: and how sayest thou (so, why are you saying that), The Son of man must be lifted up? who is this Son of man?

35 Then Jesus said unto them, Yet a little while is the light with you (I will be with you for just a little bit longer). Walk while ye have the light (take advantage of this time), lest (for fear that) darkness come upon you: for he that walketh in darkness knoweth not whither he goeth.

36 While ye have light, believe in the light (believe in me), that ye may be the children of light (in order that you might become my righteous followers; compare with Mosiah 5:7). These things spake Jesus, and departed, and did hide himself from them.

37 But though he had done so many miracles before them, yet they (the majority) believed not on him:

38 That the saying of Esaias (Isaiah) the prophet might be fulfilled, which he spake (Isaiah 53:1), Lord, who hath believed our report (who believes us prophets anyway)? and to whom hath the arm of the Lord been revealed (who recognizes the hand of the Lord in things)?

39 Therefore they could not (did not)

believe, because that Esaias (Isaiah) said again (it is just as Isaiah was told by the Lord when he received his call to preach to hard-hearted Israel; see Isaiah 6:10),

40 He hath blinded their eyes, and hardened their heart; that they should not see with *their* eyes, nor understand with *their* heart, and be converted, and I should heal them.

Note: Referring to verse 40 above, it is important to understand that God does not make people spiritually blind nor harden their hearts. They are given agency and can become that way by ignoring the gospel.

41 These things said Esaias (Isaiah), when he saw his (Christ's) glory (Isaiah 6:1-5), and spake of him (spoke of Christ).

42 Nevertheless among the chief rulers also many believed on him; but because of the Pharisees they did not confess *him*, lest they should be put out of the synagogue: (By now, many of the chief religious rulers of the Jews had come to believe that Jesus was the Messiah, but they would not admit it for fear of being excommunicated.)

43 For they loved the praise of men more than the praise of God.

44 Jesus cried (spoke loudly) and said, He that believeth on me, believeth not on me, but on him that sent me. (If you believe in me, you believe in the Father.)

45 And he that seeth me seeth him that sent me (if you see me, it is as if you were seeing the Father).

Note: While the message above is

clear, namely, that if you believe in the Savior and follow him, you are, in effect, believing in the Father and following him, there is a literal aspect also to verse 45. We are told by the Apostle Paul, in Hebrews 1:3, that Jesus is "the express image" of the Father. In other words, the Savior and his Father are exact look-a-likes. See McConkie, *Doctrinal New Testament Commentary*, Vol. 3, page 138.

46 I am come a light into the world, that whosoever believeth on me should not abide in darkness (will not live in spiritual darkness).

47 And if any man hear my words, and believe not, I judge him not (it is not yet time for final judgment; such people may still rethink and repent): for I came not to judge the world (at this time), but to save the world.

48 He that rejecteth me, and receiveth not (does not accept) my words, hath one that judgeth him: the word that I have spoken, the same shall judge him in the last day. (People are made accountable when they hear and understand the gospel to some degree. Therefore, the words of the Savior will be a witness against them on final Judgment Day, if they have not repented.)

49 For I have not spoken of myself (on my own); but the Father which sent me, he gave me a commandment, what I should say, and what I should speak.

50 And I know that his commandment is life everlasting (leads to eternal life): whatsoever I speak therefore, even as the Father said unto me, so I speak.

JOHN 13

1 NOW before the feast of the passover, when Jesus knew that his hour was come that he should depart out of this world unto the Father, having loved his own which were in the world, he loved them unto the end.

2 And supper being ended (they had finished eating the Passover meal), the devil having now put into the heart of Judas Iscariot, Simon's *son*, to betray him;

3 Jesus knowing that the Father had given all things into his hands, and that he was come from God, and went to God (and would return to God);

4 He riseth (arose) from supper, and laid aside his garments; and took a towel, and girded himself.

5 After that he poureth water into a bason (basin), and began to wash the disciples' feet, and to wipe *them* with the towel wherewith he was girded.

Note: This must have been an especially tender time, when the Master of all demonstrated that he was the servant of all. The washing of the dusty, tired feet of guests was a gesture of hospitality and service in the culture of the Jews. Among other things, the Savior was demonstrating by his actions that he was a humble servant to his apostles.

6 Then cometh he to Simon Peter: and Peter saith unto him, Lord, dost thou wash my feet (are you going to wash my feet too)?

7 Jesus answered and said unto him, What I do thou knowest not now (you don't understand now); but thou shalt know hereafter (but later you will

understand).

8 Peter saith unto him, Thou shalt never wash my feet (JST "Thou needest not to wash my feet."). (Peter apparently felt that it was not necessary for Jesus to wash his feet.) Jesus answered him, If I wash thee not, thou hast no part with me. (Symbolically, if I don't cleanse you, you will not be with me in eternity.)

9 Simon Peter saith unto him, Lord, not my feet only, but also *my* hands and *my* head. (In that case, please wash me completely.)

10 Jesus saith to him (Peter), He that is washed (is clean spiritually) needeth not (needs no more) save (except) to wash *his* feet, but is clean every whit (every bit, in other words, Peter, you are spiritually clean, and all I need to do is wash your tired dusty feet here this evening as a token of my being your servant; more is not necessary): and ye are clean, but not all (you apostles are "clean", except for Judas Iscariot).

11 For he knew who should (would) betray him; therefore said he, Ye are not all clean.

12 So after he had washed their feet, and had taken his garments, and was set down again, he said unto them, Know ye what I have done to you?

13 Ye call me Master and Lord: and ye say well; for so I am. (You are correct in calling me Master and Lord, because I am.)

14 If I then, *your* Lord and Master, have washed your feet; ye also ought to wash one another's feet. (You ought to serve one another.)

15 For I have given you an example, that ye should do as I have done to you.

16 Verily, verily, I say unto you, The servant is not greater than his lord (no servant is greater than his master); neither he that is sent greater than he that sent him (the messenger is not greater than the one who sent him).

17 If ye know these things, happy are ye if ye do them.

18 I speak not of you all: I know whom I have chosen: but that the scripture (Psalm 41:9) may be fulfilled, He (Judas Iscariot) that eateth bread with me hath lifted up his heel against me (has become my enemy).

19 Now I tell you before it come (I tell you this before it happens), that (so that), when it is come to pass (has happened), ye may believe that I am he (JST "the Christ").

20 Verily, verily, I say unto you, He that receiveth whomsoever I send (my servants, missionaries, apostles etc.) receiveth me; and he that receiveth me receiveth him that sent me (my Father).

21 When Jesus had thus said, he was troubled in spirit (was sad), and testified, and said, Verily, verily, I say unto you, that one of you shall betray me.

22 Then the disciples looked one on another (at one another), doubting of whom he spake (trying to figure out which one of them he meant).

23 Now there was leaning on Jesus' bosom (laying his head on Jesus' chest) one of his disciples, whom Jesus loved (John).

Note: John, the author of this Gospel (this book in the Bible), is so humble that he never directly gives his name in his writing.

24 Simon Peter therefore beckoned to him (motioned to John), that he should ask who it should be of whom he spake. (Peter signaled to John, who was leaning his head on the Savior at the moment, to quietly ask him who it was that would betray him.)

25 He then lying on Jesus' breast (had his head on Jesus' chest or on the front of his shoulder) saith unto him, Lord, who is it (which one of us is it)?

26 Jesus answered, He it is, to whom I shall give a sop (a small chunk of bread, used to dip into gravy, juice or whatever), when I have dipped it. And when he had dipped the sop, he gave it to Judas Iscariot, *the son* of Simon.

Note: Jesus must have whispered the answer to John, because none of the others at the table seemed to have heard his answer, see verse 28.

27 And after the sop (after Judas had taken the sop) Satan entered into him (Satan's influence came upon him strongly). Then said Jesus unto him, That thou doest, do quickly (what you have in mind to do, do quickly).

28 Now no man at the table (none of the others) knew for what intent he spake this unto him.

29 For some *of them* thought, because Judas had the bag (the money purse; apparently Judas handled the finances for the twelve apostles), that Jesus had said unto him, Buy *those things* that we have need of against (for) the feast; or, that he should give something to the poor.

30 He (Judas) then having received the sop (accepted the sop from Jesus) went immediately out: and it was night.

31 Therefore, when he was gone out (when Judas had left), Jesus said, Now is the Son of man (the Son of God; Son of Man of Holiness; see Moses 6:57) glorified, and God is glorified in him. (The time has arrived for my Atonement, in which I shall be glorified, and in which I will bring glory to my Father.)

32 If God be glorified in him, God shall also glorify him in himself, and shall straightway (right away) glorify him.

33 Little children (my dear apostles, who still have much to learn), yet a little while I am with you. Ye shall seek me: and as I said unto the Jews, Whither (where) I go, ye cannot come (you can not come to heaven with me now); so now I say to you.

34 A new commandment I give unto you (I renew a very old commandment), That ye love one another; as I have loved you, that ye also love one another.

35 By this shall all *men* know that ye are my disciples, if ye have love one to another.

36 Simon Peter said unto him, Lord, whither goest thou? Jesus answered him, Whither I go (where I am going), thou canst not follow me now (in other words, Peter can't follow Jesus to heaven now); but thou shalt follow me afterwards (after you have finished your mission, you can come to heaven).

37 Peter said unto him, Lord, why cannot I follow thee now? I will lay

down my life for thy sake. (Peter apparently thinks Jesus is telling him that he, Jesus, must go it alone in Jerusalem, and Peter wants to stick close to him and defend him with his life if necessary.)

38 Jesus answered him, Wilt thou lay down thy life for my sake? Verily, verily, I say unto thee, The cock (rooster) shall not crow, till thou hast denied me thrice (three times).

Note: Denying knowing the Savior is not the same as denying the Holy Ghost. Denying the Holy Ghost, as described in D&C 76:31-35, is an unforgivable sin. Peter's denying that he knows the Savior and has been one of his followers for three years is not unforgivable, though so doing brought Peter deep anguish and tears.

JOHN 14

1 LET not your heart be troubled (don't worry): ye believe in God (the Father), believe (have faith) also in me.

2 In my Father's house are many mansions: if *it were* not so, I would have told you. I go to prepare a place for you.

Note: Joseph Smith explained the meaning of verse 2 above, wherein it says "In my Father's house are many mansions". He said it should be, "In my Father's kingdom are many kingdoms." Also, "There are mansions for those who obey a celestial law, and there are other mansions for those who come short..." (*Teachings of the Prophet Joseph Smith*, page 366.) We know from D&C 76 that there are

three degrees of glory, each of which has some degree of reward and glory. Even the telestial kingdom is so glorious that it "surpasses all understanding" (D&C 76:89). We know from D&C 131:1 that even the celestial kingdom has three "mansions" or degrees. Thus, the Father's "house", or kingdom, does indeed have "many mansions" or categories. Obviously, Jesus will prepare a place for his faithful apostles, whom he will leave shortly, in the highest mansion (exaltation) of his Father (see verse 3 below).

3 And if I go (JST "And when I go") and prepare a place for you, I will come again, and receive you unto myself; that where I am, *there* ye may be also.

4 And whither I go ye know, and the way ye know. (You know where I am going, and how to get there yourselves.)

Note: These wonderful apostles are still undergoing intensive training by the Savior. To those of us who are familiar with the concepts in these verses, because we have been taught them most of our lives, there may be a temptation to wonder why it is taking so much time and repetition for these brethren to catch on. We must remember that they grew up in an environment of apostate Judaism, very foreign to these simple truths.

5 Thomas (one of the apostles) saith unto him, Lord, we know not whither thou goest; and how can we know the way? (We don't know where you are going, so how can we know the way to

get there?)

6 Jesus saith unto him, I am the way, the truth, and the life (I have everything you need): no man cometh unto the Father, but by me (except through me).

7 If ye had known me (if you had truly known me and understood me and what I have been teaching you), ye should have (would have) known my Father also: and from henceforth (from now on) ye know him, and have seen him (because you have seen me).

8 Philip (one of the apostles) saith unto him, Lord, shew us the Father, and it sufficeth us (and that will be sufficient for us).

9 Jesus saith unto him, Have I been so long time with you, and yet hast thou not known me (and you still don't understand), Philip? he that hath seen me hath seen the Father; and how sayest thou *then* (so why do you say), Shew (show) us the Father?

10 Believest thou not that I am in the Father, and the Father in me? the words that I speak unto you I speak not of myself: but the Father that dwelleth in me, he doeth the works. (Don't you understand that the Father and I are a team and we work together in perfect unity? Everything I do is, in effect, what the Father is doing for you.)

11 Believe me that I *am* in the Father, and the Father in me: or else believe me for the very works' sake. (In other words, if you can't believe that I and my Father are perfectly unified in the work we do, at least believe me because of the works you have seen and heard me do, which could come from no one but the Father.)

12 Verily, verily, I say unto you, He that believeth on me, the works that I do shall he do also; and greater (more) *works* than these shall he do; because I go unto my Father.

Note: The word "greater" in verse 12 above, can have at least two meanings. In addition to meaning more significant or more spectacular or more powerful, higher etc., it can also mean "more" or on-going, continued etc. It is used this way in D&C 7:5 where the Savior tells Peter that John the Beloved will stay on the earth until the Second Coming, and thus "do more, or a greater work" than he has done up to now. For more on this, see *Strong's Exhaustive Concordance of the Bible*, word # 3187, where "greater" is also defined as "more". There is also another aspect of the word "greater" as used by the Master in this promise to his apostles. When they are exalted, and have become gods, they will indeed do greater works, in the normal sense of the word. They will have spirit offspring, will create worlds, and as gods, will do even greater, more magnificent and higher things than they ever saw Christ do while he was among them. See Joseph Smith's teachings on this in *Lectures on Faith*, pages 64-66.

13 And whatsoever ye shall ask in my name, that will I do, that the Father may be glorified in the Son.

14 If ye shall ask any thing in my name, I will do it.

Note: Verses 15-26, below, will speak of two different "Comforters". One of these Comforters is the Holy Ghost.

The other is the Savior himself and includes the Father on occasions. Verses 16, 17, and 26 speak of the Holy Ghost. Verses 18, 21, 23, and 28 speak of the Savior. For more on this, see *Teachings of the Prophet Joseph Smith*, pages 149 to 151.

15 If ye love me, keep my commandments.

16 And I will pray the Father, and he shall give you another Comforter (the Holy Ghost), that he may abide (be) with you for ever;

17 *Even* the Spirit of truth; whom the world cannot receive (the world, meaning those who are not members of the Church, cannot receive the Gift of the Holy Ghost), because it seeth him not, neither knoweth him: but ye know him; for he dwelleth with you, and shall be in you.

18 I will not leave you comfortless: I (Jesus) will come to you. (This is spoken of as the "Second Comforter". See McConkie, *Doctrinal New Testament Commentary*, Vol. 1, page 738.)

19 Yet a little while, and the world seeth me no more (I will be crucified and gone, as far as most people are concerned); but ye see me (you will see me after I am resurrected): because I live (resurrect), ye shall live also. (Because of my Atonement, you will resurrect also and have eternal life.)

20 At that day ye shall know that I *am* in my Father, and ye in me, and I in you. (Jesus is still responding to Thomas' question in verse 5 and to Philip's request in verse 8.)

21 He that hath my commandments, and keepeth them, he it is that loveth me: and he that loveth me shall be loved of my Father, and I will love him, and will manifest myself to him (as the "Second Comforter").

22 Judas (one of the faithful apostles) saith unto him, not Iscariot (not Judas Iscariot who has already left to betray Jesus), Lord, how is it that thou wilt manifest thyself unto us, and not unto the world?

23 Jesus answered and said unto him, If a man love me, he will keep my words: and my Father will love him, and we will come unto him (the "Second Comforter", and make our abode with him.

24 He that loveth me not keepeth not my sayings (does not keep my commandments): and the word (gospel) which ye hear is not mine (did not originate with me), but the Father's which sent me (originated with the Father who sent me).

25 These things have I spoken unto you, being yet present with you (while I am still with you).

26 But the Comforter, *which is* the Holy Ghost, whom the Father will send in my name, he shall teach you all things, and bring all things to your remembrance, whatsoever I have said unto you. (This is a description of some of the things the Gift of the Holy Ghost can do for us.)

27 Peace I leave with you, my peace I give unto you: not as the world giveth, give I unto you. Let not your heart be troubled, neither let it be afraid.

28 Ye have heard how I said unto you, I go away, and come *again* unto you. (The Apostles had the "Second Comforter" for forty days, after

Christ's resurrection, see Acts 1:3, as the Savior ministered to them and taught them.) If ye loved me, ye would rejoice, because I said, I go unto the Father: for my Father is greater than I.

29 And now I have told you before it come to pass (I have told you ahead of time that I will be arrested, tried, crucified and resurrected), that (so that), when it is come to pass (after it has all happened), ye might believe.

30 Hereafter I will not talk much with you (we can't keep talking much longer): for (because) the prince of this world cometh, and hath nothing in me (JST "for the prince of darkness, who is of this world, cometh, but hath no power over me, but he hath power over you."). (In effect, the Savior is saying, "We can't talk much longer because Satan is bringing Judas Iscariot and the high priests with their soldiers to arrest me. Satan has no power over me, but you are still vulnerable to his temptations.")

31 But that the world may know that I love the Father; and as the Father gave me commandment, even so I do. Arise, let us go hence (let us go to the Garden of Gethsemane).

Note: Mark 14:26 tells us that they sang a hymn at this point. Luke 22:39 tells us that Jesus then led his eleven remaining apostles to the Mount of Olives. Matthew 26:36 informs us that they went to Gethsemane, a garden with olive trees, near the foot of the Mount of Olives. The time is getting short, because, as Jesus knows, Judas Iscariot and the high priests and their soldiers will be coming shortly.

JOHN 15

1 I AM the true vine (grape vine; symbolic of the fact that the true gospel comes from Christ), and my Father is the husbandman (farmer, owner; symbolic of the fact that the Father owns the earth)

2 Every branch (branch growing from the vine; symbolic of people) in me that beareth not fruit (people who live wickedly) he taketh away (the wicked will be destroyed): and every *branch* (every person) that beareth fruit (who lives righteously), he purgeth it (prunes it, cuts out inappropriate behaviors and sin etc., nourishes it, shapes it etc.), that it may bring forth more fruit (symbolic of continuing progress in the lives of the Saints).

3 Now ye are clean (you have become clean) through the word (the gospel with the Atonement) which I have spoken (taught) unto you.

4 Abide in me, and I in you (stay with me and I will stay with you, or, live with me and I will live with you). As the branch cannot bear fruit of itself, except it abide in (stay attached to) the vine; no more can ye, except ye abide in me. (Just as a branch of a vine cannot live without remaining attached to the vine, so you cannot live righteous lives unless you stay with me.)

Note: The beautiful symbolism in verse 4 above is vitally important for us. How do we attach ourselves to the "vine" so that we can remain securely fastened to Christ? Answer: "...ye shall bind yourselves to act in all holiness before me--" (D&C 43:9.) How do we "bind" ourselves to the true vine

(Christ, verse 1, above)? Answer: We make and keep covenants. Thus, by making covenants, we bind ourselves securely to the true vine, receive constant nourishment from His roots, and are privileged to be pruned, shaped and strengthened by the Husbandman so that we can return to live with Him forever.

5 I am the vine, ye *are* the branches: He that abideth in me, and I in him, the same bringeth forth much fruit (produces much good): for without me ye can do nothing.

6 If a man abide not in me, he is cast forth as a branch (is cut off and thrown away), and is withered (and dries up); and men gather them, and cast *them* into the fire, and they are burned (symbolic of the destruction of the wicked).

7 If ye abide in me (if you stay faithful to me), and my words abide in you (and you are faithful to my gospel), ye shall ask what ye will (want), and it shall be done unto you.

8 Herein is my Father glorified (here is how my Father is glorified), that ye bear much fruit; so shall ye be my disciples. (This reminds us of Moses 1:39 which says "For behold, this is my work and my glory–to bring to pass the immortality and eternal life of man.")

9 As the Father hath loved me, so have I loved you: continue ye in my love (remain faithful to me).

10 If ye keep my commandments, ye shall abide in my love; even as I have kept my Father's commandments, and abide in his love.

11 These things have I spoken unto you, that my joy might remain in you,

and *that* your joy might be full.

12 This is my commandment, That ye love one another, as I have loved you.

13 Greater love hath no man than this, that a man lay down his life for his friends. (This is exactly what Jesus will do in a few hours.)

14 Ye are my friends, if ye do whatsoever I command you.

15 Henceforth (from now on) I call you not servants; for the servant knoweth not what his lord doeth: but I have called you friends; for all things that I have heard of my Father I have made known unto you (I have taught you everything). (This is a significant change of status, from servants to friends. The Savior said the same thing to early members of the Church in our day in D&C 84:77.)

16 Ye have not chosen me, but I have chosen you, and ordained you, that ye should go and bring forth fruit (bring converts into the Church), and *that* your fruit should remain: that whatsoever ye shall ask of the Father in my name, he may give it you.

Note: "Ye have not chosen me, but I have chosen you, and ordained you," in verse 16 above is a most important matter for people to understand. We do not set up our own church and then choose the Savior to be our leader. It is the other way around. He is the leader, and invites us to join him for our salvation. Unfortunately, all other churches have been built up by people. The authority of the priesthood flows from Christ to us, not from us to Christ.

17 These things I command you, that

ye love one another.

18 If the world hate you, ye know that it hated me before *it hated* you. (If you were not doing what is right, the world would not hate you.)

19 If ye were of the world (if you were worldly and wicked), the world would love his own (the world would love you because you would be just like they are): but because ye are not of the world, but I have chosen you out of the world, therefore (that is why) the world hateth you.

20 Remember the word that I said unto you (remember when I taught you), The servant is not greater than his lord (Matthew 10:24). If they have persecuted me, they will also persecute you; if they have kept my saying (obeyed my teachings), they will keep yours also.

21 But all these things will they do unto you for my name's sake, because they know not him (the Father) that sent me.

22 If I had not come and spoken unto them, they had not had sin (they would not have been accountable): but now they have no cloke (cover or excuse) for their sin.

23 He that hateth me hateth my Father also.

24 If I had not done among them the works which none other man did, they had not had sin (they would not have become accountable): but now have they both seen and hated both me and my Father.

25 But *this cometh to pass*, that the word might be fulfilled that is written in their law (this is a fulfillment of the prophecy, They hated me without a cause (Psalm 35:19).

26 But when the Comforter (the Holy Ghost) is come, whom I will send unto you from the Father, even the Spirit of truth, which proceedeth from the Father, he shall testify of me:

Note: The Holy Ghost was functioning on earth during the Savior's ministry as exemplified by the Holy Ghost's descending like a dove at the Savior's baptism. See also Luke 4:1. Apparently, though, the full power of the Gift of the Holy Ghost was not present. See Bible Dictionary, page 704.

27 And ye also shall bear witness, because ye have been with me from the beginning.

JOHN 16

1 THESE things have I spoken unto you, that ye should not be offended (stumble, crumble under the coming pressure and persecution, fall away).

Note: The word "offended", as used in verse 1 above, means to stumble, to crumble under pressure, to fall away, to apostatize. It is used the same way as in Matthew 11:6, where the Savior says "And blessed is he, whosoever shall not be offended in me." Footnote a, for Matthew 11:6, sends the reader to Isaiah 8:14 and Matthew 24:10 where the above definitions are verified.

2 They shall put you out of the synagogues (Jewish church buildings and centers of learning): yea, the time cometh, that whosoever killeth you will think that he doeth God service.

3 And these things will they do unto you, because they have not known the Father, nor me.

4 But these things (these warnings of your coming persecutions) have I told you, that when the time shall come, ye may remember that I told you of them. And these things I said not unto you at the beginning (of my mission), because I was with you.

5 But now I go my way to him that sent me (to the Father); and none of you asketh me, Whither goest thou?

6 But because I have said these things unto you, sorrow hath filled your heart.

7 Nevertheless I tell you the truth; It is expedient (necessary) for you that I go away: for if I go not away, the Comforter (the Holy Ghost) will not come unto you; but if I depart, I will send him unto you. (See note, following John 7:39, about whether or not the Holy Ghost functioned on earth during Christ's mortal ministry)

8 And when he is come, he will reprove (convict) the world of (with respect to) sin, and of (with respect to) righteousness, and of (with respect to) judgment: (After the full Gift and power of the Holy Ghost has come upon you, he will inspire and direct you and bear witness through you such that your teachings and deeds will stand as a witness against the wicked of the world for rejecting righteousness and refusing to believe that the day of judgment will come.)

9 Of (with respect to) sin, because they believe not on me; (They will be accountable, convicted, of their sins because the Holy Ghost will bear witness to them as you preach.)

10 Of (with respect to) righteousness (your teaching of me and my gospel), because I go to my Father, and ye (JST "they") see me no more; (They will be held accountable for your testimonies and teachings, because I am no longer here to teach them.)

11 Of (with respect to) judgment, because the prince of this world (Satan, see John 12:31, footnote a) is judged. (They will reject the witness of the Holy Ghost which will accompany your testimonies and will thus be judged for their sins, like Satan, whom they choose to follow, is judged for his sins.)

12 I have yet many things to say unto you, but ye cannot bear them now (you are not ready for them now).

13 Howbeit (however) when he (the Holy Ghost), the Spirit of truth, is come (has come upon you in full power), he will guide you into all truth: for he shall not speak of himself; but whatsoever he shall hear (from Heavenly Father and Jesus), *that* shall he speak: and he will shew (show) you things to come.

14 He shall glorify me (bear witness of me): for he shall receive of mine (he gets his instructions from me and my Father, see verse 15), and shall shew *it* unto you.

15 All things that the Father hath are mine: therefore said I (that is why I said), that he shall take of mine, and shall shew *it* unto you.

16 A little while, and ye shall not see me: and again, a little while, and ye shall see me, because I go to the Father.

17 Then said *some* of his disciples among themselves, What is this that he

saith unto us, A little while, and ye shall not see me: and again, a little while, and ye shall see me: and, Because I go to the Father?

18 They said therefore (they continued to wonder, among themselves), What is this that he saith, A little while? we cannot tell (understand) what he saith.

19 Now Jesus knew that they were desirous to ask him, and said unto them, Do ye enquire among yourselves of that I said (about what I just said), A little while, and ye shall not see me: and again, a little while, and ye shall see me?

20 Verily, verily, I say unto you, That ye shall weep and lament (when I am crucified), but the world shall rejoice: and ye shall be sorrowful, but your sorrow shall be turned into joy (when I am resurrected and you see me again).

21 A woman when she is in travail (is in labor) hath sorrow, because her hour is come (because the time for her baby to be born has arrived): but as soon as she is delivered of the child (as soon as her baby is born), she remembereth no more the anguish, for joy that a man is born into the world.

22 And ye now therefore have sorrow (you will indeed have sorrow because of what will happen in the next few hours): but I will see you again, and your heart shall rejoice, and your joy no man taketh from you.

23 And in that day ye shall ask me nothing (JST "And in that day ye shall ask me nothing but it shall be done unto you."). Verily, verily, I say unto you, Whatsoever ye shall ask the Father in my name, he will give it you.

24 Hitherto have ye asked nothing in my name (up to now, you have not had to ask Father for things in my name, because I have been here with you): ask, and ye shall receive, that your joy may be full.

Note: Obviously, these good men have said prayers throughout their lives. But the Savior is teaching them that from now on, they must pray to the Father in his name, in other words, in the name of Jesus Christ.

25 These things have I spoken unto you in proverbs (with examples and illustrations): but the time cometh, when I shall no more speak unto you in proverbs, but I shall shew you plainly of the Father.

26 At that day ye shall ask in my name: and I say not unto you, that I will pray the Father for you: (Then, you will pray directly to the Father, in the name of Jesus Christ, rather than having me contact the Father for you.)

27 For the Father himself loveth you, because ye have loved me, and have believed that I came out from God.

28 I came forth from the Father (I am the Father's Son), and am come (have come) into the world: again, I leave the world, and go to (return to) the Father.

29 His disciples said unto him, Lo, now speakest thou plainly, and speakest no proverb. (Yes! Now you are speaking clearly without relating it to other things we understand.)

30 Now are we sure that thou knowest all things, and needest not that any man should ask thee: by this we believe that thou camest forth from God.

31 Jesus answered them, Do ye now believe?

32 Behold, the hour cometh (the time is coming), yea, is now come (in fact, has now arrived), that ye shall be scattered, every man to his own, and shall leave me alone: and yet I am not alone, because the Father is with me.

33 These things I have spoken unto you, that in me ye might have peace. In the world ye shall have tribulation (many troubles): but be of good cheer (be happy, optimistic); I have overcome the world.

JOHN 17

Note: Thursday evening (see Talmage, *Jesus the Christ*, page 593), the Passover meal, known as the Last Supper, was eaten by Jesus and the twelve apostles. During the evening, Jesus introduced the sacrament and tenderly washed the apostles' feet. Sometime during the evening, Judas Iscariot left to betray Jesus to the Jewish high priests and their soldiers. After Judas had left (John 13:31), Jesus began teaching the remaining eleven apostles great doctrines which stretched their minds and strengthened their understandings. These teachings are recorded, beginning with John 13:31 and continuing to the end of John, chapter 16. Sometime, during or after this teaching, the Savior led the eleven to the Mount of Olives, just outside of Jerusalem, where he "lifted up his eyes to heaven" and gave what is known as "The Great Intercessory Prayer". It is recorded in John 17:1-26. After finishing this prayer, the Master will lead his little band of faithful apostles back down the Mount of Olives to a garden which was named Gethsemane, where he will suffer and bleed at every pore. Shortly thereafter, the Savior will be arrested and taken to the ruling high Priest's palace for trial.

1 THESE words spake Jesus, and lifted up his eyes to heaven, and said, Father, the hour is come (the time to begin the Atonement has arrived); glorify thy Son, that thy Son also may glorify thee:

2 As thou hast given him (Christ) power over all flesh (over all people), that he should give eternal life (exaltation) to as many as thou hast given him.

3 And this is life eternal, that they might know thee the only true God, and Jesus Christ, whom thou hast sent.

Note: In D&C 132:24, the phrase "this is life eternal" is given as "This is eternal lives", which emphasizes the fact that the faithful Saints who earn "eternal life" will have "eternal lives", meaning there will be no end to the spirit children they will have in eternity. See last two lines of D&C 132:19.

4 I have glorified thee on the earth: I have finished the work which thou gavest me to do.

5 And now, O Father, glorify thou me with thine own self with the glory which I had with thee before the world was.

6 I have manifested thy name unto the men (the apostles) which thou gavest me out of the world: thine they were, and thou gavest them me; and they have kept thy word (the eleven have remained faithful).

7 Now they have known that all things whatsoever thou hast given me are of thee.

8 For I have given unto them the words which thou gavest me; and they have received (accepted) *them*, and have known surely that I came out from thee, and they have believed that thou didst send me.

9 I pray for them: I pray not for the world (I am not referring to the world at this point of my prayer), but for them which thou hast given me; for they are thine.

10 And all mine are thine, and thine are mine; and I am glorified in them.

11 And now I am no more in the world (I am leaving), but these are in the world (my apostles have to stay here), and I come to thee. Holy Father, keep through thine own name those whom thou hast given me, that they may be one, as we are.

Note: It is obvious that the Savior is speaking so that the apostles can hear him. You may wish to imagine, in your mind's eye, the faces of these humble eleven as they listen to this powerful prayer, given in their behalf.

12 While I was with them in the world, I kept them in thy name: those that thou gavest me I have kept, and none of them is lost, but (except) the son of perdition (Judas Iscariot); that the scripture might be fulfilled.

13 And now come I to thee; and these things I speak in the world (within hearing of my apostles, while I am still here on earth), that they might have my joy fulfilled in themselves.

14 I have given them thy word; and the world hath hated them, because they are not of the world (they are not worldly), even as I am not of the world.

15 I pray not that thou shouldest take them out of the world, but that thou shouldest keep (protect) them from the evil.

16 They are not of the world, even as I am not of the world.

17 Sanctify them (make them holy, pure and fit to be in thy presence) through thy truth: thy word is truth.

18 As thou hast sent me into the world, even so have I also sent them into the world.

19 And for their sakes I sanctify myself, that they also might be sanctified through the truth.

20 Neither pray I for these alone, but for them also (everyone) which shall believe on me through their word (through their teachings);

21 That they all (all the righteous) may be one (united in purpose); as thou, Father, *art* in me, and I in thee, that they also may be one in us (so that all of them can be united in purpose with us): that the world may believe that thou hast sent me.

22 And the glory which thou gavest me I have given them; that they may be one (united), even as we are one:

Note: The Prophet Joseph Smith taught that the word "one", as used in these verses, means "agreed as one". See *Teachings of the Prophet Joseph Smith*, page 372.

23 I in them, and thou in me, that they may be made perfect in one (agreed, in unity, harmony); and that

the world may know that thou hast sent me, and hast loved them, as thou hast loved me.

24 Father, I will (desire) that they also, whom thou hast given me, be with me where I am (live with me in celestial glory); that they may behold my glory, which thou hast given me: for thou lovedst me before the foundation of the world (in the premortal life).

25 O righteous Father, the world hath not known thee: but I have known thee, and these (apostles) have known that thou hast sent me.

26 And I have declared unto them thy name, and will declare it: that the love wherewith thou hast loved me may be in them, and I in them.

JOHN 18

1 WHEN Jesus had spoken these words, he went forth with his disciples over the brook Cedron, where was a garden (the Garden of Gethsemane), into the which he entered, and his disciples.

Note: "Gethsemane" means "oil press". There is significant symbolism here. The Jews put olives into bags made of mesh fabric and placed them in a press to squeeze olive oil out of them. The first pressings yielded pure olive oil which was prized for many uses, including healing and giving light in lanterns. In fact, we consecrate it and use it to administer to the sick. The last pressing of the olives, under the tremendous pressure of additional weights added to the press, yielded a bitter, red liquid which can remind us of the "bitter cup" which the Savior

partook of. Symbolically, the Savior is going into the "oil press" (Gethsemane) to submit to the "pressure" of all our sins which will "squeeze" his blood out in order that we might have the healing "oil" of the Atonement to heal us from our sins.

2 And Judas also, which betrayed him, knew the place: for Jesus ofttimes resorted thither (went there) with his disciples.

3 Judas then, having received a band *of men* (soldiers) and officers from the chief priests and Pharisees, cometh thither (there) with lanterns and torches and weapons.

4 Jesus therefore, knowing all things that should come upon him, went forth, and said unto them, Whom seek ye?

5 They answered him, Jesus of Nazareth. Jesus saith unto them, I am *he*. And Judas also, which betrayed him, stood with them (the soldiers etc.).

6 As soon then as he (Christ) had said unto them, I am *he*, they went backward, and fell to the ground.

7 Then asked he them again, Whom seek ye? And they said, Jesus of Nazareth.

8 Jesus answered, I have told you that I am *he*: if therefore ye seek me, let these go their way (let my apostles go free):

9 That the saying might be fulfilled, which he spake, Of them which thou gavest me have I lost none.

10 Then Simon Peter having a sword drew it, and smote (struck) the high priest's servant, and cut off his right ear. The servant's name was Malchus.

(Malchus was a relative of the high priest. See John 18:26.)

11 Then said Jesus unto Peter, Put up thy sword into the sheath: the cup which my Father hath given me, shall I not drink it? (Should I not go ahead with the Atonement? Then Jesus healed the ear, Luke 22:51.)

12 Then the band and the captain and officers of the Jews took Jesus, and bound him,

13 And led him away to Annas first; for he was father in law to Caiaphas, which was the high priest that same year.

Note: Annas had served as high priest, which was the chief religious office among the Jews, for several years, before being taken out of office by the Romans. Even though his son-in-law, Caiaphas, was now the chief officer, Annas still had tremendous influence. By the way, it appears that Annas had kept much of the tithing given by people during his time in office, and thus had become tremendously wealthy. See Bible Dictionary, page 609.

14 Now Caiaphas was he, which gave counsel to the Jews, that it was expedient (necessary) that one man should die for the people.

15 And Simon Peter followed Jesus, and *so did* another disciple: that disciple was known unto the high priest, and went in with Jesus into the palace of the high priest.

16 But Peter stood at the door without (outside). Then went out that other disciple, which was known unto the high priest, and spake unto her that kept the door (guarded the door), and brought in Peter.

17 Then saith the damsel (young lady) that kept the door unto Peter, Art not thou also *one* of this man's (Jesus') disciples? He saith, I am not.

18 And the servants and officers stood there (in the courtyard), who had made a fire of coals; for it was cold: and they warmed themselves: and Peter stood with them, and warmed himself.

19 The high priest then asked Jesus of (about) his disciples, and of (about) his doctrine. (The illegal trial by night begins.)

Note: To read a full account of the illegal aspects of Christ's trial, see Talmage, *Jesus the Christ*, pages 644-648.

20 Jesus answered him, I spake (spoke) openly to the world; I ever (constantly) taught in the synagogue (in the Jewish churches), and in the temple, whither (where) the Jews always resort (go); and in secret have I said nothing.

21 Why askest thou me (why ask me about my doctrine)? ask them which heard me (ask the people), what I have said unto them: behold, they know what I said.

22 And when he had thus spoken, one of the officers which stood by struck Jesus with the palm of his hand, saying, Answerest thou the high priest so (how dare you talk like that to the high priest!)?

23 Jesus answered him, If I have spoken evil, bear witness of the evil (tell me what I said that was not

correct): but if well, why smitest thou me (if what I said was true, why did you slap me)?

24 Now Annas had sent him bound (still tied up or in chains or whatever the soldiers had used to make sure he could not escape) unto Caiaphas the high priest.

25 And Simon Peter stood and warmed himself. They said therefore unto him, Art not thou also *one* of his disciples? He denied *it*, and said, I am not.

26 One of the servants of the high priest, being *his* kinsman whose ear Peter cut off, saith, Did not I see thee in the garden with him? (This man had good reason to recognize Peter!)

27 Peter then denied again: and immediately the cock crew (the rooster crowed).

28 Then led they Jesus from Caiaphas unto the hall of judgment (to the Roman governor's place): and it was early; and they themselves went not into the judgment hall, lest they should be defiled (be made unclean); but that they might eat the passover.

Note: It is ironic and sad to think that, even while they were turning the "Lamb of God" over to be executed, they themselves were being very careful not to become unclean in any way that might prevent them from finishing Passover worship, in which they showed gratitude for blessings received by the shedding of the blood of sacrificial lambs, representing Christ.

29 Pilate then went out unto them, and said, What accusation bring ye against this man (what are you accusing Jesus of)?

30 They answered and said unto him, If he were not a malefactor (criminal), we would not have delivered him up (turned him over) unto thee.

31 Then said Pilate unto them, Take ye him, and judge him according to your law (you handle it). The Jews therefore said unto him, It is not lawful for us to put any man to death (under Roman law, we Jews cannot execute anyone):

32 That the saying of Jesus might be fulfilled, which he spake, signifying what death he should die.

33 Then Pilate entered into the judgment hall again, and called Jesus, and said unto him, Art thou the King of the Jews?

34 Jesus answered him, Sayest thou this thing of thyself, or did others tell it thee of me (are you asking because you, yourself, want to know, or because others have told you I am) ?

35 Pilate answered, Am I a Jew (how should I know what is going on; I am not a Jew)? Thine own nation and the chief priests have delivered thee unto me: what hast thou done?

36 Jesus answered, My kingdom is not of this world: if my kingdom were of this world (if this were my time to be king on earth), then would my servants fight, that I should not be delivered to the Jews: but now is my kingdom not from hence (here on earth). (The time will come, during the Millennium, when Christ becomes everyone's King here on earth, literally. But that time has not yet come at the time Pilate is questioning the Master.)

37 Pilate therefore said unto him, Art thou a king then? Jesus answered, Thou sayest that I am a king. To this end was I born (for this purpose I was born), and for this cause came I into the world, that I should bear witness unto the truth. Every one that is of the truth heareth (hears and obeys) my voice.

38 Pilate saith unto him, What is truth? And when he had said this, he went out again unto the Jews, and saith unto them, I find in him no fault *at all* (I do not find Jesus guilty of anything).

39 But ye have a custom (you have a tradition), that I should release unto you one at the passover (that every year, at Passover time, I release a criminal of your choosing): will ye therefore that I (would you like me to) release unto you the King of the Jews?

40 Then cried they all again, saying, Not this man, but Barabbas. Now Barabbas was a robber.

Note: The name "Barabbas" means "son of the father" (see Bible Dictionary, page 619). This may be symbolic in that the "imposter", Satan, stirred up the multitude to demand the release of an "imposter", Barabbas, while the true "Son of the Father" is punished for crimes which he did not commit.

JOHN 19

1 THEN Pilate therefore took Jesus, and scourged *him* (had him whipped).

Note: Scourging involved tying the victim to a frame or column, with the arms pulled tightly upward to put tension on the back muscles, and then whipping him with a whip which was made of leather strips with sharp bits of metal, bone etc. fastened to them. Often, a victim of scourging did not survive to continue on to be crucified.

2 And the soldiers platted (wove) a crown of thorns, and put *it* on his head, and they put on him a purple robe (mockingly symbolic of his being "King of the Jews"),

3 And said, Hail, King of the Jews! and they smote (hit) him with their hands.

4 Pilate therefore went forth again, and saith unto them, Behold, I bring him forth to you, that ye may know that I find no fault in him (I do not find him guilty of any crime).

5 Then came Jesus forth (where the crowd could see him), wearing the crown of thorns, and the purple robe. And *Pilate* saith unto them, Behold the man (just look at the man)!

6 When the chief priests therefore and officers saw him, they cried out, saying, Crucify *him*, crucify *him*. Pilate saith unto them, Take ye him, and crucify *him*: for I find no fault in him.

7 The Jews answered him, We have a law (a law against blasphemy [mocking God] making it punishable by death), and by our law he ought to die, because he made himself (claimed to be) the Son of God.

8 When Pilate therefore heard that saying, he was the more afraid;

9 And went again into the judgment hall, and saith (said) unto Jesus, Whence art thou (where do you come from)? But Jesus gave him no answer.

10 Then saith Pilate unto him, Speakest thou not unto me? knowest

thou not that I have power to crucify thee, and have power to release thee? (Don't you think you ought to answer me. Don't you realize I have power to have you crucified or to set you free?)

11 Jesus answered, Thou couldest have no power at all against me, except it were given thee from above: therefore he (Caiaphas; see McConkie, *Doctrinal New Testament Commentary*, Vol. 1, page 809) that delivered me unto thee hath the greater sin.

12 And from thenceforth (from then on) Pilate sought (tried) to release him: but the Jews cried out, saying, If thou let this man go, thou art not Cæsar's friend: whosoever maketh himself a king speaketh against Cæsar. (If you release him, you are not loyal to Caesar, because Jesus claims to be the king, instead of Caesar.)

13 When Pilate therefore heard that saying (that it could appear that Jesus was undermining the Roman government), he brought Jesus forth, and sat down in the judgment seat in a place that is called the Pavement, but in the Hebrew, Gabbatha.

14 And it was the preparation of the passover, and about the sixth hour: and he saith unto the Jews, Behold (look) your King!

15 But they cried out, Away with *him*, away with *him*, crucify him. Pilate saith unto them, Shall I crucify your King? The chief priest (Caiaphas) answered, We have no king but Cæsar.

16 Then delivered he (Pilate) him (Jesus) therefore unto them to be crucified. And they took Jesus, and led *him* away.

17 And he bearing his cross went forth into a place called *the place* of a skull, which is called in the Hebrew Golgotha:

18 Where they crucified him, and two other (the two thieves) with him, on either side one, and Jesus in the midst (middle).

19 And Pilate wrote a title, and put it on the cross. And the writing was, JESUS OF NAZARETH THE KING OF THE JEWS.

20 This title then read many of the Jews: for the place where Jesus was crucified was nigh (near) to the city: and it was written in Hebrew, and Greek, and Latin.

21 Then said the chief priests of the Jews to Pilate, Write not, The King of the Jews; but that he said, I am King of the Jews. (Don't write "King of the Jews", rather, write "He claimed to be King of the Jews".)

22 Pilate answered, What I have written I have written (I will not change it).

23 Then the soldiers, when they had crucified Jesus, took his garments (clothes), and made four parts (and divided them into four piles), to every soldier a part; and also *his* coat: now the coat was without seam, woven from the top throughout, (was woven as one continuous piece of fabric).

24 They said therefore among themselves, Let us not rend it (tear the coat), but cast lots (gamble) for it, whose it shall be: that the scripture (Psalm 22:18) might be fulfilled, which saith, They parted my raiment (clothing) among them, and for my vesture (clothing) they did cast lots. These things therefore (to fulfill prophecy) the soldiers did.

25 Now there stood by the cross of Jesus his mother (Mary), and his mother's sister, Mary the *wife* of Cleophas, and Mary Magdalene. (Mary was a very beautiful and common name among the Jews.)

26 When Jesus therefore saw his mother, and the disciple (John the Beloved apostle) standing by, whom he loved, he saith unto his mother, Woman, (a term of great respect in Jewish culture) behold thy son!

27 Then saith he to the disciple (John), Behold thy mother! And from that hour that disciple took her unto his own *home*. (The Savior asked John to take care of his mother from then on, and he did.)

28 After this, Jesus knowing that all things were now accomplished (knowing that he had now finished everything which the Atonement required of him as a mortal), that the scripture might be fulfilled, saith, I thirst.

29 Now there was set a vessel full of vinegar (JST adds "mingled with gall"): and they filled a spunge with vinegar, and put *it* upon hyssop, and put it to his mouth.

30 When Jesus therefore had received the vinegar, he said, It is finished: and he bowed his head, and gave up the ghost (and left his body).

Note: Jesus uttered a total of seven recorded statements from the cross. The references for these statements and the statements themselves follow, and are in chronological order:

1. Luke 23:34 "Father, forgive them; for they know not what they do."

2. Luke 23:43 "Today shalt thou be with me in paradise."

3. John 19:26-27 "Woman, behold thy son!" Behold thy mother!"

4. Matthew 27:46 "My God, my God, why hast thou forsaken me?"

5. John 19:28 "I thirst."

6. John 19:30 "It is finished."

7. Luke 23:46 "Father, into thy hands I commend my spirit."

31 The Jews therefore, because it was the preparation (time to make preparations for the Sabbath), that the bodies should not remain upon the cross on the sabbath day, (for that sabbath day was an high day,) besought Pilate that their legs might be broken, and *that* they might be taken away.

Note: Among the Jews at this time in history, the days of the week, Monday, Tuesday etc. went from about sundown to about sundown of the next day, rather than from midnight to midnight. Therefore, the Jewish religious leaders were very concerned about violating one of their laws which said people should not be crucified on the Sabbath. Their Sabbath (Saturday) would start at about six in the evening. Jesus and the two thieves had been crucified at about nine that morning (Friday). Persons being crucified often lived two or three days. Therefore, these religious rulers of the Jews asked Pilate to have soldiers break the legs of the three "criminals" to kill them with additional pain and shock, so that their bodies could be taken off their crosses in order to avoid violating the Sabbath. Pilate agreed and sent soldiers to do the deed.

32 Then came the soldiers, and brake (broke) the legs of the first (one of the thieves), and of the other (thief) which was crucified with him.

33 But when they came to Jesus, and saw that he was dead already, they brake not his legs:

34 But one of the soldiers with a spear pierced his side, and forthwith came there out blood and water.

35 And he (John; see John 19:25, footnote 35a) that saw it bare record, and his record (the Gospel of John) is true: and he knoweth that he saith true, that ye might believe.

36 For these things were done, that the scripture (Psalm 34:20, Numbers 9:12) should be fulfilled (in order to fulfill the prophecy which says), A bone of him shall not be broken.

37 And again another scripture (Zechariah 12:10) saith, They shall look on him whom they pierced.

38 And after this Joseph of Arimathæa (from Ramah; a member of the Sanhedrin, see Bible Dictionary, page 717), being a disciple of Jesus, but secretly for fear of the Jews, besought (asked) Pilate that he might take away the body of Jesus: and Pilate gave *him* leave (permission). He came therefore, and took the body of Jesus.

39 And there came also Nicodemus, (one of the Jewish religious rulers, see Bible Dictionary, page 738) which at the first came to Jesus by night (John 3:2), and brought a mixture of myrrh and aloes (costly spices with which to prepare Christ's body for burial), about an hundred pound *weight*.

40 Then took they (Joseph and Nicodemus) the body of Jesus, and wound it in linen clothes with the spices, as the manner (custom) of the Jews is to bury.

41 Now in the place where he was crucified there was a garden; and in the garden a new sepulchre (tomb), wherein was never man yet laid (which had never been used).

42 There laid they Jesus therefore because of the Jews' preparation *day*; for the sepulchre was nigh (near) at hand. (There was an urgency to get Jesus' body into a tomb, because of the approaching Sabbath, and this tomb was close by.)

JOHN 20

1 THE first *day* of the week (Sunday) cometh Mary Magdalene early, when it was yet dark, unto the sepulchre (Christ's tomb), and seeth the stone taken away from the sepulchre (JST adds "and two angels sitting thereon").

Note: Mark 16:1 tells us that Mary, the mother of James, and Salome accompanied Mary Magdalene.

2 Then she runneth, and cometh to Simon Peter, and to the other disciple (John), whom Jesus loved, and saith unto them, They have taken away the Lord out of the sepulchre, and we (the ladies mentioned above) know not where they have laid him.

3 Peter therefore went forth, and that other disciple (John), and came to the sepulchre.

4 So they ran both together: and the other disciple did outrun Peter (John outran Peter), and came first to the sepulchre.

5 And he stooping down, *and looking in*, saw the linen clothes lying; yet went he not in. (John waited for Peter to arrive.)

6 Then cometh Simon Peter following him, and went into the sepulchre (tomb), and seeth the linen clothes lie (saw the strips of linen which Joseph and Nicodemus had used to wrap the Savior's body in),

7 And the napkin (burial cloth), that was about (was wrapped around) his head, not lying with the linen clothes, but wrapped together (folded) in a place by itself.

8 Then went in also that other disciple (John), which came first to the sepulchre, and he saw, and believed.

9 For as yet they knew not (did not understand) the scripture, that he must rise again from the dead.

10 Then the disciples went away again unto their own home.

11 But Mary (Mary Magdalene; see verse 1) stood without (outside) at the sepulchre weeping: and as she wept, she stooped down, *and looked* into the sepulchre,

12 And seeth two angels in white sitting, the one at the head, and the other at the feet, where the body of Jesus had lain.

13 And they say (said) unto her, Woman, why weepest thou? She saith unto them, Because they have taken away my Lord, and I know not where they have laid him. (Someone has taken Jesus' body away, and I don't know where they put it.)

14 And when she had thus said, she turned herself back (away from the angels), and saw Jesus standing, and knew not that it was Jesus.

15 Jesus saith unto her, Woman, why weepest thou? whom seekest thou? She, supposing him to be the gardener, saith unto him, Sir, if thou have borne him hence (if you have taken his body somewhere), tell me where thou hast laid him, and I will take him away.

16 Jesus saith unto her, Mary. She turned herself, and saith unto him, Rabboni; which is to say, Master.

Note: This is a very tender moment. Mary is very concerned about where the Savior's body has been taken. After turning away from the tomb and the two angels therein, she sees a man whom she assumes is the caretaker. The question comes up as to why she did not immediately recognize Jesus. Several possibilities exist. One is that she had been crying and was so distraught that she didn't even take a good look at Jesus at first. Another possibility is that she hadn't turned all the way around from the tomb. She "turned herself back" from the tomb and the angels in verse 14, yet she "turned herself" in verse 16, implying that she had not turned completely toward where Jesus was standing when she first turned from the tomb. Whatever the explanation, when Jesus said "Mary", she recognized his voice, apparently looked again, and her sorrow was over.

17 Jesus saith unto her, Touch me not (JST "hold me not"); for I am not yet ascended to my Father: but go to my brethren, and say unto them, I ascend unto my Father, and your Father; and *to* my God, and your God.

Note: The Joseph Smith Translation change in verse 17 above, may solve a bit of a problem otherwise encountered when reading Matthew and John. The normal understanding of verse 17 is that the resurrected Lord told Mary not to touch him. Yet, Matthew 28:8-9 informs us that some women (perhaps without Mary Magdalene's being with them) were met by Jesus as they ran from the empty tomb to tell the disciples that the Master's body was gone. They were allowed to hold him by the feet and worship him. So why was Mary Magdalene not allowed to touch him (John 20:17)? The answer may be, "She was." The JST changes "touch me not" to "hold me not." The Greek, which was translated as "touch me not" in our New Testament, is often translated as "do not hold me" or "do not hold on to me". The Greek word itself is "harpazo", which is the continuous action of holding. *Strong's Exhaustive Concordance* #0680, defines it as "to fasten one's self to, adhere to, cling to". Thus, it is possible, using the JST as a reference, that Jesus was, in effect, telling Mary "Don't keep holding me. I must leave." Whatever the case, we will certainly get clarification on it some day.

18 Mary Magdalene came and told the disciples that she had seen the Lord, and *that* he had spoken these things unto her.

19 Then the same day at evening, being the first *day* of the week (Sunday), when the doors were shut where the disciples were assembled for fear of the Jews (the disciples were afraid that the Jews would arrest them too), came Jesus and stood in the midst, and saith unto them, Peace be unto you.

20 And when he had so said, he shewed (showed) unto them *his* hands and his side. Then were the disciples glad, when they saw the Lord.

21 Then said Jesus to them again, Peace be unto you: as my Father hath sent me, even so send I you.

22 And when he had said this, he breathed on *them*, and saith unto them, Receive ye the Holy Ghost:

Note: In the Jewish culture, "breathed on them" is very significant. The same word is used in Genesis 2:7, where God breathed on Adam and he became a living soul. The symbolism in verse 17 above, seems to be that of "breathing" additional life or "power" into the apostles. In April Conference, 1955, Apostle Harold B. Lee suggested that it was at this time, after the Savior's death, that he confirmed them and gave them the Gift of the Holy Ghost. This would certainly fit in with Christ's promise to his apostles that, after he had gone, he would send them "another Comforter" (the Holy Ghost). See John 14:16.

23 Whose soever sins ye remit (forgive), they are remitted unto them; *and* whose soever *sins* ye retain, they are retained.

24 But Thomas, one of the twelve, called Didymus, was not with them when Jesus came.

25 The other disciples therefore said unto him, We have seen the Lord. But he said unto them, Except I shall see in

his hands the print of the nails, and put my finger into the print of the nails, and thrust my hand into his side, I will not believe. (This is how Thomas came to be known as "Doubting Thomas.")

26 And after eight days again his disciples were within (inside the house), and Thomas with them: then came Jesus, the doors being shut, and stood in the midst, and said, Peace *be* unto you.

27 Then saith he to Thomas, Reach hither (here) thy finger, and behold (look at) my hands; and reach hither thy hand, and thrust *it* into my side: and be not faithless, but believing.

28 And Thomas answered and said unto him, My Lord and my God.

29 Jesus saith unto him, Thomas, because thou hast seen me, thou hast believed: blessed *are* they that have not seen, and yet have believed.

30 And many other signs truly did Jesus in the presence of his disciples, which are not written in this book:

31 But these are written, that ye might believe that Jesus is the Christ, the Son of God; and that believing ye might have life (eternal life, exaltation) through his name.

JOHN 21

1 AFTER these things Jesus shewed (showed) himself again to the disciples at the sea of Tiberias (the Sea of Galilee); and on this wise shewed he *himself* (and this is how he showed himself to them).

Note: The Savior had told his disciples that, after his crucifixion and resurrection, he would meet them in Galilee (Matthew 28:16). As we get to verse 2,

next, several of the disciples have already journeyed to Galilee in anticipation of meeting the Savior there.

2 There were together Simon Peter, and Thomas called Didymus, and Nathanael of Cana in Galilee, and the sons of Zebedee, and two other of his disciples.

3 Simon Peter saith unto them, I go a fishing. They say unto him, We also go with thee. They went forth, and entered into a ship immediately; and that night they caught nothing.

Note: In the days of Jesus, it was common for fishermen to fish at night on the Sea of Galilee, when the fishing was best. Peter, having been a professional fisherman on that lake before the Savior said "Come follow me," now takes his fellow disciples and they fish all night, with absolutely no success. The "sons of Zebedee", verse 2 above, were James and John, and they, too, had been professional fishermen, before being called by Jesus to follow him. It must have been extra frustrating for these professionals to have zero success fishing.

4 But when the morning was now come, Jesus stood on the shore: but the disciples knew not that it was Jesus. (He was apparently far enough away that they didn't recognize him.)

Note: Something quite wonderful is now going to happen. The tired disciples have had absolutely no success fishing throughout the night. In the morning, a stranger on the shore asks them if they have had any luck. He then tells them to simply cast their net overboard on the other side of the ship. Perhaps there are few things worse than a stranger telling professionals how to do their work. Nevertheless, they do what he says and suddenly the net fills with so many fish (153 big fish, see verse 11) that they could hardly pull it in. This rings a bell. An almost identical thing had happened three years ago when he first called Peter, Andrew, James and John (see Luke 5:1-11). Jesus had come by, and because of the crowd, had requested that Peter take him a little way out from the shore in his ship. When he was through speaking to the crowd, he told Peter to go out farther into the lake and let down his nets. He replied that they had fished all night with no success, but, since Jesus said to do it, he did. Their net filled with so many fish that the net began to break. James and John quickly brought their ship out to help, and the large number of fish almost sank both ships. Now, the same thing is happening again. Could it be the Master who is on the shore now?

5 Then Jesus saith unto them, Children, have ye any meat (have you caught any fish)? They answered him, No.

6 And he said unto them, Cast the net on the right side of the ship, and ye shall find. They cast therefore, and now they were not able to draw it for the multitude (because of the large number) of fishes.

7 Therefore that disciple whom Jesus loved (in other words, John the

Beloved Apostle) saith unto Peter, It is the Lord. Now when Simon Peter heard that it was the Lord, he girt *his* fisher's coat *unto him*, (for he was naked [stripped to the waist],) and did cast himself into the sea (Peter jumped in and swam to shore).

8 And the other disciples came in a little ship; (for they were not far from land, but as it were two hundred cubits [about a hundred yards],) dragging the net with fishes.

9 As soon then as they were come to land, they saw a fire of coals there, and fish laid thereon, and bread.

Note: This is a very touching scene. No one in the universe could be busier than the Savior. Yet he had taken the time to cook breakfast for his weary, discouraged disciples.

10 Jesus saith unto them, Bring of the fish which ye have now caught.

11 Simon Peter went up, and drew the net to land full of great fishes, and hundred and fifty and three: and for all there were so many, yet was not the net broken.

Note: There is symbolism here. Jesus told the apostles, when he called them, that he would make them "fishers of men" (Matthew 4:19). The fact that the Savior helped them have such success with actual fish is symbolic of the fact that he will help them have great success in bringing souls into the gospel net and unto the Father.

12 Jesus saith unto them, Come *and*

dine. And none of the disciples durst ask him, Who art thou? knowing that it was the Lord.

13 Jesus then cometh, and taketh bread, and giveth them, and fish likewise.

14 This is now the third time that Jesus shewed himself to his disciples, after that he was risen from the dead.

15 So when they had dined, Jesus saith to Simon Peter, Simon, *son* of Jonas, lovest thou me more than these (do you love me more than these fish)? He saith unto him, Yea, Lord; thou knowest that I love thee. He saith unto him, Feed my lambs.

16 He saith to him again the second time, Simon, *son* of Jonas, lovest thou me? He saith unto him, Yea, Lord; thou knowest that I love thee. He saith unto him, Feed my sheep.

17 He saith unto him the third time, Simon, son of Jonas, lovest thou me? Peter was grieved because he said unto him the third time, Lovest thou me? And he said unto him, Lord, thou knowest all things; thou knowest that I love thee. Jesus saith unto him, Feed my sheep.

18 Verily, verily, I say unto thee, When thou wast young, thou girdedst thyself (dressed yourself), and walkedst whither thou wouldest (and went wherever you wanted to): but when thou shalt be old, thou shalt stretch forth thy hands (you will be crucified), and another shall gird thee, and carry *thee* whither thou wouldest not (where you don't want to go).

19 This spake he, signifying by what death he should glorify God. (Jesus thus indicated to Peter how he would die when his mortal mission was over)

And when he had spoken this, he saith unto him, Follow me.

20 Then Peter, turning about, seeth the disciple (John) whom Jesus loved following; which also leaned on his breast at supper (at the last supper), and said (asked the question), Lord, which is he that betrayeth thee?

21 Peter seeing him (John) saith to Jesus, Lord, and what *shall* this man *do* (what will happen to John)?

22 Jesus saith unto him, If I will that he tarry till I come (if I want him to remain alive until my second coming), what *is that* to thee? follow thou me.

23 Then went this saying abroad among the brethren, that that disciple (John) should (would) not die: yet Jesus said not unto him, He shall not die; but, If I will that he tarry till I come, what *is that* to thee?

Note: Because of the wording of verses 22 and 23 above, it is not clear whether or not John was allowed to remain on earth until the Second Coming. However, through modern revelation in D&C 7:3, we know that John was allowed to remain. He was translated and will not die until the Lord's coming. Joseph Smith gave us more information in History of the Church, volume 1, page 176. He said that at that time, 1831, John was working with the lost Ten Tribes, preparing them for their return. More information about translated beings can be found in 3 Nephi 28, where details about the Three Nephites are written.

24 This is the disciple which testifieth of these things, and wrote these

things: and we know that his testimony is true.

25 And there are also many other things which Jesus did, the which, if they should be written every one, I suppose that even the world itself could not contain the books that should be written. Amen.

This concludes Part 1 of *The New Testament Made Easier*.

Part II of *The New Testament Made Easier* covers

the remainder of The New Testament,

from Acts through Revelation,

and will be available in the Spring of 2003.

About the Author

David J. Ridges

David J. Ridges has been teaching for the Church Educational System for 35 years and has taught for several years at BYU Campus Education Week and Know Your Religion programs. He has also served as a curriculum writer for Sunday School, Seminary, and Institute of Religion manuals.

He has served in many positions in the Church, including gospel doctrine teacher, bishop, and stake president. He currently serves as stake patriarch.

Brother Ridges and his wife, Janette, are the parents of six children and make their home in Springville, Utah.

9 26575 76380 8